NATIONALISM AND HISTORY

NATIONALISM AND HISTORY

ESSAYS ON OLD AND NEW JUDAISM

SIMON DUBNOW

EDITED WITH AN INTRODUCTORY ESSAY
BY KOPPEL S. PINSON

Meridian Books
THE WORLD PUBLISHING COMPANY
Cleveland and New York
THE JEWISH PUBLICATION SOCIETY OF AMERICA
Philadelphia

Simon Dubnow

Simon Dubnow was born in White Russia in 1860 and carried on his literary, scholarly, and journalistic activities in St. Petersburg, Odessa, Vilna, Berlin, and Riga, where he was murdered by the Nazis in 1941. Among his monumental works are a history of Hasidism, a history of the Jews in Russia and Poland, and a universal history of the Jewish people.

Koppel S. Pinson

Koppel S. Pinson was Professor of History and Chairman of the Division of the Social Sciences at Queens College. Among his numerous publications are: *Pietism and the Rise of German Nationalism*, *Essays on Antisemitism*, and *Modern Germany: its History and Civilization.* Professor Pinson died early in 1961.

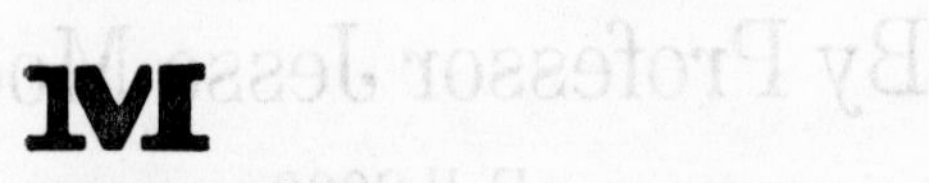

MERIDIAN BOOKS

The World Publishing Company, Cleveland and New York
The Jewish Publication Society of America, Philadelphia
First Meridian printing April 1961

Library of Congress Catalog Card Number: 58-5590
Printed in the United States of America

To the memory of the sainted Jewish scholars and sages who met their death at the hands of the Nazis

CONTENTS

PART I

ON NATIONALISM

PART II

ON HISTORY

EDITOR'S PREFACE

The name of Dubnow is not entirely unknown to the American reader. His *Essay in the Philosophy of Jewish History* was published by the Jewish Publication Society as far back as 1903 and the Society solicited and finally published Dubnow's three-volume *History of the Jews in Russia and Poland*. Dubnow's name also recurs over and over again in discussions of modern Jewish ideologies. His major works, however, have thus far not been accessible to the English reader.

Dubnow not only wrote history but also felt impelled to give explicit and coherent statement to his general philosophy of history, and to the philosophy of Jewish history in particular. In his now classic "Letters on Old and New Judaism" he developed his philosophy of nationalism and its specific relation to the role of the Jews in the modern world and to the position of the enlightened Jewish intelligentsia in a secular and modern society. Though written over fifty years ago, these essays have as much meaning and relevance as they did when they first appeared. The destruction of the Jewish centers in eastern Europe and the creation of the State of Israel give only greater cogency and interest to Dubnow's views on nationalism and history. His positions (for he changed his views on history) on the writing and philosophy of Jewish history are clearly formulated and expounded in the above-mentioned Essay and in his Introduction to the *World History of the Jewish People*. These writings, together with a number of shorter essays here collected, present the integrated philosophy of the chief exponent of Diaspora spiritual nationalism.

The initial impetus to the collection and translation of these essays as well as the final realization of the project is in large measure due to the urging and continued interest of the Jewish Publication Society. The financial assistance of the Conference on Material Claims against Germany made the publication of the volume possible. Thanks are also due to Mrs. Sophie Dubnow-Ehrlich, daughter of the historian, for her kind co-operation.

The translations of the materials in this volume were all prepared especially for this collection, with the sole exception of the *Essay in the Philosophy of Jewish History*, which is here reprinted in the excellent translation of Henrietta Szold. I wish to express my thanks and appreciation to Dr. Herbert A. Strauss, of the Academic Department of the Juilliard School of Music, for his collaboration in the translation of most of the materials included here; and to Miss Esther Pinson, Librarian of the Jewish Teachers' Seminary, for her able assistance in checking our translation of the "Letters" with the Russian original. The Editor, however, assumes full responsibility for the final text. My thanks are also due to Mrs. Eveline Kanes for her assistance in the preparation of the Index.

It is my fervent and sincere hope that the publication of these essays will create sufficient interest in Dubnow to stimulate the publication of an English translation of his most important work, the ten-volume *World History of the Jewish People*. To this day this work still remains the most authoritative, most readable and most stimulating narrative account of the history of the Jewish people. No serious work in any phase of Jewish history and culture can be done without referring to it. Translations have appeared in Hebrew, Yiddish, German, Russian and Spanish. Only the most wealthy and most influential Jewish community in the world has thus far lagged behind. I trust that sufficient energy and financial backing can be mustered in this country to make this masterpiece of Jewish historiography available to the English reading public.

K. S. P.

New York, January 10, 1958.

SIMON DUBNOW: HISTORIAN AND POLITICAL PHILOSOPHER

by Koppel S. Pinson

I. *The Man and the Historian*[1]

It is a tragic irony of history that Dubnow, the first Jewish historian to rebel against the historiography that viewed Jewish history as primarily the history of literature and martyrdom,[2] himself became one of the heroic martyrs in the Nazi war against the Jews. On the night of December 8, 1941, the eighty-one-year-old Simon Dubnow, caught in Riga by the invading Nazi hordes, was driven into the street together with all the other aged and feeble Jews and ordered into a waiting bus. Dubnow, sick and in high fever, did not move quickly enough for his Aryan masters: whereupon a drunken Latvian guard fired a bullet into him. The venerable scholar died instantly. He was buried in a mass grave in the Jewish cemetery in Riga.

Simon Dubnow, distinguished historian, literary critic, essayist and social philosopher, is best known for his numerous works in the field of Jewish history. By his studies in the history of the Jews in Russia and Poland he raised the historiography of east-European Jewry to a scientific level comparable to the standards of the science of Judaism in Germany and central Europe; by his great synthesis of the entire range of Jewish history he inherited the mantle of Heinrich Graetz as the national Jewish historian. But Dubnow was not only a scholar; he was vitally concerned with the living and contemporary Jewish life. As such he aimed to provide current Jewish life with a philosophy which would supply it with the necessary foundation for carrying on Jewish community existence and retaining Jewish national values in a secular and enlightened world. This he did in his theory of autonomism, of which he was the founder and leading protagonist. While it is true that similar ideas of Jewish autonomy were developed independently at the same time by Chaim Zhitlovsky, the latter was active as a revolutionary exile outside of Russia and Poland and hence did not reach the attention of the wide Jewish masses until long after Dubnow's ideas were already well established.[3]

Dubnow's writings cover a span of over fifty years. He began his scholarly and literary work when the great masses of Jews were still untouched, for the most part, by the spirit of western civilization and were concentrated in the pale of tsarist Russia and in the crowded towns and villages of the Galicia of the Habsburgs. He lived to see two world wars, the break up of the Austrian and Russian empires, the dissolution of the traditional patterns of Jewish existence, the tremendous surge of secularization and the final catastrophe of European Jewry brought on by the Nazis. When he started writing, Palestine and Zionism were but nascent dreams in the fantasies of youthful visionaries; he lived to see the mass colonization of the land, the Balfour Declaration and the development of a genuine and full-fledged Jewish national community in the Holy Land. To all these varying and changing historical events, Dubnow reacted keenly and with a wise combination of integrity, consistency of principle and mature and intelligent flexibility. His basic approach to Jewish life and thought remained fairly consistent; but he was always historically alive to recognize the forces of changed conditions and circumstances.

Simon Dubnow was born on the second day of Rosh Hashana in the year 5621 (September 10, 1860) in Mstislav, in the province of Mohilev, in White Russia. His forebears had lived in Dubno in the province of Volhynia, from the middle of the seventeenth to the second half of the eighteenth century. After the first partition of Poland in 1772 they had settled in Mstislav. According to the genealogy compiled by S. A. Horodetzky, Dubnow's ancestry goes back to the MaHaRaL of Prague and to a long line of learned scholars and kabbalists. His great-great-grandfather, Rabbi Joseph-Yoske, who became rabbi in Dubno in 1698, was renowned for his piety, saintliness and great love of the Jewish people. His deep humility, high ethical principles and devotion to Israel and to the Torah were just as evident in a secularized form in the life and work of his descendant Simon Dubnow. The keen sense for social justice and the preoccupation with social conditions that were to characterize the work of the historian were already apparent in the denunciations by Rabbi Joseph-Yoske of the greedy and avaricious communal leaders who lived in splendor while the masses of Jews suffered want and privation.

They live in luxury and splendor [he wrote in his Yesod Yosef*] and do not bear the burden of taxes and other communal levies. They impose heavy burdens upon others and lighten their own burdens.*

They take the lion's share of all honors and distinctions . . . and the congregation of God, the children of Abraham, Isaac and Jacob, are crushed and humiliated, left naked and barefoot by the burden of heavy taxes. The tax collectors come to their homes and cruelly grab and rob them of all they find. They are left naked and without any utensils and clothing that were prepared for wife and children. Everything is removed and sold to cover the taxes. The straw is taken out from the beds of the poor and they are left in the cold and rain, shivering and crying, each in his corner—husband, wife and children.[4]

Rabbi Joseph-Yoske died in Dubno in 1702. His son Bentsion became rabbi in Gorodok and his grandson Bentsion is the first of the family to be found in the official records of the Mstislav Jewish community. Bentsion's son Zev-Wolf was famous as a scholar and talmudist, and the latter's son Bentsion was the grandfather of Simon Dubnow.

Simon was one of nine children of Meir-Jacob and Sheyne Dubnow. His father Meir-Jacob (1833-1887), a quiet and sickly man, was in the employ of his father-in-law, a lumber merchant, and was away from home most of the time. His mother ran a petty crockery shop to supplement the family income, but the sum total for the family was still constant poverty and need.

The patriarchal head of the family and the formative influence on young Dubnow was his paternal grandfather Bentsion Dubnow, a man who had tried his hand unsuccessfully at business, and then gave it up to devote himself to study. For forty-five years Bentsion Dubnow, a convinced misnagged, gave a regular lesson (*shiur*) in Talmud in the synagogue, after the style of the Gaon of Vilna. Although the young grandson was to rebel against the traditional ways of the grandfather, the impress of devotion to study for its own sake, of *Torah lishmah*, which characterized the whole life and being of the elder sage, left a lasting impression on the young boy and throughout his later years he always referred to his grandfather with the greatest reverence and deepest affection, conscious of the fact that he himself was a true heir to the inner spirit that had motivated his traditionalist ancestors. "I felt," wrote Dubnow in later years, "that I owe much thanks to this spiritual giant who bequeathed to me my attachment to the tents of the Torah, even though it was another torah, a broad and free one."[5] In the words of Horodetzky we may say that:

Simon Dubnow was the last bearer of the family standard, the last heir of the spirit that informed the family for centuries. Radically different from his forefathers, he nevertheless possessed many of their traits. The great love for the Jewish past, for the Jewish people as a whole and for each individual, Simon Dubnow inherited from his great-great-grandfather Rabbi Joseph-Yoske of Dubno. Like his forebears, Simon Dubnow too was a great ethical personality. He accepted completely the legacy of Rabbi Joseph-Yoske, which called for humility, contentment with little, avoidance of pride and vainglory, love and friendship for each individual.[6]

Dubnow was initiated as a young child into the traditional educational process then customary among orthodox Jews. He was sent to a typical *heder* and was soon studying Bible and later Talmud. At the age of nine, however, he began to rebel against this conventional pattern of education. He discovered a copy of the medieval Hebrew chronicle of *Josippon* and devoured it. He also studied the prophetic books of the Bible with special feeling and emotion. Later he came upon Moses Mendelssohn's *Biur* and not only pored over it himself but also taught it to his fellow students. From now on the road to *haskala* was irreversible. While formally continuing his talmudic studies under his grandfather, he clandestinely read the works of the *haskala* writers. When his older brother married and left home, he secretly left to Simon a book by Kalman Shulman. From other *maskillim* in the town Simon secured other *haskala* works. He was overwhelmed by Eugene Sue's *Mysteries of Paris* (in Hebrew translation) and then by Abraham Mapu's *Ayit tsavua*. His first lesson in science came from the *Sefer habrith* of Pinkhas Hurwitz and history and geography from Kalman Shulman's works. During this time he read with special enthusiasm the *Hashahar* of Peretz Smolenskin and the poetry of Micha-Joseph Lebenson. At the age of twelve he composed a Hebrew diatribe against religious fanaticism and in behalf of enlightenment, which he called *Hazon sefat hakodesh*. What troubled him most were the formalized aspects of traditional orthodoxy.

Assigned as his *bar mitzva* discourse a pupilistic exercise on the subject of how a left-handed person is to wear his *tefillin,* he demurred and refused to deliver the speech. This as well as his other unorthodox intellectual pursuits soon gained for him the reputation in the town as a "heretic" (*apikoyres*). From the son of the synagogue sexton he learned arithmetic and in 1874 Simon entered the official government Jewish school in his home town and here for the first time was exposed to the languages and literatures of Russia and the West. He became enamored with the poetry of Pushkin and Lermontov and his love of the Russian classic poets remained with him until the end of his days. He also studied French and soon came upon the works of Ludwig Börne in Russian translation. These had a tremendous influence upon him. In his autobiography Dubnow later wrote: "For the first time I heard the voice of protest against despotism. . . . For the first time I experienced the magic of the revolutionary spirit. I was especially enthusiastic over Börne's battle for freedom of thought, a battle that was close to my own experience."[7]

Dubnow, however, never became a revolutionary. He was not impressed with Aaron Lieberman's articles in the *Haemet,* which represented the first attempt to organize a Jewish Socialist movement, nor did he follow the example of other young Jewish intellectuals who enlisted in the ranks of the Russian revolutionary movement. Capable though he was of deep emotion and sentiment, yet throughout his life sober and practical realism always triumphed over romantic enthusiasm. Dubnow always remained a moderate humanitarian reformer. And this is what he dreamed of in these early years. In his autobiography he speaks of his ambition at that time to become "a reformer within the bounds of Judaism." He came to Vilna for the purpose of entering the Vilna Jewish Teachers Institute but was refused admission because he was four months too old and would not be able to complete his course before the time for induction into military service. Incidentally, he was to be rejected later for military service because of poor eyesight. He went on to the gymnasium in Dvinsk where he lived and studied in great privation. His diary entry for January 9, 1878, reads: "It is more than one and one-half months since I have had any meat and live only on bread, herring and tea."[8] These material hardships made it necessary for him to interrupt for a time his preparations for entrance to the university, until he was able to resume his studies in Smolensk. He finally completed his preparations for admission to the university but he was not able to pass the examination in mathematics. This failure depressed Dubnow so much that he never made another attempt to receive a university education. From then on he continued his studies as an autodidact. Thus this great scholar and historian amassed his store of learning and scholarly techniques by his own disciplined life of study and practice.

Unlike most other Russian Jewish intellectuals Dubnow's European influences came not via German literature and scholarship but rather through the culture of France and England. The positivism of Comte and the classic liberalism of John Stuart Mill were much more in keeping with his sober realism than German idealistic philosophy and its metaphysical systems, whether those of Hegel or of Marx. He read Buckle and Darwin and cultivated a cosmopolitan approach. In 1878 he read Hettner's history of French literature and the world of Voltaire, Diderot, Condorcet and of deism took hold of him. These writers, as he later wrote, destroyed his religious beliefs altogether. He learned Latin, Greek and English. Draper's *Intellectual Development of Europe* was another book that stirred him. But it was Comte's *Philosophy of Positivism* and John Stuart Mill's *On Liberty* that gave systematic formation to his world view and fashioned his approach to scholarly and intellectual problems. Mill's essay remained one of his favorite works to the end of his days. His break with religion was now complete. He gave up his dream of becoming a religious reformer and his plan to attend the theological seminary in Breslau. He decided to devote himself to the study of Jewish history, but at the same time he reveled in the role of "heretic" and "free thinker" after the model of Elisha ben Abuyah in the Talmud.

There is a moving description in Dubnow's autobiography of the dramatic conflict of the old and new world views that took place when he returned to his native Mstislav for a visit on the eve of the High Holy Days in 1884. The great question was whether the young heretic would attend services in the synagogue or not. His father was away from home and his mother did not dare to broach the subject to her son, but she induced the grandfather to sound out Simon. The old sage summoned the young man and tactfully inquired at which synagogue Simon would pray. Dubnow was noncommittal. The old man rose from his chair, walked up and down the room and, stopping suddenly, he said in a sad and moving voice: "Shimen, the time will come when you will say with the prophet Hosea: 'I will go and return to my first husband, For then it was better with me than now.'" The young "Acher" did not go to the synagogue. "The town of traditional piety," writes Dubnow, "witnessed an unheard-of experience: the grandson of Rabbi Bentsion, the spiritual leader of the community, appeared in the synagogue neither on Rosh Hashana nor on Yom Kippur, days on which even the most 'wicked Jews' attended services." Dubnow tells of how the townspeople cast evil glances at him as he walked through the streets on the Sabbath with a cane in his hand. Youngsters would call after him: "Carrying a cane on the Sabbath! Heretic! (*Mit'n shtok um shabes, apikoyres!*)"

Dubnow in his autobiography continues to contrast the two worlds —his own and his grandfather's:

One could thus see the following picture in our quiet provincial town following the fall of 1884: in two parallel streets, each in his study, surrounded by books, sat grandfather and grandson. One cultivated the wisdom of the Talmud and the rabbis and transmitted it to his hearers; the other dug just as assiduously into the new wisdom of the century and also had his auditory, a numerous but distant one, with which he could communicate only through the printed page. Both grandfather and grandson lived as hermits who were fulfilling a solemn vow. The meaning of life was intellectually different for each one, but ethically it was the same.[9]

It was during the same year 1884 that he wrote a violent attack upon the traditional *heder*, which he published in the *Voskhod*.

The entire pale is filled with thousands of children's prisons. These children are criminally tortured both in spirit and in body. Emaciated youngsters leave these institutions. They know nothing of childhood, fields, meadows or blue skies. They pass away their finest years of childhood within four walls, in sticky air, in spiritual tension that is far too much for their meager energies, under the rod of ignoramuses. An enormous Babylonian storehouse of wisdom is forcibly injected into the brains of these youngsters. They are told nothing about the real world, about nature and life, but only about the next world and about death.[10]

In the early 1880s, as Dubnow was approaching the age of maturity and decision, several paths were taken by Russian Jewish intellectuals leaving the confines of traditional orthodoxy. Some, like Leon Goldenberg, Pavel Akselrod, Juri Martov and Leo Deytch, became so imbued with the ideal of liberating the Russian people from their yoke of tyranny that they abandoned Jewish interests entirely and cast themselves, with all their ardor and energy, into the Russian revolutionary movement just beginning to emerge. Others, interested primarly in their own scholarly and professional development, left eastern Europe altogether and emigrated to seek their fortunes in the universities of Zurich, Berlin, Heidelberg or Paris. Still others, like M. L. Lilienblum, Leo Pinsker and Ahad Ha-Am, constituted the founders of the "Lovers of Zion" movement and the precursors of modern Zionism. They cultivated the modern Hebrew idiom, developed the Hebrew press and literature, and worked actively for the colonization of Palestine. Dubnow selected none of these paths. His major decisions throughout his life were never extreme. His reactions were never violent. Although he had been subjected to the traditional *heder* and although he wrote violently against it, he nevertheless was emancipated from this type of education at a very early age. His life was never that of the typical "*yeshiva boher*" who later vented all his resentments and frustrations upon this type of existence. When Dubnow suffered privation as a student, it was while preparing for gymnasium and university and not at the candlelight and on the hard bench of the *klaus*. Dubnow therefore at an early age achieved a much greater harmony and synthesis of his Jewish and non-Jewish worlds than was the case with those Jewish intellectuals whose "emancipation" traversed the hard road of material want combined with intellectual and spiritual frustration. Despite his early reaction against traditional and formal orthodoxy Dubnow never lost his deep attachment to Jewish lore and Jewish learning. A secularized image of his grandfather Bentsion was always before him. At the same time he acquired at an early age a deep attachment to the Russian language, to Russian literature and to Russia as the land of his Jewish forebears. Never, until after World War I, did Dubnow seriously contemplate emigration from Russia.[11] And when he did leave, in 1922, he chose to remain as close to the country of his birth as possible. As a scholar and writer Dubnow from the start adopted the Russian language as his vehicle of expression and he wrote all his major scholarly works in Russian. Even his history of Hasidism, which was the only work to appear first in Hebrew, was based on earlier essays originally published in Russian.

Dubnow therefore rejected both the way of the Jewish revolutionary as well as the way of the early Jewish nationalist. He never joined any revolutionary group nor was he hypnotized by Socialist literature. At the same time his general cosmopolitan outlook led him to reject the *Hibbat Tsiyon* movement of Lilienblum and Pinsker. His psychological and intellectual development was of the kind to favor the intermediate position of a synthesis of the Jewish and the non-Jewish environments in the form of "autonomism," although definite crystallization of these ideas did not come until a decade later.

On June 20, 1880, at the age of twenty, Dubnow came to try his fortune in the capital city of St. Petersburg. Since Jews were not allowed to live in the city without a special residence permit, Dubnow was forced to assume the fictitious status of house servant to an attorney. These legal problems of residence became still more complicated when, a few years later, he married Ida Friedlin. But it was during these first years in St. Petersburg that Dubnow began his literary and scholarly career. His first published article, a piece on his home town Mstislav, appeared in 1880 in the Russian-Jewish journal *Russkii evrei*. Duvnow also submitted an autobiographical novel, but it was rejected. Deeply embedded in Dubnow's emotional being was a desire to be an imaginative writer. While in his scholarly works he came to curb his literary and artistic imagination, in keeping with the scientific positivism that he espoused, one finds a glowing appreciation of nature and a definite attempt at literary-esthetic expression in his letters, in his diary entries and in his autobiography. But Dubnow soon came to throw in his lot with history. His first extended essay was on "Moments in the Historical Development of Jewish Thought," also published in the *Russkii evrei*, in 1881. For the next two years he contributed regularly to the *Rasvyet*, another Russian-Jewish periodical published in St. Petersburg.

At the end of 1882 he began his important association with the journal *Voskhod* which lasted for almost twenty-five years. The *Voskhod* occupied a central role in the life of Russian Jewish intellectuals. It counted the most creative talents of Russian Jewry among its contributors, and the whole pre-war Jewish intelligentsia in Russia derived a large part of their intellectual fare from its columns. Although Dubnow's relations with the publisher, Adolf Landau, were not always cordial and there was constant bickering about terms and honoraria, hardly an issue of the *Voskhod* appeared without something by Dubnow. Beginning with his first contribution, on Sabbatai Zevi, Dubnow published here most of the original studies for his history of hasidism, for his philosophy of history, much of the materials that later went into his *World History of the Jews*, his "Letters on Old and New Judaism" and a host of miscellaneous studies. Under the pseudonym "Criticus," Dubnow also assumed the role of a literary critic and made known to the Russian world the new talents and new creations in Yiddish literature.[12]

By the end of the 1880s, Dubnow had crystallized his life's ambition—to study and to write. With pictures of Heine, Börne, Shelley and Byron on the walls of his room, he carried on systematic and methodical self-education. Thirteen hours every day he studied history, sociology, philosophy and literature, while at the same time he made his living by writing. It was not until 1887, however, that he realized that Jewish history was to be his chosen field. In his autobiography he writes of that period:

At that time a struggle began in my innermost being between centripetal and centrifugal ideas, between the national and cosmopolitan principles. I felt that the birth pangs of my self-determination were coming to an end and that I would finally have to settle down to one of the many life projects that beckoned to me from different directions. The twenty-seventh year of my life was the decisive one for me. Up to that time my ideas were still diffused in general and universal literary projects, although actually I was working in the field of Jewish literature. Trouble with my eyes gave me a chance to ponder more deeply concerning these problems. I became convinced that true creativity unconditionally requires the process of self-limitation . . . that my road to universalism runs definitely by way of the national area in which I was working. . . . It became clear to me that acquired general knowledge and universal aspirations can lead to fruitful results in connection with the accumulated treasures of Jewish knowledge and the not yet crystallized national ideals. From then on dates my interest in the great themes of Jewish history—from a broadly conceived "History of Hasidism" and a complete history of east-European Jewry to a still broader plan for a general history of the Jewish people.[13]

Writing a few years later in his diary in Odessa he described his ideological road to historicism:

In historicism I found a counterforce to both religious and philosophical dogmatism. . . . I reasoned as follows: I am an agnostic in religion and philosophy . . . but I might learn how humanity lived . . . and what were its ways to find truth and justice. I lost my faith in individual immortality and . . . the study of the Jewish past binds me to something eternal. . . . Historicism led me out of the circle of individual problems to the broad avenue of social questions that are not as deep but are more immediate. . . . Here there opened for me the path to national synthesis which would merge the best elements of the old thesis and the new antithesis—the Jewish and the universally human values, the national and the humanistic.[14]

His diary entry for New Year's Day 1892 reads:

My life's task has become clear to me: to spread historical science and work especially on the history of the Russian Jews. I have become a missionary for history.[15]

In 1890 Dubnow came to Odessa. The thirteen years that he spent here may be considered the happiest in his life and the years in which he ripened and matured into the illustrious scholar and public figure. Here, at the shores of the Black Sea, where nature was richer and sunnier, despite all the political disabilities and outbreaks of violence against Jews, a rich, pulsating and colorful Jewish cultural life was in the exalted state of initial creativity. Here were gathered a galaxy of the leading figures in Hebrew and Yiddish literature. Here Dubnow met Mendele Mocher-Seforim, already a man of sixty, but full of sparkling wit and rich imagination. Neither Dubnow nor Mendele were members of any partisan group, and this immediately created a strong bond of friendship and sympathetic intimacy between them. In Odessa, in 1891, Dubnow first met Ahad Ha-Am and established a relationship that endured until the latter's death. Then there were the Russian and Yiddish poet Simon Frug, Sholem Aleichem, the essayist and publisher Ravnitski, the Hebrew writer Ben-Ami and later the newly acclaimed Chaim Nachman Bialik and the young talmudic scholar Chaim Tschernowitz. A circle of ten or twelve people began to come together, first informally and then in a more regular fashion. They would meet either in Dubnow's or Mendele's home on Saturday afternoons. During the summer they would gather in the beautiful suburbs of Odessa. Dubnow describes one such gathering in his autobiography:

We sat . . . up late at night, drinking wine, engaging in lively conversation and singing folksongs. Mendele was full of energy. He reminisced and brought out some original ideas. Frug sang a hasidic parody beautifully. Ben-Ami, who felt peaceful that evening, sang a sad hasidic tune and we all sang with him. The Jewish folksongs echoed through the sleepy German colony, and we had the resounding waves of the sea for accompaniment. We all felt so good that night, all of us who are so sad, so worried and so oppressed by our own troubles and by the troubles of our people.[16]

Out of this informal and literary circle later developed a new official body known as the "National Committee," of which Dubnow became chairman. The chief purpose of this committee was to combat assimilation among the Russian Jewish intelligentsia. For by this time Dubnow had been completely freed of his abstract cosmopolitanism and was beginning to formulate his theories of Jewish nationalism. Out of these activities emerged eventually his "Letters on Old and New Judaism," which he began publishing in the *Voskhod* in 1897 and which he continued till 1903 and then published in book form in 1907. The "National Committee" would also hold public meetings and Dubnow frequently appeared at such as chief speaker. In his autobiography Dubnow later recalled a typical session of the committee in his home:

There is Ahad Ha-Am, walking up and down the room, with the customary cigarette or a glass of tea in his hand, outwardly calm and listening more than talking; then the energetic Dizengoff, the quiet Ravnitski, and Ben-Ami always pouring abuse; then the secretary of the Palestine Committee, the lively and active Druyanov, the liberal talmudic scholar Chaim Tschernowitz, the essayist Lewinski and many others.[17]

In this intensive and exalted Jewish atmosphere Dubnow was first and foremost the Jewish historian. Here in Odessa matured the various facets of his historical lifework—the collector and organizer of Russian Jewish historiography, the student of autonomous institutions, the historian of hasidism, the great synthesizer of world Jewish history. He had already started the publication of his first essays on hasidism in the *Voskhod* in 1888. Now he began the systematic collection of hasidic and anti-hasidic materials. It was a completely uncharted field when Dubnow began his researches. He approached the problem not with the hostility of the earlier *maskilim*, nor with the mystical idealized love of Horodetzky or Buber later on, but with his characteristic sober mixture of sympathy and critical analysis. He sought above all to uncover the social foundations of the movement. He traveled to Warsaw and ransacked the old bookshops for rare hasidica. In 1897, on his way to Switzerland, he visited Galicia and traversed the strongholds of the hasidism of his day. The positivist and rationalist "Litvak" confessed to a feeling of strangeness and even revulsion at the typical hasidic life of his own day. An entry in his diary, recorded in Lemberg in 1897, reads as follows:

Last night I sought out one of the hasidic synagogues during services. There was crowding, disorder, shouting, strange howling instead of song, dirt, sticky air. . . . The train ride to Lemberg had taken me through Zloczow, Zbaraz and other historical places in hasidic history. In the forests and defiles that we passed I believed I saw a vision: the Besht as he was praying amidst nature and gathering medicinal herbs, or the shades of Mikhl of Zloczow, Wolf of Zbaraz and others. Have they not put to sleep for a whole century this dark human mass in long kaftans with wide sashes? . . . I feel strange here. This feeling in an important historical site of my brethren is peculiar, but I have so little in common both in language and in ideas with this living remnant of the past that the feeling of estrangement involuntarily creeps into my heart.[18]

In a letter dated February 20, 1939, to Samuel Linik, an American student of Salo W. Baron's who had sent to Dubnow a copy of a dissertation he had written on him, Dubnow explained that all his published works up to 1886 were only compilatory and amateurish in character and that his first works that could be called scholarly were his essays on hasidism published in the *Voskhod* between 1888 and 1893.[19] At this time Dubnow's historical philosophy and methodology were still under the influence of Heinrich Graetz. In 1892, on the death of Graetz, Dubnow published a long obituary on him in the *Voskhod*. "My essays," wrote Dubnow later in his autobiography, "were permeated with the sorrows of the present and the pathos of the past."[20] He projected a three-volume Russian abridgment of Graetz's *History* and wrote a long essay on "What is Jewish History, An Attempt at a Philosophical Analysis," which was to serve as the introduction to the Graetz volumes, but which was first published in the *Voskhod* in 1893. The Graetz project never materialized, but the philosophical essay was later translated into German by Israel Friedlaender and then into English by Henrietta Szold.[21] It was the first work by Dubnow to be acclaimed abroad. While critical in some respects of Graetz, Dubnow was inspired by Graetz's conception of the Jews as a spiritual people. In two important respects he deviated from the master. In contrast to Graetz's disparagement of mysticism and hasidism, Dubnow's first historical studies, as we have seen, were on Sabbatai Zevi and then on hasidism. More important still, Dubnow set it as his goal to correct the negative and indifferent attitude of Graetz and other western Jewish scholars to the history of the Jews in eastern Europe. He made it his life's ambition to bring the study of the history of the Jews in Russia, Poland, Lithuania and White Russia to the same plane of scholarly and scientific quality as that achieved by the *Wissenschaft des Judentums* in the West.

During this time too he began his historical investigations into the various communal and autonomous Jewish institutions in eastern Europe which went hand in hand with the development of his political philosophy of autonomism for contemporary Jewry. Dubnow himself delved into archives, dug out old minute books and continued to publish long studies on Russian Jewish history in the *Voskhod*. But he realized very early that the task called for a national communal effort rather than the work of a few individuals. In 1891 he published a long essay in the *Voskhod* on "The Study of the History of Russian Jews and the Establishment of a Russian Jewish Historical Society," in which he called for the systematic collection of source materials on Russian Jewish history as a necessary step for the writing of a solid and scholarly history of Russian Jewry. The essay was republished as a separate pamphlet and later in an abridged form in Hebrew under the title *Nahpesa v'Nahkora. Kol kore el hanevonim baam hamitnadvim leesof homer lebinyan toledot yisrael bepolin uverusiya.*

> *I appeal* [wrote Dubnow] *to all well-meaning persons, Jews and non-Jews, to help create a Russian-Jewish historiography. This is a sacred duty for us. We Russian Jews wish to demonstrate that we are not only a branch of the most historical of all peoples but that we too have a rich historical past. We also wish to demonstrate that we understand how to evaluate our past. An old people that has grown up and become gray in rich experiences cannot give up its unique historical past.*[22]

Dubnow's call for the organization of a historical society was not realized until many years later, in 1908, when Maxim Vinaver and Baron Günzburg organized the Russian Jewish Historical Ethnographic Society in St. Petersburg. But his call for the gatherings of source materials found immediate response throughout all parts of the Russian empire. Young Jewish intellectuals in all parts of the pale, even those not capable of scholarly work themselves, found both intellectual and Jewish national satisfaction in digging out source materials and sending them on to Dubnow. Throughout his long life Dubnow became the recipient of such materials from all over eastern Europe and thus was able to build up his enormously rich archival collection. Later, when the Yiddish Scientific Institute was established, the same passion for the collection of source materials as a sacred national duty became part and parcel of its network of *zamlers* or collectors of materials. We may even say that this call for the collection and preservation of source materials was behind the passion of the tragic victims of Nazi liquidation, who in their last moments of martyrdom risked all in order to record, collect and preserve the records of their experiences. It was the spirit that inspired Zelig Kalmanovich in Vilna as it did Emanuel Ringelblum in Warsaw and all the unknown and simple Jews who in the ghettos, concentration camps and later in the DP centers continued to carry out Dubnow's call of *Nahpesa v'Nahkora*.

Dubnow was no cloistered scholar. He was constantly torn between the quiet of the study and his books and archives on the one hand, and the battle for Jewish rights and the arena of current issues agitating the Jewish scene, on the other. This is what helped to fashion his conception of history as living history. "The essence of historicism," he wrote, "is to embrace the past with the vitality of the swiftly moving moment and the present is to be viewed historically."[23]

After a visit to Abraham Harkavy, the distinguished academic scholar and historian of the old school, he wrote in his diary: "Everything here is congealed; a mummy of history is buried in a cellar among books and papers. . . . Our paths really diverge. For me history is a spring of bubbling life, of struggle, of creation, a source of world views."[24] But the situation was becoming too tense for Dubnow in Odessa. The public controversies, the concern with current issues came to divert too much of his energy from his historical work. This situation became even more aggravated after the Kishinev massacre of 1903, when Dubnow together with the other Jewish intellectuals was active in organizing measures of defense and counterpropaganda.

As a result, Dubnow reluctantly decided to leave Odessa in 1903. Over thirty of his friends took leave of him at a gathering at which many chided him for going away. Mendele reviewed the whole period of Dubnow's stay in Odessa and recalled with especial fondness the earlier days when, in place of official "sessions" and debates, they carried on their quiet and friendly conversations regarding the "higher problems of life and literature."

The Odessa period [wrote Dubnow in his autobiography] was the high summer time of my life. It is still a long way to autumn, but the best years of my life are behind me. . . . I have left the sunny south, the warm sea, my friends and co-militants. . . . Seeking rest for my wearied soul and quiet for my scholarly work, I have changed my place. Unfortunately it is not up to me to change the times, and the succeeding years of my life coincide with an epoch of social storm and stress.[25]

Dubnow lived for three years, between 1903 and 1906, in Vilna. This period witnessed the Russo-Japanese war and the first Russian revolution. While carrying on his research and scholarly writing, Dubnow could not avoid involvement in the great movement for Jewish emancipation in Russia that began on the eve of the revolution. He participated in the organizational meeting of the League for the Attainment of Equal Rights for Jews in Russia, which was established by the gifted Jewish communal leaders and lawyers, Maxim Vinaver and Henryk Slyozberg, both of St. Petersburg. Together with B. Goldberg and Shmaryahu Levin, Dubnow was elected to the Vilna section of the committee. He was especially pleased at the acceptance by this all-Russian Jewish committee of his program of Jewish autonomous rights.

The early success of the revolution in 1905 and the manifesto of the tsar promising Russia a constitutional regime filled Dubnow with glowing hopes for the future. In his diary at the time he wrote as follows: "In my soul sings the quiet music of nature in bloom and of the new Russia on the march. . . . At noon the newspapers arrive. I attack them and devour the news. . . . The majority is in a mood of opposition, the battle for liberty is being prepared. . . ." He later recalled those days: "Only the people of my generation, who for a quarter of a century, while chained in slavery, dreamed of a constitution, of a constitutional assembly, only they can understand the mood of the spring of 1906 when the harassed soul was yearning for faith in a new Russia and a renewed Judaism in it."[26]

In September 1906 Dubnow moved to St. Petersburg to occupy a special chair for Jewish history created in the newly-organized Russian progressive university known as the "Free University of Professor Lesgoft." The university was soon dissolved by the police as the early progressive winds of the revolution began to give way to a return to reaction. But Dubnow now managed to remain in the capital city and stayed there until he left Russia in 1922. This period marks for him a new epoch of creative historical work, in which the process of synthesizing his earlier studies begins to absorb the major part of his activity. A much greater feeling of peace with himself and resolution of inner conflicts are now apparent. His diary in 1910 records the following entry:

God is so near to me. He is in me, in every urge of mine to eternity, in my entire tense spiritual striving. . . . This is the way a person who is a servant of the spirit must live. . . . This is the way my grandfather, R. Bentsion, lived, and this is the way I have been living from that moment when grandfather and grandchild, along two parallel streets of Mstislav, in the stillness of their libraries, each in his way was seeking eternity. . . . The soul of my grandfather is so close to me! It may be hovering over me now—no, it lives on in me in a second metamorphosis of the soul.

I have returned, although without the ritual and the dogmas, to the source of the spirit from which we both drew. . . . I have continued to repeat my most beloved verse of the Psalms, which described the essence of my grandfather's life as it does of mine. "One thing I have asked of the Lord, that I will seek after: that I may dwell in the house of the Lord all the days of my life." I always interpreted those words to mean unending spiritual creativity.[27]

It was during this St. Petersburg period of his life that Dubnow did most of the work that later went into his great, ten-volume, general history of the Jews. In 1910 appeared the first volume, dealing with the ancient period of Jewish history, and in 1914 the first volume of his *Recent History of the Jewish People,* which was to appear later in a three-volume edition in German even before the entire ten volumes had been published. A source of financial benefit as well as of great pedagogic influence came from his preparation of a textbook in Jewish history for use in modern Jewish schools. It was soon translated into Hebrew, Yiddish and later also into English, and for over a quarter of a century to follow generations of young Jews in Russia, Poland, Lithuania, the United States and wherever eastern European Jews settled were to acquire their knowledge of Jewish history from this text.

In 1907, when the League for the Attainment of Equal Rights fell apart and different factions organized themselves separately, Dubnow and his followers established the Folkspartay. This was Dubnow's sole attempt at political and communal leadership and it was not a very successful one. The party was revived under different leadership in Poland after World War I and was more successful at that time. These communal stirrings, however, led Dubnow to bring together his "Letters on Old and New Judaism" that he had published in the *Voskhod,* to re-edit them, add new material and publish the whole in book form, which appeared in a stout volume in 1907. "You will find much that is new in the old," he wrote to Ahad Ha-Am in telling him of this publication.[28] At the same time he also agreed to join the editorial board of the new Russian Jewish encyclopedia which was projected on the model of the *Jewish Encyclopedia* of America. Dubnow had already contributed a number of articles to the American encyclopedia. He was always forced by financial worries to digress from his main scholarly work to more popular or educational projects, although he never demeaned himself in any way for the sake of earning more money. The Russian Jewish encyclopedia was a project that was close to his heart and he consented to co-operate and at the same time was assured of a fixed salary of 5,000 rubles a year for five years. In his diary he commented as follows on this problem:

I have never chased after large honoraria. I have always preferred poverty with the work I like to riches with work that is not to my liking. But the work of the Encyclopedia does interest me and without me the project might collapse. . . . So what then? Shall I sacrifice five of the few years I have to live? And I am always afraid that I will not be able to complete my work.[29]

In the fall of 1908 Vinaver reorganized the Historical-Ethnographic Society, realizing Dubnow's dream of seventeen years earlier, and Dubnow became vice-chairman of the Society. After the *Voskhod* was closed by the authorities two new Russian Jewish journals began to appear in St. Petersburg and they were even more to Dubnow's taste than the earlier one. They were the *Evreyskaya starina* and the *Evreyskii mir*. The first was a purely scholarly journal, the second a journal of opinion on current issues. Dubnow was active in both, and the *Evreyskaya starina* is a mine of historical materials from the pen of Dubnow himself and from other authors whom he attracted. Dubnow never cultivated a school of historians in the academic sense of the term, since he was active in university posts only at intermittent and for very brief periods. But his influence was felt by the persons whom he attracted to the publications or by circles in which he enjoyed a position of leadership. This was true of the contributors he assembled for the Russian Jewish encyclopedia and even more so of the scholars he gathered around the *Evreyskaya starina* to deal with the history of the Jews in Russia and Poland. Among the contributors were Meir Balaban, Yitzhok Shipper, Moshe Shor, Yuri Hessen, Mark Wischnitzer, S. Anski and others. To these might be added the names of Solomon Zeitlin and Zalman Rubashov. The latter were not disciples of his in a literal sense but they were profoundly influenced by his historical method and by his philosophy of Jewish life.

In far-off United States, Dubnow had acquired a different sort of apostle and admirer. Israel Friedlaender had already come to admire Dubnow when he was a student in Germany and in 1898 had translated into German Dubnow's essay on Jewish history. He also translated the first two "Letters" into German in 1905. On coming to the United States, Friedlaender, although a Zionist and a member of the faculty of the Jewish Theological Seminary, saw the applicability of Dubnow's work to American Jewry along two lines. Despite his official Zionist affiliations Friedlaender accepted Dubnow's analysis of Diaspora nationalism and saw the possibility of applying Dubnow's autonomist doctrines to the American scene. This no doubt was the philosophical basis for Friedlaender's activities in behalf of a Kehillah in New York City. As a product of east-European Jewry and one who never sought to conceal the fact or to revile this part of his past, as so many figures in official American Jewish life did at the time, Friedlaender saw the great need of building a bridge between American Jewry and the Jews of Russia and Poland, from which the greatest part of the Jewish immigration had been coming since 1880. The first prerequisite for such a bridge was knowledge of the old-world past of these Russian and Polish Jews. Friedlaender therefore conceived the plan of asking Dubnow to prepare a history of the Jews in Russia and Poland and he induced the Jewish Publication Society of America, headed at that time by one of the stalwarts of the German-Jewish leadership in this country, Judge Mayer Sulzberger, to publish the work. The acceptance of the project by the Society speaks highly for both the persuasiveness of Friedlaender and the open-mindedness of Judge Sulzberger. On December 6, 1910, after preliminary negotiations, Friedlaender wrote definitely to Dubnow regarding the project, promising him an honorarium of $2,000 for the manuscript. Dubnow accepted the offer and wrote to Friedlaender on December 26, 1910, as follows: "What attracts me most, is your principal argument: the desire to connect the American branch of Jewry, which is continually developing and occupying an important place in the future of our people, to its ancient root in the east of Europe."[30]

Out of these negotiations emerged Dubnow's three-volume *History of the Jews in Russia and Poland*, which was finally completed, after interruption by war and revolution, with the publication of the third volume in 1920. The ironical aspect about this work is that Dubnow, the great historian of Russian Jewry, actually never published a complete and separate history of the Jews in Russia in his own country. This work was prepared especially for the American publishers and was translated by Israel Friedlaender.

When World War I broke out, Dubnow, despite his hostility to the tsarist regime and despite his bitterness at the Jewish disabilities in Russia, was far-sighted enough to see the dangers that would come from a victory by the Central Powers and he supported the Russian war effort. "The defeat of Germany," he wrote in his diary at the time, "this militaristic spider that has spun its web over all of Europe, will bring salvation to the world. The joint victory of Russia, France and England will not strengthen the reaction in Russia. On the contrary, it will purify the atmosphere."[31] On the other hand, he was filled with chagrin at the numerous instances of violence against Jews at the very time they were shedding their blood for the Russian fatherland and he was never able to suppress his sorrow over the fact that Jews were killing other Jews on the various battle fronts. In a series of articles under the title "Inter Arma," published in the *Novii voskhod* and *Evreyskaya nedelye,* Dubnow laid bare the tragedy of the Jewish people, still deprived of their civil rights in Russia, and he looked toward the long overdue rectification of this situation as one of the important results of the war. He took the allied declarations on the rights of small nations as the basis for demanding also national rights for the Jews. Dubnow's articles made an especially profound impression on Russian liberal writers like Maxim Gorki, Leonid Andreyev and Fedor Sologub, who in 1915 organized the League to Combat Antisemitism. Pogroms, persecutions and disturbances, however, continued to harass the Jewish population and to grieve Dubnow as well as the other communal leaders in Russia. On top of this came the news of the passing of several of his closest friends: of Sholem Aleichem in 1916, then of Simon Frug a few days later. All these tense developments were hardly conducive to calm and detached scholarship. Yet Dubnow continued to work on his general history of the Jews during those disturbing years. He always showed an amazing capacity for carrying on his scholarly studies even under the most trying physical and material conditions.

The revolution which came in March 1917 brought only a very brief period of relaxed tension for Dubnow. He was not as enthusiastic and hopeful in the early stages of the 1917 revolution as he had been during the earlier revolution in 1905. He was full of anxiety regarding the dangers of anarchy and he was oppressed by the continuation of the war. His diary entry for February 28, 1917 (old style), concludes with the sentences: "My soul is filled with the greatness of the historical moment. Perhaps the year 1917 will finally bring the realization of our hopes." But on March 8 he writes:

There is something strange about this revolution. It is like the current weather, spring sun and yet cold. The sun sends off its rays but it does not warm. Terrible things are going on at the fronts. The counterrevolution is beginning to be active. At the moment everything is fine: equal rights for Jews came overnight. What we have been fighting for for decades has been attained. The disgraceful police state is overthrown. Our Jewish leaders, Vinaver, Gruzenberg and others have been invited to become senators. Nonetheless spring does not seem to want to come to my soul. The nightmare of the war weighs heavily upon the revolution.[32]

March 21, the date of the official manifesto by the Provisional Government proclaiming Jewish emancipation in Russia, is noted in the diary as "the completion of the dream of his whole lifetime" and "the realization of the goal of the fight" but he comments also: "War and anarchy must come to an end first, before we can enjoy the blessings of this liberation. At present we still have the crass contrast between the exalted character of the revolution and its powerlessness against hunger."[33] He was soon to feel the full effects of hunger and privation.

Dubnow from the start saw the grave dangers of the Bolshevist agitation and the perils to the revolution from the activities of Lenin. On May 1, 1917, he wrote in his diary: "The dictatorship of the proletariat is spreading like a contagious disease; following the plan of Lenin and his followers it can only lead to violent expropriations." On June 9 of the same year he appeared as one of the speakers at a large Jewish gathering in St. Petersburg. In this speech, which contains the gist of Dubnow's lifelong political philosophy, he said:

We have been overtaken, to our surprise, by the anarchy now dominating our road from the revolution that liberated us to the constituent assembly that is to set down the forms of our future existence. We have barely had a chance to express publicly our feel-

ings on the proclamation of our civic emancipation and our thoughts regarding our future national constitution, when the course of events has forced us, at this first general Jewish assembly, to take a stand on the unhealthy situation between revolution and counter-revolution. Can the oldest cultural people, which had its own "social revolutionaries" in its Prophets over two thousand years ago, which dared to say to its kings what we today are saying to the dethroned tsar, can such a veteran of culture accept without protest this anarchy, this children's disease of culturally backward peoples? It is true that a few demogogues, who have joined up with the street heroes and the preachers of forcible expropriation, have come out of our midst too. They appear under Russian pseudonyms, because they are ashamed of their Jewish origins (Trotsky, Zinoviev and others). But it would be better to say that their Jewish names are pseudonyms; they are not rooted in our people. Under the flag of the democratic republic we will march together with those who will keep our democracy clear of excesses from both left and right. As pacifists by historical tradition we will fight for the kind of conclusion of the present war which will destroy the rule of militarism. We will support the position that the class principle must be subordinated to the national principle.[34]

The triumph of the Bolshevists in November 1917 brought on Dubnow a period of the greatest physical want and spiritual suffering. He gave vent to his feelings against the regime in his diary; he came to regard the diary as his greatest treasure, but likewise as a source of great danger to him should agents of the Cheka ever come in possession of it. He compared his secreting it from the Bolshevists to his former hiding it from the agents of the tsarist regime, and he added significantly: "Then I would have faced Siberia; today I am in danger of being shot."[35]

Dubnow remained under the Bolshevist regime until April 23, 1922. For the first time he toyed with the idea of emigrating and leaving the land of his birth. The dictatorship and terror of the Bolsheviks shocked and horrified him. Physical want was wasting his energies. For a while he was able to carry on Jewish scholarly work, but the activities of the Jewish Communists were making this increasingly difficult. An entry in his diary for December 12, 1918, gives a picture of the privation he and his family were enduring:

I got up quite early, got dressed, put on my winter coat, rubbers and hat (in the room the temperature was 7 degrees Centigrade) and sat down to work. With frozen fingers I wrote about the Dominicans and the French inquisition of the thirteenth century. At ten o'clock I had a bite, looked at the daily paper and set out for the Fuel Division of the regional soviet to get a requisition for wood. I got into a line of hundreds of persons. The line extended over the steps of the lower entrance to the huge building. . . . I stood for two hours amidst the crowd of unfortunate and excited individuals and, like hundreds of them, I too went away empty-handed. The requisitions were exhausted before they got to us. . . . I returned home all broken up. On the way back I bought a pound and a half of bread. . . . In the courtyard of our house there was both good fortune and trouble. A friend of ours did us a favor and sent us some wood. . . . Night was already beginning to fall. Wearied I resumed my interrupted work. I finished a paragraph and I sat and thought: we are fortunate, we shall have wood to heat the kitchen (I myself carried up a few heavy logs) and poor Ida will not have to freeze or run to some neighbor in order to cook something. . . . We suffer more from cold than from hunger.[36]

In the meantime his friends and students in the newly-established independent state of Lithuania had been trying to secure Dubnow's emigration from Russia. Jewish national rights had been established in the little state and a Jewish Minister for Jewish Affairs was in the cabinet. Through his intervention the University of Kovno addressed a formal invitation to Dubnow to become professor of Jewish history at their institution and requested the Soviet government to allow him to leave. The request was initiated in January 1921, but more than fifteen months of negotiation, delays, investigations and red tape had to pass before Dubnow was finally able to leave Russia on April 23, 1922. On June 18, 1921, the entry in his diary reads:

I am leaving Russia for ever—this is the basic melody of these days. I would like to say good-bye to all the things to which I am attached in this country. How I long to see once more my old native town, wander through the streets of the town in which I was born and shed tears at the graves of my grandfather and parents.[37]

On April 21, 1922, he writes: "I have the even stronger feeling that I am fleeing, not from Egypt, but from Sodom."[38]

In March 1922, Dubnow finally secured his exit visa from the Soviet authorities. A problem that gave him endless concern was how to take along his books, archives and above all his "dangerous" diary. In all his travels and migrations, down to his last days, Dubnow was always attached to his personal library and archives and never moved without them. In this case there was also grave political danger. An interesting coincidence saved him at this time. Permission was given that his baggage be examined at his home instead of at the frontier, and the official sent to do the examining was not a trained customs official but a young history student. Dubnow engaged the young student in conversation about some of the books and manuscripts that lay on top of the heap and the young student was so enraptured by the conversation that he did not bother to look at the materials under the top heap and automatically ordered the police official who was with him to seal up all the trunks and approve them for exit all the way to Kovno. In this way Dubnow was able to salvage his entire library and all his archives and all the materials that were later to go into his ten-volume history, as well as his autobiography and his other writings.

Dubnow did not remain in Kovno long. The intellectual climate and the scholarly facilities were too limited in this tiny republic. In September 1922, he moved to Berlin. Here too he was not spiritually very happy. In a letter to Ahad Ha-Am dated April 22, 1924, he complains of the barrenness of Jewish life in Berlin. "I have no spiritual hold on the life of the present, for formlessness and void reign here," he writes.[39]

It would seem that he too, like many a refugee from Russia, was waiting for the day when the hated Bolshevist dictatorship would collapse and he would be able to return to Russia. In a letter to Maxim Vinaver of July 30, 1922, however, he expressed contrary sentiments. To Vinaver, who had emigrated to Paris, Dubnow writes from Danzig:

After all, dear friend, we are both emigrés. True, we are citizens of a world Diaspora, members of the historical international created before the days of Alexander the Great. Nevertheless, one feels the pain of a nest destroyed. I do not even have the faith which still keeps you going: the faith in the revival of a Jewish center in Russia.[40]

Writing to Ahad Ha-Am in 1924, he says: "One thing can stand in the way of redemption, namely, the wicked regime of the new Russia, which has inherited all the tyranny of the old Russia and added to it its own good measure."[41] His hatred of the Bolshevist regime increased even more as Stalin took over the mantle of control from Lenin. However, he did find in Berlin a circle of devoted followers and friends who made his intellectual and personal existence more agreeable. Among these were Joseph Meisel, Simon Rawidowicz, Jacob Leshtchinsky, Aaron Steinberg, his former student Mark Wischnitzer, the poet Daniel Charny and, above all, his devoted disciple Elias Tscherikower and his wife. Among German-Jewish scholars he established cordial relations with Ismar Elbogen, David Koigen and Aaron Freimann. Always a diligent correspondent, he maintained contacts with all his close friends of former years now scattered in all corners of the globe. From Berlin too he participated in the founding of the Yivo, or Yiddish Scientific Institute, in Vilna and until his death this institution was dearest to his heart. He participated in its organizational meetings and in its general conferences, and contributed to its publications. If Dubnow can be said to have left behind a school of historians, then the scholars gathered around the Yivo are those most accurately described as such. An interesting description of Dubnow as he appeared during his life in Berlin has been recorded by Wolf Rabinovich, author of a study on Karlin hasidism and a disciple of Dubnow, who describes his impressions of a visit to Dubnow's home in 1929.

Dubnow received me cordially the way one receives a friend and colleague. His home was modest, as was its furniture. His study was small and it seemed as if there was harmony between his lean figure, his modest bearing and his simple living quarters. He was dressed in a simple Russian jacket, and on his writing table were many papers and books, all neatly arranged. We conversed in Russian and talked of hasidism in rabbinist Lithuania. . . .

In his meetings with young scholars he showed, not only his readi-

ness and willingness to guide us and assist us, but also his humility and modesty, qualities that were not too often found among our Jewish scholars in western Europe. We young scholars knew that he had no preferences other than devotion to historical truth. . . . When we walked out of his study we felt that the door to his home was always open to us for advice and counsel. Dubnow was also close to us because he was the only Russian-Jewish scholar of stature that we, descendants of east-European Jews, found in those days in Germany. We sensed the great difference between him and the western Jewish scholars. We knew that he was one of the founders of the Jewish national movement, of which we were the products, and he also served as a symbol to us of that liberal Russian culture that was also close to our hearts.[42]

It was during his stay in Germany that Dubnow brought to completion his great historical works. Here he published in 1924 his edition of the *Pinkas* of the Lithuanian Council. Here he contributed articles on his chosen fields of interest to the various encyclopedias being published in various parts of the world—the Hebrew *Eshkol* encyclopedia, the German *Enciclopedia Judaica* and *Jüdisches Lexikon* and the American *Encyclopedia of the Social Sciences.* In Berlin he finally saw the full publication of his ten-volume *Weltgeschichte des jüdischen Volkes,* translated from the Russian manuscript by Dr. A. Steinberg and issued by the Jüdischer Verlag between the years 1925 and 1929. With this work Dubnow took over the mantle of Jewish national historian from Graetz. Dubnow's *Weltgeschichte* may in truth be called the first secular and purely scholarly synthesis of the entire course of Jewish history, free from dogmatic and theological trappings, balanced in its evaluation of the various epochs and various regional groupings of Jewish historical development, fully cognizant of social and economic currents and influences, and, above all, sane and realistic in its approach.

In Dubnow's approach to all historical as well as current problems the element of healthy common sense always was dominant. A product of White Russian Jewry, he embodied in his person a synthesis between the cold, rationalist, *true* "Litvak" and the unbridled and super-emotional Ukrainian or Polish Jew. He had genuine warmth, true affection, real sympathy—but always in the right proportions, with the proper balance and the proper measure of sanity and common sense. Whether it was this basic emotional approach that attracted him to the English school of thinkers and to the empirical traditions of English liberalism, or whether he developed these approaches to human problems as a result of the British influences is immaterial; the combination of the two resulted in a basic sanity characteristic of all his work and writing. One never finds in him sickly national romanticism; there is no mystical quest for God, no wrestling with demons. One cannot combine his theories or philosophy with existentialism or with Kierkegard. It stubbornly resists all mystical or metaphysical affiliations.

No matter what differences one may have with the plan of periodization of his history, or the national theory underlying the work, it remains a lasting monument of great erudition, sober scholarship and research, amazing synthesis and at the same time a model of literary historical writing in the best tradition. No one dealing with the problems of Jewish history can afford to dispense with it. And so it has been translated into many languages, English, alas, being one of the few exceptions. Baruch Krupnik prepared a Hebrew translation; Zelig Kalmanovich initiated a Yiddish translation which has now been completed by a group of American translators working under the auspices of the Congress for Jewish Culture, although the actual publication of the volumes has taken place in Argentina. A Spanish translation is also under way and in the very last days of his life Dubnow saw through a Russian edition published in Riga. One must be careful in using the various editions of this work. Dubnow never just let a translation go through as is. He always reworked and re-edited each edition as it came out. According to his own testimony the German edition is the definitive version of the history,[43] but in the Russian edition published in Riga, Dubnow added an epilogue on events after 1914 which was not found in the original text. This epilogue is now also included in the Yiddish translation. Similarly one finds enlightening comments in the prefaces that he wrote for the various linguistic versions of his history.

In Berlin, Dubnow also brought to final fruition his long preoccupation with the history of hasidism. He had promised Ahad Ha-Am that he would write at least one work originally in Hebrew, and this he did with his final history of hasidism. The original version of this is the Hebrew, but here too there are Yiddish and German versions that were published with the full co-operation of the author. Hasidism was Dubnow's first love. He began his scholarly studies with essays on hasidism published in the *Voskhod* and his history of hasidism is the last product of his scholarly life. The Hebrew edition was published under the title *Toldot hahasidut bitkufat tsemihata vegidula al yesod mekorot rishonim nidpasim vekitve yad* (The History of Hasidism in the Period of its Growth and Development Based on Original Sources both Printed and Manuscript) in two volumes, in 1931-1932. In the preface to the Yiddish edition he writes:

I had to gather the building material all by myself, dig for sand, clay, make the bricks and then erect the building according to a definite architectonic plan. I used the entire hasidic literature, both the learned works and the legendary materials, and I attempted to find some system in the maze of the various hasidic currents and tried to reveal the kernel of truth present in the naive folk tales. I sought for a verification of my hypotheses in the literature of the misnagdim. . . . In this manner I found a way of bringing the statics of hasidism into relationship with the dynamic process of Jewish life.[44]

Dubnow has been found wanting by some hasidic enthusiasts as being too rationalistic in his approach to the history of hasidism; he has also been criticized for his complete disparagement of developments in hasidism after the first decades of the nineteenth century. While he is undoubtedly right in insisting that the creative period of hasidism ended about 1815, it is odd that this social historian should not have seen also the important social elements in the popular hasidic rabbis of the nineteenth and twentieth centuries and should not have carried his studies down through the more recent period. His work is a pioneer study in the field and is indispensable for any study of the subject, but it has already been supplemented by the work of younger scholars and will need still further supplementation for the period since 1815.

The coming to power of Hitler in January 1933 brought the seventy-three-year-old Dubnow face to face with emigration once again. East-European Jews seemed to sense the full meaning of Nazism before the native German Jews did, and their status as either stateless persons or citizens of other countries made them more immediately subject to abuse and persecution. As a result they were the first to emigrate from Germany and one by one the circle of Dubnow's close associates and friends sought refuge in other lands. Dubnow was full of sadness at having once again to dig up his moorings and find a sanctuary for himself and his wife and for his library and archives. From all sides came suggestions to go to Paris, to Switzerland, to America, to Palestine. He rejected them all in favor of Riga, in Latvia. There is a curious ambivalence in Dubnow's attitude toward emigration to Palestine. His diary and his letters are full of contradictory sentiments on that subject. As far back as 1919 he wrote in his diary of his dream to end his days in Palestine "in order to give his historical work the garb of the national language," but, he continued to muse, he is afraid the dream will never come true. "It is decreed," he wrote then, "that I shall die in the wilderness and on the verge of death to hear the voice say to me! 'Thou shalt not go over thither!' How I would like to be among the saved ones, but how can I leave those that are perishing?"[45]

Abraham Levinson, his Hebrew translator, urged him again in 1934 to go to Palestine. He appealed to his sense of historical concreteness to emulate Graetz and Eduard Meyer, who had felt an obligation to visit the scene of ancient Jewish history. Dubnow replied: "I move easily in time, but not in space. In my researches I can move swiftly from period to period, from the twelfth to the sixteenth century, for example; but to move several thousand kilometers from Riga to Jerusalem is not within my powers."[46] And so, when urged in 1933 to come to Palestine he refused. "Years ago," he wrote to Tscherikower, "I would have gone. But now it is too late to break up my life." "There are many arguments in favor of Riga," he wrote again to Tscherikower. "The environment is not as alien. I shall be near the children—in Soviet Russia and in Warsaw. We live a sad life here—outwardly calm but full of internal agitation. The transition is hard, the mood is one of emigration. Our friends in Eretz Yisrael wonder why I do not want to settle there. They do not understand that at my age the change in climate, in language, and in the whole way of life would mean simply to ruin my remaining energy and kill any hope of achieving something."[47]

In August 1933 the Dubnows left Berlin for Riga. Here they found a still functioning Jewish cultural autonomy, of the sort that he had preached all his life, and a warm, although provincial, Jewish atmosphere. But the advent of Nazism in nearby Germany also furthered the spread of Latvian chauvinism and the political climate was anything but tranquil. The reactionary elements triumphed in Latvia in 1934 and ousted the more liberal regime. In January 1934 his lifelong companion Ida died and he was left alone to seek comfort and consolation in his work. His optimism did not forsake him even under the most trying conditions. Writing to Tscherikower from Riga he said:

I would be plunged into melancholy if not for my beloved work and that poetry of thought that reveals itself to me in moments of solitary meditation and which has saved my spirit in the most severe moments of my life. I look with philosophic calm even upon the insanity of the present-day world. I only wonder whether our generation will live to see the end of this epidemic.[48]

To Mordecai ben Hillel Hakohen in Palestine he writes on October 31, 1933: "Even in my isolation I have not ceased following and observing all that goes on in our world. I read many newspapers, I hear a great deal from visitors who come to see me in Kaiserwald and I exchange correspondence with friends and acquaintances in all corners of the earth."[49] His long-standing devotion to *Torah lishmah*, which he shared with his grandfather Bentsion, stood him in good stead in these last trying years. On October 6, 1936, he writes to Joseph Meisel in Palestine: "I devote myself to study out of desire for self-preservation. For in these topsy-turvy days of ours it is as impossible for a thinking and sentient being to continue to exist outside the atmosphere of 'Torah' as it is for a fish to live out of water."[50] He devoted himself chiefly during these years to writing his autobiography. This he again wrote in Russian as his last monument to the

Russian Jewish life of which he was a product. Three volumes of this work appeared under the title *Kniga zhizni* (The Book of My Life). Here Dubnow also arranged for the publication of the Russian edition of his *World History of the Jewish People* and even added the new epilogue on events after 1914. From many sides again came pleas to emigrate to Palestine or to the United States. Jewish intellectuals began leaving Riga and urged Dubnow to follow suit. He refused. Latzki-Bertoldi, a Diaspora-nationalist disciple of Dubnow, decided to leave for Palestine and he wrote to Dubnow inquiring whether this was not a form of negation of the Diaspora. Dubnow replied as follows:

When you ask me, as an old comrade of the Folkspartay, whether this movement in our own ranks to settle in Palestine is not a negation of the Diaspora, I must reply that it really is that, that it is a sort of despairing of the Diaspora, a desire to abandon our unfortunate, large family in the Diaspora in order to find refuge amidst its tiny portion in Eretz Yisrael. My friends in Palestine incessantly keep demanding that I go there. But I answer them: As an "affirmant of the Diaspora" I cannot participate in the "emptying of the Diaspora," in voiding the Diaspora of its spiritual forces. We must not forget the fifteen million Jews because of the one million. . . . We have more than enough intellectuals there. . . . True, here they will have their troubles. . . . But their spiritual energies will have their effects upon the people. It is a great sin to draw this energy away from the Diaspora. Not long ago I wrote to an old friend in Jerusalem that I wish all the best to our tribes of Judah in Eretz Yisrael, but I do not want our ten tribes in the Diaspora to get lost and the Jewish world-nation to disappear from the scene. . . . This is the very basic principles of our Folkspartay and we dare not sin against this fundamental dogma. Obviously each individual can and sometimes must allow himself such action, but as a movement it is not to be countenanced in our ranks.[51]

The founder and chief theoretician of Diaspora nationalism thus bravely adhered to his own principles in his conduct even when it involved risking his very existence. At the same time, however, he also resisted emigration to another part of the Diaspora, to the United States. When the Jewish National Workers' Alliance secured an

American visa for him after the Russians had moved into Latvia, he wrote to them:

Believe me, it was very difficult for me to reject your American plan, which would have rescued me from all European troubles and cares. I must do so, however, not only because of reasons of health—the impossibility of such a difficult journey for a man of my years under such difficult conditions—but also because of social reasons. The union of Vilna with Lithuania has posed for me the question of moving to Vilna in order to help in the restoration of our Yiddish Scientific Institute, which has suffered much from the war, especially from the destruction of Poland. I will do that in the coming spring when things grow calmer in Vilna. If conditions change so as to involve danger for me in remaining in the Baltic area, then I will have to use the American visa, which I will try to have extended. Let us hope, however, that the situation improves and we see a liberated Europe.[52]

For the same reasons he opposed the plan to transfer the Yivo to America. "We dare not set up a tombstone for the European center," he wrote to Daniel Charny, "when the better world is fighting for a new Europe."[53] Not only was he filled with undying devotion to the east-European Jewish centers, but he was to his last days full of optimism regarding the ultimate victory of the Allied powers over the Nazi barbarians. He refused to become a party to the despair and disillusionment that were spreading among Jewish intellectuals who were voicing their utter disillusionment in the achievements of emancipation. He gave expression to this in one of his last published works, his "Letter to His Friends" in *Oyfn Sheydveg.*[54]

His long-range historical optimism and his belief in the ultimate triumph of right and justice were eventually vindicated, but unfortunately he himself did not live to see the day. He was utterly wrong in his short-term evaluation of the situation and fell victim to his devotion to his principles. On July 1, 1941, the Nazi hordes entered Riga and Dubnow's doom was sealed. The last letter we have from him is to Joseph Meisel, dated Riga, March 5, 1941. We give it in its entirety:

Your letter of January 1 reached me about two weeks ago and, like all letters that come from abroad, it was an eventful occasion in the life of a person shut up in the prison of Europe, which is embroiled in warfare all around, even in the neutral countries. So our camp in Palestine is overjoyed with the British victories in Africa (may they multiply) and there is hope that the plague of world destruction will not reach you and will not desecrate the Holy Land! I have also benefited from the merit of the Holy Land, for from time to time I receive some written lines or printed matter from there, while from America I have not received even one letter of the alphabet since the end of the summer of the year 5700 [1940]. I also received the book by Eshkoli on David Reubeni and I sent him a detailed reply to his letter. From a young Jerusalem student, a Mr. Shwarzbaum, I also received his dissertation and a letter which I answered right away. I hope that through a miracle my replies arrived to the proper addresses. In general we are well used to miracles. By a miracle we continue to live in a world full of angels of death (in modern scientific terminology, death bombs), and angels of destruction of all sorts even outside the battlefields. We are completely isolated from the sources of our spiritual life. Thus, after a long search, I was able to secure only a small Jewish calendar for the year 5701. This is the entire fruit of our "literature" this year. Newspapers from abroad do not come here and we know only about one part out of a thousand of what is going on in the wide world. This, too, is in a special form, adapted to the sources of information in our area. And you, affluent ones, complain of the decline of literary productivity in your land!

Twenty years ago, in the year 5681, I sat in troubled times in my native land and waited for liberation, for "the year to come" in Berlin. And now I wait for nothing. There is no going out and no coming in. All the doors are shut to me. Berlin has become transformed into Sodom and our other centers in Europe are destroyed and uprooted by the men of Sodom. From two ends of the earth, Eretz Yisrael and America look towards me and my eyes are directed to them. But I know that I shall not reach their borders and that it is ordained that I remain in this "great and terrible wilderness." My "Talmud" was already closed during the last years with the last edition of the Russian version of all the ten volumes of my large History (Riga 1936-39) and also the accessories to my "Torah," the Book of My Life, of which *the last volume (the Berlin epoch) was published in 5700. Unfortunately it is impossible for several reasons for me to send it to you or to my other friends. Now I write nothing for publication. I read the world's literature and make some notes for myself insofar as my impaired eyesight permits.*

My friends worry about my fate. But I worry about one thing: how to preserve the portions of my archives that still are in my possession. There is danger that they will suffer if turned over to public control. This storehouse was originally intended for the two institutions: the Jerusalem of Lithuania [Vilna] and the old Jerusalem. Under the new condition I would like to divide it between the national library in Jerusalem and the Yivo in America, which has changed from merely a branch to the central headquarters. But my good intention to set this down in my last will and testament will undoubtedly meet with resistance on the part of the leaders of the place in which I am—and this is the reason for my worry. Here you will also find an answer to your detailed project of transferring a number of documents to the archives of the Bezalel Museum. If the cedars have fallen to the flames what shall the moss on the wall do? Thousands of letters on public issues and literature over the course of sixty years and hundreds of other important historical documents belong only in a central national archive. And the harrowing question tortures my mind: shall I succeed in doing this after the war's end and shall I myself survive to see this end?

My family is scattered now over the face of the entire globe. My daughter and her children, refugees from Warsaw, escaped to Lithuania and are proceeding through Russia and Japan to the United States. Those who had previously remained in the Soviet Union have not yet received permission to come to the Baltic countries to visit me. I send my greetings to the celebration of your family reunion in Eretz Yisrael and to that dark-complexioned young girl with the sparkling eyes that is now Mrs. Yardena. And how are your wife and your son Saul? Has he completed his studies in Eretz Yisrael and become an expert in radiology? Since you live in Gan Rehavya I will ask you to transmit my greetings to your neighbors, the family of Mordecai ben Hillel Hakohen and especially to his daughter, the lawyer, Rosa Ginsburg. I wrote to her several weeks ago but I do not know if my letter got to her. Write me about what is happening in Jerusalem and at the university, that is undoubtedly suffering as a result of the times. I have not received a copy of Kiryat Sefer *during the course of the past year. In general, everyone who writes to me about affairs in our land will be blessed and praised by the mouth of the isolated resident in the Baltic forests—your devoted friend from the days of Berlin to this day.*

S. Dubnow

P.S. *Please let me know where Dr. Katzenelson of the Jüdischer Verlag is. I have not heard from him in several years.*[55]

When the Russians came into Latvia, Dubnow was afraid that they would not spare him because of his well-known anti-Bolshevist record. But to his surprise they did not molest him. Perhaps it was because they did not remain long enough. In any case, when the Nazis entered Riga the fate of all the Jews there was sealed. We have several versions by refugees from Riga about Dubnow's last days. They vary in details. But the main course of events was apparently along the following lines. When the Nazis entered Riga they evicted Dubnow from his home and seized his entire library. They summoned him for questioning at Gestapo headquarters and then placed him in a home for the aged. After a short period of ghetto organization the Nazis liquidated the ghetto at the end of October 1941 and a month later they carried out their first "action" against the Riga Jews. Dubnow was seriously ill, but friends managed to conceal him for a while. On the night of December 7-8 the Nazis carried out their second "action." All the old and sick as well as the women in advanced pregnancy were herded together in buses. Dubnow was also taken outside to be squeezed into one of these overloaded buses. He was in high fever at the time and was hardly able to move his feebled legs. A Latvian militiaman then advanced and fired a bullet in Dubnow's back and the sainted martyr fell dead on the spot. The next day several friends buried him in the old cemetery in the Riga ghetto. A story went round that the last words that Dubnow muttered as he was being led out to the bus were: "Brothers, don't forget! Recount what you hear and see! Brothers make a record of it all!" His sense of history and the spirit of *Nahpesa v'nahkora* did not forsake him even to his bitter end.[56]

II. *Dubnow's National Theories*[57]

GENERAL THEORY OF NATIONALISM

The key to the understanding of Dubnow's theory of nationalism is to be found in his historicism. His interpretation of the Jewish past, his analysis of contemporary issues, his program of action and, above all, his hopeful optimism for the future are all rooted in his historical approach to all problems. Those who, unlike himself, lacked historical perspective, he admonished in the following words: "There is one prescription for those who have little faith as well as for those who believe in nonsense—to probe deeply into the law of the survival of the people of Israel in all its details." To those who despaired of the spiritual revival of Jewish life he said: "You look only within the narrow confines of recent history and you are terrified by what you see. You think there never was another period in Jewish history like this one—a period of assimilation and conversion! You are mistaken!" Look at Alexandria, at Syria, at the Caliphate, at Spain. "Despite everything, the law of survival has never stopped working things out in its own way."[58]

Dubnow distinguishes three stages of national type: (1) tribal, (2) political territorial and (3) cultural-historical or spiritual. His definition of nationality is pretty much the same as that of Ernest Renan. But, as with so many nineteenth-century theorists of nationalism, there is in his system some contradiction between static and dynamic factors as well as between subjective and objective criteria. He insists that "the decisive factor for the destiny of a nation is not its external power but its spiritual force."[59] Cultural-spiritual factors are by their very nature subjective factors and Dubnow explicitly accepts subjective criteria as decisive for his definition of nationality. Nevertheless, when discussing the relation of the Jewish nationality to other nationalities, he writes: "A person is not *made into* a son of this nation or that, but *born* into it. . . . One may be made a member of some artificial, legal or social-political grouping. . . . But it is impossible for a person to be made a member of a *natural* collective group, of a tribe, or people, except through mingling of blood (through marriage) in the course of generations." A French Jew cannot be a Frenchman of the Mosaic faith because no one can be called a Frenchman "unless he is born a Frenchman, unless he is a son or grandson of Gallic stock or of a related stock, or is so linked with the French for many generations that he has inherited all the qualities and characteristics that are the fruit of the historical development of the French nation."[60]

The most important aspect of Dubnow's general theory of nationalism is the distinction he makes between *state* on the one hand and *people* or *nationality* on the other. In this, of course, Dubnow is not original. He follows in the footsteps of the progressive nationalist theorists of the late nineteenth century, especially those of the Austro-Marxist school. This distinction for Dubnow, however, is the foundation for his entire theory of Judaism and Jewish national survival. As a follower of the evolutionary school of social theory, Dubnow considers the various national types as specific stages in the history of mankind. The lowest stage is that of tribe and the highest stage is the cultural-historical or spiritual nation. In the latter stage the connection between state and nationality disappears and the nation becomes a purely spiritual phenomenon. "The state is an external social organization designed only to protect the needs of its members. The nationality is an inner and natural form of the social collectivity. The state, in keeping with its entire character, can be changed at all times; the nationality is fixed and unchangeable."[61]

With such an approach Dubnow strenuously opposes any sort of national oppression or national expansionism. Like other great humanitarian nationalists, such as Herder, Mazzini and Masaryk, Dubnow distinguishes sharply between a positive and negative kind of nationalism. Positive nationalism is humane, an expression of national individuality and, above all, liberating in its effect. Negative nationalism is national egotism; it is the *sacro egoismo*, with its *energie nationale*, its *appel au soldat* and its *Machtstaat*; it is a nationalism that is motivated not by a desire to generate freedom and liberate the creative forces of a people but rather one of struggle and forced assimilation.[62] The entire course of history, according to Dubnow, is in the direction of multinational states, made up of more than one nationality. "The function of a 'ruling nationality' in the state," he predicts, "will be relegated to the same position occupied today by a 'ruling church' in a free state. This is not just a myth but a historical necessity based on the development of our legal and political science. It is upon this historical necessity that I base my hope that the struggle of the Jews for their national rights will succeed."[63]

Dubnow lived to see this theory accepted by the peace makers of Versailles in 1920 and incorporated into the minority provisions of the treaties with the succession states.[64] But he also lived to see them give way before the onslaught of extreme monolithic statism. "The worst plague of our times," he wrote in the *Zukunft* in 1935, "is that the world is returning once again to political unitarism." And just as religious unitarism in the past brought on inquisition and religious wars so will this political totalitarianism lead only to new inquisitions. What he wrote in 1901 he continued to cling to to the end of his days: "Despite the present reaction, the course of history is directed, not toward the subjection of national groups, but toward their liberation. In the same way that the principle of a ruling Church gave way after a bitter struggle, so too the principle of a ruling nationality is bound to be discarded. . . . The struggle by nationalities for this ideal will not cease until it is crowned with victory. Israel is not alone in this struggle. Its path is the path of history moving toward the noble goal. . . ."[65]

The present political climate in the world is certainly not in keeping with Dubnow's national theories. Ever since the breakdown of the League of Nations system of minority rights and particularly since the close of World War II the entire trend of political organization has been in the direction of the monolithic and highly unified nationalistic state. This does not necessarily invalidate Dubnow's theories, however. For all reputable political thought today holds as Dubnow held that, when the world returns to some semblance of sanity, monolithic nationalism will have to give way to varying forms of federation and hence to multinational states. In such multinational states minority rights and autonomism will be the only sensible and feasible way to combine national freedom with international peace and understanding. Even the most radical and deep-seated territorial cleavages of our day, the division between India and Pakistan and the partition of Palestine, will someday have to be rectified by federation combined with national autonomism.

THE CHARACTER OF JEWISH NATIONALISM

The most distinguishing characteristic of Jewish nationalism for Dubnow is its spiritual quality. The Jews are the clearest expression in history of a nation based primarily and exclusively on spiritual ideals. Dubnow declares:

> *When a people loses not only its political independence but also its land, when the storm of history uproots it and removes it far from its natural homeland and it becomes dispersed and scattered in alien lands, and in addition it also loses its unifying language; if despite the fact that the external national ties have been destroyed, the nation still maintains itself for many years, creates an independent existence, reveals a stubborn determination to carry on its autonomous development—such a people has reached the highest stage of cultural-historical individuality and may be said to be indestructible, if it but clings forcefully to its national will. We have many examples in history of nations that have disappeared from the scene after they had lost their land and become dispersed among other nations. We find only one instance, however, of a people that has survived for thousands of years despite dispersion and loss of homeland. This unique people—is the people of Israel.*[66]

This, says Dubnow, is not due to a miracle. It is the product of Jewish historical development. In the course of 2,000 years of its history the Jewish people has been converted from just a nation into the very essence of nationhood, i.e., pure and distilled spirituality, the highest stage of nationalism.[67]

The theme of a "spiritual nation" runs like a constant thread through Dubnow's writings, from his first youthful preoccupation with religious reform to the last words he wrote before his death. In his diary for January 1, 1894, we find the following entry: "The idea of a spiritual nation—that is what elevates my spirit as Jew and as man. I shall carry out this ideal in all my works because I consider it to be the anchor for all progressive Jews."[68] In his essay on Jewish history of 1892 he refers to the Talmud as the "spiritual weapon" needed by a "spiritual people." The clearest expression of this view, however, is found in the interpretation given by Dubnow in his *Weltgeschichte* to the conflict between the Pharisees and Sadducees. For him the difference between these two sects was more than a theological controversy regarding the validity of the oral law. It was rather a conflict between the advocates of a "spiritual nation" and those of a "political nation." Dubnow's delineation of a Pharisee might almost serve as a description of Dubnow's own position. In his discussion of the revolt of the Pharisees against the warlike policies of Alexander Jannaeus he says:

This was not the kind of state dreamed of by their predecessors, the hasidim, when the independence of Judea was attained and when the star of the Hasmoneans first began to gleam. Had Judea battled against the Syrian yoke, sacrificed for a quarter of a century its material goods and the blood of its best sons, only in order to become, after attaining independence, a "despotism" or warrior state after the fashion of its pagan neighbors? The Pharisees believed that the Jewish nation was created for something better; that in its political life it was not to strive for the ideal of brute force but rather for the lofty ideal of inner social and spiritual progress.[69]

This is no different from Dubnow's own idea of national morality proclaimed in his *Letters:* "There is absolutely no doubt that Jewish nationalism in its very essence has nothing in common with any tendency towards violence." "As a Jew," says Dubnow, "I utter the word 'national' with pride and conviction because I know that my people, because of the special conditions of its existence in the Diaspora, is not able to aspire anywhere to primacy and dominance. My nationalism can be only purely individualistic and hence completely ethical."

"It is fitting and proper," he exclaims, "for the descendants of the Prophets to raise aloft on their flag the unsoiled national ideal that combines the visions of the Prophets of truth and justice with the noble dream of the unity of mankind."[70]

Dubnow's theory of Jewish nationalism is distinguished from other theories of Jewish nationalism developed in his day by its more all-embracing and all-inclusive character. Unlike the assimilationists who

...ist, unlike the Zionists who were con-
...sh future, and unlike the Jewish social-
...ey of the Bund or of Zhitlovsky's Yiddishist persuasion, who were preoccupied only with the Jewish present and for whom Jewish history began only with the emergence of the Jewish proletariat and the beginnings of Yiddish literature, Dubnow with his profound historical approach, weaves into his autonomist theories all the strands of Jewish present, past and future.

We, proponents of autonomism [writes Dubnow in the Letters*] do not wish to break the chain that unites the nation's present with the nation's future, just as we do not separate both of these from the nation's past. We are true evolutionists and our strength lies in our recognition of the natural process of historical development and a faith in the power of the national will that is revealed in the history of our people. The strengthening of this will, the deepening of this recognition and the striving for civil and national freedom for our people in all the lands of dispersion—all these are well within the realm of possibility and actuality. The very striving for this alone is a clear sign of the beginnings of an inner rebirth.*[71]

In his essay on "The Secret of the Survival and the Law of Survival of the Jewish People," written in 1912, Dubnow wrote:

Every generation in Israel carries within itself the remnants of worlds created and destroyed during the course of the previous history of the Jewish people. The generation, in turn, builds and destroys worlds in its form and image, but in the long run continues to weave the thread that binds all the links of the nation into the chain of generations. The spirit of each generation turns about continually in its circuit and the spirit returns again to its circuit, the point of the nation's existence. The soul of each generation (a generation is for a nation what an individual is for society) emanates from the soul of the (collective) "body" of all the preceding generations, and what endures, namely, the strength of the accumulated past, exceeds the wreckage, the strength of the changing present.[72]

This accounts for the positive attitude that Dubnow has toward religion in Judaism. Dubnow rejects the factor of religion as the supreme criterion of Jewish nationalism. Judaism, for him, is not merely a religion but a "system of culture." But he insists just as strongly that a Jew cannot abandon the religion of Judaism and still remain a Jew.

By aspiring to secularism, by separating the national idea from religion, we aim only to negate the supremacy of religion but not to eliminate it from the storehouse of national cultural treasures. If we wish to preserve Judaism as a cultural-historical type of nation, we must realize that the religion of Judaism is one of the integral foundations of national culture and that any one who seeks to destroy it undermines the very basis of national existence. Between us and the orthodox Jews there is only this difference: they recognize a traditional Judaism, the forms of which were set from the beginning for all eternity, while we believe in an evolutionary Judaism in which new and old forms are always being assumed or discarded and which adjusts itself . . . to new cultural conditions.[73]

That is why, according to Dubnow, it is impossible for a Jew converted to Christianity to remain a Jew by nationality and become a Christian by religion. "The exit from Judaism by acceptance of the Christian religion," he says definitely and incisively, "means exit from the Jewish nation."

Not only is Dubnow always striving to encompass present, past and future in the history of the Jewish people, but his nationalism is also tolerant of all parties and shades of opinion that have a positive attitude toward Jewish national life. "Judaism," he says, "is broad enough and variegated enough so that any man in Israel can draw from its source according to his spirit and outlook." The concept of *Klal Yisrael* is more important for him than anything else. What he wrote of Nathan Birnbaum on the occasion of his fiftieth birthday in 1915 may well be said of Dubnow himself: "He bears in his soul the woes and yearnings of all Jewish generations." And in his greetings to Birnbaum on the latter's sixtieth birthday in 1925 he listed three forms of contemporary Jewish nationalism: (1) political nationalism in the form of modern Zionism; (2) cultural nationalism in the form of autonomism; and (3) religious nationalism in the form of extreme orthodoxy. Which of these three theories will triumph? asks Dubnow. And his answer is:

The question should not be put in this form but rather as follows: In what way is the triumph and survival of the people better guaranteed? Here we find the gage by which we can measure all theories. Everything is good which is advantageous to the existence of the national germ seed, whether it assumes the form of a Jewish land for one part of Israel, or the form of religious discipline for the community of believers, or in the form of an internal autonomous organization in the entire Jewish people. Each of these theories is good if it adds new means in the struggle for national existence and does not lessen them. . . .

Which road should the people then choose? That road which leads to the union of all parts of the nation in one aspiration: the immortality of the national soul. This road branches out into three paths adapted to the three parties in Israel. Each of these parties may proceed in its own path but may not abandon the road that leads to the preservation of the nation in its totality.[74]

Dubnow stood above parties in Jewish life. The national goal was supreme for him. That is why he could participate in greetings to Birnbaum as well as greetings to Dr. Zhitlovsky and Ahad Ha-Am. That is why he was accepted as the Jewish historian by the most varied groups in Jewish life ranging from left to right, in Germany and Central Europe as well as in Poland and Russia, in Palestine as well as in the United States. He does reject, however, the class interpretation of history and attacks the Jewish Marxists for their emphasis on the class struggle. Of all the general political parties in Russia he found the Constitutional Democrats the closest to his own views. In 1906 he pointed out the weakness of those who believe that Jewish national rights are inextricably bound up with the triumph of socialism.[75] That is also why he refused to join in the celebration of the fortieth anniversary of the Bund in 1937. He accused the Bund of isolating itself and not joining the community of Israel in recognizing that the rebuilding of Palestine is "the greatest miracle of Jewish history." At the same time he added that the Zionists too must be opposed for their denial of the *galut* and for their exaggerated sense of national mission and chosen people.[76]

JEWISH AUTONOMY

Dubnow's theory of autonomism is derived from his conception of Jewish history as a succession of autonomous centers of Jewish national creation. The destruction of the Jewish state, holds Dubnow, forced Jews to create "in place of political autonomy a social and cultural autonomy."[77] Jewish law, the life in the ghetto, messianic hopes and dreams were but "external manifestations of forms of national survival."

These were not fixed forms but forms that changed and were altered in the course of history. Quite apart from these, the source of vitality of the Jewish people consists in this—that this people, after it passed through the stages of tribal nationalism, ancient culture and political territory, was able to establish itself and fortify itself in the highest stage—the spiritual and historical-cultural, and it succeeded in crystallizing itself as a spiritual people that draws the sap of its existence from the natural or intellectual "will to live." All this only because in the play of forces that sustained Jewish nationalism those elements not dependent on territory counted more than those dependent on territory. In the measure that the positive political factors declined, the spiritual factors increased in importance, in the same way, for example, that the sense of touch or hearing of a blind man is sharpened at the expense of his defective sense of sight.[78]

Perhaps the most succinct exposition of Dubnow's historical view of Jewish autonomy is found in the introduction to his edition of the *Pinkas of the Lithuanian Vaad.* The council of the leading communities or "the council of state" in Lithuania writes Dubnow,

is one link in the chain of autonomy—the essential source of power of the Jewish communities in all lands. Were it not for this chain, which encompasses all parts of the Diaspora, Israel would not have survived all these generations after the destruction of its state and its land. The secret of national survival is dependent on the positive command of the ancient prophecy: "The scepter shall not depart from Judah." It is indeed possible to say that kingship never ceased in Israel. It merely shed one form to assume another. Reconstruction and destruction alternate in the history of our people. The earliest tribes join together into one national body and concentrate in a separate state or kingdom. The state is destroyed, and the national body separates into its parts—the communities. In this way the people build for themselves in every place something like a kingdom in miniature. Our enemies in all generations cry out: "There is a certain people scattered abroad and dispersed among the peoples and their laws are diverse from those of every other people." In modern times they call it "a state within a state." But the congregation of Israel goes on in its historical path and says: "Indeed, a state within a state," an internal autonomous group within an external political group, and the nature of things sanctions it.[79]

Because Jewish history has been a succession of shifting centers, emigration is always a major problem in Jewish communal life. Already at the close of the nineteenth century Dubnow looked to America as a future great center for Jewry and as a potential savior for the Jews should Europe become intolerable for them. "Our strength," he wrote, "is great in this respect that in our war for liberation we have two positions, one in Europe and one in America. If Esau will fall upon one position we will receive him properly, but in the event of the worst possible extremity the second position will be left for Jacob and 'the remaining camp will be able to escape.' "[80]

Dubnow organized a political party, the Folkspartay, to further the cause of national autonomy for the Jews in Russia. This party developed a series of demands that in later days became the basis for the practical program of Jewish national minority rights in the succession states after World War I. But these practical demands are not the important thing in Dubnow's system. He omits them from the Hebrew edition of his *Letters*, published in 1937. What is important is the general proposition that autonomism, the modern synthesis between the thesis, isolation, and the antithesis, assimilation, must become the basis for Jewish survival in a secularized world. The chief axiom of autonomism is that Jews in each and every country, who participate in an active measure in the civic and political life of the country, enjoy all the privileges given to the citizens not only as individuals but also as members of their national group.[81] The Jew says in effect: "As a citizen of my country I participate in its civic and political life, but as a member of the Jewish nationality I have, in addition, my own national needs. In this sphere . . . I have the right to speak my language, to use it in all social institutions, to make it the language of instruction in my schools, to order my internal life in my communities and to create institutions serving a variety of national purposes; to join in the common activities with my brethren not only in this country, but in all countries of the world, and to participate in all organizations which serve to further the needs of the Jewish nationality and to defend them everywhere."[82]

Although Dubnow prescribes certain forms of autonomy for his own time and for the country in which he lives, he does not intend these to be fixed and eternal forms. Every age will devise its own forms of autonomy, dictated by the dynamic forces of Jewish life and by the special conditions then prevailing.

THE LANGUAGE QUESTION

Dubnow's nationalism, like his general world outlook, was free from national mysticism and national romanticism. Just as he had no feeling for those mystical associations of people with land—so, likewise, did he not have any of the notions, developed by literary nationalists, of the deep irrational connections between a people and its language. National content is always more important for Dubnow than national form. Hence his broad tolerance and eclecticism in the language struggle that went on in Jewish literary circles during his lifetime. Hebrew he considered the most important of Jewish national languages; to Yiddish he had the warmest and most personal attachment; Russian was the language in which he wrote almost all of his major scholarly works. Russian too was the language of the last and most personal of all his works, his autobiography. His history of hasidism was the only major work he wrote in Hebrew. He explains in the preface to this work that he had promised his lifelong friend Ahad Ha-Am, that he would write this work in Hebrew and he adds: "I felt for a long time already the need to write at least one book in our national language, to which I owe the first literary impressions of my childhood."[83]

There is no doubt that Dubnow considered Hebrew to be the most important national language of the Jewish people. He published shorter essays and articles in Hebrew in *Hashiloah, Heathid* and *Haolam,* and he hailed the renaissance of Hebrew in Palestine as a great miracle.[84] Even when defending Yiddish against its detractors he does not place it on the same level with Hebrew. He compares the Jewish people to a cripple with one natural and one artificial leg. "Hebrew is our natural leg, but it is only one leg and not two. The second one was cut off by the *galut.* . . . In place of the missing leg came the artificial leg, Yiddish. On these two legs our people has stood and survived for many generations just as in former years it stood on the language dualism of Hebrew and Aramaic." Hebrew, then, is the natural leg and Yiddish the artificial leg. But Dubnow is interested in utilizing all means to strengthen Jewish autonomous life and he finds in Yiddish a strong bastion against cultural assimilation. Dubnow wrote against Dr. Pasmanik:

Among the forces which are the basis of our autonomy in the Diaspora I also set aside a place for the powerful force of the folk language used by seven million Jews in Russia and Galicia, which for several generations now has been fulfilling the function of a spoken language, the language of instruction in the school (the heder *and* yeshiva*) and to an appreciable degree has been also a language of literature. Let our relation to the "Jargon," or more correctly to Yiddish, be what it may, we dare not abandon one of the foundations of national unity in the very hour that the languages of the peoples around us rob our people of thousands and tens of thousands of its sons, so that they no longer understand the language used by their parents. . . . There being no hope of converting our ancient national tongue into the living and daily-spoken language in the Diaspora, we would be committing a transgression against our national soul if we did not make use, in our war against assimilation, of the great counterforce stored up in the language of the people. . . . Insofar as we recognize the merit of national existence in the Diaspora, we must also recognize the merit of Yiddish as one of the instruments of autonomy together with Hebrew and the other factors in our national culture.*[85]

Dubnow was one of the first among the Russian Jewish intellectuals to take up the cudgels in behalf of Yiddish and give encouragement to the budding Yiddish literati. In 1881 he published an article in Russian on the necessity for a newspaper in Yiddish, and this heralded the initiation of the *Yiddishe Folksblat* in St. Petersburg. He it was who first called attention to the great talent of Sholem Aleichem, as revealed in *Dos Meserl*, and his article in 1888 on "Zhargonishe Literatur," published in the *Voskhod*, may be said to have made Yiddish literature respectable among the Russian Jewish intelligentsia. In a letter, dated August 1889, Sholem Aleichem expressed his appreciation of and indebtedness to Dubnow: "You are the only writer," wrote Sholem Aleichem, "who shows a human and sympathetic attitude to the poor Jargon. It is difficult to express the feeling of gratefulness that I owe to you."[86]

With all his theoretical and practical support of Yiddish as well as his deep emotional attachment to the living language of the large masses of eastern European Jewry, Dubnow was a sharp critic and opponent of Yiddishism as a formalized dogma, as represented by Dr. Chaim Zhitlovsky and others. His objections were based not only upon his opposition to any kind of "linguistic chauvinism," but also upon his wish to protect and conserve the Jewish national values found in those Jews who used neither Hebrew nor Yiddish, but rather the language of the country in which they resided. Referring to his comments on the resolutions of the Tschernowitz Conference of 1908, which had proclaimed the principle that only Yiddish and Hebrew are the national languages of the Jewish people, he wrote in his autobiography:

I had to defend the rights of the Russian language in our literature against the Yiddishists and the Hebraists. I maintained that one dare not stigmatize the cultural instrument of those broad elements of Jewish intellectuals who read and speak Russian. I was ready to agree that from a national standpoint Yiddish and Russian are not equal, nevertheless they must be recognized as such from the standpoint of instruments of culture.[87]

Dubnow reasserted this principle when, in commenting on the autonomism of Dr. Chaim Zhitlovsky, he wrote:

History shows us that had the Jewish people rested only on the foundation of language no trace of it would have remained by now. . . . The future of a people must be built on all the foundation-stones of its cultural autonomy and not solely upon one of them—one which has endured only for a few hundred years and which may, in a few hundred years, lose its supporting force. Yiddish is dear to us and we must use it as a uniting force for the greater half of our people in the coming generations; but, to erect our entire national culture upon "Yiddishism" means to cast off from us immediately millions of Jews who do not speak this language and to prepare millions of others for bankruptcy at a later time.[88]

In the same year (1929), in the preface to his collected writings on Yiddish, Dubnow predicted that Hebrew would become the dominant language in Palestine and that Yiddish would play the leading role in the Jewish press, literature and school in Eastern Europe and America. But, he went on to add:

It is obvious that the "foreign languages" in the various countries will continue to play an important role in our culture, simply because these languages have become mother tongues to great numbers of our people, and the contents of Jewish culture must be poured into these language vessels, just as the Jews have always done in their long journey among peoples and lands. . . .

One must not be caught up in language chauvinism and believe that Jewish culture can be saved only in this way. We must not disregard the eternal role of our old-new language and the great value of the European-American languages that have in fact become the cultural languages of various parts of our people.[89]

Thus in the language question, too, we find Dubnow to be consistent. In his last writings on this subject in 1929 he adheres to the same position expressed in his call for a three-language Jewish literature for Russian Jewry, proclaimed in his earliest article in *Voskhod*, in 1888.

ZIONISM

Dubnow's attitude toward political Zionism underwent certain modifications, from earlier skepticism to later acceptance of the

Balfour Declaration and the rebuilding of Palestine as one of "the great miracles of Jewish history." Historically, he correctly interpreted Zionism as a secularized form of messianism. Just as mystical messianism in the past was one of the ways in which earlier Judaism reacted against dangers of oppression and resultant apostasy, so modern Zionism was an answer to the present-day *Judennot*.

Political Zionism is merely a renewed form of messianism that was transmitted from the enthusiastic minds of the religious kabbalists to the minds of the political communal leaders. In it the ecstasy bound up in the great idea of rebirth blurs the lines between reality and fantasy. Here, too, we find the continuing effects of secularization. In the same way that the Jewish national idea in its completeness now divests itself of its religious form and takes on a secular form, so does messianism pass over from the religious to the political sphere.[90]

In his *Sixth Letter* (1898 [1907]) he is still skeptical enough to ask: "Will the results of the political messianism be more real than those of mystical messianism?" And in 1898 as well as in 1907 he still finds fantastic in Zionism, "the dream of the creation of a Jewish state, guaranteed by international law, . . . the dream of finding a solution to the Jewish problem in this manner."[91] The Zionist dreamers, at least for part of this "dream fantasy," proved to be wiser than Dubnow. And to Dubnow's credit it must be said that he admitted it later in life.

It is also true, however, that Dubnow never doubted the great positive elements in the Zionist movement, just as he continued to point out that the gravest weakness of political Zionism is its "denial of the *galut*." To this extent he is right when he says in 1937, in his preface to the Hebrew edition of his *Letters:* "With all the sharpness of my objections to political Zionism I never was opposed to its positive and practical sides—the upbuilding of the land—but only to its negative side—the denial of the *galut*." And even with the present-day triumph of the ideal of Jewish statehood those who have a deeper historical perspective may still warn those who stake the entire future of the Jewish people upon the realization of a Jewish state in Palestine in the words of Dubnow:

Do not forget that extreme Zionism of this kind may inflict damage if bitter realities fail to come up to glowing hopes. . . . One must take into account what will happen to the group of Zionists if the hope that influences their spirit is dissipated by unforeseen deceit or is turned into empty messianism. What will happen if the dissipation of the dream brings with it also the destruction of the national idea bound to it and nothing remains in the soul but terrifying emptiness?[92]

Zionism represents a healthy national movement for Dubnow only if it understands that "the *return to Judaism* is the primary goal, and not merely an indirect goal, of the return to a Jewish state." Without this, any failure of political Zionism will result in greater disillusionment than even the failure of assimilation. "Zionism is useful if it serves as a transition to a higher world-view, to a spiritual nationalism, the fruit of the development of generations in Judaism."[93]

PALESTINE VS. DIASPORA

The greatest problem created by Zionism and the establishment of a Jewish state is the relation of Palestine to the Diaspora. On this question Dubnow and Ahad Ha-Am carried on a debate for many years, a debate that began in the circles of that wonderful period of the "sages of Odessa"[94] and continued in the columns of the leading periodicals and in private letters.[95] Both Dubnow and Ahad Ha-Am clarified their views on this subject as a result of the extended debate; both respected and admired each other and both came closer to each other in the end. Dubnow in referring to his differences with Ahad Ha-Am said: "In the field of national ideology I am closer to him than to any other writer of our times,"[96] and Ahad Ha-Am reciprocated by writing that people like Dubnow "are much closer to me in spirit than those new Zionists who begin from the end of ends and whose entire nationalism is based upon a 'Jewish state.' "[97]

Both Dubnow and Ahad Ha-Am believed that even after the establishment of a center in Palestine the majority of the Jews would remain in the Diaspora. Both agreed in theory that it was necessary to maintain the national consciousness of the Jews in the Diaspora. Ahad Ha-Am rightly pointed out that in Dubnow's first formulation of his autonomist theories there was a serious ambiguity. Dubnow had not made clear whether he hoped that Jews could carry on a full and complete national life in the Diaspora or whether he envisaged merely the "best possible" national life under the circumstances. As a result of Ahad Ha-Am's prodding, Dubnow was forced to accept the latter formulation, thus bringing him closer to Ahad Ha-Am. For Ahad Ha-Am likewise recognized such a goal as desirable even though he had some doubts as to its feasibility. The real divergence between the two, however, was not one of basic theory but rather of subtle difference in emphasis. Dubnow, closer to the masses, with his historical approach and with his all-inclusive view of the Jewish community, could not help being deeply concerned with the Jewish destiny of millions of Jews. Ahad Ha-Am, the intellectual artistocrat, concerned much more with Judaism than with Jews, did not feel deeply enough the urge to formulate a program for saving the Jews in the Diaspora other than through his idea of a cultural-spiritual center in Palestine. "I agree," wrote Dubnow, "with the idea that the handful of Jews in Eretz Yisrael will live a fuller national life than those in the Diaspora and I look forward to this rebirth with joy, but I also am worried about the lot of that great remnant of Israel. . . . Perhaps the land of Israel might be converted into a Noah's Ark in which only a portion of Jewry will be saved from the great flood, while the rest sink in its waves?"[98] Dubnow accepted Ahad Ha-Am's distinction between "subjective denial" of the *galut*, in which the *galut* is rejected because of preference of values, and "objective denial" of the *galut*, which is based merely on the possibility or impossibility of the Jew's position, irrespective of subjective evaluation.

The autonomists and the spiritual Zionists [wrote Dubnow] *stand together against those who completely negate the Diaspora. Both of us "affirm the Diaspora." In what way do we affirm it? I agree with Ahad Ha-Am that it is not in a subjective sense, because of the recognition of the good and the blessings of a* galut *existence. It is self-evident that if we had the power to transfer the entire Diaspora to a "Jewish state" we would do this with the greatest joy. We acquiesce in the Diaspora only because of historical necessity and we strive to preserve and develop the national existence of the greater part of the nation which will remain there.*[99]

Jewish national life in the Palestine center, he admits, will be more intensive and fuller than Jewish life in the Diaspora. Dubnow is ready to agree fully with Ahad Ha-Am were he to accept the following formulation of the problem:

The difference between Palestine and the Diaspora will be quantitative and qualitative. In Palestine there will be a none too numerous minority of the Jewish people that will be distinguished by a richer and more complete national culture, while the Diaspora will be weaker but will make up in quantity for quality. The reciprocal influence of the two centers will create the mean for the national development of Judaism.[100]

In his last word on the subject, in an article in *Hashiloah* in 1914, Dubnow summarized his position as follows: "The autonomist nationalists admit the value and influence of the cultural center in Palestine and consider it their duty to incorporate into the sphere of their program activity in behalf of strengthening and perfecting this center, on the one condition that this activity be joined with *all* activities designed to strengthen national culture and communal autonomy in all countries 'up to the limits of possibility.'" Dubnow rightly claims, and this is most crucial today, that there is an inextricable connection between a strong national existence in the Diaspora and a healthy Jewish Palestine. If the Diaspora cannot live a full national life without the center in Palestine so likewise is a strong Jewish center in Palestine, built on secure foundations and endowed with stability and endurance, not possible without an active Jewish life in the *galut*. This formulation was accepted by many political Zionists after World War I, when they joined in the activity in behalf of Jewish minority rights in Europe. It is also being emphasized by many groups in the Zionist movement today, when the problems of the Jewish State of Israel have become more actual than ever.

JEWS AND THE WORLD

Dubnow's sociological and national theories are deeply rooted in the historical optimism of the nineteenth century with its faith in humanity which it inherited from the Age of Enlightenment. In his reminiscences of Mendele, Dubnow tells of a gathering at Mendele's home in Odessa on Passover 1891, right after the expulsion of the Jews from Moscow. A deep sadness hovered over the entire gathering. One speaker proposed Palestine colonization as the solution; another, emigration to America. Dubnow's proposal was "a propaganda tour of Europe to stir up the world against despotic Russia."[101] To the end of his days he believed in a conscience of humanity that could be moved by truth and justice. In 1939, on the eve of the great Jewish catastrophe, he wrote to his disciple Tscherikower: "An international people of several million, full of hatred for fascism and Nazism, can serve as a powerful ferment to stir up the world against these murderous movements and arouse the world conscience."[102] Dubnow was not naive enough to rely only on such moral support. In the days of the tsarist pogroms he called for the creation of Jewish self-defense units, and in his last call of 1939 against Nazism he advocated the economic boycott and active military action by Jews against the Nazis. Dubnow was not a follower of Tolstoi in the sense of advocating passive resistance.[103] But his profound historical knowledge provided him, as it did the Italian anti-fascist philosopher, Benedetto Croce,[104] with a healthy historical optimism. In the last analysis everything depends on the faith that there is a conscience in humanity; that a small nation like the Jews must endeavor above all to enlist the help and co-operation of the better and more humanitarian elements in the nations in whose midst they dwell.

Until his very last days, surrounded already on all sides by the cruel hordes of Nazi barbarism, Dubnow never lost his historical perspective. Writing in the *Zukunft* in 1935 his "Melancholy Observations on our Sorrowful Times," Dubnow said: "I believe that this is only a transition period between the World War that brutalized millions of people and the normal conditions of the future. A day will come when this black-red insanity will be remembered as one of the greatest catastrophes in world history." Dubnow recounts the talmudic legend of the fright of Adam in the Garden of Eden when he experienced the first setting of the sun. The next morning, however, Adam saw the sun rise again and he understood that there is order in the universe. "Yes," adds Dubnow, "there is a certain order also in the social world. It does not remain in one place. It revolves. Often there are volcanic explosions; but the world develops according to certain laws that are grounded in human culture. Our sages used to say that the human soul is the scene of an eternal struggle between the 'evil inclination' and the 'good inclination,' and that it is the task of religion and ethics to give added strength to the 'good inclination.' We say the same thing in different words: There are times when large masses of humanity are beset by the evil principle, by the beast in man. In such times all the others must organize themselves in order to strengthen the good principle, the human conscience, the categorical imperative."

Dubnow was fully cognizant of the widespread disillusionment and cynical despair of the fruits of enlightenment and emancipation that had taken hold of many Jewish intellectuals as a result of the rise of Hitlerism. But he castigated such cynics most severely. In one of his last published writings he says: "In our epoch of counter-emancipation we dare not posit the ironic question, well, what has emancipation brought us? True it brought assimilation, but also freedom and human dignity. It revived the free person in the Jew. . . . We stand or fall with the progress or regress of all mankind and not with a few of its degenerate parts."[105]

Dubnow thus may serve as an ideal model for the Jew seeking to create a synthesis of living as Jew and as man in a secular society. His supreme ideal is summed up in his phrase "to educate the man and the Jew at one and the same time." This message Dubnow preached, in the words of Ahad Ha-Am, "in clear language and with full vigor; with the dignity of a man who recognizes his own worth as a person and as son of his people and without any trace whatsoever of that 'inner slavery' of that canting and self-derogation toward the outer world that is so frequently found in the articles of our writers in the European languages."[106] In speaking of Bolshevism and the life of the Jews in the Soviet Union, Dubnow defended his steadfast opposition to Bolshevism on the grounds that it was void of all ethical elements and he added: "True, Jews are the equals of all other persons in the Soviet land, but the human being as such is debased there and without rights and enslaved. The *human being in the Jew* is destroyed and his spirit broken. What good is the Jew when the human element in him has been annihilated?"[107]

DUBNOW AND AMERICAN JEWRY

Dubnow's philosophy of Jewish life should be particularly relevant to American Jews today. Although Dubnow himself never visited America, he saw long before the breakup of the European Jewish centers that in the United States there was emerging one of the great concentrations of modern Jewish populations. After World War I he referred frequently to America and Palestine as the two new focal points of Jewish life. The coming of the Yivo to the United States brought to these shores a whole group of disciples of Dubnow who continue to work along the lines laid down by him. But Dubnow's influence on Jewish scholarship in the United States long antedated these developments. We have already referred to the publication of his *Essay on Jewish History* and to the appearance of his *History of the Jews in Russia and Poland* and to the work of Israel Friedlaender. While the older Jewish scholars in the United States during the first decades of the twentieth century were much closer to the "mummified scholarship" of Abraham Harkavy than to the living history of Dubnow, and while Dubnow's larger historical works were never translated into English, the newer and younger Jewish scholars that developed after World War I showed plainly the influence of Dubnow's historical approach.

There were several reasons that accounted for this. In the first place, Dubnow's approach to history paralleled in many ways the development of the "new history" of James Harvey Robinson, Charles Beard, Carl Becker and others in the United States. Like them, Dubnow revolted against the purely political and narrative chronological history and sought to find vital meaning in history; like them, he sought to find in the history of the past instruments for the understanding of the present and for coping with the problems of the present; like them, Dubnow brought into the writing of history the study of institutions, of social and economic affairs, the significance of everyday life as opposed to the more dramatic and sensational, and the integration of history with the other social science disciplines. The result was that when the new generation of American Jewish historians came into contact with the American "new history" and reacted against the older, theologically-oriented American Jewish scholarship, they found in Dubnow a ready guide and master for the application of their own viewpoint to Jewish historiography. While such influence cannot always be proven to have been immediate and direct, there is no doubt that it pervaded the climate in which they worked. Such influence could be said to appear in the general Jewish history by Solomon Grayzel, in the work of Oscar I. Janowsky on minority rights, of Louis Finkelstein on Jewish self-government in the Middle Ages and on the sociological background of the Pharisees, and in Abraham A. Neuman's study of the institutional life of the Jews in Spain. Salo W. Baron brought with him from Vienna the same reaction against the "lachrymose conception" of Jewish history as expressed by Dubnow and the same interest in the social and institutional history of the Jews and the Jewish community.

Much more significant, however, is the parallelism of cultural and emotional conditions of American Jewish life and the national theories of Dubnow. The secularization of American Jewish life as well as the coming into their own of the east-European Jewish immigrants helped to create a receptivity to Dubnow's ideas. Here, too, direct influence is not wanting. The influence of Israel Friedlaender on American Jewish life still awaits its proper evaluation and assessment. But there seems to be no doubt that Friedlaender, the champion of Dubnow in this country, played a very crucial role in the development of the *kehillah* movement in New York and, as chairman of the Board of Trustees of the Bureau of Jewish Education of the New York Kehillah, exercised a profound influence on Judah L. Magnes, Mordecai M. Kaplan and the group of educators of the Dushkin-Berkson-Golub school. One scans the literature of this group during the early 1920s and one can almost believe that Dubnow was the author. Take, for example, the following extract from a piece by I. B. Berkson. "The Jews," wrote Berkson in 1920, "are conceived of not as living in an isolated locality but scattered throughout the country. Together with other nationalities they engage in commerce, in political and social life . . . they contribute in whatever way they can to the development of America in all its phases, economic, political and cultural. Over and above this participation in the common life of the country, wherever Jews live to make communal life possible, the Jews are conceived of as having their own communal machinery organized specifically for conducting schools to preserve what is most essential in the life of the group—namely the Torah."[108] This is nothing but the application of the principles of Dubnow's autonomism to the American scene and the expression of Dubnow's theory of the Jews as a "world nationality."

Here again, as in the case of Jewish historiography, direct influence merges with parallel social and psychological conditions. For, apart from the political disabilities that Russian Jews suffered when Dubnow wrote his *Letters on Old and New Judaism*, there is a significant parallelism between the emancipated, secularized Jewish intellectual in Russia—who no longer was able to live his life within the bounds of traditional orthodoxy, who resisted psychologically the way of "inner slavery" that characterized assimilationism and who remained deeply attached to the life and culture of the Jewish people, who at the same time also felt an attachment to the land and culture in which he was living and hence rejected the radical Zionist solution of emigration to Palestine—with the present-day status of those American Jews, who even when adherents of either Conservative or Reform Judaism come fully under the category of secularized Jews as Dubnow saw them, who continue to feel a deep attachment to Jewish history, to Jewish culture and to Jewish life, and who, even when they are Zionists, feel themselves to be an integral part of the American scene. For the same reasons Dubnow's approach to the language question seems so peculiarly applicable to the American scene. All one need do is substitute English for Russian.

Many an American Jew is but vaguely conscious of these tendencies and conflicts within him and needs theoretical formulation and philosophical grounding to help him clarify his position as a Jew in the United States. To these groping, unaffiliated American Jewish intellectuals the call that Dubnow made to the Russian Jewish intelligentsia after the Kishinev massacre in 1903 may be appropriately addressed today:

However much the camp of the fighters for national emancipation has grown during the last decades, it still is small and weak compared to our intelligentsia remaining outside the camp. Thousands of educated and gifted Jews continue to labor in foreign vineyards, turn their backs on their lost brethren and defect to camps where their participation is not sought, perhaps also not desired. Since they were brought up in a spirit alien to Judaism, they are carried away by the social and literary currents of the alien environment. . . .

Those who will look deeply into the complex chaos of our national catastrophe will not go over to the camp of the peaceful and the light-hearted, nor to the camp of those who dream of things that are remote from the burning needs of the hour. Our national catastrophe, which is as vast as the sea, must cure our estranged intelligentsia. It offers it a sacred and exalted ideal and will give meaning and purpose to its life.

May all the vital elements of our people, all those in whose souls the "spark of Judaism" is not yet extinguished, all those who strive for the preservation and revival of our nation, unite over the fresh graves of our new national martyrs! May every educated Jew look upon himself as a soldier in a united army, the only army in the world which has fought for two thousand years against powerful enemies with spiritual weapons which have sustained us and enabled us to reach this time.[109]

EPILOGUE

In one of the earliest entries in his diary, in the year 1877 when he was in Dvinsk, the seventeen-year-old Dubnow wrote: "Here they do not understand my attachment to the Jewish nation. On the contrary, I notice hostility and disparagement of it. In me, however, the love for our nation, which the youth here cast aside as something undesirable, is constantly increasing."[110] This deep and abiding love of the Jewish people may well be said to have determined Simon Dubnow's basic approach to Jews and Judaism. If we may say that Ahad Ha-Am typified *Gedulat Yisrael*, the "majesty of Israel," majesty frequently combined with a measure of condescension; if Nathan Birnbaum personified the character of *Tiferet Yisrael*, "the splendor of Israel"; then Dubnow without doubt was the very incarnation of *Ahavat Yisrael*, of "love of Israel." In his anniversary greeting to Ahad Ha-Am, Dubnow gave expression to the hope that out of Ahad Ha-Am ("One of the People") there might develop the *Meahed Ha-Am*, the unifier of the people. What Dubnow expected of Ahad Ha-Am he himself became. Dubnow the "lover of Israel" for that very reason was the great "unifier of Israel," the great synthesizer of conflicting factions and ideologies in Jewish life. This was his strength, but this was also his weakness. In the practical and everyday life of modern political and social struggles, when it is necessary to exert influence over large masses of people, the ability to see elements of truth in your opponent's point of view is a source of weakness. It is much more advisable to be one-sided in the expression of one's convictions. Balanced synthesis and broad view often paralyze action in the arena of social and political battles. Dubnow, therefore, was never successful as a practical political leader in his own day. His influence was enormous but almost exclusively on the intellectual classes and on the leaders of the Jewish people. There is no doubt, however, that his influence will become even more apparent as time goes on.

Dubnow tells us in his autobiography of the last time he visited his eighty-five-year-old grandfather in Mstislav. It was in the year 1890, at a time when tsarist reaction was at its height. The Jews of Mstislav had been subjected by the local officials to most humiliating abuse. Dubnow on learning of this situation published a sharp letter of protest in the *Voskhod*, in which he exposed the intolerable situation. So effective was this exposé that it resulted in the elimination of the tension and the clearing of the atmosphere in the town. Before returning to St. Petersburg, Dubnow came to take leave of his grandfather Bentsion. "I heard, Shimen," said the old sage, "that you have done a good deed and that you have defended the honor of Israel. People in town say of you: There are some who acquire eternal life in one hour. I know that you were really never estranged from our people in your innermost being. May God grant that you continue to work in behalf of your people."[111]

Dubnow fulfilled the expectation of his beloved grandfather. He acquired eternal life not only with the "one hour" but with the eighty-one years of his life and creative activity. And as he became a sainted martyr in Israel through his tragic end, so he achieved the position of a "sage of Israel" through his historical and philosophical works, which will serve for a long time as a "guide to the perplexed" of our own day and of future generations.

A NOTE ON THE ESSAYS INCLUDED IN THIS VOLUME

I. On Nationalism

1. LETTERS ON OLD AND NEW JUDAISM

These letters were first published in serial form in the Russian Jewish journal Voskhod, between the years 1897 and 1906, under the title Pisma o starom i novyom evreystvye. In 1907, Dubnow collected these letters, re-edited them and added to them the article on "The Goals and Tasks of the Folkspartay," which he had published in 1907, first in Russian in the Raszvyet and then in Yiddish in Der Fraynd, and issued them in St. Petersburg under the original title, in a volume of 370 pages with an introduction of eight pages. In 1937, the Hebrew edition of these letters appeared in Tel Aviv, as translated by Abraham Levinson with the collaboration of Dubnow himself. Several important changes were made in this new version. Dubnow went over the entire text himself and eliminated repetitious elements, expressions and evaluations that he now considered too harsh against personalities of the time, and materials that were relevant only to the practical Jewish political scene of the earlier period and that had lost their significance by then. Three letters of the original Russian version were left out in their entirety in the Hebrew edition: one on "Changing Tendencies in Russian Jewish Journalism," published in 1899; another on "Division and Unity in the National Party," published in 1901; and a third on "The Confused Intelligentsia," published in 1902. An addition was made to the Hebrew edition with the inclusion of the article "The Affirmation of the Galut," a reply to Ahad Ha-Am's "Denial of the Galut," which Dubnow had published in 1909 in the Evreyskii mir. In addition Dubnow added to the Hebrew version a new preface and a number of footnotes.[112]

It is this Hebrew version that has been used for the present English translation. However, with the assistance of Miss Esther Pinson, I have compared the Hebrew with the Russian edition of 1907. In all instances of more than minor deletions in the Hebrew version I have indicated such deletions by three dots. Incidentally, to avoid confusion, I have completely eliminated from the present edition Dubnow's use of dots to indicate hesitation or an uncompleted thought. The presence of three dots in this English text, therefore, always means the deletion of material from the original Russian text. Much of these omissions are purely repetitious materials. Writing for a current periodical there was bound to be a great deal of repetition throughout the series and these Dubnow eliminated in editing the Hebrew version. I have not attempted to restore these. On the other hand, there are many interesting sidelights that he cut out. I have interpolated these either in the form of direct translations or in summarized statements as footnotes to the text. In order to avoid confusion between the footnotes that Dubnow himself wrote and those that I have seen fit to insert, I have left all Dubnow's own footnotes on the same page together with the text and indicated them by asterisks, while I have collected all my own footnotes at the end of the volume and indicated them by numbers. In the footnotes that I have added I have not tried to bring Dubnow's ideas up to date or supplement his bibliographical references with more recent studies. Apart from the footnotes of omitted materials, the others are only intended to aid the present-day reader to understand allusions to personalities and events that might not be as familiar in our day and in this country as they were to the original readers of the Letters.

2. "NEGATION AND AFFIRMATION OF THE DIASPORA IN AHAD HA-AM'S THOUGHT"

This essay, the final contribution by Dubnow to the long exchange between himself and Ahad Ha-Am on Jewish nationalism, appeared in the special issue of the Hebrew periodical Hashiloah commemorating the 25th anniversary of the publication of Ahad Ha-Am's famous essay, "Lo ze haderekh." It was published under the title "Shelilat hagalut vehiyuba betorat Ahad Ha-Am," in vol. xxx, no. 2, February, 1914, of Hashiloah, pp. 206-10.

II. On History

1. JEWISH HISTORY. AN ESSAY IN THE PHILOSOPHY OF HISTORY

This essay was written originally to serve as an introduction to a projected three-volume, abridged Russian edition of Graetz's History of the Jews. The Graetz edition never materialized, but the essay was published in the Voskhod in 1893 under the Russian title of "Chto takoye evreyskaya historiya? Opyt filozofskoy charakteristiki" ("What is Jewish History? An Attempt at a Philosophic Analysis"). It was Dubnow's first attempt at setting down his philosophy of history. During this time he was still under the dominance of the spiritual interpretation of history as exemplified by Graetz. He later abandoned this view of history in favor of the "sociological" interpretation, which formed the basis for all his later important works. In the Introduction to his Weltgeschichte he even goes out of his way to disparage his youthful effort.[113] But it became widely disseminated outside of Russia, largely as a result of the German translation prepared by Israel Friedlaender in 1898. A second edition of this German translation was published in Frankfurt-am-Main in 1922. The Friedlaender version was in turn translated by Henrietta Szold into English and published by the Jewish Publication Society in 1903. It became very popular in this country, but has been out of print for some years. The English version we publish here is a reprint of the Szold translation together with the preface to the German edition by Friedlaender. It appears in exactly the same form, except for changes in style sheet made to conform to the style of this entire volume. We have included it in this selection because of its intrinsic value and because it is an important document in the evolution of Dubnow's historical thinking.

2. THE SURVIVAL OF THE JEWISH PEOPLE. The Secret of Survival and the Law of Survival

This essay, a synthesis of philosophy of history and nationalism, was written by Dubnow in response to an invitation in 1911 by the brilliant Hebrew journalist Sh. I. Hurewitz, editor of the Heatid, to representative leaders of Jewish thought and ideological groupings to express their views on "Judaism and its Prospects." Among those, other than Dubnow, who participated in this symposium were Micha Joseph Berdichevski, Eliezer ben Yehuda, Martin Buber, Nathan Birnbaum, S. A. Horodetzky, Joseph Thon, David Neumark, Nahum Sokolow, David Frishman, A. Kaminka, A. Coralnik, Ludwig Stein, Ludwig Geiger and Max Nordau. All the replies, including this essay by Dubnow, were published in vol. iv of the Heatid in 1912. The entire set of volumes of the Heatid were reprinted after World War I in 1922. Dubnow's essay appears in vol. iv of this set, pp. 111-20.

3. THE SOCIOLOGICAL VIEW OF JEWISH HISTORY

This essay in the philosophy and problems of Jewish historiography, which is the introduction to Dubnow's magnum opus, the ten-volume Weltgeschichte, is the definitive pronouncement by Dubnow of the "sociological" view of Jewish history which he developed as the basis for all his mature scholarly work. An abridged English translation of the essay appeared in the Menorah Journal, vol. xiv (1928), pp. 257-67, but the translation included here is an entirely new one and presents the essay without deletions of any kind. The version used for the translation was the German edition of the Weltgeschichte, but the Yiddish and Hebrew versions were used in conjunction with the translation for purposes of comparison and clarification.

4. WHAT SHOULD ONE DO IN HAMAN'S TIMES?

This essay, one of the last published works by Dubnow, is a moving statement by the aged scholar of his national and philosophical credo in the most critical period of Jewish history. Just before the outbreak of World War II, Elias Tscherikower and several other Jewish scholars and journalists, under the impact of the rise of Nazism, had established a Yiddish periodical in Paris called Oyfn Sheydveg. The purpose of the literary venture was to enable Jewish writers and thinkers to re-evaluate the whole course of Jewish development since the coming of emancipation. In the circle were many who turned their backs on the fruits of emancipation and preached a return inward by the Jewish people and a rejection of the humanitarian and world ideals on which the hopes of secularized Jews had been founded during the preceding generations. Tscherikower, devoted disciple of Dubnow, wrote to Dubnow in Riga asking him to contribute to this re-evaluation. As seen from the piece that is published here, Dubnow refused to be party to such an intellectual project and addressed a letter to the editors of the journal instead of writing the article requested. He subsequently consented to have the letter published, together with a reply by Tscherikower. It appeared in Oyfn Sheydveg, number 2, Paris, August 1939.

PART 1 · ON NATIONALISM

LETTERS ON OLD AND NEW JUDAISM

(1897-1907)

AUTHOR'S PREFACE TO THE HEBREW EDITION

My theory of nationalism as presented in *Letters on Old and New Judaism* gained wider publicity through its interpreters and critics than in its original version. At the time of their publication (in the Russian *Voskhod*, St. Petersburg, 1897-1906, and later, in 1907, collected in a separate volume) the "Letters" were used in their original form only in Russia. In other countries only fragments were available: the first two chapters were published in Berlin in a German translation.* Many writers on the history of the Jewish national movement judged my theories on the basis of what others wrote (and sometimes dreamed) about it. After the great Jewish center that gave birth to the national movement was destroyed, I contemplated writing an abbreviated version (a *Kitsur shulhan arukh*) of the "Letters" in a form which could serve as a source for the principles of my system,

* This translation (Berlin, Jüdischer Verlag, 1905) by the late Israel Friedlaender was prepared from the first version, the version which was revised later when the essays were published in collected form. The revised version of the "First Letter" was published in *Der Jude* (Berlin, 1926), in a German translation by Dr. Elias Hurwicz, as the first step in the publication of the whole collection. The complete project, however, never materialized.

for its development in the chain of the events of that period, and for the general history of the national movement. For the past ten years the book was being prepared in the new version, and translations were made from it into German and Hebrew. Neither the revised text in the original Russian nor the German translation has as yet been published. Both rest among my manuscripts "until the coming of Elijah." Only the Hebrew translation has found a redeemer, in the person of Abraham Levinson, an eminent Zionist and one of the critics of this book when it first was published. I have worked together with the translator and have provided additions and corrections to the text (for the most part abbreviations of materials of only passing significance).[1]

Readers of the new generation will now be able to judge the ideas and actions of one of the writers of the preceding generation by his own words. I should like this book to serve, not only as a systematic exposition of ideas and beliefs, but also as a storehouse of information on the history of the period in which it was written. The first part is designed to explain the principles of the idea of nationalism in general and of the Jewish national idea in particular, ideas accepted by most of the parties in the Jewish community. The second part will guide the younger generation through the war of ideas waged among the Jewish nationalist parties, the various Zionist currents, the assimilationists and the Socialists who rejected nationalism. The reader will find here an adequate commentary on the controversies I carried on for decades with the leaders of Zionism, especially with Ahad Ha-Am, the greatest of the Zionist theorists. Notwithstanding my severe objections to political Zionism, I was never opposed to its positive and practical side, the rebuilding of Palestine, but only to its negative aspect, the rejection of the *galut*. This was the central point in my long controversy with Ahad Ha-Am, the closest to me in spirit among my friends. He was in the end forced to make some concessions to my point of view and to differentiate between objective and subjective negation of the Diaspora (see his last essay "The Negation of the Diaspora," in *Al perashat derakhim*, vol. iv, pp. 106-16). In the present volume the reader will also find my answer to that excellent essay by Ahad Ha-Am (this was published originally outside the framework of the "Letters"), with which the controversy was closed (Eighth Letter, "The Affirmation of the *Galut*").

In the new version of the "Letters," I have deleted some of the harsh expressions directed against the opposition parties which were appropriate only at the time, in the heat of battle. And if the reader still finds occasional remnants of this kind I hope he will understand that I have no intention at this time of hurting anyone but aim only to state the truth as I see it.

Kiryat-Yearim, near Riga (Latvia), July 7, 1936.

First Letter

THE DOCTRINE OF JEWISH NATIONALISM

I. The course of the development of the national type: tribal foundations, territorial, political, and cultural-historical or spiritual.—The transition from material to spiritual culture in the growth of a nation. —The test of the internal strength of a nation: its loss of statehood and territory.

II. This development in Judaism: the early beginnings of the growth of the spiritual nation in the period of the Prophets, its continued growth during the era of the Second Commonwealth and its final realization in the Diaspora (autonomism, Diaspora centers).—The nation as both the creator and the product of its history; the crystallization of national types.

III. The transition from objective to subjective criteria in scientific definitions of the term "nation."—Spiritual affinity as more important than blood relationship; essential basis of the nation.

IV. The negation of Jewish nationalism: Confusion of religious and national foundations and the secularization of the Jewish national idea.—The assimilationist current; religious nationality and religious group.—Minimum of Judaism and the limits of nationalist rejection.

V. National individuality and national corporate personality.—The Jewish national idea as an expression of enlightened individualism.—The national foundation as midway between the individual and the social foundations.—Fundamental theses.

I

In investigating the evolution of national types we discover that development proceeds from the material to the spiritual and from external simplicity to inner complexity. On lower cultural levels the differences between peoples are largely natural in character; on higher levels the differences are historical-cultural in character. On the basis of the predominant characteristics of each period we can distinguish the following stages in the evolution of national types: (1) the tribal type, (2) the territorial-political or autonomous type, (3) the cultural-historical or spiritual type. Each type is combined with the succeeding one in either mechanical or organic fashion, that is, the earlier may be preserved in the later type in its original form, or it may disappear and take on a new form. Let us examine each of these types separately.

In the earliest stage of civilization the racial or tribal group is merely a product of nature.[2] Common origin, territory and climate leave their stamp on the physical and mental characteristics of the members of the family group, who may be concentrated in one territory or in many (in fixed settlements or nomadic). Thus the "nation," in original and biological sense (*natio*, from *nasci*, to be born), comes into being. General tribal characteristics become crystallized, as the law of heredity operates over many generations, and in this way a fundamental pattern is established, the natural or tribal stage of nationality.

Even in this stage of development, however, the influence of material culture begins to compete with the influence of nature. Gradually the influence of nature over man decreases, as man gains mastery over it. Cultural factors weaken the more obvious effects of territory and climate and they obscure somewhat the more dominant characteristics of the tribal type (later on the same effects are produced by migrations, intermarriage, etc.). As the reciprocal influences between man and nature grow more complex, the cultural pattern creates a more complex individuality. The more the tribe adjusts itself to its natural environment and, in turn, adapts the environment to its essential needs, the more will its economic needs find expression in various forms of co-operation, thus planting the seeds of the social organization of the future. As the struggle for survival takes on definite forms, common tendencies, habits, attitudes and beliefs become fixed among the members of the whole tribal group. Common language is one of the strongest forces cementing the members of the group and setting it apart from other tribal groups. Thus the transition from material to spiritual culture becomes marked and the second stage of nationality, the cultural, emerges from the natural or tribal foundations.

The growing social cohesion, which results from economic co-operation and other forms of human association, leads necessarily to a unified and stable organization in the form of a civic union or state.

The territory, hitherto only part of the natural environment, becomes a political factor which unites the various tribes into a nation. An organized political authority subjects the whole state to fixed laws and protects its frontiers against the attacks of foreign nations. Political life educates the nation along certain definite lines. Social discipline, well-defined duties and rights of citizens (equal at least within each class and party) and the setting off of the state from other states—all these create for the members of the political community numerous new needs, preferences and aspirations. The unifying force is the concept of native land, with the will to defend or strengthen it. The heroic deeds of patriots and the legends of the great men who won eternal fame in the annals of the nation become a powerful factor in the development of the historical consciousness during this early period.*

The territorial-political type of nationality emerges in various stages and forms which are conditioned by the level of civilization of the group and by the degree of its self-government. The annals of human history contain frequent examples of small states being swallowed up by big states. As a result, the conquered nations, whose national-cultural character was not too well developed, lose all or some of their characteristics and become fused with nations of a clear-cut and distinct type. Spiritually and culturally strong nations, however, preserve their identity, even under conditions of political subordination, thanks to their social autonomy, that is, their ability to order their communal self-government in keeping with their historical traditions and inner needs. The conquering nations on their side are themselves often endangered by political hypertrophy. Through conquests and forceful annexations of territory they create polyglot empires of alien and often hostile national groups. Thus arise those inner tensions which lead to the breakup of absolutist monarchies and to the destruction of the conquering nation as well (Assyria, Babylonia, Persia, ancient Rome). The ruling nation, powerful in a political sense, dis-

* The formulation which most closely resembles this scheme of development of national types is that by Alfred Fouillée in his *Esquisse psychologique des peuples européens*. In the section on "Factors of National Character," Fouillée lists the following "three great factors" as most important for the development of the physical and psychic structure of a people: (1) accumulated inherited tradition; (2) adaptation to the physical environment; (3) adaptation to the social milieu.

appears often precisely because the element of political power outweighs its spiritual resources. After a period of social and ethical decline it comes to be absorbed in the family of younger nations, who bear within them the seeds of sound cultural development. From this we see that the decisive factor for the destiny of a nation is not its external power but its spiritual force, the quality of its culture and the inner cohesion of its members.

The culture of the political or social stage is higher and more differentiated than that of the earlier tribal stage. The growth of material culture is intimately related to the advance of its spiritual creativity. Social life gives rise to altruistic ideas and emotions. Religion is elevated to a comprehensive world view. The moral sense becomes deepened and takes on well-defined forms of ethical ideals as expressed by priests and sages. Language, up to then only a means of communication among the members of the tribal group, now becomes a tool for spiritual intercourse and for the creation of literary and scientific values. . . . History and legend no longer glorify exploits solely of conquest or defense, but also spiritual strength, dedication to lofty cultural values, to freedom of thought, religion and conviction. These historical traditions inspire succeeding generations and unite the nation in a powerful bond of common feelings of love and hatred.* The earlier tribal foundation and the chain of historical traditions, when joined with the spiritual progress of the people, create

* This high point of national evolution is related to Renan's well-known characterization:

"Une nation est un principe spirituel résultant des complications profondes de l'histoire, une famille spirituelle . . . Deux choses qui, à vrai dire, n'en font qu'une constituent cette âme, ce principe spirituel. L'une est dans le passé, l'autre dans le présent. L'une est la possession en commun d'un riche legs de souvenir; l'autre est le consentement actuel, le désir de vivre ensemble, la volonté de continuer à faire valoir l'heritage qu'on a recus indivis. . . . La nation, comme l'individu, est l'aboutissant d'un long passé des efforts, de sacrifices et de dévouements. . . . Une passé heroïque, des grandes hommes, de la gloire . . . voilá le capital social sur lequel on assied une idée nationale. Avoir des gloires communes dans le passé, une volonté commune dans le présent; avoir fait de grandes choses ensemble, vouloir en faire encore, voilá la condition essentielle pour être un peuple. . . . La souffrance en commun unit plus que la joie. En fait des souvenirs nationaux, les deuils valent mieux que les triomphes; car ils imposent des dévoirs; ils commandent l'effort en commun." (E. Renan, *Qu'est ce qu'une nation?* [Conférence faite en Sorbonne, le 11 Mars, 1882, Paris, S. Levy, 1882] pp. 25-27).

a broad basis for national consciousness. From this moment the future of the nation depends mainly on the depth of this consciousness, on the strength of the national spirit, on the power of the cultural foundations created over generations and on the ability of the nation to further develop its creative powers. The natural instinct of national self-preservation creates for itself forms of autonomous development, and if they prove inadequate in the political sphere they are directed to the social or cultural spheres, to all areas of life and thought.

A test of the full development of the national type comes in the case of a people that has lost its political independence, a factor generally regarded as a necessary condition for national existence. A people that has been deprived of its political liberty, though remaining on its own territory but subject to alien rule, undoubtedly gives evidence of a strong national will and a store of vital spiritual energies if it persists in carrying on a social life of its own and aspires as far as possible to internal autonomy. History records many nations that found themselves in such a condition but succeeded for a long time in preserving their identity, beginning with Judea and Greece during the period of Roman expansion and up to Ireland and Poland in modern times. There is, however, a still more rigid test for the maturity of a nation. When a people loses not only its political independence but also its land, when the storm of history uproots it and removes it far from its natural homeland and it becomes dispersed and scattered in alien lands, and in addition loses its unifying language; if, despite the fact that the external national bonds have been destroyed, such a nation still maintains itself for many years, creates an independent existence, reveals a stubborn determination to carry on its autonomous development—such a people has reached the highest stage of cultural-historical individuality and may be said to be indestructible, if only it cling forcefully to its national will. We have many examples in history of nations that have become dispersed among other nations. We find only one instance, however, of a people that has survived for thousands of years despite dispersion and loss of homeland. This unique people is the people of Israel.

This fact must not be viewed as a historical miracle. The Jewish people went through the same stages of national development as did other peoples. Due to its unique historical destiny, however, the elements which condition the national type became crystallized in different forms and value-relationships. Due to this unique destiny, the spiritual elements outweighed decisively the material and political elements. A cursory survey of the course of Jewish history will demonstrate this point.

II

Up to the period of the Kings in the history of Israel, the tribal element was decisive for the development of the Jewish national type. From various semitic groups (the sons of Terah, Abraham, etc.) a number of nomadic tribes emerged and came to be known as "Children of Israel." Their habitat in Mesopotamia, Palestine, Egypt, and the Sinai desert left its imprint upon these blood-related tribes. Their character was formed by a struggle, not only with nature, but also with men (their slavery in Egypt). The conquest of Canaan gave the Children of Israel a fixed territory and thus a powerful instrument for unity. During the period of the Judges the skeleton of tribal organization was still discernible in the dominance of the family patriarch and in the division into tribes. But the skeleton gradually became covered with the skin of a common territory. The moment of political unification was approaching. It was realized during the period of the first kings: Saul, David and Solomon.

The brilliant flash of a "great power" status lighted up the Jewish commonwealth and the ambition lured it on to conquer the neighboring tribes in order to secure its frontiers. However, under the political conditions prevailing in the Near East shortly before the emergence of the huge empires of Assyria and Babylonia, the role of conqueror was too much for the powers of the tribes of Israel. Internal divisions still alive among the tribes and the struggle for hegemony within the nation broke up the unity of their state. The period of the divided kingdom, of the two kingdoms of Judah and Israel, followed.

In the meantime a new unifying force emerged, the force of a unique spiritual culture in which religion predominated. Out of the embryo of a tribal monotheism (Jahwe, the God of Israel), which differed from the idolatry of the other nations more in degree than in essence, there developed after much agitation and stumbling the concept of universal monotheism (Jahwe, the God of all mankind) with Israel as its standard bearer. This religious nucleus served as the basis for a system of social and ethical ideas that was infused into the life stream of the people through the flaming words of the Prophets. The Prophets strove to combine the universal national elements into one harmonious whole and were forced to seek new paths to secure the inner strength of the nation. In the face of the growing power of the aggressive empires of Assyria and Babylonia and the danger of the impending political destruction of the weak Kingdom of Israel, the Prophets acted energetically to shift the center of gravity of national survival from the political sphere to the social and spiritual spheres. They taught that political weakness or even the loss of statehood were no danger as long as the people were united and bound together by inner spiritual energy, for the state was merely the shell placed around the kernel, which was the nation. The Prophets sought to lift Judaism at one stroke to the highest level of national existence; but they were ahead of their times. Of necessity the struggle for national survival led to a natural selection: the weaker elements (the Kingdom of the Ten Tribes) in the nation could not withstand the pressure of the national catastrophe and most of them were assimilated into the neighboring peoples, while the stronger elements (the Kingdom of Judah) avoided annihilation and with slow but sure steps continued their path toward the creation of a new type of spiritual nation.

This type showed its vitality for the first time in the brief period of the Babylonian exile, after the Kingdom of Judah had lost its political independence as well as its land, and somewhat later, during the prolonged period of Persian and Greek rule, when the land but not political independence was restored. Although the theocracy (or better: hierocracy, that is, the rule of the priests) of that period was still a far cry from the lofty ethical standards of the Prophets, yet it succeeded in establishing Jewish national existence on the two firm principles of social and cultural self-rule. The "People of the Book" came into being (after the time of Ezra the Scribe), drank from the stream of its earlier spiritual creations and produced new cultural values. In spite of internal differences, a definite national form emerged, fixed like a solitary island rock in the stormy sea of the neighboring peoples. As if by a powerful force, all parts of the Jewish Diaspora in the Near East and in North Africa were drawn to this island and when a new storm was unleashed by history—Greek culture extending its magic influence over the idols of Asia and its peoples—it was able to shake this Jewish island, but not to destroy it. A historical moment without parallel in the history of mankind arrived: not two political states but two cultures, two world views, Judaism and Hellenism, stood facing each other.

The triumph of Judaism for a time restored even political independence to Judea and led to the establishment of the Hasmonean kingdom. Once more the struggle for supremacy was renewed between the principles of political and spiritual nationalism, with the Sadducees as the protagonists of political and military power while the Pharisees asserted the primacy of spiritual culture and internal self-rule for the national community.[3] The iron hand of Rome contributed to the victory of the Pharisees and their rule of the Law (nomocracy). Since the resistance of the political zealots could not break the Roman hold, a period of spiritual resistance began which was crowned with success. The destruction of the Second Temple did not lead to the annihilation of the nation. The roots of the weakened and dispersed nation continued to remain attached to its native territory, Roman Palestine, and it was here that a new center of social and spiritual self-government arose (the period of the Patriarchate) that provided sustenance to the far-flung branches of the Diaspora (the hegemony of Palestine).

History, however, once more put the national maturity of Israel to a severe test. Up to that time the Diaspora had merely been a dependency of Palestine. In the Middle Ages nothing but the Diaspora remained and the hegemony of Palestine vanished. The native land became a minute geographic point on the map of the three continents over which the Jews were dispersed. The nation without a state also became a nation without a territory. The great period of the migrations, the political conquests of Islam in the East, and of Christianity in the West split up and weakened the Jewish Diaspora. Could such a scattered and dispersed national organism exist for long? History answered in the affirmative and the organism continued on its course. The period of the hegemonic centers of the Diaspora had arrived.

In those countries where the Jews were numerically strong, concentrated centers of national-spiritual energies were created, repositories of vital cultural forces, to which the smaller centers of the Jewish Diaspora looked for leadership. In this way there came the development of the great centers of the Jewish Diaspora in Babylonia (from the fifth to the eleventh centuries), Spain (from the eleventh to the fifteenth centuries), Germany and Poland (from the sixteenth to the eighteenth centuries). In each of these centers autonomous communal organizations came into being that embraced many diverse aspects of the social and cultural life of the people (the Exilarchs and the Geonim in Babylonia, the *Aljama*[4] in Spain, the rule of the *kahal* and of associations of communities with their central institutions or "Councils of the Lands" in Poland). . . . The Jewish nation, deprived of geographical boundaries, staked out for itself social and spiritual limits in all the countries of the dispersion. . . . In place of political autonomy it created for itself social and cultural autonomy. All through this period the Jewish nation passed through a variety of stages: prosperity and stagnation, progress and mere survival, full and retarded growth. The nation as a whole, however, lived and developed as one, as a definite national personality, in all parts of the Diaspora.

What force, then, was it that kept alive this dispersed nation, without state and without territory, all these centuries? Was it the written law of the Bible, the ordinances of the Talmud and the decisions of the rabbis, the isolation of the ghetto, inner autonomy, faith in the coming of the Messiah? All of them indeed contributed, but they were only external manifestations of forms of national survival. These were not fixed forms, but forms that changed and were altered in the course of history. Quite apart from these, the source of vitality of the Jewish people consists in this: that this people, after it had passed through the stages of tribal nationalism, ancient culture and political territory, was able to establish itself and fortify itself in the highest stage, the spiritual and historical-cultural, and succeeded in crystallizing itself as a spiritual people that draws the sap of its existence from a natural or intellectual "will to live." All this came only because in the play of forces that sustained Jewish nationalism those elements not dependent on territory counted more than those dependent on territory. In the measure that the positive political factors declined, the spiritual factors increased in importance, in the same way, for example, that the sense of touch or hearing of a blind man is sharpened at the expense of his defective sense of sight. Over a period of many generations, unique characteristics, emotions, and historical tendencies, the effects of the sufferings and pains of the past, were brought out by the law of heredity. The collective personality grew deeper and the power to resist the leveling influences of an alien environment waxed stronger. The weapons used by the nation in its struggle for survival were adapted to more difficult conditions. In this struggle there were critical and dangerous moments, periods of separation of the chaff from the grain, when the weaker parts of the nation were cut off and assimilated with other peoples (assimilation in varying degrees is a constant factor throughout Jewish history). In the end, however, the healthy kernel of the nation survived and drew its strength from a determined national will.

To the degree that a people creates its own history it is itself in equal measure created by it. In each generation it creates its own culture and is itself in turn the product of the creative efforts of all past generations. A nation is not merely an aggregate of individuals, but also of successive generations, a community of the living and the dead. Therefore, the law of heredity, the common denominator of various historical transformations operating below the threshold of consciousness, directs the course of development of national life and copes with the influences of the external environment.

Two forces interact in a living nation: the accumulation of culture and accumulated culture, the efforts of the living generation and the cultural storehouse and creative tools of the preceding generations. In time a national individuality becomes crystallized and leaves its imprint on the life of the individual. This national personality, however, is subject to a natural limit which emanates from the influences of the international environment to which the nation must adapt itself. A nation will survive, therefore, only if it develops a very strong individuality; otherwise it must degenerate through assimilation and be absorbed by other nations. A nation that has the protective arsenal of a native land and state, a national language, schools and other cultural institutions, will be secure in its independent development even if it should be wanting in a pronounced national personality. But if these protective elements of the national type are lacking entirely or in part, they can only be replaced by a strengthening of inner defenses, that is, through a strong national will to develop cultural autonomy and through determined resistance against the assimilating influence of the external environment. This is the lesson to be learned from the history of the Jews in the Diaspora.

III

What is the distinguishing mark of nationality? This question has up to most recent times aroused sharp controversy both in theory and in practice. I shall not dwell on the details of the controversy. I wish to underscore but one fact: the scientific definitions of the concept "nation" exhibit the same transition from the material to spiritual factors as the concrete historical development of nations. Philosophers of the old school looked upon nationality as the product of biological elements, climate and territory. Contemporary legal philosophers and political scientists frequently confuse the terms "nation" and "state." For them the typical nation is the uni-national state and, where they find a multi-national state, they condemn the national minority to assimilation and fusion with the ruling majority (this opinion originated during the French Revolution and was for a long time widely accepted in jurisprudence). More liberal political theorists benevolently accord the right of cultural autonomy to national groups which do not have a state of their own but have not yet lost their territory and their language. Lately, however, the view has gained ground that a nation may be defined as a historical-cultural group which is conscious of itself as a nation even though it may have lost all or some of the external characteristics of nationality (state, territory or language), provided it possesses the determination to continue developing its own personality in the future. Objective criteria of nationality are giving way in the scientific definitions of the concept to subjective factors.*

Theoretical sociologists and political scientists have arrived at the conclusion that subjective or spiritual factors are supreme in the development of the national type, while all the material factors are but stages leading to the highest point of this development, namely, the crystallization of a well-defined and conscious national individuality. In the same way in which spiritual affinity is a more important factor than blood relationship in families of higher cultural circles (there are numerous instances of families being broken up because of profound differences in ethical and spiritual aspirations among their members), so also in higher types of national families the common spiritual aspirations are the unifying and cohesive forces.†

* Fichte (in his *Reden an die deutsche Nation*) was the first to emphasize the spiritual basis of the national type, although he did not separate it from the territorial-political elements and thus confused the concept "patriotism" with the concept "nationalism." Renan (*op. cit.*), as pointed out above, stressed the element of subjective will in national consciousness more clearly and made the excellent observation, especially applicable to Judaism, that in the sum total of historical impressions and emotions the unifying effect of suffering is greater than that of the experiences of happiness, Fouillée closes his study of "Factors of National Character" with the following conclusion: "A nation is, above all, a group of individuals who recognize themselves as a nation; it is a spiritual creation of those who create it without cessation. The essence of the nation is its consciousness." The latest conclusion reached by Rudolf Springer (Karl Renner), who has devoted himself to the study of the national question, reads: "Nationalism is a feeling of spiritual and cultural community," and its importance is established by the will and its public manifestations. (*Staat und Nation*, 1899, published under the pseudonym Synopticus.) . . .[5]

† Renan, who wanted to refute antisemitism scientifically, showed the mixed composition of the Jewish racial type in his address "Le Judaisme comme race et comme religion" (Paris, 1883). Since I find his arguments exaggerated and since I see in Jewry the relatively purest of all existing racial types, I find no basis whatsoever in Renan's rejection of the Jewish national type. A Jewish nationalist can wholeheartedly accept the following conclusion in Renan's address:

"The racial basis has no decisive importance for the question of nationality. The ethnographic basis, so important in the early days of mankind, loses its value slowly

What is the supreme moving force in the national struggles of our time for political freedom and communal autonomy, if not this desire of nations to preserve their spiritual possessions and to develop freely their historical personality? The German War of Liberation against Napoleon I at the beginning of the nineteenth century and similarly the subsequent struggle of the Italians against Austria were battles against the injection of foreign national culture into the national life of the Germans and Italians. In all liberation movements of oppressed peoples, in all uprisings against political tyranny, a strong sense of national self-preservation is manifested which claims for itself the right to free cultural development. Usually the shell of political or territorial independence is placed around this precious kernel—the freedom of the nation—in order to protect it. From time to time, however, a nation is forced to forego this protective shell of political autonomy and to remain content with social and cultural autonomy. In place of the external instruments of nationality, which it had to give up, it strengthens its inner resources, the consciousness of its identity, the collective will, and the common aspirations necessary for building up its autonomous organizations and institutions, its language, its educational system and its literature. If this struggle is carried on successfully over a long period, it is safe to predict that it will also succeed in the future, provided the utmost is done to increase and strengthen national unity.

IV

After what has been said above it should be clear to all how greatly mistaken are those Jews and non-Jews who deny to the Jews of the Diaspora the right to call themselves a nation, only because they lack the specific external marks of a nationality which were taken

---

and increasingly with advancing civilization." Renan thus contradicts himself when he postulates the rule "that the Jews will of necessity assimilate with other nations." He fails to recognize the cultural-historical structure that rises above the racial foundation, brings nationalism into being and strengthens it particularly "with advancing civilization." A definite proof of this can be seen in the national alienation of the Karaites from Judaism, which followed their religious separation from the Jewish community. A branch of the Jewish family became estranged from our people after it turned away and strayed from the path of its historical development. The blood ties were severed at the same time the spiritual ties were cut.

from them or which became weakened during the nation's long history. Only he who completely fails to understand the nature of the national "ego" and of its development can refuse to accord nationality to this old historic community which, during the last 2,000 years, has been transformed from a simple nation into the very archetype of a nation, a nation in the purest and loftiest sense, which has attained the highest stage of nationality.

The rejection of Jewish nationalism among Jews stems from two opposing camps, the orthodox and the freethinkers. Since religion completely dominated all spheres of Jewish life for two thousand years, the mass of orthodox Jews accepted the idea that Judaism is not a nationality in the accepted sense but a religious community living according to sacred traditions, laws and commandments that encompass the life of the individual and the community. The mass of the people who do not understand the interdependence of historic events failed to see that all the ancient national values of the Jewish nation—the historical festivals, customs and usages, laws, social institutions, the whole system of self-administration retained in the Diaspora—all had been incorporated gradually and artificially into the sphere of religion. The national body became wrapped in the garb of religion so that . . . its true form was unrecognizable.

In essence the views of the orthodox may be formulated as follows: "Judaism is a religious nation, its members are held together by religious ordinances and practical commandments; whoever violates this religion removes himself from the national community." This view is not opposed to the concept of a spiritual or cultural nation. It is mistaken only in the sense that it confuses the concepts of "spiritual" and "cultural" with "religious." It is the result of a limited perspective characteristic of men who do not distinguish between fossilized tradition and living, creative development. Let the mass of the orthodox consider nationality and religion as one, for the time being; . . . let them be satisfied with this partial understanding as long as they cannot arrive at a full and complete understanding based on theoretical analysis and research. In the end they too will see the light. The observing and believing Jew will realize that there are many Jewish freethinkers who, while disregarding the religious laws and commandments, are nevertheless true and dedicated members of their people and that they not only remain within the fold of Judaism but strive with all their power to strengthen and exalt it. From this realization it is but one step to theoretical analysis and research. These Jews will then come to differentiate religion from nationality, and the scientific study of history will reveal to them how these concepts came to be confused. When that happens the movement of the secularization of the national idea, which has already begun among an important segment of the community in modern times, will gain ground among the broad strata of the people.

While the mass of old-type orthodox Jews sees itself in practice as a religious nation and resists assimilation in the surrounding nations by the force of its faith, the assimilationist intelligentsia, on the other hand (mostly freethinkers or the neo-orthodox of the West), sees in Judaism only a religious community, a union of synagogues which imposes no national duties or discipline whatsoever on its members. According to this view, the Jew can become a member of another nation and remain a member of the Mosaic faith. He is a German Jew, for example, in the same way that there are German Protestants or German Catholics. It follows logically from this premise that a freethinking or non-religious Jew must be excluded from the community of Jews of the Mosaic faith. This corollary is usually glossed over so that whatever remains of Jewish "unity" may not be disturbed. I shall discuss this doctrine, which was in vogue only a short time ago but has recently lost ground among its adherents, in greater detail in the following Letters. Here I only wish to point out that it contradicts both the traditional view of many past generations that the "religious nation" must be kept pure, and the scientific view of the non-assimilability of the spiritual or cultural nation. This kind of doctrine comes neither from religion nor from science. It is the invention of naive ideologues, or calculating opportunists, who seek to justify by means of this artificial doctrine their desire to assimilate into the foreign environment in order to benefit themselves and their children.[6] This is but a repetition of the process of natural selection and of the weeding out of those weak elements of the nation which are unable to bear the pressure of the alien environment.

The natural tendency to strip the Jewish national idea of its religious cloak is liable to lead to still another extreme position. While the orthodox say: "The Jewish religion is the sole foundation of our nationality," the freethinkers can claim: "The Jewish religion is not at all a necessary condition of nationality; it can exist without it by virtue of the law of psychic heredity and cultural-historical factors." In practice this theory would make it possible to justify religious apostasy. A Jew could give up Judaism, embrace another religion, and still remain a Jew by nationality. Those who hold this view are guilty of a grave and dangerous error. By aspiring to secularism, by separating the national idea from religion, we aim only to negate the *supremacy* of religion, but not to eliminate it from the storehouse of national cultural treasures. If we wish to preserve Judaism as a cultural-historical type of nation, we must realize that the religion of Judaism is one of the integral foundations of national culture and that anyone who seeks to destroy it undermines the very basis of national existence. Between us and the orthodox Jews there is only this difference: they recognize a traditional Judaism the forms of which were set from the beginning for all eternity, while we believe in an evolutionary Judaism in which new and old forms are always being assumed or discarded and which adjusts itself unceasingly to new cultural conditions. Their main concern is holiness,[7] ours is creative freedom. Here I may be asked: "And what of those who do not accept religion in general and the Jewish religion in particular?" This is a most important question and demands special attention.

Historical Judaism is not merely a religion, like Christianity or Islam. Judaism is a body of culture. Unique historical conditions which brought the life of the Jewish nation under the dominance of religion converted Judaism into an all-embracing world view which encompasses religious, ethical, social, messianic, political and philosophical elements. In each of these areas history has piled up layer upon layer. The Bible, the Talmud, Rabbinic Judaism, rationalist Jewish theology, Jewish mysticism are not merely chapters in Jewish religious teaching but also stages in the development of Judaism. Judaism is broad enough and variegated enough so that any man in Israel can draw from its source according to his spirit and outlook.

The orthodox Jew accepts all the principles of religious faith and practice formed in the course of generations and rigidly set down in the codes of law and in the ordinances of the rabbis. The "reformed" Jew rejects the decisions of the rabbis and even the laws of the Talmud and accepts only the religious principles, laws and obligations of the Bible. Adherents of rationalist theology find satisfaction in the religious philosophy of the Middle Ages. The freethinking Jew who accepts only ethical teaching can find an exalted moral and social world-view in the teachings of the Hebrew Prophets. The ethical teachings of the Prophets can well become the "religion of the future," the moral doctrine of a free society.* All those who base their religion on poetic content will find in the Bible and in medieval Jewish literature a source of poetry that fills the soul with magic splendor. Followers of mysticism will find a great treasure house in the kabbala and to a greater degree in hasidism, the "religion of the heart." Thus one may be a Jew according to the teaching of the Prophets or of the Talmud, according to Moses Maimonides or the *Shulhan Arukh*, according to Moses Mendelssohn or the Besht, according to Geiger or Samson Raphael Hirsch, as long as one does not reject entirely the national idea, which is not a matter of theory but a historical fact.†

In the end those Jews to whom any form of religion is alien will prefer to remain within the Jewish fold rather than embrace another faith. The enlightened among us, who in the main tend toward rationalism and scientific positivism, will not betray the Covenant of Abraham out of conviction and submit to the yoke of another religion for the simple reason that, if the principles of the Jewish religion, which are so closely related to rationalism, do not suit them, the symbols and mysticism of Christianity surely will not do so. Diderot once said that the way of science leads from Christianity to

* The famous orientalist James Darmesteter made such an attempt in his *Les Prophètes d'Israel* (Paris, 1892).

† I believe that even Spinoza would not have turned away from his people if he and the Jews of Amsterdam had understood history well enough to realize that it was possible to be a national Jew without retaining traditional religion. The seventeenth century was not yet advanced enough, however, to understand the secular Jewish national idea.

Judaism and thence to philosophical Deism. In any event, a rationalist in search of ethical ideals will turn to the philosophy of life of the biblical prophets rather than to the other-worldly doctrine of the Gospels.

A non-believing Jew may be counted as an adherent of Judaism so long as he does not identify himself with any other faith that conforms to his philosophical views. He may also join the "dissidents," or *Konfessionslose*, who do not believe in any religion. In any case he cannot attach himself to another Church out of sincere conviction. Absence of faith takes the Jew out of the national community only if he believes in complete national assimilation. In practice, conversion to another faith, under conditions prevailing in the Diaspora, means also separation from the Jewish nation. If this may not apply to the apostate himself, it certainly does to his family, which has no choice but to assimilate with the non-Jewish environment in the national as well as the religious sense. A convert of this kind may consider himself in his innermost heart as a "Christian son of the Jewish nation"; in fact, however, the tie between the two is broken. This does not apply, of course, to the marranos of Spain who, under a Christian cloak, clung to Judaism and educated their children in its spirit. In general, a Jew may be a son of the Jewish faith potentially or actually, or he may be without any religion at all; but exit from Judaism by acceptance of the Christian religion means exit from the Jewish nation.[8]

In his "Historical Letters," the Russian publicist Lavrov[9] (Mirtov) discusses the theory that each nation realizes its own distinct idea in the course of the general progress of mankind. More precisely, he raises the question whether there is a typical national idea which "is not limited only to a definite period but embraces and links all epochs in the life of a nation?" The author answers the question in the negative, and supports his position by pointing to the example of two "historical nations," the Jews and the French. "The Jews," says Lavrov, "despite their small numbers, fulfilled a historic role in the ancient world and in medieval Europe. Even in our own day they have not lost their historic worth. . . . The names of Jewish Socialists are so deeply inscribed in both scientific literature and in the annals of the modern Socialist movement that it is difficult to deny their influence, which can hardly be separated from their nationality. . . . However, is it possible to assume, even for a moment, that the Prophets of the first Exile and the medieval kabbalists, the rabbis of the Talmud and the translators of Ibn-Roshd, and the generation of Heine, Rothschild, Meyerbeer, Marx and Lassalle, all expressed the same idea in history? And there is hardly a nation in which separation from the environment and tradition were of such overriding importance as with the Jews." The author concludes . . . : "There is no such thing as a general idea running like a silk thread through the entire history of a nation. . . ."

I do not intend to contradict this general conclusion, especially since I myself have drawn attention to the many changes in the Jewish cultural pattern which goes by the name of "Judaism." I am equally removed from the doctrine of a predetermined national "mission" and of a "national spirit" forced into a definite mold. . . . I agree with the Russian sociologist Struve that "every attempt to identify the content and the form of the national spirit with one constant principle is liable to stunt its growth, to petrify it and to fix its content for all time." I further agree with him "that the national spirit continues to develop in the workshop of national life."* However, this does not preclude the possibility of singling out *a posteriori* one or more character traits typical of the history of a nation. In the history of Judaism, for example, there is no single definite idea which runs through all periods like a silk thread. There are various ideas, with increasing cultural creativity and deep yearning for social progress in every generation. A people which, in the course of the thousands of years of its existence, amassed a working capital of spirituality, a people which has developed uninterruptedly without recourse to savagery or lawlessness, has reached a level the like of which cannot be found even among nations that reached the highest stage of cultural development.

I am convinced, therefore, that every nation has the right to extol its past achievements, its historic deeds and the values which it

* Struve, Peter, "What is the Essence of True Nationalism?" in his *Na razniya temi* (St. Petersburg, 1902) pp. 533, 535.

contributed to the store of mankind in order to justify its right to national existence. . . . This fact alone should be enough to make anyone blush who dares to maintain that this old historic people, which witnessed the development of Europe from its savage prehistory to its period of culture, which has given to humanity two world religions and which continues to advance proudly on its beaten path—that this people could or should blot out its own peculiar features and become absorbed in other nations whose culture is briefer in time and inferior in experience. Against such a shameful demand we must advance, not some unique "mission" of Israel, but rather the determined will of the nation to continue its free historic development under the necessary conditions of autonomy.

We subordinate the Jewish national idea neither to a "mission" idea nor to the traditional forms of the Jewish law, but bind it to the free growth of the nation on its spiritual soil. The future of the nation depends on its autonomous culture; it is not predetermined but develops incessantly, and such autonomous culture will, as a matter of course, also be a national culture, a continuation and perfection of everything the nation created in the course of its previous historical existence.

V

The charges usually leveled against nationalism in general are also directed against Jewish nationalism. The chief point made is that it runs counter to the fundamental principle of the progress of humanity. . . . The basic error in these arguments arises from a confusion of terms, from the failure to distinguish between the two forms of nationalism, national individualism and national egotism.

National individualism, whose historical and psychological roots we have discussed above, involves the striving by every people to retain its originality and to preserve the necessary internal or external cultural or political autonomy in order to insure its own free development. It is the fruitful and creative will of a national group to remain true to itself, to improve and to adorn its historical forms, and to defend the freedom of its collective personality. This definitely is in keeping with the principles of ethics and social progress symbolized in the slogan of Liberty, Equality and Fraternity. The freedom of the national individual flows from the freedom of the individual as a human being. Just as the individual enjoys freedom in the community, the nation also needs to be free in the international community. The principle of freedom implies the principle of equality, which sets limits to liberty. All national cultural groups, irrespective of their size or political conditions, are equal with respect to the sanctity of their national rights; and if several national groups are joined together into one state, no single dominant nationality has the right to suppress the individuality of the national minority. Only then is national "fraternity," that is, the quiet and peaceful coexistence of various nationalities, possible, if no group tries to suppress or devour the others and if none must fear attack on its existence. This is the meaning of national individualism.

National egotism, on the other hand, means the complete rejection of all these progressive principles. It represents the ambition of the ruling nationality to dominate over the dependent national groups, the desire of the national majority of a state or region to force its culture upon the national minority (the majority forcing the minority to accept its language, its educational system, its social organization and its economic institutions). It constitutes the negation of freedom and equality in relations between nationalities. National egotism is characterized by strife, hostility and aggression; national individualism fights only in self-defense. The former assumes the form of "national imperialism" and "national rivalry" and stands condemned by the moral principles of humanity. The latter was always looked upon with favor by enlightened circles and manifested itself either in the form of a political liberation movement . . . or in the defense of the inner autonomy of national minorities living under strong nations. . . . On the whole, people always knew in practice how to differentiate between true and false nationalism, between nationalism as a liberating force and aggressive and oppressive nationalism. It is only in theory that confusion of terms in this area still prevails and that clarification and elucidation is needed.[10] In one of the following Letters I shall deal in detail with the problem of "national ethics." At present I can only outline in a general way the ethical standards on which Jewish nationalism rests.

There is absolutely no doubt that Jewish nationalism in essence has nothing in common with any tendency toward violence. As a spiritual or historical-cultural nation, deprived of any possibility of aspiring to political triumphs, of seizing territory by force or of subjecting other nations to cultural domination (language, religion and education), it is concerned with only one thing: protecting its national individuality and safeguarding its autonomous development in all states everywhere in the Diaspora. It has no aggressive national aspirations even of the kind found among other peoples that lack political independence but live on their own soil and show the tendency to wipe out the national minorities living in their midst (for example the behavior of the Poles toward the Jews in Russian Poland, and toward the Ruthenians and Jews in Austria). The Jewish nationality is an outstanding example of a collective individuality which protects itself against attacks from the outside but never stops to attack on its own and is not able to do so. A nationality of this kind manifests the highest sense of social justice, which demands that the equality of all nations be recognized as an equal right of all to defend themselves and their internal autonomous life.

Does this, however, imply isolation and separation from the world at large, a withdrawal into a national shell? To be a true and useful member of a community one does not have to hide his face and his personality and to lower his character and his ambitions to fit a general pattern. Mass character types of this kind are not a creative element in the community, but rather a passive and slow-moving mixed multitude. A nation whose features have become indistinct has no cultural values within the family of nations. A nation that is uprooted from its spiritual soil withers and degenerates into sterility and is unable to create new cultural values for the enrichment of mankind. . . .[11]

. . . The national principle stands between the individual and the social principle. It is not the abstract man, but man as a member of a definite nationality, that is the actual member of the social organism. The individual finds expression in the state and in society with all his individual characteristics, and to these belong also his national characteristics. Every human group appears to the rest of the world in its own national physiognomy, which is connected with the inner structure of its life, and only as an individual collectivity does it become a cultural and social force. The instinct of national self-preservation grows stronger as the dangers which threaten it increase. . . . In a nation without land or state and in danger of being absorbed by other peoples, the national instinct takes on the form of eternal vigilance and impresses its stamp upon all manifestations in the life of both individual and community. As the pressure from without increases, each member of a cultural nationality, not protected by state frontiers or armed might, must reaffirm the moral imperative: "Act in such a way as to preserve the autonomy of your people and its perfection!" This imperative must become the supreme criterion in the life of Jewry, exposed as it is to dangers from every side. This imperative must rouse and strengthen the national will. The absence of such strength in any part of the persecuted nation would indicate a diseased will in one part of the national organism. To diagnose precisely this disease and to prescribe the necessary therapy is one of the important tasks for our writers in this period of transition in which we live.

* * *

All that has been presented in this Letter leads us to the following general theses:

(1) A nationality, in its over-all development, is a cultural-historical collectivity whose members are united originally by common descent, language, territory, and state, but who after some time reach a spiritual unity based upon a common cultural heritage, historical traditions, common spiritual and social ideals and other typical characteristics of development.

(2) A nationality which went through all these stages of development in the past, which disposes of a store of common ideas, sentiments and needs in the present, and which gives expression to aspirations of independent development in the future must have autonomy in one form or another (political or social or cultural), in keeping with its position in the family of nations.

(3) The consciousness of the nationality itself is the main criterion of its existence. "I think of myself as a nationality—therefore I am" is the formula of the national-cultural group. This consciousness mani-

fests itself concretely in the strengthening of the national will to protect and defend its autonomy in its various social forms. A nationality which lacks the defensive protection of state or territory develops, instead, forces of inner defense and employs its national energy to strengthen the social and spiritual factors for unity which serve it as weapons in the struggle for national survival.

(4) The Jewish nationality which fulfills all these conditions is the highest type of cultural-historical or spiritual nation. Its long and unique historical development toughened the nation and energized its vital strength even though it had neither a unified state nor a territory. It will continue to exist as a nationality and strengthen its national will as it has done in the past, although the forms will be different and more in keeping with modern cultural conditions.

(5) In point of fact, the Jewish people exists as a cultural nationality in the consciousness of the majority of its members who still think of themselves as a "religious nation" since national culture was identified with religion, and since religion dominated the life of the people for many generations. The inevitable secularization of the national idea will in due time change the traditional religious consciousness into the historical evolutionary consciousness. The rejection of Jewish nationality in favor of the concept of a "religious group" ("the Jews are a religious group among every nation of the world") is rooted in assimilation and represents merely an attempt of certain parts of Diaspora Jewry to fuse with the ruling people. . . .

(6) The teachings of Judaism, the creation of a national culture, approximate the culture of humanity through the principle of evolutionary development and not of tradition. The rejection of Judaism in this form by means of a change of religion means in fact exodus from the national community, separation from the congregation of Israel.

(7) Morally, Jewish nationalism must be understood as a manifestation of national individualism which has no connection whatever with national egotism.

These theses, presented thus far only in theoretical formulation, will be clarified in detail in the following Letters on the basis of data drawn from life in the past as well as the present.

(1897-1906).

Second Letter

THE JEWS AS A SPIRITUAL (CULTURAL-HISTORICAL) NATIONALITY IN THE MIDST OF POLITICAL NATIONS

I. The error of the assimilationists: they sacrifice their own national individuality for a foreign national individuality.—The difference between the concepts "Frenchman, German . . . of the Mosaic Faith" and "French citizen, German citizen . . . of the Jewish nationality."—The historical contributions of the Jews as ancient Roman settlers on European territory.—In western and eastern Europe this right is based not on the law of possession, but on the law of colonization and cultural activity.—Is it possible to combine Jewish national feeling with patriotic devotion to country?—The natural love of land of birth is a constant one and does not change, the civic basis of love of fatherland depends on the civic and national freedom of the nationality.—Membership in a formal political union does not conflict with membership in a spiritual-national union.—Jews are not a state within a state but a nationality among nationalities, a spiritual nationality (cultural-historical) among political nations.—They demand not only civic rights but also national rights.

II. The beginnings of assimilationism.—The rejection of Jewish national rights in the period of the French Revolution and the giving up of national rights in order to receive civil rights.—Slavery amidst freedom.—The degeneration of assimilationist ideology.—The limits of amity with other nationalities.—The equal worth of nationalities.

I

In the preceding Letter we established the point that the Jewish national idea not only does not contradict the social and ethical ideals of mankind but that, on the contrary, it is dependent on them and derives from them. It seemed clear to us that all those who gather under the banner of justice and progress support this idea, while those who oppose it are enemies of enlightenment and incline to violence and reaction.

As we weigh this simple truth we come to realize how erroneous and perverted was the concept of nationality which prevailed among enlightened Jewish circles in western Europe and in Russia, and how greatly mistaken were those who, supposedly in the name of human progress, rejected completely the progressive principle that each historic nationality had the right to develop freely. They confused the contradictory concepts of national individualism and national egotism, and they forgot that the curtailment of the freedom of another nationality is as much a crime as the protection of the freedom of national individuality is a moral duty. While fighting for the principles of liberty and equality for all, they themselves gave cause for the violation of these principles by renouncing their own rights and submitting their fate to foreign mercies. By acknowledging the right of neighboring peoples to swallow up the Jews the representatives of newly emancipated Jewry legalized the rule of the strong nationality over national minorities within its borders. . . . In rejecting their own nationality, they believed they were carrying out the commandments of mankind as a whole, until bitter experience taught them that individuality is respected by others only if it respects itself, if it does not efface itself before others and if it does not allow others to blot out its own character.

When their ideological arguments had been demonstrated to be false, the opponents of Jewish nationalism seized upon arguments based on "practical wisdom." They argued as follows: "What are we to do? Can we reconcile the Jewish national idea with the fact that Jews live among other peoples and are dependent on other social and political groups? Can the Jews, who in some countries enjoy equal political rights with the Christians and who are about to receive equal rights in other countries, assert that they do not belong to the families of nations which adopted them? Can the Jews maintain that they are members of a separate Jewish nationality, united in its dispersion, without giving rise to the dangerous accusation of segregation?"

Here we arrive at the main supporting argument of the antinationalist politics of emancipated Jewry, an argument meriting more detailed attention.

To one of the questions raised above I should like to respond with a counter-question. To the question whether the Jews dare assert that they do not belong to the nationalities which adopted them, I counter with the question: Can the Jews claim with real conviction that they have in truth become members of the nationalities that "adopted them," that is, which recognized them or are about to recognize them as citizens with equal rights? It is enough to recall the simple definition of the term "nationality" in order to understand how erroneous it is to assume that emancipated Jews in France have become in their very nature Frenchmen, those of Germany—Germans, etc. A person is not made a member of this nationality or that, but is born into it. (The word *nation* is derived from the verb *nasci*, "to be born.") One may become a member of some artificial, legal or social-political grouping, but it is impossible for a person "to be made" a member of a natural collective group, of a tribe, or people, except through mingling of blood (through marriage) in the course of generations, through the prolonged process of shedding one's national individuality. Does it follow that because a Jew emancipated, for example, in France considers himself to be "a Frenchman of the Mosaic faith," that he is in truth a member of the French nationality but of the Jewish faith? By no means. No one can be counted a member of the French nationality unless he is born a Frenchman, unless he is a son or grandson of Gallic stock or of a related stock, or is so linked with the French for many generations that he has inherited all the qualities and characteristics that are the fruit of the historical development of the French nation.

A Jew, however, who is born and lives in France still remains a member of the Jewish nationality and consciously or instinctively bears the stamp of Jewish historical development. Therefore the term "a Frenchman of the Mosaic faith" has only one meaning: a native or resident of France or a citizen of the French state of the Mosaic faith. If such an individual cannot be considered as belonging to the French nationality to which nationality does he belong? He belongs, of course, to the Jewish nationality. And if Judaism or any other positive faith runs counter to his convictions, to which faith does he belong? To neither. Does he, because of this, cease consciously or unconsciously to belong to the Jewish nationality? No, because the theology of Judaism (as demonstrated in the preceding Letter) is not the only cultural factor in Jewish nationality and because "Judaism" as such is more than merely the religious element. It follows that a Jew of this kind will, under any condition, be a French citizen of the Jewish nationality. This is the term that should be used in such cases instead of the confused, unrealistic and ambiguous term "Frenchman of the Mosaic faith." When for brevity we use terms like "German Jew" or "Russian Jew," we mean a native or citizen of Germany or Russia belonging to the Jewish nationality.

Can an individual who separates himself from the ruling nationality of the state be a good citizen and be devoted to the country of his birth? It is strange that this kind of question is raised only with regard to the Jews, but not with regard to other nationalities living in multinational states. . . . A member of a national minority will be a faithful citizen of his country and will work for the common needs of the state as long as his national rights are not curtailed and his national individuality and inner freedom are not trod under foot. All inhabitants who have lived on their territory since time immemorial are loyal citizens of their country only to the degree to which it protects their basic human rights. The essence of a civic union is contained in precisely such protection. It should be recognized that the state is an external social organization designed only to protect the needs of its members. The nationality is an inner and natural form of the social collectivity.* The state, in keeping with its entire character, can be changed at all times; the nationality is fixed and unchangeable. . . . A nation that has lost its political independence as a result of a historical catastrophe must not therefore also lose its national individuality. There are examples of nationalities which freely combined into one state, as in the case of Switzerland, where three nationalities—German, French and Italian—form one commonwealth, while each preserves its own national individuality. If, thus, in a normal multinational state each group is assured national autonomy, the Jews, too, have the right to demand the rights of citizenship in the countries in which they live, together with special national rights as members of the Jewish nationality.

Some argue as follows: The Jews find themselves in an extraordinary situation. They are not a territorial nationality living on their own soil even after they were conquered by others, but a people

* Herder already differentiated between artificial political bodies and natural, national organisms.

uprooted and exiled from their land a long time ago and wandering about in strange lands. The Jew thus deprived of his land either ceases to be a member of the Jewish nationality and must, therefore, be absorbed by the peoples among whom he dwells, or else, if he stubbornly persists in considering himself a member of the Jewish nationality, he must renounce his citizenship rights in the countries where not even a handbreadth of land can be called his own.

The view that since the Jews were exiled from their ancient homeland in Asia Minor they have no moral or legal right to European territory is so widespread that it is used not only by antisemites but also by political Zionists in their propaganda. Yet there is no more dangerous and likewise no more anti-historical error than the view that the Jews are "strangers" and foreigners in Europe. History proves that the Jews are old inhabitants of Europe, that they had established themselves in Europe even before the growth of European civilization and the spread of Christianity. From the time of Alexander the Great the fate of the Jews was strongly intertwined with the fate of the two world-empires of western Europe, Greece and Rome. The Seleucid rule in Asia drove a great number of Jews from Judea already during the period of the Second Commonwealth and Jewish cultural centers of the Diaspora thus came into being in Syria, in Egyptian Alexandria, and all along the Asiatic shores of the Mediterranean. When Rome extended its rule over Judea, it accepted the Jews as a matter of course among the subjects of the Roman empire and gave them the right to reside in the metropolis and in all the provinces, that is to say, in most of western Europe, without restricting their settlement to any "pale." . . . At the close of the period of the Second Commonwealth there were already Jewish settlements in the city of Rome and in the coastal cities of Italy, from where they slowly penetrated into the European provinces of Rome, into Gaul, Germany and Spain. When, after the destruction of Jerusalem and after the unsuccessful rising of Bar-Kokhba (70-135 C.E.), the hope of establishing a Jewish state had to be abandoned, the Jews scattered in great numbers into all the provinces of the powerful Roman empire. In addition to the autonomous center which remained in Palestine in the period of the Patriarchate, there were also Jewish communities in both the eastern and western parts of the Roman empire. The Jews witnessed the conversion of pagan Rome to Christianity . . . and they soon felt the iron rod of the first Byzantine emperors who came under the influence of the clergy.

When the Roman empire broke up, the European states which were erected upon its ruins divided among themselves the territory of the empire and with it also its Jewish inhabitants. As Christianity spread, the Jews were persecuted, not because they were foreigners or strangers (as Roman subjects they had been living there long before), but because they were the only group among the local inhabitants who refused to embrace the new faith. Not national but religious animosity alone was thus at the basis of the persecution of Jews in Ostrogoth Italy, in Merovingian France and in Visigothic Spain. (It is noteworthy that the persecution of the Jews in Spain began only after the Visigothic kings had abandoned Arian Christianity—a form not too far removed from Judaism—and embraced Catholicism, toward the end of the sixth century.) Charlemagne, who attempted to re-establish the Roman empire, protected the Jews not only in the interest of trade but also because of a vague notion that together with the Jewish population that he had inherited from the Roman empire he had also inherited certain obligations toward them. The breakup of western Europe into petty feudal kingdoms obliterated these obligations of rulers and peoples toward the Jews, their living inheritance from ancient Rome. Only the medieval rulers of the Holy Roman Empire of the German Nation remembered it, only to turn the Jews into *Kammerknechte* (serfs of the Imperial Chamber) and commercial slaves. The expulsions that followed each other in rapid succession and that brought upon the Jews the evil and oppressive system of medieval government, the endless migrations from country to country—from Italy to France, from France to Spain and Germany, from Spain to Italy, the Low Countries and England, from Germany to Poland—all these implanted in the minds of the nations the belief that the Jews were a species of eternal wanderers who always had been foreigners and strangers in every country. Thus was created in the imagination of the peoples the legend of Ahasuerus, "the Eternal Jew."

All these events were but the fruit of lawlessness and violence which erased the historic rights of scattered Israel from the memory of the nations. The Jews could have said to the Christian peoples of Europe: "You have no right to deprive us of the territory on which our forefathers had settled in early times as subjects of the Roman empire, after we had been driven from our homeland in the east. We are descendants of the first Jewish colonists who settled in the European provinces of the Roman empire. At the time of the great migrations, that historic moment when the nations and states of Europe began to take shape, we were already established in the various countries. When your culture was still in its infancy and you were still primitive pagans, we, your neighbors, were the possessors of an old culture and religion from which your faith, too, was derived. Why is our portion any less than that of the Huns, Goths and other uncivilized tribes who divided up among themselves the heritage of ancient Rome? Is the right to territory established only by the use of the sword and the fist and not through the natural efforts of colonization and the peaceful works of culture carried on over many generations?"

. . . All that has been said in respect to the history of western Europe, the direct heir of ancient Rome, can also be established for eastern Europe. The Slavic nations entered history later than the Romanic-Germanic peoples. But they, too, in the early period of their history, encountered Jews already settled on their soil from earlier times. The remains of ancient Panticapaeum (present-day Kerch) bears witness to the existence of Jewish communities or synagogues on the north shore of the Black Sea in the Crimea as early as the first century before the Christian era. Early during the spread of Christianity a number of Jews were driven out by the eastern Roman Empire in Byzantium to the shores of the Black and Caspian Seas. They later congregated in southern Russia. The princes of early Kievan Russia paid tribute to the rulers of the Khazars who had been converted to Judaism. A great number of Jews came to Poland from Germany and Bohemia as soon as a stable kingdom had been established there. Into this land of little culture the Jews introduced commerce and trade. They taught the natives how to exploit the resources of their soil (mining for salt and minerals), brought far-off Poland into commercial relations with the world market and thus helped bring it into contact with the enlightened world. At a time when Muscovite Russia—reduced to inertia by Byzantine influence and isolated from western civilization by the Tartar conquest—prohibited the Jews, who could have brought it great advantage, from entering into its territory, the Polish rulers recognized their usefulness and afforded the Jews all possible protection.

The policy of the medieval Church left harsh memories in Poland also. The Jews were frequently oppressed, they were deprived of the elementary rights guaranteed to them in the ancient privileges of the kings, they were shamed and humiliated and assigned to a separate social status based on special regulations rather than on the general laws of the country. In spite of all this, however, the Polish rulers could not help recognizing the Jews as an organic part of the state, fulfilling their set social functions. When rumors spread in 1539 that the Jews of Lithuania were making ready to settle permanently in Turkey, Sigismund I became worried and ordered a careful investigation. He relaxed only when the rumor turned out to be without foundation. Thus the Jews in Poland played their usual role as cultural intermediaries for many generations until the partitions of Poland among its three neighbors. Russia received the largest slice of Polish territory and with it a crowded Jewish settlement. It thus inherited definite obligations toward the Jews of the country it annexed. How Russia lived up to these obligations is only too well known—with shameful denial of rights to the Jewish masses, with oppressive laws, persecutions and pogroms. In the recent past the condition of the Jews in eastern Europe has again come to resemble those characteristic of the Middle Ages in western Europe. . . .

Even in a formal sense, therefore, the Jews are entitled to demand for themselves the rights of long-established inhabitants of Europe. It is true that, unlike other peoples who lack political independence, they do not live in compact masses in definite areas but form a national minority wherever they are. This, however, does not detract from their right to be called native Europeans. Europe has been the home of the majority of the Jewish people for two thousand years. The remains of our fathers and grandfathers have found their last resting places in its earth. Here, as Roman colonists, we witnessed the growth of Christian civilization. Here we developed our own spiritual and economic civilization whose influence extended also to our Christian neighbors. After all this we are called foreigners and strangers, and some of our own people are ready to agree with our enemies and to justify thereby the expulsion of the Jews from Europe! Shall we, instead of protesting against the unjust curtailment of our historic rights, ourselves renounce them? The conclusion is clear. If, as even the more severe critics admit, territorial nationalities that are deprived of their political independence are still entitled to retain their nationality, then the same right also belongs to the Jews, since they are definitely a territorial nationality except for the fact that their territory in Europe is divided up into small fragments instead of being concentrated into one province. The Jews are inhabitants of Europe since ancient times and their territorial rights are based not on property title but on colonization and cultural influences.*

Can the Jewish group, as a national entity, become an integral part of the political organism in which it lives? In other words, can the nationalist Jew feel love and patriotism for his homeland? Does not the national feeling of the Jew clash with loyalty to state and with citizenship?

Patriotism is a complex emotion, composed of two elements: the natural feeling of love for one's homeland and the civic consciousness of the common needs of all members of the state. Since Europe has become the second fatherland for the majority of the Jewish people, they have developed a natural feeling of love of fatherland wherever they settled.[12] . . . Not only nature but also the remains of the national past link us to the lands where many generations of

* What has been said of Europe can, *mutatis mutandis*, also be applied to America. Even if we do not take into consideration Columbus' Jewish companions who took part in the discovery of the new world, the colonization of North and South America by Jews developed without interruption and parallel with the colonization by other European emigrants beginning with the sixteenth and, especially, the seventeenth centuries. The Jews participated actively in the foundation of commercial settlements and industrial centers in the American states, and, together with other nationalities, created American civilization.

Jews have lived. Long stretches of our history are bound up with Germany, Italy, France, England, Poland, Russia, and the other European countries. Can anyone doubt the attachment of the Jew to his land when all the conditions that naturally create such attachment are present? Let us pass then, to the second element of love of country, the civic consciousness, that is, the feeling of unity among all the members of the body politic. This feeling depends upon the social situation of the individual in the state. If all citizens are equal before the law, if the fatherland does not divide its citizens into children and stepchildren, if the inner freedom of national or religious groups is guaranteed by general agreement and not subordinated to the demands of a "ruling" nationality, then a common feeling of civic unity and of devotion to the political community will permeate all the different groups forming the state. If these conditions are absent, however, civic feeling will be destroyed altogether or take on different forms among different groups. . . .

What are the demands of the Jews in the dispersion? The Jews as inhabitants of Europe since ancient times demand equal political and civic rights; as members of a historic nationality united by a common culture, they demand as much autonomy as is appropriate for any nationality that strives to develop freely. If these two demands are satisfied, the patriotism of the Jews in all the different countries will be beyond doubt. The Jew who lives a life of peace and quiet in his fatherland, can well be an English, French, or German patriot and can, at the same time, be a true and devoted son of the Jewish nationality, which, though dispersed, is held together by national ties.*

* Conflicts between general national feeling and local patriotism are, of course, possible. It is not easy to portray, for example, the tragedy in the souls of the Jews who, in 1870, fought in the opposing French and the German armies. An even greater tragedy was experienced by the Jews and the Poles in the World War. However, such occurrences, which have their origin in the rule of militarism, can be considered out of the ordinary. When I speak of patriotism, I exclude, of course, reactionary "patriotism," which springs from base chauvinistic motives and is defiled by the policies of the antisemites in Germany and Austria, of the "nationalists" in France, and the "Black Hundred" in tsarist Russia. The Jew can never be a "patriot" of this kind, be it only because this species of patriotism is usually linked with hatred of Israel.

The state, as we explained, is an external community; the nationality is a spiritual community. The members of the former are united by common needs; those of the latter, by common emotions and attitudes. For this reason one can be a loyal member of both communities at one and the same time and give each its due. . . . As a matter of fact, the Jews usually try hard to tip the scales in favor of their sense of civic duty. . . . We still remember the decision made by the Reform leaders in Germany to delete all references to the return to Zion from the prayerbook in order not to sin, God forbid, against the German *Vaterland*. . . . The emancipated Jews of western Europe of that time demanded their liberty not as free men but as slaves; their appeal for equal rights came with timidity and obsequiousness; they thought that civic rights required the sacrifice of their souls and the offering up of the holy treasures of their nation. After they had obtained equal rights, they were just as frightened as they had been before without rights.

Thus we see that spiritual or cultural nationalism is not at variance with the general civic obligations of the various Jewish groups in the different countries. Just as every individual can be both a devoted member of his family and a loyal citizen of his state, so each Jewish group can stay linked to its national family and watch over its needs, and still participate in the civic life of the state in which it dwells and minister to its needs, provided it enjoys full and equal rights with all the other inhabitants. For the Jews are not a state within a state but a nationality among nationalities. . . .

Once a state recognizes the civic rights of the Jews, it must also recognize their national rights: i.e., their right to free internal development which is implied in their free self-determination. It is our duty to fight against the demand that Jews give up their national rights in exchange for rights as citizens. . . . Such a theory of national suicide that demands that the Jews make sacrifices for the sake of equal rights, the like of which are not demanded of any other nationality or language group, contradicts the very concept of equal rights and of the equal value of all men, and is merely a transitional stage from slavery to freedom in the consciousness of both the emancipated and their oppressors.

II

We shall now analyze the origins and nature of assimilationist theory which dominated enlightened circles in the recent past, up to the advent of the present grave crisis.

Assimilation came upon the heels of the sudden transition that Jews made from a condition in which they had no rights at all to that of full citizenship. It struck root in western Europe after the first wave of emancipation in France (1791) and, especially, after the second period of emancipation in Germany (1848). When the Jewish question was under discussion in the National Assembly in Paris in 1789, Clermont-Tonnerre, one of the protagonists of the Jewish emancipation, declared: "From the Jews as a nation we must take everything, but to the Jews as individuals we must give everything. . . . We cannot have a nation within a nation." Abbé Maury, speaking for the opposition, based his conclusions and arguments against emancipating the Jews on the idea that "the name Jew denotes not a religious sect but a nation," and that a Jew faithful to his national traditions could not be a Frenchman. Liberals and conservatives were at one in their belief that the Jew had to renounce his nationality in order to obtain equal rights, and that he could only remain a Jew by religion if he became a Frenchman by nationality. The only difference between them was that the liberals believed that such assimilation was possible and therefore demanded equal rights for the Jews, while the conservatives did not think it was possible and therefore fought against giving rights to the Jews. Neither of the factions understood that national rights are a part of the freedom of the citizen. The Jews themselves, torn between hope and fear, did not raise the demand for complete emancipation. They still failed to distinguish between national and religious elements and they were thus able to conceal the former under the disguise of the latter in order to salvage their civic rights. When these civic rights which had been granted to them by the Revolution appeared to be in danger during the Napoleonic period (1807), their representatives declared, in the Grand Sanhedrin in Paris, that "from now on the Jews are no longer a nation since the honor had been bestowed on them to become part of the great

[French] nation and they see in this their full political liberation."* In the other western countries the Jews achieved their emancipation likewise through open renunciation of their nationality or by silently consenting to its loss.

A considerable part of the Jewish masses which thus regained their rights only in a curtailed form looked upon this emancipation, not as an act of right and justice toward a persecuted nation, but rather as a gift bestowed by the ruling Christian nations at the price of national self-destruction. For this favor many Jews paid the price of partly or fully obliterating their national individuality through assimilation with Germans, French, etc. They did not join their Christian neighbors on the basis of equality, but tried hard to make themselves resemble them, to imitate their customs, to adapt themselves to their national cultures and even to intermarry with them. The first generation of emancipated Jews accepted the new nationality only in name; among later generations, however, assimilation progressed in various degrees. This tendency, in a very limited form, was even apparent among the upper circles of Russian Jewry when the winds of emancipation first began to blow there in the 1860s. After generations of bondage, of self-abasement and of limited intellectual horizon, the Jews had to blaze a path for themselves to enlightenment, to spiritual and social regeneration and to a widening of horizon, on the foundations of a common humanity with the progressive nations of Europe. In practice, however, they artificially suppressed their own national individuality in favor of that of an alien people. "Assimilation" of this kind was but a change in form—and a morally inferior one—of the previous state of bondage of the Jews. The Jew of the Middle Ages bent only his back before his oppressors, but he never dealt falsely against himself nor did he ever renounce one iota of his national rights. The modern Jew, however, who had been given the opportunity to become a proud member of the society of peoples, bartered away his soul and perverted his own national type so that he could be like the ruling nationality. This is nothing but a change in the form of servitude, the substitution of inner for external humiliation.

* *Cf.* Dubnow, *Dibre yeme yisrael badorot haaharonim* (Berlin-Tel Aviv, 1923), vol. i, par. 22.

In all fairness the fact must be mentioned that, in addition to the practical-minded assimilationists, who sought quick adjustment to their new environment, there were also idealistic assimilationists who looked upon assimilation as a contribution to human progress. Some of these negated their nationality for the sake of the idea of cosmopolitanism; but they did not realize that they were becoming citizens, not of the cosmopolitan community of their imagination, but of the alien national group with whom they were connected by political and territorial ties. The theoretical rejection of the national principle meant, in practice, merely a substitution of their own natural nationality for a foreign nationality, and this before the advent of the messianic era with its fusion of all nations into one abstract "humanity." . . . Only in most recent times has the Jew gained the deeper insight that no one has the right to demand of him that he be untrue to his nationality; that the curtailment of the national rights of the Jews, like the previous degradation of their status as citizens, is tribute extorted by wicked and crude government. True emancipation means, not only liberation of the individual human being, but also of the individual nationality. . . .

Must the Jews then isolate themselves again and set up for themselves a spiritual pale in place of the walls of the medieval ghetto which has been destroyed for good? Not by any means. I do not advocate any kind of artificial isolation or separation from the community. But each being, individual or group, needs natural isolation, in the sense of stress on its own individuality, if it wishes to preserve itself. The Jew who enters into close contacts with a member of another nationality has no need to subordinate his own national personality to that of the other; both must accept the basic principle that all citizens have equal value. And if the non-Jew is unwilling to accept this approach on the basis of equality, the self-respecting Jew should declare that close relations on such terms are impossible and undesirable. Such an attitude may, it is true, contain an element of isolation; but it is an isolation made necessary in order to preserve the freedom and the honor of the nationality. It is an attitude—I would call it "protective isolation"—which in tsarist Russia was taken by the best elements of the Jewish people who thus preserved their inner freedom. I bow my head before the proud isolationism of these men who prefer to remain outside the safe camp of the national majority to being admitted to it on terms that are humiliating to their honor and that offend their individual and national sense of values. During the course of many periods of its national history, Jewry found itself in the position of splendid isolation within its spiritual fortress.

We conclude therefore that assimilation leads, not only to the abandonment of the national needs of Judaism, but also to a denial of the individual freedom of the Jewish nationality and of its equal worth in the family of nations. It is both a theoretical and practical mistake caused by the social prejudice and the moral shortcomings of both the assimilationist Jews and of those who demand that the Jews assimilate. Whatever his motivations may be, the assimilationist Jew who subordinates his own national individuality to the will of strangers is always an unconscious victim of oppression, of that psychological disease which also becomes a moral scar when people run away from the down-trodden and persecuted and desert to the camp of those who are happy and secure. In the demand by non-Jews that Jews assimilate there is a modicum of the scorn which the "strong" have for the "weak" and of the idea that the Jews, oppressed for many years, must pay for their equal rights (that is, for the restoration of rights of which they had previously been deprived) with the annihilation of their national individuality. Those who make such demands and those who yield to them violate the basic principle of social ethics: the equal value of all nationalities.

Beginning with the first period of emancipation in 1791, we have been fighting only for civil and political rights in the countries of the Diaspora. The time has now come to claim also our national rights. . . .

The whole course of the development of mankind leads us to one decisive alternative: national extinction or national revival. Many in our camp took the path of extinction. During the nineteenth century the center of activity of the leading groups of the community shifted from our inner national life to the outside environment, to the sphere of the needs of other peoples. The center of gravity has been moved outside of our national circle; thus the equilibrium has been upset and we are in a perilous state of national vacillation. This vacillation can only be stopped if the center of gravity is restored to its natural place—the area of national needs. The restoration of our national balance is the main precondition for our rebirth. To this lofty task of national rebirth we must dedicate all our strength, all our thoughts, all the inner resources that we have inherited from the many generations of fighters and martyrs who, by their heroism, saved the ark of Judaism from the crushing winds of the deluge of world history.

January 1898 (1906).

Third Letter

THE ETHICS OF NATIONALISM

I. The results of false association.—The Dreyfus Affair and the anti-semitic nationalists in France.—Nationalism is divested of its ethical character.

II. Analogy between the national and the religious idea.—The crisis of the national idea.—Its ethical character: the difference between national egotism and national individualism.

III. The ethical approach of Solovyev.—The difference between national and "nationalist." Defensive nationalism and aggressive nationalism.—Confusion of the two concepts.—The plain words of a national Jew.—The line of separation.

IV. The national idea can be combined with the universal idea.—The universalism of Israel and the messianic ideal of the Prophets.—The maximum "Christian" approach of Solovyev and the approach of living reality.—The national idea can be combined with internationalism.

I

No attempt at an evaluation of ethical behavior arouses as many problems and difficulties as the national question. Some denounce nationalism as a reactionary movement; others laud it as a progressive movement of liberation. This is due in part to the complex content of the national idea and in part to the variety of forms in which it is expressed. Here more than in any other question we make frequent and erroneous use of the method of association of ethical ideas which judges this or any other idea, not according to its real meaning or all its various manifestations, but rather according to those accidental manifestations and factors which are dominant at the given moment. The national idea finds favor when it appears mainly as a liberating or defensive force, but it arouses aversion when it is given political expression in wanton aggression by nationalist extremists and fanatics of ruling nations or of nations with ambitions to rule. We are now in the midst of such a period, with danger to mankind in general and to Jewry in particular.

Not so long ago there appeared upon the European political horizon a movement which contributed to pervert the correct understanding of the national idea. I am referring to the new "nationalist" party founded in France in 1898, which came up like a whirlwind or like murky foam in a boiling kettle amidst the storm of political passions aroused by the Dreyfus affair.* The fearless heroism of Emile Zola and his group, who stood up to protect the soiled honor of French justice, met with determined resistance on the part of those Frenchmen whose world was confined to the sphere of an illusionary patriotic fanaticism and to plans for military *révanche*. . . . The Dreyfus case was for them merely a pretext to persecute and denounce everything that did not bear the stamp "French" and "Catholic" and to plant in the hearts of the masses hostility and contempt for "Jews, Protestants, and Free Masons," in keeping with the triple slogan of the nationalist hate doctrine. The names of the leaders of this party, those who headed the men of violence in the legislature and in the press (Déroulède, Rochefort, Drumont), testified to its savage behavior. . . . In the short time it was in existence the new party succeeded in attaining scandalous notoriety by its actions throughout the European world. . . .

The propaganda of the French nationalists was condemned by all decent people and only temporarily impeded the onward march of truth and liberty in the realm of political affairs. In the higher spheres of human thought, however, it inflicted more lasting damage. Propaganda of this kind plants in the human mind a false association of ideas by juxtaposing the concept of nationality with concepts of reaction, violence and moral degeneracy. What evaluation of the national idea will be drawn from all these events by those who followed closely all these years the various turns taken by the Dreyfus case? A definitely unfavorable attitude, without doubt. The noble and lofty idea is perverted and disfigured by ugly manifestations that are purely accidental. In order to avoid erroneous generalizations it is necessary to differentiate, in a theoretical analysis, between local or passing manifestations of the national idea and its substance. But not

* This was written in the spring of 1899, when the Dreyfus affair approached its climactic end. Now innumerable examples like the Dreyfus case can be cited.

everyone is sufficiently capable and qualified to make such an analysis. . . . Subconscious confusion of ideas is immeasurably stronger than logical analysis, and even dispassionate individuals are not always able to free themselves of the influence of constantly recurring associations. . . .

At the moment I am concerned with the following problem: what influence does such an association have on the comprehension and ethical evaluation of the national idea among Jews? The fact that for the moment French nationalism in the Dreyfus case has taken on an openly antisemitic character could well suggest to Jews the following conclusion: "French nationalism is our deadly enemy, a cruel, crude and bloodthirsty enemy; the nationalist parties in other countries also openly hate us; it follows, therefore, that the national idea in its very essence must contain something which engenders in its partisans hate of other nationalities. Every people must, therefore, carefully guard itself against it in its own environment." . . . Thus among the better elements in the community there is an ever-growing and violent rejection of the national idea in general that springs from moral revulsion. There is grave danger in a generalization of this kind. It is important to point out that such a conclusion is based upon a fundamental error.

The readers of my previous Letters will not need further proof. If they agreed with the author's psychological interpretation of the national idea, they will also agree with the ethical evaluation which follows below.

II

Despite differences in psychological origin we find great similarities in the development of the two powerful spiritual forces and historical influences: the religious idea and the national idea. Religion, born out of man's psychological need to find an answer to the riddle of the universe, passed through a number of stages of development as it adapted itself to the conditions of growth and spiritual culture. Beginning with primitive man, who peopled the world he knew with hidden forces and magical and miraculous deeds, up to the scientist of our own time, for whom the ways of the known world hold no secrets, generation after generation has been dominated by religious creativity expressed in a variety of forms. Here, too, we observe the gradual transition from material to spiritual foundations which we found in the development of the national idea (First Letter). In the same way in which the nationality passed from the primitive influences of tribe, territory and climate to social and political factors to become crystallized at last into a spiritual or cultural type, so religion also developed from crude idolatry to polytheistic worship of beautiful images and then to lower or higher forms of monotheism in which religious ritual and church ceremonies predominated; in the end, however, religion was liberated from accumulated external forms and appeared to the enlightened world as a mighty and creative spiritual force striving to express the highest goals of life.

There was a time when rationalist philosophy and later on scientific positivism rejected completely any religious view of life. The devotees of philosophy, however, intoxicated as they were by the triumphs of science, forgot altogether that, in addition to the world that could be clearly apprehended and whose boundaries had been greatly expanded by mankind, there continued to exist the world of mystery in which the creative force of religion reigned supreme over the spirits of the believers in a variety of forms. All who understand the psychological need for the existence of religion as one type of inner understanding will not dismiss it; on the contrary, they will include it in the storehouse of creative spiritual culture. The same is true for the national idea: scientific thinkers no longer reject or dismiss this idea. They have begun to accept it and study it as a powerful cultural-historical factor which has made its own valuable contribution to the development of mankind.

In addition to this psychological affinity, the religious and national ideas also show a moral similarity. The war against the religious outlook which commenced in the eighteenth century was, without doubt, not only an expression of protest of liberated reason, but also a revolt of the moral sense. . . . The freethinkers of the period recalled the terrors and atrocities committed in the name of religion during the Middle Ages—the torture chambers of the Inquisition, the tyranny of the dignitaries of the Church, the breaches of morality by the clergy, the fanatical suppression of intellectual and religious dissent—and they concluded that religion in its very nature is a deadly and destructive force that must be rooted out completely in the interests of mankind.

Those who held such views did not realize that they had been misled by the usual association of ideas which resulted only from temporary historical conditions. They judged religion by the forms of its ceremonial or by the way of life and behavior of its representatives. Very frequently these included men who falsified the essence of religion either because they lacked understanding or because they were plain greedy. The followers of the Enlightenment forgot that even sacred and exalted truths can be converted by evil and wicked men into violence and corruption. If we recall that the reformer John Hus, who died as a martyr on the stake, and the grand-executioner Torquemada both spoke in the name of Christianity in the same century, we will also be able to understand how the aspiration toward the triumph of the moral sense together with the complete perversion of this goal can both be associated with religion. We conclude from this that the reason for all these contradictions did not derive from the religious idea itself, but rather from the differences in understanding and uses to which it was put under changing cultural and social conditions. . . . In our own time only superficial minds can still believe that religious thought or emotion is in and for itself opposed to morality. On the contrary, it becomes increasingly clear that purified religion, which already at the time of our ancient Prophets advocated lofty ethical ideals, is also destined to fulfill the function of a powerful ethical force in our scientific age.

The serious crisis which left the religious idea unharmed did not bypass the national idea. National intolerance is glorified in our own day with the same savagery as was religious intolerance in the past. One need only point to the bitter national conflict between Germans and Slavs in Austria, to the extreme nationalism of Prussians and Poles in the province of Posen, to the antics of the nationalists in France and, finally, to the pogroms in Russia, in order to understand the great danger inherent in nationalist passions. No wonder, then, that decent and fair-minded people are imbued with a skeptical attitude toward nationalism in general and that others find fault with it and condemn it as a dangerous force inimical to all positive social principles.

Among enlightened Jews, especially, opposition to nationalism has been widespread, since they learned from experience that every outbreak of nationalist passions among the peoples of the world led first of all to a deterioration of the status of the Jews living in their midst. The cosmopolitan tendency which has permeated our educated circles in the recent past can be explained primarily as a result of their abhorrence and loathing of the crude manifestations of nationalism. It is not the national idea as such that repels people but the lawlessness and violence which accompany it, that is, the ethical perversion of this idea. The time has indeed come to rid ourselves of the influence of this erroneous association of ideas. . . . Should one doubt the religious faith of Hus because Torquemada also fought under the banner of religion? Are the national ideals of the great liberator Garibaldi discredited because the Russian conservative Pobedonostsev[13] also spoke in the name of nationalism? In one case an individual fought for his sacred religious convictions, and in the other case the individual's aim was to eradicate all religious convictions different from his own and force his own views upon them. In one case the fighter is defending the freedom of his people, in the other a despot is attempting to crush the freedom of another nation. Do they not contradict each other from an ethical point of view? You have psychological striving for freedom on the one hand, aspiration to tyranny on the other; fighters for right and justice on one side, worshipers of the mailed fist on the other—and all in the name of "nationalism"! We must, therefore, find an ethical standard which will enable us to draw the line between the good and the evil in nationalism.

A standard of this kind was already established in the previous Letters, in which various designations were assigned to the positive and negative poles of nationalism. The former we called "national individualism," the latter, "national egotism." The former is a moral gain, the latter a moral loss. The defense of individual freedom must be undertaken by each highly developed individuality, whether it be a single person or a whole nationality. Whoever suppresses the free individuality of either the individual person or the whole nationality, and superimposes his own personality upon them, commits a crime comparable to that of the fanatics of the medieval Church who tried to force their faith upon the members of another religion. Such compulsion and conflicts are possible only where national egotism rules supreme. These conflicts take on two forms: (1) a struggle between two national egotisms, that is, between two peoples, each striving to gain decisive advantage or supremacy over the other. This is a battle between two aggressors that leads to violent and devastating wars and to the plague of militarism which afflicts our time; (2) a conflict between national egotism and national individualism, that is, an attempt by a despotic nationality to deprive a weaker nationality of its political freedom or of its cultural autonomy and to impose its dominion upon it. In a case like this the aggressor has violated the ethics of society and those who protect themselves and defend their freedom and individuality are fighting for right and justice.

It follows that the defense of national individuality against national egotism is a necessary condition of human freedom and progress. Now the question arises: in what forms is a conflict between two national individualisms possible? Individuality means the striving of the individual to defend his internal and external liberty on condition that it in no way curtails the freedom of other individuals (for otherwise individuality would turn into egotism). To meet this condition it is necessary to set the limits of the legal autonomy of each individual nationality, and the line must be drawn beyond which begins the curtailment of the autonomy of others. The point at which the limits of autonomy should be fixed are debatable; but as soon as the limits are clearly established by law and have been firmly recognized in international law, the danger of conflict is diminished while the probability of peaceful relations between nations increases. And although pure individualism, free of admixtures of egotism, is a rare phenomenon, it must, in any event, be accepted as an ideal to be approximated and for whose realization we must strive.

Jewish nationalism approximates this ideal more than any other, since it is by nature spiritual and seeks only to defend itself, not to attack or to oppress. Even the advocates of humanitarian universalism are forced to admit that "a nationality fighting for its survival presents a brilliant scene of heroic deeds and noble spirit,"* that "the national idea is exalted when it strives for spiritual values which by their very nature cannot be achieved through unethical means."† What was all of Jewish history in all its many periods if not the heroic struggle of a cultural nationality for its inner freedom—a struggle waged not by force of arms but by the spirit, a struggle for those lofty spiritual values which by their very nature cannot be achieved through discreditable means? The ideal of a spiritual nation is basically an ethical one, and such is the national ideal of Judaism.

III

The Russian philosopher Vladimir Solovyev[14] defines the ethical value of the uncorrupted national idea in the following words:

Let it be granted that the immediate object of the moral relation is the individual person. But one of the essential peculiarities of that person—direct continuation and expansion of his individual character—is his nationality (in the positive sense of character, type, and creative power). This is not merely a physical, but also a psychical and moral fact. At the stage of development now reached by humanity the fact of belonging to a given nationality is to a certain extent confirmed by the individual's self-conscious will. Thus nationality is an inner, inseparable property of the person—something very dear and close to him. It is impossible to stand in a moral relation to this person without recognizing the existence of what is so important to him. The moral principle does not allow us to transform a concrete person, a living man with his inseparable and essential national characteristics, into an empty abstract subject with all his determining peculiarities left out. If we are to recognize the inner dignity of the particular man,

* This is the formulation of one of the founders of the Deutsche Gesellschaft für ethische Kultur, Professor Friedrich Wilhelm Foerster, in his Zur *Ethik* des *Nationalismus und der Judenfrage* (Berlin, 1893), p. 7.

† Solovyev, Vladimir, "The Justification of the Good. An Essay in Moral Philosophy" (St. Petersburg, 1897), p. 362 [Engl. translation by N. A. Duddington, New York, 1918].

this obligation extends to all positive characteristics with which he connects his dignity; if we love a man we must love his nation which he loves and from which he does not separate himself. The highest moral ideal demands that we should love all men as we love ourselves. But since men do not exist outside of nations (just as nations do not exist apart from individual men), and since this connection has already become moral and inward as well as physical, the direct logical deduction is that we must love all nations as we love our own.*

With this definition of national morality the philosopher-idealist took the definite step from the minimum demand of national altruism (love for the members of other nations) to a maximum demand. If we leave aside for the time being the maximum demand, which may be questioned by some (and which we will discuss later), we can all agree that according to the minimum assumption (concerning which there are no doubts) the ethical relationship toward the individual also includes the recognition of his national characteristics and of his right to make use of them and to give expression to them in ways which do not violate the accepted principles of law and justice. The following proposition must be used as a test of legality in such a judgment: the realization of my national rights must never go beyond the point at which the rights of my neighbors, members of other nationalities, begin to be impaired. If we thus recognize the basic ethical and legal character of the nationality, we must also accept nationalism as a system of thought resting on this principle. However, popular writers usually differentiate between the two terms "nation" or "nationality," which they use in a positive sense, and "nationalism" which they use in a negative sense. Solovyev himself, in his political writings, differentiates between "national" movements as progressive and "nationalist" movements as tending toward reaction. For him, national feeling or "national character" is a positive force belonging to the nation as a whole and manifesting itself among its best members; "nationalism," however, he considers to be a fanatical and exaggerated concern for one's own nation, a particular manifestation of national egotism. The conclusion drawn from this distinction is that

* *Ibid.*, ch. ix, "The National Question from the Moral Point of View, p. 387 ff. [Engl. trans. by Nathalie A. Duddington, *l.c.*, p. 297.]

national character is an uncorrupted ideal while nationalism is idolatry.*

It seems to me that such oversharp distinctions have no place in scientific terminology because they are liable to increase the theoretical confusion which already besets the problem of nationality. The high-minded Russian philosopher is ashamed of the term "nationalist," a term used with pride by Mazzini and Garibaldi, although all three accept the lofty concept of the pure form of nationalism. On the other hand, when you read the news reports that in both France and Ireland the "nationalists" won in the parliamentary elections, you are torn between mixed feelings: you rejoice in the victory of the Irish nationalists and deplore the victory of the French deputies known by the same name. Why is this? Because you are dealing here with two opposing types of "nationalism": liberating and oppressive nationalism, defensive and aggressive nationalism; national individualism and national egotism.

Solovyev, the representative of the Russian people, is right in rejecting the "fanatical concern for one's own nation." He is right from the point of view of *his* nationality, since the ruling Russian nationality does not need such concern; it is useful only to the fanatics who have adopted the slogan of "Russia for the Russians." But Solovyev would be entirely wrong were he to extend his condemnation also to the national minorities in Russia, who can only maintain themselves if they are "concerned for their own national individuality." In the case of a nationality which is persecuted or which lacks political liberty it is perfectly reasonable to encourage a group of nationalists, because such a nationality must fight for its national character and its autonomy against the ruling nationality which seeks to weaken it or swallow it up. When the ruling nationality in the state, however, sets up groups of "nationalists" of its own, it is bent not on defense but on attack, and it seeks to strengthen its rule by crushing the freedom of the subject nationalities; it wants to turn its national minorities into Germans, Russians, Poles, etc., and to force them to adopt its lan-

* Solovyev, "The National Question in Russia," pp. 19, 66 (St. Petersburg, 1884; clearer in the 2d ed., 1894). See also his article "The National Movement" in the Brockhaus-Efron Encyclopaedia.

guage, its educational system, its political aspirations. . . . We are all in the habit of associating this kind of nationalism and patriotism with violence and oppression and with political despotism, and we understand perfectly well why our liberal friends among the ruling nationalities emphatically declare: "We are not nationalists, and we are not 'patriots'!" The word "patriots" is put in quotation marks to indicate that there is also a reputable kind of patriotism. . . . It would be advisable to use quotation marks also for the extreme nationalism of aggressive groups.

To all these proclamations by the high-minded individuals of the nations of the world the Jew might answer: "From your own point of view you are absolutely right. If I were in your place, if I were a Russian, a Prussian, a Frenchman, I would be ashamed of the term 'nationalist,' the armor of political oppression with which the powerful nations oppress the weak. I would be especially ashamed of the kind of nationalism that is primarily concerned with a policy of Russification, Germanization or similar forced assimilation, that is, the annihilation of the national identity of national minorities. Even if I were a Pole or a Czech, that is, a member of a national minority within a state, I would use the term 'nationalist' only under carefully defined conditions, because experience has taught me that these nationalities, too, while defending their own national liberty, are not very mindful of the national individuality of the smaller national groups among them, whom they oppress with force. . . . But as a Jew, I utter the word 'national' with pride and conviction, because I know that my people, because of the special conditions of its existence in the Diaspora, is not able to aspire anywhere to primacy and dominance. My nationalism can be only a pure form of individualism and hence completely ethical. . . .

"Thus, we, the representatives of nations defending themselves, as well as you, representatives of nations attacking the others, use the same generally accepted term to express two contradictory ideas. If some artificial language would coin a new word for our ethical nationalism, we would gladly leave to you the old disreputable and hollow term. As long as such a word is still lacking, however, it is our duty to establish by exact definition how the existing term should be used."

The two opposing concepts are indicated in the following table of the two types of nationalism, positive and negative, in line with the discussion presented in the preceding Letters:

Positive Type	*Negative Type*
(1) National individuality	(1) National egotism
(2) Defensive or liberating nationalism	(2) Aggressive nationalism or national striving for forced assimilation

IV

When the aggressive nationalism of strong nations disappears, there will, of course, be no need any longer for the extraordinarily concentrated energy of defensive nationalism. This does not mean, however, that nationalism will disappear altogether. Gone will be that sharp feeling and intense anxiety for self-preservation which are aroused by danger; but the healthy and normal feeling of self-preservation will remain, as will the quiet and measured individualism and the striving of a people for the free development of its culture. Then it will become apparent that the national idea is fully compatible even with the ideals of universalism. It is, of course, incorrect to confuse universalism with "cosmopolitanism." The latter rejects the psychological and ethical foundations of nationalism and does not recognize any intermediate links between the individual and humanity. Universalism, on the other hand, recognizes that each individual is a member of a people, and that each people is a member of the family of nations or of mankind, and demands therefore that the same brotherhood prevail between the peoples of the community of mankind as exists between individuals in each people.

Expressed in the form of a messianic vision, this was the spirit of the Prophets of Israel, who were the bearers of a universal but never of a cosmopolitan ideal as is sometimes erroneously thought. The Prophets taught that the national mission of the people of Israel is to spread the knowledge of God and of social justice among the nations. They called Israel a "light to the nations," an eternal light which shall never be extinguished. They taught that every Jew must do his utmost to fulfill the spiritual mission of the people of Israel, and that it is the task of the whole nation to bring the other peoples, that is, all "mankind," to spiritual perfection. To the Prophets this was the highest moral justification for the existence of the Jewish people. Since we find the justification for our existence in the right of each nation to self-determination, we do not feel any need to defend it by setting up a "mission" for it from the beginning. . . . The ultimate moral goal will only be reached when this principle has been realized in practice in a way which will not accentuate the tensions between peoples but, on the contrary, when the yearning for brotherhood strongly permeates all circles of mankind. It would be idle to hope that members of different nationalities would be united in feelings of sympathy and attachment in the same measure as are the members of one nationality; but it is entirely within the range of possibility to have mutual feelings of friendship that spring from common human aspirations and amicable relations between equal members of the world community of nations.*

In this sense I find it necessary to correct Solovyev's doctrine of national altruism or universalism which teaches: "Love all the nations as your own." This commandment does not agree with the substance of his definition that "the fundamental characteristic of each individual is his nationality" as a "psychological and ethical fact." From this proper definition we must conclude that individuals who share common national characteristics will feel closer to each other than to members of another nation. This is actually what we find in real life. The man who loves his people because he is linked with it by ties of blood and spirit cannot love in the same degree members of other

* Professor Moritz Lazarus establishes the relationship between national particularism (isolation) and universalism on the basis of Judaism in his work *Die Ethik des Judentums* (Berlin, 1898), pp. 157-61, in the following manner: "The adherents of these two systems differ from each other not so much on ethical but on psychological grounds. The controversy is not over abstract purpose or the future of mankind, but the actual path and the present state of Judaism. . . . The advocates of particularist nationalism think in a realistic way only about the present; the adherents of universalism think in an idealistic way about the future, too. . . . But there is no doubt that the principal ideas of both these systems have a common moral basis." . . .

nations to whom he is not bound by such ties. Any postulate which would equate a person's love for another people with that of his own people is bound to remain in the category of a *pium desiderium*. Instead of this ethical abstraction I would submit the following concrete proposition: *Recognize the freedom of each national group as you recognize your own national freedom;* or: *honor the national individuality of others as you do your own.*

The logical conclusion from the concept of national individuality is that, if I accept the right and, what is more, the duty to protect my own national individuality, I must accord the same right to members of other nationalities. And if my own national aspirations and tendencies have ethical value in my own eyes, then I must also respect the national aspirations and tendencies of other peoples and honor them as much as my own. I wish to emphasize the point that it is "honor" not "love," because I cannot love if I do not fully make the aspirations of others my own, and if I did this I would become a member of two nationalities at one and the same time—which is impossible—or I would abandon my own nationality for another—which would be little short of national treason.

The difference of opinion between the "Christian philosopher" Solovyev and myself reveals once more the difference between national outlooks on life. It is the old controversy between *love*, the subjective principle of the Gospels, and the objective standard of *justice* embedded in the Jewish ethical tradition. Judaism never set up ethical postulates which were incapable of realization. It never built systems which were "not of this world." It formulated ideals which could be reached and hence demanded with all the severity of the law that they be carried out. . . .

All that has been said here about universalism can also be said in relation to internationalism. This term, which is common in Socialist literature, was used with different meanings at different stages of its development. Marx and Engels used the term internationalism almost interchangeably with cosmopolitanism in the sense of a rejection of the national idea which, to them, appeared like a historical malady, a luxury that was unnecessary for the "proletariat which has no fatherland." Since wars between nations tended to obscure the class struggle, the early Marxists rejected national wars and demanded political centralization, the subjection of the smaller nations to the stronger and more centralized ruling nation, in order to achieve "cultural unity." (Marx, for example, strongly condemned the aspirations for national autonomy of the Slavs in Austria, excepting only the Poles). More recently, as the liberating effect of national movements was brought into stronger relief, Social-Democratic leaders corrected the error of their predecessors. At Socialist party congresses and in Socialist literature they now acknowledge that the aspirations of suppressed nationalities to political autonomy and national culture are justified as long as they do not weaken the class consciousness of the proletariat. Along the same lines the term internationalism has been redefined by present-day Socialists. It is no longer confused with abstract cosmopolitanism, but approximates the concept of universalism as developed above. . . .[15] Those who fight for class emancipation can now join with the fighters for national liberation in a common effort to realize this ideal of internationalism in an association of autonomous national groups with equal rights.

If the national idea in general can thus be combined with the ideal of humanity, the Jewish national idea, which can never become aggressive and warlike, will be in even closer harmony with it. Its kind of nationalism is derived from the basic principles of social ethics: the equal worth of all nations in the family of mankind. . . .

It is fitting and proper for the descendants of the Prophets to raise aloft on their flag the unsoiled national idea that combines the visions of the Prophets of truth and justice with the noble dream of the unity of mankind.

May 1899 (1906).

Fourth Letter

AUTONOMISM, THE BASIS OF THE NATIONAL PROGRAM

I. The thesis of isolation; antithesis of assimilation; synthesis of autonomism.

II. Autonomy and heteronomy.—The tradition of Jewish autonomy.—The community as the historical core of self-administration.—The old type of religious community as the core of the "religious nationality."—The "community of the synagogue" of emancipated Jewry.—The need for secularization: the national community.—Prospects for autonomy.

III. The answer to opponents: autonomy and the war for liberation.—The merit of cultural "isolation."—The fight against political nationalism.

I

The nineteenth century, which began with a wave of glowing youthful hopes, came to a close worn out and enfeebled and in the esthetic and ethical condition described by the term *fin de siècle*. One of the powerful antitheses of Jewish history created by this turbulent century is now gradually drawing to its close.*

* In order to avoid misunderstanding I should point out that the threefold scheme of development of thesis, antithesis, and synthesis (that is, positive theory, negative theory, and deciding theory) which I shall use in this and the following chapters is different in nature from Hegel's law of dialectics. In my system it does not have any formal-logical content, but represents the psychological process of combining partial truths which are scattered among different stages of thought and feeling. The three stages constitute the complete cycle of development and each of them has a corresponding basic idea which is a balancing force in every period. The thesis, or the accepted theory, is the tradition inherited from past generations, a point of view or a faith which has become rooted and fixed in its ancient form, a positive dogma which allows for no examination or criticism. The antithesis is the striving to become liberated from the yoke of the dogmatic thesis, to break it down completely without leaving even the modicum of historical truth which led to its being established; it is radical criticism, the complete denial of the past, a counter-ideal. The synthesis is not "the negation of the negation" (as in Hegel's dialectic), but a balancing theory which results from a more comprehensive creation of ideas. In this creation all those partial truths that were contained in the

In Jewish history the nineteenth century was the "epoch of the antithesis," which had declared war upon the old thesis known as "isolation." . . . Up to the period of the Enlightenment and the French Revolution, at the end of the eighteenth century, this thesis had served as the most important foundation for the life of the Jews. Complete isolation from the alien environment in the areas of individual and community life, internal self-government in the Jewish communities and the status of strangers with respect to the external state government—these were the outstanding features of the old order of Jewish life. With all its shortcomings, this old order had one great virtue: it was a complete and consistent way of life. Since the state merely tolerated the Jews as rent-paying tenants, and the Christian masses behaved either as complete strangers to them or were hostile to them, it was quite natural that the Jews should not feel any love for their unfriendly neighbors. In this way a sort of mutual "toleration" was established between the two sides, although not of the same character on each side.

Du duldest, dass ich atme,
Dass du rasest, dulde ich.
—*Heine*

The Jews paid to the state numerous taxes that were out of pro-

---

thesis and the antithesis are fused into one idea, cleansed of their dross of extremism and adapted to the demands of life in the new period. . . . The conservative masses who do not analyze or question, the orthodox community of the old school, still cling to the thesis. The mass of *maskilim,* especially the youth in whom the old beliefs and views are weakened and undermined, take up the antithesis. Only men of limited vision are satisfied with negation alone in this period of transition. Those who search more deeply pass from the antithesis to the synthesis and thus complete the cycle of development. It is obvious that the synthesis, too, as it is assimilated into the consciousness of the masses, is in time converted into dogma and tradition, that is, into a thesis whose essence is lost in alien admixtures and under the new layers which are piled upon it. Then a new antithesis will appear in opposition to it; and finally a new synthesis will be created which will supersede the former in the profusion of its forms. Thus the wheel of history turns and creates at every stage concepts that are more balanced and tested, refined in the crucible of the experience and criticism of the chain of the generations. This is the law of the evolution of *Weltanschauungen,* the law of spiritual progress. I hope to discuss in detail the psychological and sociological manifestations of this scientific law in a separate study.

portion to the niggardly rights which were granted to them, but beyond that they considered themselves free of all obligations toward the state which treated them as strangers. They acquiesced in their lack of political rights and in the curtailment of their rights as citizens, and they stood guard over the only right they had, which was more important to them than "all the treasures of this world," the right of the freedom of their national life as realized through communal self-government. This internal rule served them in place of state and citizenship. The Jew who was a slave and of little value outside the ghetto was a free man inside the ghetto, within his pale of settlement, in his community, in his spiritual realm. In Poland, the main center of Jewry from the sixteenth to the eighteenth centuries, the Jews created a broad and well-ordered social organization, with communities and associations of communities, and with a complex network of religious, social and cultural institutions. . . . The national and cultural value of this autonomy was very great. The autonomy provided strength and unity to the outcast nation and, at the same time, gave it culture and laws and educated it in the spirit of discipline and self-rule. The Jew felt that he was a part of a living national body. He stayed within his social and cultural circle, a restricted circle indeed, but it was his own and it satisfied all his needs. . . . Every Jew willingly or unwillingly sacrified part of his personal freedom in order to strengthen the national discipline. Only extraordinarily high-spirited individuals, who could not endure the burden of such severe discipline, fought against the community ordinances to preserve their individual freedom. This tragic struggle left its mark especially during the period of transition which followed.

The nineteenth century was initiated with the sound and fury of the Revolution and the call for "Liberty, Equality, and Fraternity." The enlightened Jews in western Europe had absorbed the spirit of liberty even before the walls of the ghetto fell. On the eve of the French Revolution a movement for cultural renaissance began in Germany under the influence of the humanistic spirit of the "Mendelssohn period." The rays of sunshine of the approaching springtime of society melted the layers of the ice of isolation which had accumulated during many generations. The spring floods increased;

the great flood of "assimilation" spread. The thesis, the old fossilized order of Jewish life, broke down, and on its ruins arose another extreme, the antithesis. . . . In the beginning, the great mass of Jews in eastern Europe still resisted this trend; but in the second half of the nineteenth century the upper circles of east-European Jewry were also drawn into the current of the western antithesis.

The humanitarian movement, drunk with success, everywhere broke down the walls of history. Man, freed from the heavy fetters of tradition, raised his head high. But what did the Jew stand to gain? Here the antithesis of the new century brought catastrophe. The very concept of Jewry as a living nationality, taking its own place in the world of culture, was dissembled; among enlightened circles the national idea was placed under a complete ban. In place of the former call: "To your tents, Israel!" they now began to call: "Rise and go forth! Out of your tents, Israel!" Intermingling with the nations became the basis of a new world-view. . . . Many were convinced that Jewry as a nationality was already dead and that nothing was left for it but to merge with all mankind, or, since mankind is divided into various nations, to become absorbed into other national bodies and retain only its religious traditions in greater or lesser degree. The extreme of isolationism was followed by the extreme of assimilationism. The force of the antithesis, according to psychological law, balanced the force of the thesis.

By its very nature, however, the antithesis cannot exist for long. To tear down is easier than to build up. Assimilation was bound to expose itself as a doctrine of national suicide. The antisemitism of the last decades of the nineteenth century revealed the folly of the assimilationist motto: "Thou shalt cleave unto the nations of the world," since numerous members of these nations began to eliminate from their midst the Jews who "cleaved" unto them and let them understand that intermingling requires the approval of both parties. . . . Better elements in the Jewish community began to wonder: What have we achieved in the period of the antithesis? We have become alienated from our own people, without being able to become integrated into the nations around us. Assimilation turned out to be in practice psychologically unnatural, ethically damaging, and practically useless. We gave up autonomy, the vital artery of every national body, and exchanged for it the principle of heteronomy, an alien law of development. We lost the center of our inner life, we transferred it to an alien environment, and we thus lost our balance. . . .

Our sense of honor was stronger sevenfold during the period of the old thesis—when the center of our life was still found in our own midst and not outside of it; when isolation, although it could not protect us against blows from the outside, saved us from inner disintegration and tension and made us members of equal worth within our own national body. True, our isolation of those days was extreme: it had an evil influence, not only upon the Jews as Jews, but also upon man as man; it crushed the individual under the burden of its discipline and chained the spirit of freedom with the fetters of tradition. This loss was made up in some small measure during the period of the antithesis, and this was its chief advantage. For this epoch broadened the area of individual freedom, accustomed us to political and civic life, aroused within us the need for renewal and for inner reform. But the net result of the epoch was that it brought the Jew close to humanity, while at the very same time it alienated him from his own nationality.

Experience has demonstrated that both the thesis and the antithesis are one-sided. It revealed to us that the hour has come for new combinations of forces which will bring the demands of humanity into harmony with the demands of progressive nationalism. The way is open for a broad synthesis which must unite in itself all the solid and vital elements of the two previous stages of development and, once extremism has been overcome, create from them the basis for a new order of life. The thesis was called "isolation," the antithesis "assimilation"; the synthesis is called "autonomism." . . .

II

Every living nationality strives to preserve the individual and original qualities with which it was endowed by its historical development, as well as the means which contributed to such preservation.

It defends its territory and its political freedom without regard to danger; and if both are lost, it defends with equal vigor its language, culture, literature, education and religion, its self-administration, its particular institutions, and in general everything which strengthens the inner association of its members. When the determination of a nationality to preserve its historical type is joined with a striving to perfect its development, we have a case of autonomy adapting itself to the spirit of the times.

The more complex and original the historical development in question, the stronger is the force which leads it to "laws of its own" (this is the meaning of the word "autonomy") and to resistance to "alien laws" (or heteronomy), which forces it to accept the substance and form of alien development. Autonomy as a historic claim is thus the firm and inalienable right of each national individuality; only its forms depend on the status which a nationality has within a multi-national state. . . . In view of its condition in the Diaspora, Jewish nationality cannot strive for territorial or political isolation, but only for social and cultural autonomy. The Jew says: "As a citizen of my country I participate in its civic and political life; but as a member of the Jewish nationality I have, in addition, my own national needs, and in this sphere I must be independent to the same degree that any other national minority is autonomous in the state. I have the right to speak my language, to use it in all my social institutions, to make it the language of instruction in my schools, to order my internal life in my communities, and to create institutions serving a variety of national purposes; to join in the common activities with my brethren not only in this country but in all countries of the world and to participate in all the organizations which serve to further the needs of the Jewish nationality and to defend them everywhere."

During the "period of isolation" the Jews enjoyed in great measure the right of national autonomy, although in outmoded forms, but they lacked civic and political rights. During the "period of assimilation" they began to participate in the civic and political life of the countries in which they lived, but many became alienated from the chosen inheritance of the nation, from its internal autonomy, which, in their limited view, did not accord with civic emancipation already granted or about to be granted by law. In this manner old Jewry sacrificed its civic rights for its national rights, and new Jewry its national rights for its political or civic rights. The period of autonomy now approaching does not tend to either of the two extremes of the previous epochs, which had rendered the life of the Jewish people defective and impaired. The new epoch must combine our equal civic and political rights with the social and cultural autonomy enjoyed by other nationalities whose historical conditions resemble our own. The Jews must demand simultaneously all civic, political and national rights, without renouncing one for the other as had been the case in the past.

The chief axiom of Jewish autonomy may thus be formulated as follows: Jews in each and every country who take an active part in civic and political life enjoy all rights given to the citizens, not merely as individuals, but also as members of their national groups.

Now that we have succeeded in establishing the principle of autonomy, we must analyze the problem of how it can be realized under the conditions in which the Jewish nationality finds itself. Here we have to differentiate between two kinds of national minorities in a multi-national state: (1) a territorial minority, which is a minority as compared with the total population of the commonwealth, but which constitutes a majority in its own historical state or province; (2) a non-territorial minority, scattered over various provinces without being a majority in any. Nationalities of the first kind require regional autonomy where they are settled, nationalities of the second kind must have communal and cultural autonomy.

Up to the nineteenth century the community (*kehilla*) was the basis of Jewish autonomy in the lands of the Diaspora. . . . Since all our social and private life in those days was dominated by laws that operated with religious sanctions, the administration of the community also took on a religious form. The order which turned all Jewry into a type of religious nation created also the type of religious community; and in practice the nationality as a whole fulfilled tasks under the rule of religion which transcended the sphere of religion, so that all the tasks of secular organization were fulfilled in the "religious" community. The *kahal* took care of matters of communal welfare, supervised economic life, education, and tax collection for the government, while the rabbinic tribunals adjudicated cases involving family and financial matters. . . . The synagogue and the rabbis occupied the central position in all these institutions in name only; in practice the community was a kind of Jewish city within the Christian city. Up to the period of emancipation communal Jewish autonomy as described above served as a substitute for government, for a state, and for citizenship, which under the old order were completely absent from Jewish life.

What, then, should modern Jewry have done after it had received its civic freedom in the West or, already before then, after it had absorbed the spirit of European culture? It should have adapted its autonomy to modern ideas, to the way of life of free citizens. Judaism, too, was now subjected to the general European process of secularization which separated the social from the religious elements. In its communal organization it, too, should have separated the core of nationality from its heavy religious shell. Even after the extent of self-administration had diminished under the influence of emancipation, a wide area of social and cultural autonomy still remained inside the community and outside—in the political associations dedicated to the ordering of the general affairs of Jewry. . . . All this, however, the assimilationist Jews forgot as they rushed into the (not always open) arms of their "liberators." The emancipated, who rejected the secular national idea and who attached to Judaism the unhappy label of a "religious group," retained only the symbols of the former autonomy: the synagogue, the rabbinate and, to a small degree, the welfare fund; everything else they assigned to the control of the state. Thus was created in Germany and Austria a greatly restricted organization which rested, not on the free national community, but on the religious community, the association of worshipers in the synagogue (*Synagogengemeinden, Cultusgemeinden*). . . . For many, membership in the community was merely a fiction, since by conviction they were distant from religious service; others severed this link as well and proclaimed themselves to be without any religious affiliation (*Konfessionslos*), thereby being freed also from the requirement to pay the communal tax. . . .

The fiction of the "religious community" was bound to be destroyed together with the fiction of the "religious society," not in the sense of a disruption of the religious service, but of a removal of the religious label from secular institutions. It is necessary to reconstruct the shattered autonomy in forms which are adapted to modern social conditions. In countries of German culture, the nationalist Jews must convert their religious communities into national communities (*Volksgemeinden*). Even before such a change can be effected officially, with the approval of the government, it is possible, on the basis of the existing laws guaranteeing freedom of association, to widen perceptibly the circle of activities of the communities, and, at the same time, to wage a parliamentary battle for the recognition of the fullest measures of secular national communal autonomy. . . . Real and broad autonomy is especially possible in countries in which the principle prevails that the government does not interfere in the private lives of its citizens, and where authoritarian governments or exaggerated concentration of power do not exist. In such countries, especially in the United States of America, Jews could enjoy even now a large measure of self-administration if they only were willing to advance beyond the confines of the "religious community." . . .[16]

There is no need to demonstrate that national-cultural autonomy is of singular value to the Jewish masses concentrated in eastern Europe. Here the Jews do not yet have full rights as citizens and, therefore, the extension of the autonomy of their communities meets with external difficulties. Over against this, however, there are strong inner tendencies in that direction among the Jewish masses which are attracted to the modern national movement. . . .

III

It is customary to oppose Jewish autonomy on the ground that it will lead to our being accused of separatism, and that it would be used to undermine our civic status. The time has come, however, to dispel the clouds of terror which darken the word "separatism" and with which both our "friends" as well as our enemies frighten us. If the old civic isolation, the product of force and violence, is, in truth, contrary to modern legal thought, national-cultural autonomy is the noblest and most humane expression of this thought. The accusation of "separatism" is the favorite weapon of all ruling nationalities in their struggle against minorities; but no self-respecting nationality will take notice of such accusations, because it considers its free development to be a sacred and inalienable right. Why are Jews alone afraid of this "accusation"?

In the most recent period it is hard to find anything more shameful than this terror which befell the last two or three generations of the Jewish intelligentsia, the fear of being rebuked for national separatism. . . . All members of persecuted nationalities pride themselves on their national stubbornness, on not assimilating with the dominant nations; but the enlightened European Jew retreats in terror before the rebuke that he did not become a Russian, Frenchman, or German! Worse still, Jews of this sort have accustomed liberal Christians also to consider assimilation as unavoidable, especially for the Jew, as a kind of price paid for equal civic rights. . . . Among Russian publicists, for example, two standards of judgment are accepted, one for the Jews and another for all other oppressed nationalities. Of Poles, Lithuanians and Armenians, the liberal journalist not only does not demand assimilation with Russians, but he also denounces any such tendency in government policy. When it comes to the Jews, however, even outstanding liberals press this demand. . . . One radical Russian journalist expressed the following opinion: "We do not take it upon ourselves to make the Jews into Russians, but we want them to do it themselves."*

. . . There are many who agree that the demands of the Jewish autonomists are historically and morally justified, but they doubt its feasibility at a time when the strength of the national state is on the increase and when political nationalism is oppressing the subject nationalities in the name of the principle used by all ruthless governments: political unity and national security. Will the Jews be strong enough to resist such force? It is true that political nationalism is hostile to all nationalities under its rule. . . . In many states the

* Yuzhkov in *Russkoye Bogatstvo*, in one of the issues of 1901. The publicist-philosopher, Struve, also expressed the same view in an interview with a journalist concerning Zionism. "For the good of Russia I would want that the Jews assimilate; I believe it would also be to the advantage of the Jews" (*Russ*, February 2, 1907). . . .

medieval watchword of "ruling religion" has been replaced by the principle of "ruling nationality." For the principle of *cuius regio, eius religio,* they have substituted the doctrine of *cuius regio, eius natio.* Among conservatives, slogans abound such as "Russia for the Russians." Such political falsehood makes no sense and it cannot be maintained for long in a multi-national state without endangering the existence of the state. A policy which is based on the suppression of national minorities and on their forced assimilation with the dominant majority can only lead to one of two results: (1) permanent turmoil and revolutionary upheavals within the persecuted nationalities, incessant "civil war" which will undermine all the foundations of law and order in the state; or (2) the break-up of the state into individual national states. Neither of these results is in the interest of the above-mentioned politicians and "patriots." After some experience with the spirit of political nationalism, these politicians will finally come to understand that they have to give up this destructive theory of wiping out national types in the interests of the safety and internal security of the state. It is in the interest of the maintenance of peace and of political security that the multi-national state must give a certain measure of autonomy to all its nationalities. . . .

Despite the present reaction, the course of history is directed, not toward the subjection of national groups, but toward their liberation. In the same way that the principle of a ruling Church gave way after a bitter struggle, so too the principle of a ruling nationality is bound to be discarded. If the nineteenth century was able to secure the legal recognition by the community of the principle of freedom of the individual, the twentieth century is faced with the task of establishing the freedom or the autonomy of the national individual. The struggle by nationalities for this ideal will not cease until it is crowned with victory. Israel is not alone in this struggle. Its path is the path of history moving toward the noble goal of liberating the national individual within the bounds of the freedom of the state based on the foundations of law and justice.

* * *

This is the practical content of the historical synthesis discussed above. This synthesis contains the best of the static elements of the thesis and of the dynamic elements in the antithesis. What we want is to preserve our national type and to perfect it in the spirit of our historical development and with the help of those means which our modern culture supplies to all peoples fighting for their survival. . . .

We are now living in the midst of great distress and we drink without wincing from the cup of sorrow. Our entire world is filled with sighing and groaning. Despair without the daring of the desperate, pain and suffering without that incentive to action generated in a living and feeling body by severe suffering—all these stay the hands and paralyze the strength of the Jewish intelligentsia. To the weak I say: "Here is a concrete ideal which will restore to your life its lost meaning. It is an ideal such as that proclaimed by the Lawgiver: "For this commandment which I command thee this day, it is not too hard for thee, neither is it far off. . . . But the word is very nigh unto thee in thy mouth, and in thy heart, that thou mayest do it (Deuteronomy, 30.11-14). Our historical life depends, not on the outside forces which oppress us today even though they may appear great and severe to us . . . , but on ourselves and our strength, "on our mouth and our heart," on all those concrete efforts which we will make everywhere step by step in the Diaspora for the preservation and defense of our people.

We must abandon the strategy of watchful waiting, waiting until we receive equal civic rights, until the antisemites have become disillusioned or strong governments show us favors. Our program is a program of action, of stubborn day-to-day effort often hidden from view; and it is at the same time an unceasing war for our human and national rights. Every exertion and effort in the present is also a step toward the future. Every institution which gives support to our autonomy, every school permeated by the Jewish national spirit, every new circle for the study of Hebrew, Jewish history and literature, brings us nearer to our sacred goal. We still stand at the threshold of this great task; but concealed within it is our immediate future, the rebirth of the spirit throughout the dispersion of Israel. . . .

December 1901 (1907).

Fifth Letter

ON NATIONAL EDUCATION

National education and its function in the development of national autonomy.—Diagnosis of the sickness of education.—The doctrine of racial and cultural nationalism and the sad state in the west.—"The Jew Werther": the "schism in the soul" of the Jews of our generation, the perversion of national feeling as a result of alien education.—The Danish nationalism of Brandes and his indifference to Judaism; his estrangement from Judaism.—Those who do not want to be and those who cannot be Jews.—The denationalization of the Jewish school in Russia.—The confession by a contemporary.—Fathers and sons.—How to overcome the dualism of racial and cultural nationalism.—The racial nationality becomes the cultural nationality of the individual by means of education.—The universal and the national needs of the individual are fashioned by education.

The internal autonomy of the Jewish nationality rests on a threefold basis: the community, the language, and the school. It is difficult to decide which of the three is the most important, since each of them is indispensable in its sphere and fulfills a definite function in the organization of the life of the people. There is no doubt that the third factor of autonomy, the national school or "national education," is strongly intertwined with the development of the soul of the people. If the autonomy of the community is especially important for the social organization of Jewry, the autonomy of the school (which includes also the presupposition of the free use of language) is a necessary condition for the development of the Jewish personality. The school, the educational methods and the curriculum directly influence the growth of the individual cells of the national body. To the same degree that the health of the body depends on the health of its cells, national education must provide the basis for the whole organization of the people. The life and death of the nation are in the hands of the school, especially so among the Jews. The educated Jew of our time is from his early youth exposed for the most part to the influence of an alien school which separates him from his nationality, or makes him uncertain of his direction. Since we are discussing the renaissance of Judaism and the health of our national body, we must carefully investigate and analyze the prolonged sickness which is eating it bare, the sickness of education, and find the means to remove its causes.

I shall not discuss the problem in abstract theoretical language. I shall call living witnesses and let them speak for me. Let us begin with the idea of the "humanitarian mission" in recent literature.

S. Lublinski,[17] a Jewish author writing in German (a journalist and the author of the book *Literatur und Gesellschaft im neunzehnten Jahrhundert*), recently invented a doctrine which justifies assimilation in a special way. This doctrine, which may be called "the devil theory of nationalism," differentiates between "racial" and "cultural" nationality. The racial nationality of all the enlightened Jews in modern Europe is the Jewish nationality to which they are bound by ties of blood; the cultural nationality is that of the people in whose state they live, whose language they speak, whose schools they attend, and in whose literature they are brought up. The opposition between these two national influences produces in the Jewish soul a painful dualism, and a "split personality" from which he must free himself. Lublinski disposes of the split without much effort. If a choice is to be made between racial and cultural nationality, supremacy must be accorded to the latter, for *Die Kultur ist mehr als das Blut*, culture is more important than blood relationship. In Germany, for example, the Jew of our time must and can consider himself a German. "A Jew who carries in his breast the German culture is a full German," more so than even a German by birth who has not been brought up as a German. "And the task of the national state," Lublinski continues, "is to unite into one organic whole the different classes, religions, temperaments [?] and races. In this large circle and general spiritual organization the Jew can freely emphasize his characteristics as much as a Catholic or a Bavarian member of the German nation. [What possible freedom is there if the "national state," according to Lublinski, is justified in working for "the mixture of races and creeds?" S. D.] Don't we often hear it said jokingly that the south-Germans and those in some regions of the Rhineland are not Germans at all, but German-speaking Celts? Yet culturally they are full Germans. It follows, therefore, that culture is more important than blood."*

The meaning of this doctrine is clear: a man who is born a Jew but educated in a German environment is a German of different race or religion, like, for example, Swabians, Bavarians, or Catholics, and since in each individual of this kind the racial and religious characteristics which create this particular type are erased by cultural influences, the Jewish element becomes indistinct and the German stands out. By analogy this is equally applicable to Russian, French, English and other Jews.

Is such an analogy tenable and is there any need to prove or disprove it? If we were concerned here with a theoretical doctrine, we would possibly have to subject it to sociological or ethical analysis. What ethical value is there to a doctrine which is built upon the recognition of the right of the "national state," to "combine classes, religions, races into one organic whole," that is, to unite by force, in the interest of the unity of the state, the different groups of its inhabitants? It is also not difficult to determine the moral value of the view of the Jew who says: "The cultural nationality to which I and my contemporaries are bound by ties of language and education is closer to me than the nationality of my birth, from which my ties are already severed because its culture, the product of a hundred generations, has become alien to my spirit." In this case it is not the theory that is important but the fact which follows from it, the revolution which was effected in the soul of the Jew under the influence of alien education. Such a Jew need not prove to us that he is a German, Russian, etc.; it is enough that he honestly states that he feels himself to be a German or Russian because he was brought up that way. You may decide that such a person is an abnormal national type, but you must give credence to his subjective feeling, unless there is reason to doubt his honesty.

One frequently meets in our time the type of intelligent Jew who is willing or is forced by the pressure of outside influence to be a national Jew, but who cannot do so because the education he received in school or at home has made him a German, Russian or

* "Ein letztes Wort zur Judenfrage," in *Ost und West*, no. 9 (1901), p. 650.

Frenchman but not a Jew. The effect of the law of historical heredity and the tribal sense create in the soul of such a person a vague leaning toward the nationality of his birth; antisemitism pushes him toward it against his will and deprives him of the right to belong to the "Aryan society"; but his education makes him clearly aware of his cultural and spiritual affinity to the nationality surrounding him, while his ties to Judaism are unconscious: blood, race, a nebulous past. This inner contradiction often causes a profound cleavage in his soul. He is torn between "racial" and "cultural" nationality, between an unconscious heritage and something he consciously absorbed through education. Usually such a conflict is decided in favor of the "cultural nation," since education and cultural environment are, indeed, stronger than the effects of the law of heredity. Lublinski, who was educated in the German spirit, was pushed for a short time by a wave of antisemitism into the Jewish national movement, and here he selected the banner which stood out with its external brilliance: the banner of political Zionism. Soon, however, the non-Jewish spirit which was planted in him by his education gained the upper hand and he left Zionism to proclaim himself a "full German." . . . Frequently, however, the inner cleavage which affects the soul of the modern Jew is not resolved peacefully but leaves the imprint of a tragic duality upon the entire life of the individual. An example of such nationalist duality appears in the work and personal biography of the short-lived German-Jewish poet Ludwig Jacobowski.[18]

Jacobowski became known in German literature only after his death. He died at the age of thirty-two of a nervous fever, in Berlin, in December 1900. He published a novel, *Werther the Jew* (*Werther der Jude*), and a collection of a few poems expressing the anguish of a crushed and tormented soul vainly searching for a perfect and happy life. The hero of the novel *Werther the Jew* is presented as the product of the psychological tensions besetting the assimilated German Jew under the impact of antisemitic expression.

The hero of the novel, the son of a Jewish merchant, who was educated at home as a "Jew of the Mosaic faith," who went to a German school and attended the university, is painfully vacillating all his life between two national feelings, the German and the Jewish.

He yearns to forget his Jewishness (to which he is attached only by childhood memories of the synagogue, of the festivals, and of an uninspiring teacher who taught him the Hebrew alphabet) and feels himself to be German to the core. His Christian environment, however, reminds him at every step that he is a Jew. The Christian girl whom he loves, her relatives, his fellow-students, all tell him directly or by hints: "You are a stranger to us, you come from a despised race, you can never be like a native German!" At times the soul of the hero himself is poisoned by the antisemitism of his environment. He sees himself victimized by the sins of his ancestors; he sharply condemns the vices of the rich Jews, but pays no attention to the shortcomings of the German bourgeoisie. Every time he becomes aware within himself of a natural feeling of attachment to Judaism he chastises himself because he views it as a bad sign that he has not become as Germanized as he should have. There are also occasions, however, when the law of historical heredity prevails. When a friend beseeches him not to concern himself so much with Judaism, he answers bitterly: "Is it possible? Does not this problem arise of itself, like a horrible monster in the soul of every contemporary Jew who looks with open eyes at the ugly reality?" How painful it is to be a Jew! "To be Jewish with every fibre of one's soul and with every drop of one's blood, and yet, from another standpoint, not to be Jewish even with one drop of blood or with one fibre of one's soul."* "Werther the Jew" is finally driven to despair by the burden of this tormenting dualism within himself and he takes his life. The external cause of his tragic end is the action of his German "friends" in expelling him from their student corporation because he was the son of a Jewish merchant who was mixed up in questionable business deals publicized in the press.

The author himself followed the example of his hero. The history of his life corroborates what we might have presumed: he put into the mouth of his hero all of his own thoughts, his sufferings and the torment of his soul. Jacobowski, too, was always torn between Judaism and Germanism, and in his case, too, his Germanism dominated over his Judaism. As if afraid of possibly being suspected of Jewish

* Lessing, Theodor, "Ludwig Jacobowski," in *Ost und West*, no. 8 (1901).

nationalism, he proclaimed in advance, in the introduction to his *Werther*: "My views on the Jewish question have remained what they have always been; the same goal has been preserved in them without change: complete identification with the German spirit and with German ways."

Jacobowski, who had buried his Jewish national feeling that weighed upon his soul like a millstone inherited from the past, addressed the German people with humble supplication:

> *Was giebst du mir, du deutsches Land,*
> *Für meine reichen Gaben?*
> *O schütte mir Liebe in die Hand,*
> *Nur Liebe möcht ich haben.*
> *O deutsches Land, du schlimmes Land,*
> *Was schenkst du deinem Knaben?*
> *Zum Leben eine Handvoll Sand*
> *Und Sand auch zum Begraben.*

Like a beggar at the door, the Jewish poet pleads and entreats for the love of an alien nationality which rejects him and he apparently does not sense how repulsive such self-abasement is. Why did he carry his love to strangers who hated him? Why did he not come to his brethren, his own kin? Why did he cling to an evil step-mother instead of to his own mother who bore him? Why was he drawn to the mighty and triumphant and not to the myriads of his unhappy brethren who would have given him their love without supplication? Because the "cultural nation" came between Jacobow-ski and his "racial nation" and weighed him down with German life and education. From early childhood he spoke, thought, read and wrote German; he knew and loved only German literature and was brought up on German ideals. Of the Hebrew language, of Jewish history and literature he had only a vague conception. This new "cultural nation," on the other hand, rejected the love of the Jew and proclaimed that he belongs to another nation which he himself does not recognize. The tragedy of "Werther the Jew" consists in the fact that he is an undesirable stepson in an alien family, while he should be, by his nature, the favorite son of the very family which he left in mourning. We have countless such "dangling limbs" in all countries and in all walks of life.

The education of the generation of the Jacobowskis and the Lublinskis coincided with the period when antisemitism flourished in Europe. This helps to explain the schism of the soul found in such men and the painful antagonism between two nationalities. Before this period, however, assimilation developed in the West under more peaceful conditions and succeeded in striking deep roots in the life of the preceding two or three generations. Most of the Jews who grew up and received a non-Jewish education in the period before the great wave of antisemitism escaped the tragic national dualism of the Jewish youth of our time. . . . They could, from the very beginning, develop a strong national feeling for the peoples in whose schools they were educated. The famous Danish critic Georg Brandes[19] furnishes proof for this. Brandes has worked all his life in the field of literary criticism; he lectures and publishes books on all the creations of European literature, even those of less advanced nations, but he has never revealed any traces of his Jewish origin nor did he interest himself in the life and literature of the Jews.* What is more, he was not even aware of the existence of modern Hebrew literature. On one occasion Dr. Marcus Ehrenpreis,[20] in a conversation, told him that such a literature existed, and Brandes expressed great astonishment. Brandes, who has command of a number of ancient and modern languages, apparently does not know Hebrew, the language of his ancestors, in which the oldest universal creations of the spirit of mankind were written. The Jewish nationality, its past and present, its agonies and sufferings, are completely foreign to him. In this respect the conversation just mentioned between Brandes and Dr. Ehrenpreis is highly instructive. Brandes, after expressing a negative opinion on political Zionism, conceded the value of its spiritual foundation, but he acknowledged it only as an unconcerned bystander. When Dr. Ehrenpreis told him that the new movement "would restore their spiritual homeland to the Jews, would give Jewish life a new content, would revive their own historical

* Only toward the end of his life, during and after the World War, did Brandes comment on the Jewish question, but even then only as a bystander.

language and culture," Brandes answered: "This is indeed a noble thought, but I do not understand it at all. I am a Dane, and I shall not allow anybody to take that right from me. All my life I have written with my very blood. I have toiled and labored for the liberty and the progress of Denmark, and I shall continue to work for her until my last breath."

Did not Brandes feel what tragedy was contained in this short confession? . . . Georg Moris Cohn, a descendant of the priests of Israel, finds special honor in working for peaceful, happy Denmark, but does not feel the moral call telling him that a man who works for his people when it is unhappy is deserving of sevenfold honors. The attitude of Jews like Brandes to Judaism is not, to be sure, due to bad intentions. It is a necessary outcome of their education, their environment and their epoch. . . . The men of Brandes' generation, who grew up in the period of emancipation following 1848, were eyewitnesses of the complete abandonment of Jewish ideals in western Europe. They were swept into the rapid stream of general European culture. As plain soldiers or as leaders they fought under all banners but the Jewish banner. When antisemitism appeared and reminded them of the existence of the Jewish nationality, they had, for the most part, become so estranged from their nationality that they could not take their places in the ranks of its fighters. . . .

Thus, in addition to those who do not want to be Jews, there is a large group who cannot be Jews because their education has implanted other national feelings in their hearts. We have illustrated this above by examples taken from the life of west-European Jewry, but the same phenomenon, although to a lesser degree, can also be found in eastern Europe. Here, too, as in the West, the theory of "denationalization" began with hollow and alluring phrases on the "enlightenment of all humanity." Those converted to this enlightenment did not understand that the concept of a general humanitarian education is merely an abstraction, which in concrete reality takes on a definite national form adapted to the language of instruction and its curriculum. In Russia they scorned the Jewish school, which could have been reformed, and went directly to the Russian school, thus supplanting their own national education by a foreign national education.

Thus began the plague of Russification which beset the second generation of the intelligentsia. The first generation, the men of the 1860s, who passed from the Jewish school to the Russian school, consciously accepted the idea of assimilation. These pioneers of the enlightenment from the very beginning sent their children to Russian schools, and there an unconscious process of assimilation began. Some of the assimilationist "fathers," influenced by the new currents that revived in them memories of their youth, repented and returned to national Judaism. Most of their children, however, are unable to steep themselves in the Jewish national spirit, although at times they want to do so because of pity for their persecuted people or because the pressure of antisemitism forces them to return to their people. Should a representative of this generation want to bare his soul and confess to us, he might say something to this effect: "You demand a Jewish national consciousness from me, but where should I get it from? I grew up in an assimilated family where Judaism was either not discussed at all or else referred to as an anachronism. They planted in me the idea that the unenlightened masses still cling to their nationality out of ignorance, but that enlightened Jews merge with the ruling nationality. My parents, as freethinkers, could not give me a religious education and, as assimilationists, they also did not provide me with a national character. The language I spoke was Russian; the first book I read was in Russian; the primary and secondary schools instilled in me a Russian spirit. I knew by heart Pushkin's poems, but had no idea of the Psalms, of the Song of Songs, of Judah Halevi and of the creations of modern Hebrew literature. . . . I read the epics of Homer and Virgil and the dialogues of Plato in the original, but I never knew the noble tales of the book of Genesis or the visions of the Prophets Isaiah and Jeremiah, which are written in the language of my ancestors which I do not understand. I know the history of many peoples and different creeds, but I do not know the history of Judaism and of the Jewish people. I first heard of equality and social justice not from the Prophets of the

Bible but from modern journalists. I became acquainted with various philosophical and ethical systems, but not with those which the sages of the Jewish people had created in the course of generations. The Hebrew language and literature were a sealed book to me, nor did I deem them worthy of study. What is more, I do not even know the spoken language of the masses, the 'Jargon' which they taught me to hate and despise, and thus I am not able to speak to the masses of my brethren in their language. All my social and cultural ideas are bound up with Russian society and Russian literature. I am drawn with all my might and soul to my 'cultural nationality' and nothing except our common political status binds me to my 'racial nationality.' With Judaism I am only connected through fetters of oppression; to Russian society, however, I am drawn by custom and culture."

Such a confession by a contemporary man might serve also as the confession of a contemporary woman and be expressed in even more painful form, since, in a national sense, the education of Jewish girls is inferior to that of boys. . . . The verse of the Bible: "Your sons and your daughters are given over to foreign people" has been fully realized in the cultural life of the enlightened circles of our people. Only a great literary master could adequately describe the tragedy of those parents who are more or less identified with their nationality and what they feel in such instances. They undoubtedly experience great pain and profound suffering, seeing the extinction of their national ideals in their children and feeling that they are the last link in the chain of generations, in those glorious millennia of Jewish history.

Is it possible to halt the course of deterioration of this great nationality? One must turn to the cause of the malady. The root of the evil is that the Jew who has been brought up away from his national environment has two nationalities, one racial, the other cultural, and that the latter swallows up the former. How can the malady be cured? The conclusion is obvious: it is necessary to soften as much as possible the contradiction between the racial and cultural nationalism which the new education has brought about. The children must be so educated and guided that the Jewish nationality will be, not only their racial, but also their cultural nationality. They must be provided with the opportunity to acquire their basic universal culture through the national channel, so that Judaism will serve as a source of national interests and a center of social and cultural ideals. Education has estranged the youth from Judaism, now it must lead them back into Judaism. The school of the recent past was used to blur the national features; now it must be turned into an instrument of nationalization and fulfill its general educational functions at the same time. We are faced with the need for a basic reform of our educational concepts. The problem of educational reform arises every time there is a cultural crisis, every time it becomes necessary to provide for the strengthening of the foundations of national life. . . . Without a basic reform we are in danger of losing our intelligentsia, our advance guard in the struggle for civic and national rights.

How far is such a basic reform of the school possible, and to what degree can it be realized? This question can first be answered in a general way. Our old schools, the *heder* and the *yeshiva*, educated only the Jew, but not the man; and even to the "Jew," they supplied only a limited education, since they influenced only his religious thinking. The new general school, on the other hand, forgets the Jew and educates only the man, that is, in practice it educates a Russian, German, etc. One is the thesis, the other its antithesis. The synthesis is self-evident: to educate the man and the Jew at one and the same time. The dual practical task of the present moment is to strengthen the universal foundations in the old schools and nationalism in the new school. The school must prepare its pupil for the struggle for his individual and national existence, because his enemies are arrayed against him as members of a specific nation. . . . We need universal enlightenment, a lofty all-inclusive moral and social ideal, and nothing is as well suited in our time to uplift and glorify the spirit of our youth as is the Jewish national idea which implants in them the awareness that it is better to work for their persecuted nation and to fight for its existence than to join a strong nation outside of our camp in the name of happiness for the individual. An enlightenment without such an ideal will not arouse moral and social sentiments in young people, but on the contrary may guide them into a path which leads toward alienation from their people and thus perverts their moral sense. The nationalization of education and instruction (on condition that the school is prepared to accept the demands of modern culture, and in connection with the reconstruction of the communities on the basis of self-government) is one of the beaten paths that will lead to the strengthening of Jewry in the near future.*

1902 (1907).

* In the Russian edition of this work there are given here detailed programs for educational reform and a review of the activities of the Society for the Propagation of Enlightenment (*Hevrat mefitse Haskala*) in Russia at the time. All these details of the *Kulturkampf* of 1901-1903 are only of historical interest now.

Sixth Letter

REALITY AND FANTASY IN ZIONISM

I. The history of Zionism.—A double reaction: against assimilation and against antisemitism.—Historical examples.—Political messianism in place of religious.

II. *Hibbat Tsiyon,* its ideologues and its practical leaders.—Pinsker's *Auto-Emancipation.*—His erroneous historical view and his loose national thinking.—The settlement in Palestine.—The beginning of spiritual Zionism.

III. Political Zionism: Herzl's *Judenstaat* and the First Congress in Basle.—The programmatic declaration by Nordau: the material and moral foundations of the *Judennot;* a return to Judaism or to a Jewish state?—The Basle program.—The utopia of Zionist diplomacy.

IV. Zionism as a shield against assimilation.—The idolatry of the national idea.—Zionism as a transition to cultural nationalism or autonomism.

I

Opposition to the theory of autonomism is found in two extreme camps: among the proponents of assimilation and among the political Zionists. The assimilationists, who utterly reject the idea of a Jewish nationality, defend only the civic rights of the Jews as members of the nations among whom they live and consider Jews to be linked with each other solely by a common religion. The Zionists recognize the Jews as a nationality, but as an abnormal one, and, for that reason, without firm grasp or foothold. They maintain that in order to preserve the Jewish nation for the future it must be transformed into a normal nation by acquiring a particular piece of territory with independent political rule. The assimilationists maintain that there is no need for autonomism; the Zionists hold that it is inadequate. In our analysis of assimilationist doctrine we have found that it rejects the principle of equality, and that it is the manifestation of a new kind of oppression, an inner bondage that has taken the place of the external bondage. Assimilationism, which once was powerful, is now slowly losing ground, at least as a social theory, if not in practice.

The awakening national consciousness is undermining it and forcing it back. Within the movement of the liberation of Judaism, political Zionism, one of the manifestations of our national revival, advances now with powerful steps. The young Zionist movement takes on a militant spirit. It is energetic, powerful, and fully confident that it holds the future destiny in its hands, and that the Jewish national idea can be realized only through the establishment of a Jewish state in Palestine. . . .

Our national movement, which had its inception in the 1880s, began in the form of "Love of Zion" (*Hibbat Tsiyon*). In the 1890s it assumed the wider form of Zionism. A certain section of our people wants not only the national-spiritual soil which was lost in the upheavals of assimilation, but also the political territory which was taken from us in the distant past. . . . Zionism is not so much a system based upon objective conclusions from the past and the present, as it is a social movement . . .[21] which arose under the pressure of bitter experience and which coincided with the subjective feelings of many Jews. This origin of Zionism requires clarification. Among the social and psychic factors that stimulated the rise of Zionism, it is necessary to differentiate between the temporary and the permanent factors in order to establish, from the beginning, which foundations of Zionism are solid and which are flimsy and ephemeral. . . .

Zionism is an answer to both the material and the moral aspects of "Jewish distress (*Judennot*), to the growth of antisemitism, and to the national degeneration brought about by assimilation. . . .[22] These two manifestations of Jewish distress existed in previous periods of Jewish history in different forms: as hatred against Israel and as the danger of "apostasy." Against this danger the Jewish people fought for its physical and spiritual existence with various strategems. In moments of severe crisis, when the situation was desperate, it was saved by mass migration; and when this too failed to heal fully the national distress, mystical messianism appeared on the scene. We are now witnessing one of the "great migrations" of the Diaspora, from Europe into America, and, at the same time, we see a powerful national trend among the people toward its ancient homeland, Eretz Yisrael.

Political Zionism is merely a renewed form of messianism that was transmitted from the enthusiastic minds of the religious kabbalists to the minds of the political communal leaders. In it the ecstasy bound up in the great idea of rebirth blurs the lines between reality and fantasy. Here too we find the continuing effects of secularization. In the same way that the Jewish national idea in its completeness now divests itself of its religious form and takes on a secular form, so messianism passes over from the religious to the political sphere. Will the results of political messianism be happier than those of mystical messianism? Let us investigate the history of this movement which developed from the modest groups of "Lovers of Zion" to the far-flung organization of political Zionists.

II

The Palestine idea, according to the concept of its originators, was far too simple to solve the entangled and complicated national question. The Palestine movement, which began in Russia in the early 1880s, at a time of violent pogroms and of unrest caused by emigration, strove to solve not so much the national-cultural as the social and economic problem. M. L. Lilienblum's[23] basic assumptions were: "The Jewish masses have been reduced to extreme poverty by old and new restrictions, quite apart from the havoc of the pogroms. As aliens and unwanted individuals we find ourselves, wherever we happen to dwell, in a humiliating, unnatural and unhealthy condition of life. Only settlement in Palestine can save our starving masses from imminent destruction."* Many accepted these assumptions and believed that Palestine colonization will not only ease the plight of thousands of settlers, but would also "save all our starving masses" and restore myriads of Jews to a "natural and normal life."

The author of the pamphlet *Auto-Emancipation* placed the national question on a broader basis. Leo Pinsker[24] set down as his main assumption that the Jewish people, surrounded by enemies on all sides, can only find help and salvation through self-liberation, that is, if it establishes the Jewish nationality on its own soil, in Palestine,

* Lilienblum, "On the Revival of the Jewish People" (Russian, 2d ed., Moscow, 1886), p. 64.

or in some other corner of the world. . . . The author of the pamphlet . . . holds that Jewry ceased to exist as a nation after it lost its state. He points to the lack of national consciousness among Jews and says: "What is the reason for this? It is the misfortune of our tribe that we are not a nation, but only Jews. We are a herd that is scattered all over the world." On another occasion Pinsker explained his ideas as follows: "The Jewish people lacks most of the attributes by which a nation is recognizable as such. It lacks a life of its own, which is unimaginable without common language, common customs and without living together on a common territory. The nations of the world have never had dealings with the Jewish nationality, but only with Jews. Yet to be recognized as a nation, the Jews lack the spirit of national individuality, which is found among all other nations and which is created by dwelling together on a common territory."

These basic ideas, which the author repeats because of their importance in the conclusions of his book, flagrantly contradict the facts of history as well as of real life. Pinsker, himself a follower of the Haskala during the period of assimilation, arrived at his judgments from the viewpoint of the social circle to which he belonged. It is as if he did not see the reality of the "original life," "the common customs," and even "the common language" of millions of Jews in eastern Europe among whom he lived. . . . Moreover Pinsker himself contradicts this hasty generalization when he says in the introduction to his pamphlet: "The Jews are an alien element among the peoples in whose midst they dwell. They are not absorbed by any other nation or language and are therefore not tolerated by them." This confusion in historical thinking is the major shortcoming of Pinsker's inspiring declaration. It is the call of a heart full of grief at the sorrow of his people, but it is not a scientific analysis. . . . The author of *Auto-Emancipation,* disillusioned in assimilation, hastened to despair of the vital forces of the Diaspora, which continued to function for thousands of years without a state and without a territory and which has witnessed the destruction of innumerable nations possessed of powerful empires.

What effect did the new messianic dreams of a return to Zion have on the solution of the world-wide Jewish problem? In practice the matter was from the very beginning limited to the support of agricultural colonization in Palestine. This colonization proceeded with difficulty. While tens of thousands of Jews emigrated from Russia to America every year, only hundreds went to Palestine. Baron Edmund Rothschild[25] saved from ruin the first colonies established in the old homeland. At the Kattowitz Conference in 1884,[26] the leaders of the Palestine colonization movement formed a unified organization. Gifts began to flow into the coffers of the colonization movement. The leaders of the movement, including Dr. Pinsker, devoted their energies to the practical organization of the work. . . . In 1890 the Conference of Odessa began its activities and was accorded official recognition by the government. Gifts and contributions were collected from the public and the work was carried on in a lively and courageous spirit. What were the results? A few more colonies were added to the first ones, and they were as insignificant as the earlier ones. . . . In the course of fifteen years (1882-1898) about fifteen colonies were founded. The Jewish population in the country, rural and urban, increased by about 15,000. This in itself is cause for rejoicing. We all look with love and good will at the growth of these small colonies in our Holy Land, so dear to us for its historical associations. What a difference there is, however, between the settlement of these few tens of thousands of Jews in Palestine as Turkish subjects and the dream of the political renaissance of ten million Jews in the Diaspora! How great is the gulf between reality and fantasy!

When a sobering process set in, many of the Lovers of Zion came to understand that their modest political activity did not come up to the great ideal they had set for themselves, and they searched for a compromise. A new current came to the fore, which I would call "spiritual Zionism," as distinguished from political Zionism. The founder of this new current of thought in Zionism, Ahad Ha-Am,[27] proclaimed that Palestine is important, not as a political, but as the spiritual center of Judaism, as a refuge "not for Jews but for Judaism," that is, for our national culture. For this reason the Zionist idea could be realized even if only a minute part of the Diaspora would settle in Palestine. The spiritual Zionists believe that it is necessary to concentrate our energies at one and the same time on both the rebuilding of the land of Israel and on the rebirth of the people of Israel. The Palestine idea must serve mainly to revitalize the national culture in the Diaspora. Political nationalism thus moved closer to spiritual or cultural nationalism. Both had one mission, the inner rebirth of the Jewish nation as an autonomous cultural unit. The only difference between them is that the spiritual Zionists hold that such an inner rebirth is impossible without the creation of an autonomous center in Eretz Yisrael, while the spiritual nationalists do not make the rebirth of the nation dependent on such a condition and they assume that the main struggle is for cultural autonomy in the countries of the Diaspora. In practice, the only difference between them is merely that the former preach the idea of national rebirth with their faces turned eastward, while the latter prophesy under the same banner with their faces directed westward. . . .*

III

The spiritual climate created by political Zionism among the Jews of Russia in the early 1880s led to a similar movement in western Europe fifteen years later. . . . The proclamation of the *Auto-Emancipation* was transformed into the *Judenstaat* of Dr. Herzl (Vienna, 1896). Once again the question of the creation of a Jewish state in Palestine or elsewhere was raised, but this time in a more positive and more definite form, with a detailed plan for the acquisition of the territory and a plan for immediate negotiations to that effect. Dr. Herzl, who was at first indifferent to the choice of a territory for his "Jewish state," embraced the Palestine idea wholeheartedly once his words had found an echo among the existing Zionist groups. A new spirit of enthusiasm animated the Zionists in both the East and the West. Veiled rumors of negotiations by Herzl with the Sultan in Constantinople and with Jewish bankers in England strengthened faith in the political idea. The notable Congress of

* For the development of the controversy between Ahad Ha-Am and me during this entire period, see below Letters Seven and Eight.

Basle, convened by the Zionists in August 1897, was to give a semblance of reality to this fantasy. Was this goal achieved?

The First Zionist Congress in Basle was intended to fulfill two tasks: (1) to proclaim before the entire world that the Jewish people recognizes itself as a nation and that it wants to live the life of a nation; (2) to demonstrate the need for creating a sovereign Jewish state or an autonomous state guaranteed by public international law. The first task, which is inclusive of the whole nation, was achieved with visible success. For the realization of the second task, the partisan one, there were naturally only programmatic declarations and various decisions to organize, to prepare, to arouse. If the Congress of Basle had been not a party congress but one representing the entire Jewish people, it could have adopted the first paragraph and then passed a resolution that the Palestine question was only part of the general national question and that it was necessary to mobilize and to organize the forces of the whole Diaspora. In any event, all the main currents of Jewish life should have been represented at the Congress, so that the voice of the people would have been heard instead of that of only one party. The Zionist Congress, however, had a ready answer to all questions. The theoretical foundation of this answer was contained in the programmatic address by Max Nordau,[28] who painted in bold strokes the sad picture of Jewish life in western Europe.

Max Nordau presented a marvelous description of the appalling "Jewish distress" as manifested in the material and moral spheres. . . . He penetrated deeply into the recesses of the soul of the contemporary Jew, who had removed himself from his own national family after "emancipation," but was rejected as an alien from the family of nations surrounding him. He recalled the days of the past when the Jew of the ghetto endured the material hardships caused by the hatred of his enemies, but was morally free because he lived in his own spiritual world. Civil emancipation, which tore down the walls of the ghetto, did indeed lighten the material burdens of the Jew, but it also subjected him morally to the Christian world. The Jew, liberated from the yoke of legal oppression, longed to integrate himself with his neighbors, his Christian fellow citizens. During the first period, for a generation or two, he succeeded in this effort to such a degree that he began to see himself as a German in Germany, a Frenchman in France, etc. Suddenly, however, the storm of antisemitism broke loose over Europe, and the Jew who thought he was enjoying equal rights with the rest of the citizens was shamefully ejected from Christian society as an alien and an undesirable. "The Jew who was emancipated in the West," Max Nordau said, "lost his Jewish characteristics; but the nations around him tell him that he had not acquired their characteristics. He left the walls of the ghetto, which had served as a kind of fatherland to him; but the land of his birth did not recognize him as its son." . . .

How, then, can one save these unfortunate emancipated Jews, oppressed as they are on all sides? The First Basle Congress provided a clear answer to this question in its resolution: It is necessary to colonize such Jews in their ancient homeland and establish a Jewish state. How wide, however, is the gulf between the correct diagnosis of the disease that Nordau gave in his address and the suggested therapy! The enlightened Jew was cut off from the roots of his people as a result of a severe historical crisis. Well, then, strengthen the forces so that he might return to them; give him the opportunity to find within his own national family the things he is seeking in an alien family! . . . The decline of national feeling among emancipated Jews appeared to Nordau a sign of decay, as if it were the final verdict of Jewish history, as if our changing historical past did not show repeated manifestation of a decline of national energy followed by the rise of new forces. . . . Nordau did well in emphasizing the thesis of separation and the antithesis of assimilation, but he forgot that a nation which passed through these two cultural stages is also prepared to enter into the third stage, that of broad synthesis. Much time was needed to adapt the national consciousness to the new conditions of life. This process of adjustment still continues in our time and is accompanied by shifts from one side to the other. . . .

The Basle Program states: "Zionism seeks to secure for the Jewish people a publicly recognized, legally secured home in Palestine. To achieve this goal, the Congress envisages the following measures:

(1) the fostering of the settlement of farmers, laborers and artisans in Palestine; (2) the organization and unification of the whole of Jewry into suitable local and general bodies, in accordance with the laws of the respective countries; (3) the strengthening of the national Jewish feeling and national consciousness; (4) the taking of preparatory steps to secure any governmental consent which may be necessary for the achievement of the goals of Zionism." . . . Are these means appropriate for the achievement of the main goal? The colonization of Palestine by Jews is already now being realized gradually within the limits of economic and political conditions. The first Lovers of Zion, after many years, had given up the hope that this tiny settlement would bring about a political rebirth, and now the western Zionists have come to renew the dream of a Jewish state. They are determined to promote an extensive mass settlement instead of gradual colonization, once they receive the consent of the Turkish government, or even after Palestine is secured for the Jews by international guarantee.

What tangible materials do they have for the realization of such a gigantic plan? . . . Granted that the Zionists will secure from the Turkish Sultan the right of free colonization in Palestine and that with the help of bank loans they will greatly expand the earlier colonization, in the hope that in due course a large Jewish center with political authority will be created there. It should be borne in mind, however, that increased colonization will be definitely limited by the economic and agricultural conditions of the country. During seventeen years of concentrated effort, under conditions of increased emigration, with huge expenditures of money and with the aid of Rothschild's millions, we succeeded in settling on the land a total of about 3,600 Jews, or about 212 per year. . . . Granted that the committees of western Zionists will operate with larger sums and that they will bring into Palestine every year not 200, but 1,000 settlers. In a hundred years the Jewish agricultural population of Palestine would then be 100,000. Let us increase this number fivefold through natural population increase and through the flow of masses of industrial workers into the cities. We will find that after a hundred years the land of Israel will have a half million Jews,* which means a population slightly larger than the Jewish population of the province of Kiev (428,000 according to the latest census). It is, of course, pleasing to entertain the hope that at the beginning of the twenty-first century there will be half a million Jews in our ancient homeland. But is it possible to solve by this means the problem of the ten million Jews in the Diaspora, which will have become twenty million in a hundred years? . . .

Political Zionism is thus a web of fantasies: the dream of the creation of a Jewish state guaranteed by international law, the dream of colonizing a great part of the Jewish people, and the dream of finding the solution of the Jewish question in this manner.

What remains of the whole Basle Program in practice? I believe only the second and third paragraphs of the Program: the "organization of the Jews" and the "strengthening of the national consciousness." These principles, which are also included in the theory of autonomism, together with the gradual extension of the settlement of Palestine, will be the outstanding results of the Zionist effort. To this end, however, the Zionists must become sober, and understand that the "return to Judaism" is the chief goal and, not a means for the (illusionary) establishment of a Jewish state. Otherwise the failure of political Zionism may cause even greater spiritual disillusionment than the despair brought about by the failure of assimilation.

IV

. . . Insofar as political Zionism is able to save certain elements of Judaism from the scourge of assimilation or indifference, its effects are all to the good. But it may also cause damage to the degree to which it falsifies the true historical perspective and the fundamental nature of the Jewish national idea. Those who speak of the saving effect of Zionism emphasize that, but for its influence, many of its

* Times have changed, and it is our good fortune to have now, 55 years after the beginning of the new colonization, an agricultural population of 70,000 and an urban population of close to 300,000. May they multiply further! Despite all this, I did not delete my old estimates, in order that it may serve as a symbol for those days, "days of little faith" in actual achievement, which aroused in us worry and doubts concerning the fate of the *yishuv* (Note of the author, 1936).

adherents would either have become completely alienated from Judaism or would not have dedicated themselves to it with the same devotion as they do now, imbued as they are with faith in its imminent political rebirth. Such a messianic faith is a cure for the pessimism which saps their vigor. In general, political Zionists do not have great faith in the vitality of the Jewish people. . . . Jewish history, which they never studied properly, never provided them with understanding of the deeper course of development of the Jewish people. It never imparted to them the faith—not a mystical faith, but a scientific one—in the eternity of Israel, in the indestructible power of the nation, if only it would continue to strengthen its national will through concrete institutional forms. The nationalists can say to the Zionists: "You do not believe in historical experience, and you want to serve the needs of the people only on condition that the people receive in the near future material security in the form of a territorial homeland. Serve the people here and now, as the hour demands, be it even out of illusionary hopes! The hour will come when you will understand the development of our people better . . . and then you will be members of an existing nation and not only 'of a nation of the future.' "[29] . . .

Some time ago I received a long letter from a young Zionist in which he took sharp issue with my theory of spiritual nationalism. The author, writing in the name of many other friends who share his views, closes his letter with the following declaration of principles: "(1) I believe in the existence of the Jewish nation. (2) I find that it is faced with the grave danger of disintegration, and that this process of disintegration began from the moment the Jews left the walls of the ghetto. (3) The Jewish nation can only be saved by a common effort which draws strength and enthusiasm from the source of its ideas. (4) I see such an effort in the realization of the Zionist idea."

The reply which I sent to my opponent may serve as an answer to many of the Zionist youth of our time. Here are some excerpts from my letter:

. . . I learn from your letter, which is full of deep insight, that you and your friends consider the Jewish intelligentsia doomed to total national degeneration unless it embraces the Zionist doctrine. In your

critique (the like of which I read and hear almost every day) I hear the cry of our confused intelligentsia: "Do not deprive us of our last refuge, of the force which spurs on our national effort and which we owe to Zionism!" My friends, we are not that cruel to take away the crutch from one who cannot stand firmly on his feet. I consider it erroneous to maintain that the Jewish community would have ceased to be concerned with national affairs had Zionism not come to its aid. . . . Resurgence and decline of national energy alternate in Jewish history. The most recent resurgence would have saved the wavering Jewish intelligentsia even without that special expression of the national movement which is called Zionism. You and your friends, however, take the opposite view. . . . This is sad from the standpoint of absolute truth but encouraging from the standpoint of practical usefulness, in that even those among us who "worship idols" are nevertheless serving the national cause and are devoting themselves to their people. Gradually, perhaps, the Zionists will advance from the lower material forms of national service to its loftier national forms. Then the true idea of nationalism, which is the outstanding and more original characteristic of Judaism, will triumph.

Thus I consider it better for people who can identify themselves with Judaism only through the ideal of a "Jewish state" to enter the ranks of the Zionists than to remain in the camp of the assimilationists. Do not forget, however, that extreme Zionism of this kind may inflict damage if bitter realities fail to come up to glowing hopes. . . . One must take into account what will happen to the group of Zionists if the hope that influences their spirit is ever dissipated by unforeseen deceit or turned into empty messianism. What will happen if the dissipation of the dream brings with it also the destruction of the national idea bound to it and nothing remains in the soul but terrifying emptiness? Zionism will be useful if it will serve as a transition to a higher world view, to spiritual nationalism, the fruit of the development of generations of Judaism. Only in this form, as a temporary factor, do I recognize the merit of the existence of Zionism among special groups in the community. . . .[30]

1898 (1907).

Seventh Letter

THE JEWISH NATIONALITY NOW AND IN THE FUTURE

I. The Jewish nationality as one that was, is and shall be.—The assimilationists reject the nationality in the present, the autonomists accept it, and the Zionists waver.—The internal contradiction in Zionism: the defamation of the image of the "present-day nationality" in order to glorify its future.—The variations in Nordau: his attack upon the non-Zionists as "clinging to a life that is lacking in honor and ideals;" passive opposition and power of martyrdom; Byron and Nordau.—The danger of fantasy in Zionism; burning bridges before the time.

II. Is the strengthening of the nationality in the Diaspora fantastic? —The ideas of Lilienblum.—National cultural autonomy is within the range of possibility.—The ideas of Ahad Ha-Am.—The answer of political reality which creates the need for cultural autonomy and the guarantee of minority rights.—The vicious circle of spiritual Zionism. —The way of true development: the nationality as an unending chain of past, present and future.

I

If we were to formulate in a few words the basic differences among the ideologies that now dominate the Jewish community, I would suggest the following simple formulation. The assimilationists view Judaism only as a nation of the past, a "nation that was." In their opinion the national existence of Jewry ceased with the destruction of the Kingdom of Judah, after which the nation was turned into several religious groups scattered through the world. The political Zionists look upon Jewry as a nation that is to be in the future: they strive to create a territorial center and, in the future, also a "Jewish state," without which the Jews, in their opinion, are only a fragmentary and abnormal nationality. The autonomists recognize Jewry, not only as a nation of the past or of the future, but also as a nation that is, of the present, which has never ceased to exist and which will never cease to exist in time to come.

On the central problem of Jewry as "a nation of the present," both assimilationists and autonomists have a clear opinion. The former deny it completely; the latter affirm it completely. Such is not the case with the Zionists. Among them there is great divergence on this issue, from the one extreme of nationalism to the other extreme of assimilation. The reason for these differences is inherent in the very ideology of Zionism, which suffers from an inner contradiction, an antinomy. On the one hand, Zionism, as a national movement, must work against assimilation and demonstrate that the Jews of the Diaspora have not become sects of a religion, but have retained all the typical characteristics of a united nationality. On the other hand, however, the fundamental idea of Zionism, that only political or territorial reconstruction can save Jewry from destruction, makes it necessary for the Zionist party functionaries and propagandists to deny the national character of the Diaspora. In their eagerness to emphasize the terrors and misfortunes of the Diaspora, they refer to the Jewish dispersion as a "herd" or as wretched fragments of a nation that are merely the raw materials out of which a nation will be built in the future. In their fanatical negation of the national character of the Diaspora, many of them even approximate the opposite pole of assimilation.

The tragic dualism in the soul of the orthodox Zionist is indeed unfortunate; but one must condemn the tactics of those "political" Zionists who belittle the "nation that is" in order to advance and glorify the "nation that is to be." . . . Such tactics are seized upon by many influential leaders of the Zionist organization in the west—men who had been uprooted from Judaism for a long time and who returned to it in our time with the tablets of the covenant of political Zionism. The waves of antisemitism swept them onto the shores of Judaism and here they stand frightened and crying with alarm: "Our last refuge is a Jewish state!" From their former assimilationist environment the impression persists among them that Judaism is moribund and from the distance they look upon their eastern brethren as upon a rabble of little value that still needs to "be made into a nation." From among these converts to Zionism we frequently hear words and declarations which falsify either our historical perspective or the conception of contemporary national Judaism.

The political speeches and essays of Max Nordau, one of the more spirited and talented leaders, may serve as excellent examples of this state of mind. In the speech he made to the First Zionist Congress at Basle and which I analyzed in the preceding Letter, Nordau criticized the present state of affairs without showing how and by what means to order the new regime. In the negative part of his speech we can still find some power of conviction. But in his subsequent speeches and essays, in which he outlines his positive ideals, he betrays his total lack of preparation. The paradoxicality of the author of *Paradoxes* is here revealed. The more we read of Nordau's written and oratorical improvisations the more we realize that his positive ideal is vague and full of contradictions. At one point he states that the belief in the coming of the messiah was a source of salvation for the Jews until our own times because it represented a faith in the future, an eschatological ideal. Since the principal failing of practical ideals comes when they are realized, "Jews need not fear this danger" as long as the messianic ideal, "which is as distant from us as the stars in heaven and as eternal as the days of the heaven above the earth, continues to live." On another occasion, however, he says that "the existence of Judaism is threatened by an immeasurable danger," and that Judaism will disappear from the world if existing conditions are not changed. "The educated," he says, "will leave and the uneducated will perish." He concludes his propaganda tirade with the cry: "My final word is: Judaism will either be Zionist or not be at all."

Even this emotional outburst is not the last word of the spirited Nordau. Six months later the skeptic in him is once again aroused and the following words escape him:

Let us assume that the impossible will happen, that Turkey and the other governments will tell us: "We open the doors of Palestine to you; come, take possession of your ancient homeland and cultivate it." I am in doubt that we would be able even then to accept this precious gift from their hands. We are not able, nor have we the right to do so, because we are not yet ready for the kind of economic and political regime which prevails in a well-organized state today. The Jewish nationality is not yet prepared to govern itself in freedom and to fulfill all the economic, political, and spiritual tasks of a well-ordered nation which stands on its own feet.

The author deduces from this premise that the Jews must first prepare themselves for their new life, that they must educate themselves anew, and he proclaims that this task of a new self-education is worthy of greater attention than the first task of acquiring Palestine. Here Nordau is converted from a political into a spiritual Zionist. Within a few months, however, the idea of the "negation of the Diaspora," in its extreme form captures his heart once again. This latest about-face of the leader of the party clearly reveals to us the nature of political Zionism, and it is worthwhile to discuss it in greater detail.

The new divine revelation of the leader was caused by an "Open Letter to Nordau" that was published in a Hebrew monthly.*

You say [*the author . . . writes, addressing* Nordau *and the western Zionists*] *that all those who oppose Zionism are estranged from Judaism or hate it. . . . You forget that in eastern Europe there are a large number of Jews who have always derived and still derive their national consciousness from the depths of their souls. And it is precisely these very Jews who also oppose Zionism, although they strive with all their soul and might to preserve the Jewish nationality. Their opposition comes from within. They do not want to make the existence of the nation dependent on so shaky and doubtful an ideal as the establishment of the Jewish state. We are Jews, and the existence of Judaism is more precious to us than anything else. We are, of course, bent on improving our existence, but if we do not succeed we shall be content with the mere fact of existence. A live dog is better than a dead lion. . . . To live, come what may, and be it even a shameful and servile life—this was the aim that stood before us during all our history. Western Zionism, giving us hope for a new and peaceful life, robs us of the opportunity to make peace with our burdensome life.*

The innocent author of this "Open Letter" expressed such a degree of self-abasement in his last lines that any one familiar with history could tell him emphatically: You are slandering the Jewish nation! Never and at no time was it the Jewish ideal to be "a live dog" and

* *Hashiloah*, vol. x (1898), pp. 377-81.

"to live, come what may, be it even a servile life." Our people, even when it was oppressed externally, was always internally free because it considered itself superior to all its oppressors and persecutors. "To make peace with a life of oppression," in any event, is not one of the attributes of modern Judaism. Nordau, however, took all these "lowly words" as a true description of the feeling of the people and in his answer berates, not the author who had entered into the discussion with him, but all non-Zionist Jews.

I have nothing to do with a Jew [he declares] *who merely wants to live, whether it be as a slave, or as a dog, provided he lives. . . . Do you want to live, just to live, without hope, without ideals, without a future, without a goal? If so, there is no more foolish path than the one you have selected. You will most certainly not live the life of either a slave or a dog, but will perish, because every sensible Jew who has had a taste of the enlightenment will immediately turn his back on a Judaism that lives the life of slaves and dogs, without a future, without purpose and without hope. If he knows Latin he will blush on reading the lines by Juvenal:* Et propter vitam vivendi perdere causas (*"To lose the purpose of life for the sake of living"*). *And if he understands German, he will feel ashamed on reading Schiller's line:* Das Leben ist der Güter höchstes nicht (*"Life is not the highest good"*). *He will look with disgust at you, cowards, who cling with all your strength to a life devoid of honor and ideals, if he compares you with other nations who value life only for the sake of its spiritual and moral purpose.*

. . . Nordau thus brands as slaves the whole Jewish people, except for its Zionist section. Only in the heat of partisan propaganda could he have allowed himself to say that "Jews cling with all their strength to a life devoid of honor and ideals," while "other nations value life only for the sake of its spiritual and moral purpose." This paradox surpasses all that the author of *Paradoxes* has ever said. Is it really possible to accuse a fugitive and wandering people—which repeatedly has suffered martyrdom, which still fights for its eternal ideal and for the honor of its flag with a moral heroism which has no match in the history of man—of lack of ideals and a sense of honor? . . . Or does Nordau find a sense of honor and spiritual content only among peoples that conquered territories and gained power in mighty empires, armed from head to foot? . . . If so, hail to the victors and woe to the vanquished! . . . When have they begun to call one a slave because he suffered from the oppression of strangers? A slave is a man who has been deprived of his sense of moral freedom, but not one who suffers persecution and punishment for the sake of this freedom, that is, who resists his oppressors, be it even by passive resistance. Surely, active resistance is better than resistance by suffering. But when you have no choice, when you are faced with a powerful enemy, even passive resistance is an expression of supreme daring and even suffering is heroism, because they prepare the soil for the active struggle of future generations. . . . Nordau forgot the noble lines of Byron's *Hebrew Melodies:*

> Were my bosom as false as thou deem'st it to be,
> I need not have wander'd from far Galilee;
> It was but abjuring my creed to efface
> The curse which, thou say'st, is the crime of my race.

. . . Political Zionism not only lowers the moral content of our national idea, but is also dangerous in a practical way in that it weakens the psychic forces in the struggle for existence by our people. Imagine a powerful family that has become impoverished, living a life of poverty and oppression, exposed to indignities at the hands of its rich neighbors. It supports itself with difficulty through manual labor and hopes for better days. Despite its great want, however, it treasures its sense of honor and its consciousness of its spiritual heritage. Then, clever salesmen come to this family, sell it a lottery ticket and confuse it by promising that the family will soon become rich again. At first, the unfortunate ones are elated; they hope; they take courage and wait. Every day members of the family sit and plan the lives they will lead, once the great prize is won in the lottery. Then the day of the drawing arrives. The poor people do not win a cent. There is grief and sorrow in the house and black despair in their hearts. Since they had become used to imagining a rich and easy life for themselves, they begin to look with contempt upon their oppressive poverty. They now grow tired of their burdensome life, since their cares had formerly been sweetened by pleasures of the spirit. Their material cares remain the same, but their purity of soul has passed and gone and has left only the terrible, bitter emptiness of despair in their souls.

Do not the political Zionists realize that exaggerated hopes are liable to reduce the masses of the people to such a state? They kindle in the hearts of the people hopes for the acquisition of a free territory in Eretz Yisrael and for a new political life, and thus for the moment lift up the spirits. At the same time, they plant in their hearts contempt for the concrete means of the immediate struggle for existence. They burn the bridges behind them before they have reached the other shore. And what will happen when the terrible hour of disillusioned hope arrives? The people will not achieve their redemption suddenly through miracles, and meanwhile the political Zionists will succeed in rooting in their souls a feeling of scorn for the persistent activity needed for the slow and continuous redemption in the countries in which they live. Do our miracle-working saviors understand what it will mean if an important part of our nation becomes dominated by aversion to life (*taedium vitae*)? . . .

II

Is there any basis for our work, which looks to the national organization of Jewry in the Diaspora? The political Zionists, who accuse others of their own sin, charge the proponents of autonomy with being utopians. . . . M. L. Lilienblum, one of the founders of the "Love of Zion" movement and who was attracted later by political Zionism, reviews my theories in a Russian pamphlet "Love of Zion, Zionism and Their Enemies" (Odessa, 1899). Lilienblum criticizes my basic idea, that Jews must fight for their national rights in the dispersion, in the following harsh words: "Dubnow is an even greater dreamer than is, in his opinion, the founder of the modern form of Zionism. If the idea of establishing an independent Jewish state in the near future be fantastic, it is nowhere near as ridiculous as the hopes that the Jews who are dispersed in many countries will finally be given the right to a free inner development, in the sense of national freedom, as demanded by the Czechs, the Irish and others." Thus my own argument that Zionism creates fantastic plans is now turned against me.

Such opposition is understandable when it comes from the Zionists. Men whose hope for progress in history has been disappointed and who hear nothing in all of world history but the one shattering cry: "Woe to the vanquished!" can only ridicule the idea of national rights for Jews in the Diaspora. Men suffering from historical myopia burden the future generations with the conditions of the period in which they themselves live. However, although the systematic oppression of national minorities by states in our own time has not yet ceased, it does not necessarily follow that such oppressive government will endure forever.

In the Middle Ages and later, in the period of the Reformation and of the wars of religion, the cruel regime of religious oppression was in force and it drenched the soil of Europe with streams of blood. There are few places today where such a regime is still retained. We see the same thing in connection with nationality. Current "political science" requires the Prussians to crush Polish nationalism in the province of Posen, the Austrian Germans to fight the extension of national autonomy for the Slavs, the Russian government to oppress the Poles, the Ukrainians, the Jews. . . . But we are now also beginning to realize how ineffective such rule of force is. The more the majority nationality tries to swallow up and assimilate the minority the greater the resistance of the minority in defense of its own originality, its language, its customs, its schools, its self-government.

Such a struggle introduces chaos into the political life of a multinational state; the destruction and disarray following in its wake prove that the time is near when the theory of oppressing minorities will be totally repudiated, since it endangers the existence and integrity of the state. . . . Not only the sense of equity and justice, but also practical considerations will develop which will call for war against the principle that "peoples are wolves to each other" within the borders of one state. In the same way that enlightened countries came to recognize that only a free citizen can be a loyal and useful member of the community, so the realization will slowly come that, in a state composed of different nationalities, a nationality enjoying internal autonomy is a stronger support for the commonwealth than a suppressed nationality made restless by constant oppression. The function of a "ruling nationality" in the state will be relegated to the same position occupied today by a "ruling Church" in a free state. This is not just a myth, but a historical necessity based on the development of legal and political science. It is upon this historical necessity that I base my hope that the struggle of the Jews for their national rights will succeed. . . .

The same arguments can also serve as an answer to the creator of "spiritual Zionism," Ahad Ha-Am, who has a deeper understanding of the positive nature of our national question than the creator of "Love of Zion." Ahad Ha-Am and I share a common philosophical-historical view of assimilation and of the shortcomings in the development of nineteenth century western Judaism.* We are also close to each other in our negative attitude toward the experiments of political or diplomatic Zionism, because we both adhere to the scientific, evolutionary view of history which does not recognize revolutionary upheavals outside of the course of nature. Although we differ in our evaluation of the influence which the spiritual center in Palestine will have on the Diaspora in the future, we agree that even after the establishment of such a center the majority of the nation will remain in the dispersion. This leads to the simple conclusion (at which Ahad Ha-Am must also arrive if he follows right reason) that the Diaspora must always strive to obtain a definite minimum of those national rights whose maximum, in my opinion, will eventually be reached only in the Palestinian center. However, at this point, right reasoning

* This view was put forward with unusual lucidity in Ahad Ha-Am's essay "Slavery in Freedom" (1891) and clarified in one of my *Letters*. In a note to his essay, as well as in a second essay (see the following footnote), Ahad Ha-Am stated that "Slavery in Freedom" appeared as an answer to my essay "The Eternal and Imaginary Ideals of Judaism" (*Voskhod*, no. 12, 1890). While I gladly acknowledge Ahad Ha-Am's superiority in his precise description of assimilation as moral slavery, I must state that, in view of the very nature of this idea, "Slavery in Freedom," was not an adequate answer to my "Eternal Ideals." I did not touch expressly upon the question of assimilation in my small bibliographical note, but pointed merely to the spiritual ideals latent in the western idea of the "mission of Israel." In opposition to Ahad Ha-Am I believe that the idea of the "mission of Israel" was a kind of unconscious nationalism for the best Jewish scholars in the west.

fails the publicist-philosopher whose thought is generally distinguished by clarity and unusual systematic rigor. In his essay on my second Letter, Ahad Ha-Am makes an effort to prove that the doctrine of national rights in the Diaspora is only a transition stage to Zionism, since the advocates of this theory will learn by bitter experience that national rights cannot be realized outside of the land of Israel. Here are his words:*

Psychological necessity is one thing, but logic and reality are another. The Jews still lift up their heads with pride and proclaim to their neighbors: "We are an ancient cultural nationality, we have the same historic rights in Europe that you have, and, therefore, we have the right to demand that you honor our national characteristics and give us the opportunity to live in your midst a separate national life in the same way you do. Give us our national rights! The people of these countries will be irritated or will laugh, but they will not accord us national rights in their midst. The reason why Jews succeeded in getting civic rights in most European countries was only because they promised to amalgamate with these peoples and to become of "one flesh" with them in the future. But national rights—this no one will doubt who does not place his fancy above reality—they will not obtain in their midst. And not only at present, when every ruling nationality strives to make its nationalism the basis of the entire life of the state, but even "at the end of days," when the trend of thought and feeling will be changed everywhere, so that the ruling nationalities will recognize the rights of others and will allow them to develop their national life according to their own will without in the least attempting to force them to assimilate, even then you will not find one nationality in Europe which will also recognize the national rights of the Jews who live among it. Proof of this can be seen in the fact that the very Poles and Czechs, who demand national rights from their common state in the name of justice, think they have the right to ask the Jews who live among them to merge with them and to surrender themselves to Polish or Czech nationalism. . . .

Even if we went still further and extended our imagination to the belief that "in the messianic era" the Jews, too, will be considered by the other nations as a separate nationality with its national rights in

* "Beshalosh madregot," in *Al perashat derakhim* (Berlin, 1903), vol. ii.

all countries, even then this will not be enough to satisfy the needs of our national life. For even justice and equity, in the name of which the weak demands his rights from the stronger, surely will never oblige the strong to yield his own rights where they clash with the rights of the weak and where it is impossible for both to exist together. No other rights are as liable to conflict and opposition as the national rights of two nationalities that live together, not side by side, as in the cantons of Switzerland, but one inside the other, as in some Austrian provinces. In all the more important affairs in the life of the state—the educational systems, the laws and customs of society, language, science, etc.—it is impossible for different nationalities to rule at the same time, for each to infuse its own spirit into them and for the aspirations of all to be satisfied indiscriminately. All such matters, therefore, are decided by the spirit of the majority and this is both necessary and just [?] and the minority must accept the verdict without complaint, in the same way that this rule prevails in a conflict of civic rights of individual citizens. Since we are in the minority among all peoples everywhere, what right do we have to hope that the day will come when we will be able to live a full national life in Europe? . . . And if so, how can these two opposites be reconciled: on one side, full participation in the cultural life which, in each country, takes on the national form of the dominant nationality, and on the other side, the full development of our own unique national life suspended in mid-air and without any support?

For this reason, I am inclined to believe that this doctrine of national rights is merely one of the intermediate steps in the ladder of the future development of our national idea, a step through which the inner consciousness of the people will pass in order finally to reach through it the end of the idea. For, indeed, the advocates of national rights, which cannot be obtained in the Diaspora, must inevitably come to see that there is only one national right which will satisfy the needs of our cultural national life, without which we will never reach our final goal. This right is: that we, too, will be the "majority" in one country under the heavens, a country where our historical right is not in doubt and does not need far-fetched proofs, and in whose historical atmosphere our national life will truly develop in keeping with our spirit, without diminution and reduction in any limited spheres. Then there will be hope also for the rest of our people scattered in other countries, for the national center will radiate its spirit and give them *strength to live by its life, even though they lack national rights where they live.*

In the previous Letters, the reader will find a chain of ideas and practical demonstrations that weaken Ahad Ha-Am's arguments. These arguments are in accordance neither with the principles of the *Rechtsstaat* nor with the political experience of many countries. Freedom of self-determination and regional or cultural autonomy for national minorities in multi-national states are accepted as established principles in political science. This principle is often, although not everywhere, violated in practice; but we have no right to assume that in our time "every ruling nationality strives to make its nationalism the basis of the entire life of the state." We know that, while reactionary Prussia oppresses Polish culture in Posen, the Austrian government has already given up the Germanization of Galicia and is offering regional and cultural autonomy to the Poles there.

I am astonished at the very way in which Ahad Ha-Am poses the problem, when he sees a "necessity" or even a measure of "justice" in the fact that in every country "cultural life takes on the national form of the dominant nationality." Does Ahad Ha-Am find such a condition normal and healthy, does he not know that there is no cultural nationality in the world which will not defend itself and resist the majority nationality which comes to obliterate its features? Do the Ruthenians not fight against the pressure brought to bear upon them by the Poles in Galicia; have they not succeeded in reaching many of their goals of autonomy, and do they not believe in their complete victory in the future? It is unscientific and unrealistic to believe that "in all the more important affairs in the life of the state . . . it is impossible for different nationalities to rule at the same time, for each to infuse its own spirit into them, and for the aspirations of all to be satisfied indiscriminately." At the same time, Ahad Ha-Am includes in these affairs of the state, together with "the laws and customs of society" also the educational system, language, science, and the like. In constitutional countries the laws are made by the national representatives of all nationalities living in the state, and, therefore, legislation is not the fruit of one "spirit" or the fruit of like-minded currents, but rather a compromise between different currents of different nationalities.

In countries in which all the subject nationalities together exceed in numbers the "dominant" nationality (as, for example, in Austria), or where they fight for their demands with singular persistence, the rulers must grant them territorial or cultural autonomy, especially in the areas of education and language. . . . The task of the *Rechtsstaat* is not to establish one "spirit" or "current" in power, but to establish a balance among all the conflicting currents and interests of its national groups. As long as this balance is not achieved, the national war of liberation will not cease in the state. After a prolonged struggle the national majority will be forced to pacify the minorities through concessions and compromises. For autonomy and the guarantee of cultural independence for national minorities are necessary conditions for the very existence of multi-national commonwealths.

Here, Ahad Ha-Am adduces still another argument. Even if all other peoples should realize their ideal of autonomy, the Jews will be unable to achieve it because they do not live *alongside* of other nationalities but in their very midst. Such an argument would be valid if the Jews were the only "nation among nations" in the world. In fact, however, there are numerous instances of small nationalities or parts of larger nationalities that are found as national minorities in different countries. (Germans among Czechs in various districts of Bohemia; Germans in Galicia; Rumanians in Hungary; Poles in Lithuania; Lithuanians in Russian Poland; "Great Russians" in the Ukraine.) Will all these minorities agree to the extinction of their national characteristics? Almost all the nationalities of a composite state are interested in this matter, including the "ruling" nationality, because it, too, constitutes a minority in the autonomous census districts. And if the rights of each national minority will have to be guaranteed by common public law in various forms, the Jews will also not be deprived of their share, if, obviously, the Jews fight with unceasing perseverance for their national-cultural freedom in the areas of communal self-administration, education and language.*

* I would like to think that if Ahad Ha-Am were writing on the question of national autonomy today, when this question has been clarified not only theoretically but also practically, he would not publish much of what he wrote in the above-mentioned essay nine years ago, in 1898. (Much less now, after the World War, when national minority rights have been guaranteed by national and international law. Note of 1929.)[31]

When the orthodox political Zionists refuse to believe in the possibility of obtaining "national rights" in the Diaspora, they are true to their system. They do not believe in gradual historical development, but strive to put an end to the "Jewish question" by revolution and through the creation of a utopian "state of the future." If an evolutionist, however, such as the founder of spiritual Zionism, expresses such an opinion, there is some inconsistency. He himself does not rely on sudden upheavals. On many occasions he has stated his belief that the expansion of national culture in the Diaspora, and the spiritual advancement and preparation of the people, are necessary for the creation of a spiritual center in Eretz Yisrael. Can this only be accomplished by striving for Zion, the spiritual center of the future? And if such a center has been established, who will guarantee that the Palestine section of Jewry will attain to the powerful influence on the whole Diaspora that Ahad Ha-Am predicts? If he assumes that the majority of the Jews will remain in Europe and America and that only a minority will be in Palestine, can he guarantee that this minority will be the chief cultural center of Judaism? What makes him so sure that Palestinian culture will direct Jewish culture elsewhere and will not itself be influenced by the latter, . . . that is, that, as the nation develops, it will bring about a reciprocal influence of the centers?

I agree with the idea that the handful of Jews in Eretz Yisrael will live a fuller national life than those in the Diaspora, and I look forward to this rebirth with joy. But I am also worried about the lot of the great remnant of Israel in the Diaspora. Perhaps the land of Israel might be converted into a Noah's Ark in which only a portion of Jewry will be saved from the great world flood while the rest sink in its waves? There surely is no place in the program of the cultural Zionists for such a devastating verdict on the Diaspora.

"The national center in Palestine," says Ahad Ha-Am, "will radiate its spirit [upon the Jews of the Diaspora] and give them strength to live by its life, even though they lack national rights where they live." Is this a practical ideal, in keeping with the evolutionary process? Out of what kind of human material do they propose to build the Palestinian center if they do not prepare this material in a national spirit in the Diaspora? And how can they preserve and develop the national spirit here without national rights—communal autonomy, language and the school? But let us assume that the center has already been established on the shores of the Jordan and that it has a magic effect on all parts of the dispersion. What is the nature of this effect? It strengthens the national spirit and the national culture in the Diaspora, that is, the will to protect them through appropriate provisions in the law of the land. You, however, decide that it is impossible for the Jews in the Diaspora to obtain national rights. Does it follow then that the stimulation which the Palestinian center will give to the Diaspora will remain without results, that it will lead to despair if the national spiritual aims are not realized in the form of concrete rights, and if its will and enthusiasm remain outside the bounds of realization? This vicious circle is tragic for cultural Zionism: it either cannot be realized, or else there will be no need for its realization.

No, if you want to save evolutionary Zionism you will have to place the principle of striving for national rights in the Diaspora at the head of your program. You must realize that this striving is necessary to prepare for the building of a spiritual center in Palestine and for the strengthening of centers outside of Palestine. In order to justify the unique idea of Zionism, you have the right to maintain that that part of the nation which will live in our historic land will realize its national rights to a greater degree, but you cannot reject the principle of national rights for the Diaspora without violating the very foundation on which you stand. . . .

We, proponents of autonomism, do not wish to break the chain that unites the nation's present with its future, just as we do not separate both of these from the nation's past. We are true evolutionists and our strength lies in our recognition of the natural process of historical development and a faith in the power of the national will that is revealed in the history of our people. The strengthening of this will, the deepening of this recognition and the striving for civil and national freedom for our people in all the lands of the dispersion—all these are well within the realm of possibility and actuality. The very striving for this is a clear sign of the beginnings of an inner rebirth.[32]

1899 (1907).

Eighth Letter

THE AFFIRMATION OF THE DIASPORA

(*A Reply to Ahad Ha-Am's "Negation of the Diaspora"*)

I have a long-standing controversy with a distinguished author to whom I am closer in the field of national ideology than to any other writer of our time. It is precisely this similarity of views between Ahad Ha-Am and myself that has provoked us both to clarify our points of agreement as well as our differences. As usual, in such cases, our differences were emphasized more than the views we hold in common. In Ahad Ha-Am's *Al perashat derakhim* and in my *Letters on Old and New Judaism* the readers will find numerous pages which contain dialogues carried on directly or indirectly between the authors of the two books. The clarification of the issues was not brought to a conclusion, and only now am I able to acknowledge Ahad Ha-Am's new attempt to get at the central point of our controversy and "to draw more precisely the dividing lines between the two opposing views," since perhaps "the difference between them is in truth not as great as appears at first sight." The essay from which the latter quotation was taken ("Shelilat hagalut," in *Hashiloah*, May 1909)* is written with that analytical precision which we have come to expect from Ahad Ha-Am's writings, and it affords us a good opportunity to probe more deeply into our problem.

Ahad Ha-Am's essay appeared as an answer to my criticism in the preceding Letter. The author analyzes the idea of the "negation of the Diaspora," of which the autonomists accuse the Zionists, and he distinguishes between two forms of negation, subjective and objective. "All Jews," he says, "negate the Diaspora in a subjective sense. All—except the few individuals who set themselves apart from the community—recognize that the condition of a lamb among wolves is an unhappy one, and all wish to put an end to this situation." Objective negation, however, means "to deny the possibility for our national existence in the Diaspora in future generations, now that the spiritual

* *Al perashat derakhim*, vol. iv, pp. 106-16.

wall that had been a protection to our ancestors in past generations has been destroyed and we have no other refuge from the current of foreign cultures surrounding us, a current which submerges our national characteristics and swallows up our national possessions."

Those who negate the Diaspora in this manner fall into two groups, depending on the conclusions they draw from this denial. One party holds that, if Israel cannot endure and is sure to be destroyed in the end, it is better that we ourselves hasten its end rather than wait until it comes by itself after painful suffering in a prolonged agony of death. It considers those fortunate who can assimilate at once with the Gentiles; those who cannot do so should make sure that their children will be able to assimilate. The second party holds that if this is the situation, we must put an end to our exile before it puts an end to our existence. In order to be able to exist in the future we must gather our dispersion into the land of our fathers, for there and only there will we be able to continue our national existence. Those who can and wish to assimilate should stay where they are, but "those who cannot or do not wish to assimilate" should go to the "Jewish state."

However, these two parties, Ahad Ha-Am adds, did not muster enough strength to attract the entire people.

It goes without saying [he writes] *that the party which negates both the Diaspora and national survival did not win the people over. But even the party which negates the Diaspora in order to affirm the continued existence of the nation was not able to secure the approbation of the will to survive in the heart of the nation. For survival cannot be made dependent on any condition, since the condition may not be fulfilled. The Jewish people as a whole feel that they have the will and the strength to survive whatever may happen, without any ifs or buts. Its natural instinct does not allow it to accept a theory that tells it that survival is conditional upon the ending of the Diaspora. Unconsciously it feels that this is a "double condition," and that the acceptance of the first half of the condition will lead also to the acceptance of the second half: "If the attempt to leave the Diaspora does not succeed, you will certainly die."*

For this reason the people as a whole "negate the Diaspora in a subjective sense but affirm it in an objective sense." The Diaspora is a very bad thing, but we shall have to live in exile until the "end of days," which is unknown and hidden from view. But here the question arises: How can we live in the Diaspora if we want to preserve ourselves as a people? The will to survive forced our people to surround itself with walls which were intended to shield it against annihilation and destruction by the alien environment. Now the old walls are crumbling before our eyes. What new walls will be erected in their place? To this, the autonomists answer: national autonomy! The next question is: To what degree? Do the nationalists view autonomy as a guaranty of a full and unimpaired life in the Diaspora, or are they satisfied with a minimum, with what it will be possible to obtain? Two things are necessary for a full national life, ability and will, but to a large degree will depends upon ability. The strengthening of the national will is not enough to preserve the nation when external conditions continually weaken this will. From this Ahad Ha-Am draws the conclusion that the autonomists also do not consider autonomy to be a source of a full and unimpaired national life in the Diaspora and that they fight for national rights only in order to secure our national life "within the limits of the possible," even though these limits will be too narrow to encompass the free development of Jewish culture.

In the opinion of Ahad Ha-Am, no national Jew can object to autonomy if it is given this "emasculated" form. The more extreme nationalists who consider national rights in the Diaspora insufficient can extend the "realm of the possible" beyond the Diaspora and seek for guarantees of a full national life outside of it. "If this [autonomist] doctrine concedes," Ahad Ha-Am says, "that autonomy is not a complete solution, but rather that we must try to attain it on the principle that 'half a loaf is better than none,' then it must also concede that we have the duty to look for still other, more 'radical,' ways to strengthen our nationalism and to expand our national life on the other principle that 'a whole loaf is better than half a loaf.' . . ." This radical cure Ahad Ha-Am sees in his doctrine of a spiritual center.

"The proponents of autonomy know," Ahad Ha-Am continues, "that for the past twenty years one Zionist group has existed among us which has answered the question as follows: The new wall for our national life in the exile must be built outside of the exile, in the land of our fathers. This group differs from the 'true' Zionists in that it does not believe in an ingathering of the exiles and does not 'deny' survival in the Diaspora. On the contrary, since it sees the exile as a permanent phenomenon which we cannot eliminate, it strives to give strength and force to our national life in the exile. But it maintains that the only way whereby this can be secured is to create a permanent center for our nationality in the place of its natural existence." Ahad Ha-Am is convinced that if the autonomists were asked whether it is possible to obtain full autonomy in the Diaspora, they would answer in the negative. Then, he writes, "They, too, will be forced to turn their eyes toward the East and to give to their doctrine a new formulation: Hold on to one thing, and do not withdraw your hand from the other! We must improve and expand our national life in the Diaspora to the utmost limits of the possible and, at the same time, search for the 'complete solution' beyond the borders of the Diaspora."

I have taken pains to present carefully the main content of Ahad Ha-Am's essay, using mostly his own words and refraining from interrupting his argument with critical remarks of my own. I shall now present the matter in the same order which my opponent used to arrange his views. I accept, first of all, the distinction he makes between the two groups who negate the Diaspora in the "objective" sense: assimilationists who deny both the Diaspora and nationalism, and Zionists who deny the exile in order to affirm their nationalism. This coincides with my idea of the two poles of assimilation and Zionism uniting in one proposition: whoever has the opportunity should save himself! It is also good to hear that the creator of spiritual Zionism has this time drawn a sharper line between himself and those Zionists whom I called "conditional nationalists." The autonomists and the spiritual Zionists thus stand together against those who completely negate the Diaspora. Both of us affirm the Diaspora. In what way do we affirm it? I agree with Ahad Ha-Am that it is not in the subjective sense of recognizing the good and the blessings of being in exile. It is self-evident that if we had the power to transfer the entire Diaspora to a Jewish state we would do it with the greatest joy. We acquiesce in the Diaspora only because of historical necessity and we strive to preserve and develop the national existence of the greater part of the nation which will remain there.

Up to this point we are in complete agreement with the spiritual Zionists in our "affirmation of the Diaspora." Differences of opinion between us begin beyond this area, with the answer to the question: how can we secure our national existence in the Diaspora? The answer to this question is contained in two propositions: (1) "A spiritual center in the land of Israel which will serve as a national point of attraction for the Diaspora"; (2) "Striving for national rights or cultural autonomy in the Diaspora." Now we must make clear whether these two propositions are really contradictory to each other, or whether it is possible to affirm them both. Is it sufficient, in order to affirm our national existence in the Diaspora, to realize one of these propositions, or is the interaction of both necessary? Here begins my controversy with Ahad Ha-Am.

Each of us finds the doctrine of his opponent inadequate, but each of us does it in his own way. Ahad Ha-Am seeks clarification from the proponents of autonomy on the question whether they consider autonomy in the Diaspora to be a complete solution of the national question or whether they are satisfied with it as the best solution under the circumstances. I am glad to clarify the point. We all recognize the tragic aspects of the Diaspora and we cannot hope to achieve in the Diaspora as full and complete national-cultural development as is possible for a nation living in its own independent state. And although we have no hope that such a state can be established in the land of Israel, we trust nevertheless that an autonomous Jewish center can be created there and that its national culture will be purer than that of the Diaspora. Nonetheless we repeat: in the Diaspora we must strive, within the realm of the possible, to demand and to attain national-cultural autonomy for the majority of the nation. In the land of Israel we will achieve it only for a minority of the nation which, at present, is insignificant but which can greatly increase in the future. In order to strengthen the Diaspora we will use the weapons of national struggle which served us for thousands of years and which are adapted to the world view of our time. You ask what wall we shall erect in place of the fallen ghetto walls? Every period has its own architecture, and the powerful vital instinct will unmistakably tell the people what style to use for building the wall of national autonomy which will replace the former religious "fence to the fence,"[33] and will not at the same time shut out the flow of world culture. In any event, those who do not negate the Diaspora have no alternative but to direct their efforts toward building up the Diaspora on the basis of autonomy. The spiritual center in the land of Israel, while exerting a force of its own for a minority, will serve the majority only as one of the factors in the strengthening of our people.

Now that we on our side have provided a definite answer to Ahad Ha-Am's questions, we may allow ourselves to pose a few questions to the spiritual Zionists. Do they believe that the cultural center in the land of Israel will muster enough strength by itself to provide the entire large Diaspora with all the national energies necessary for revitalizing the Diaspora and for securing its autonomous organization? Furthermore, how do they visualize the manifestation of these energies: in the form of a passive acceptance of the national ideals emanating from the land of Israel, or in the form of an unceasing effort to realize our national rights in all the lands of the Diaspora?

If Ahad Ha-Am were to answer the first question in the affirmative, he would align himself with the group that negates the Diaspora and with the "conditional nationalists," those from whom he had completely disassociated himself for proper reasons and motives. If he makes the national existence of the Diaspora entirely dependent on the attractive force of the Palestinian center, he must come to the conclusion that no Jewish nationality is possible without the spiritual center in the land of Israel, that is, he would repeat the mistake of the Herzlian Zionists who say that "Judaism cannot exist without a Jewish state," a mistake which Ahad Ha-Am himself has condemned. We are thus entitled to think that spiritual Zionism sees in the revival of a spiritual center in the Land of Israel, not the only, but rather the chief moving force for the Diaspora. The Diaspora will combine the energy coming from the outside with its own internal forces and use them as weapons in the fight for its national survival.

This leads us to the second question: what form will this struggle for existence assume in the Diaspora? It is clear that it is possible only in the form of the insistent demand for national rights and cultural autonomy within the limits to which they can be obtained in each separate state. On this matter the spiritual Zionists should have reached a general agreement with the proponents of autonomy. Just at this point, however, Ahad Ha-Am stands at the crossroads and does not give his final word. On the contrary, he tries in various ways to weaken the hope for the attainment of even a modified national-cultural autonomy in the Diaspora. He repeatedly protests against the methods of our efforts in this field and casts doubts on the possibility of realizing our goal. Thus we are faced with a baffling puzzle. When the Palestinian center is established, what practical methods does Ahad Ha-Am think possible to defend the national existence of the Diaspora, which he does not reject? How can the contradiction between the two sentences at the end of the above-mentioned essay be resolved: (a) "It [the party of the spiritual Zionists] sees the *only* way to it [the strengthening of the national life in the Diaspora] in the creation of a definite center for our nationality in the place of its natural existence"; (b) "We must improve and expand our national life in the Diaspora to the utmost limits of the possible and, at the same time, search for the 'final solution' beyond the borders of the Diaspora?" What "limits of the possible" does Ahad Ha-Am see beyond the battle for national rights in the Diaspora?

Again we have the vicious circle in which spiritual Zionism was caught at the beginning. The Palestinian center influences the spread of the national spirit in the Diaspora, and the nationalized Diaspora strives to transform the energy it receives from the land of Israel into activities in behalf of its national rights—communal self-government, freedom of language and education. Here, however, it is told that it is impossible to obtain national rights in the Diaspora. However, if the Diaspora cannot endure and it is destined to disintegrate, what point is there to furthering the growth of a center in Palestine? The very revival of the spiritual center in the land of Israel depends on the healthy national material which will stream into Palestine from the Diaspora; and where is this material to come from if external security for national development in the Diaspora will be lacking? If the

Diaspora cannot live a full national life without the center in Palestine, then the latter cannot possibly exist without a national Diaspora.

Only one thing can save the spiritual Zionists from the dilemma: they must recognize autonomism, or the idea of national rights in the Diaspora, extended "to the utmost limits of the possible." The difference between the land of Israel and the Diaspora will be quantitative and qualitative. In Palestine there will be a none too numerous minority of our people that will be distinguished by a richer and more complete national culture, while the Diaspora will be weaker, but will make up in quantity for what it lacks in quality. The reciprocal influence of the two centers will create the mean for the national development of Judaism.

If this is the final conclusion of spiritual Zionism, then nothing stands in the way of its amalgamation with autonomism. It is self-evident that we do not mean a formal union of parties or organizations, since these two currents together are not numerous enough to establish such organizations, but rather an amalgamation of currents of thought that have exercised indisputable influence on the world view of modern Jewry.

In concluding this essay, I should say a few words concerning one aspect of autonomism which was touched upon by Ahad Ha-Am in passing and by Dr. Pasmanik, the author of another essay in the same issue of *Hashiloah*.[34] Ahad Ha-Am thinks that, in the countries of the Diaspora, Jewish autonomy can only be realized in the low form visualized by those who admire the colloquial language, "for whom national culture exists in Yiddish literature, national education in Yiddish speech, and the national ideal on the level of the Lithuanian, Slovakian and similar nationalities." This kind of Diaspora autonomy is indeed within the realm of the possible, but it can hardly please the nationalists whose ideal rests on the foundation of the entire historical culture of many generations, who are not satisfied with the passing culture of the hour, and who refuse to impose upon the eternal people, which is richly endowed with national treasures from the beginning of time, the role of a petty and half-civilized nationality.

Dr. Pasmanik, an old Zionist, who is opposed to my theory, argues that even Yiddish as a spoken language will not save the proponents of autonomy, and he comments ironically that I have "avoided touching" upon the problem of the national language. It is not my intention, of course, that these remarks should here dispose of a problem as important as the language problem, and I shall return to it more than once or twice. And when I express my opinion on this matter, I will surely not reject our historical culture of thousands of years and substitute for it "the Yiddish culture of yesterday." Nevertheless I shall confess "my great sin" today. Among the forces which are the basis of our autonomy in the Diaspora, I also set aside a place for the powerful force of the folk language used by seven million Jews in Russia and Galicia, which for several generations now fulfills the function of a spoken language, the language of instruction in the school (the *heder* and *yeshiva*) and to an appreciable degree also a language of literature.*

Let our relation to the "Jargon" or, more correctly to Yiddish, be what it may, we dare not abandon one of the foundations of national unity in the very hour that the languages of the peoples around us rob our people of thousands and tens of thousands of its sons, so that they no longer understand the language used by their parents. We must not destroy with our own hands the power of our folk language to compete with the foreign languages, which lead to assimilation. Such destruction would amount to suicide. There being no hope of converting our ancient national tongue into the living and daily spoken language in the Diaspora, we would be committing a transgression against our national soul if we did not make use in our war against assimilation of the great counterforce stored up in the language of the people. We might then be compared to a cripple with one natural leg and one artificial leg who tossed away his artificial leg out of great esthetic enthusiasm. The Hebrew language is our natural leg, but it is only one leg, not two: the second was cut off by the exile which removed the language from living use by the masses of the people and confined it to the fields of literature, religion, and,

* In recent years Yiddish has come to occupy a central place in the literature and journalism of the Diaspora and works of Yiddish authors have been translated into several European languages.

in some measure, to education. In place of the missing leg came an artificial leg, Yiddish. On these two legs our people has stood and survived for many generations, just as in former years it stood on the linguistic dualism of Hebrew and Aramaic. Do those nationalists who affirm the Diaspora wish to remove the artificial leg, which, for some time now, has gained the strength of a natural leg, and not to use it to get a firm foothold in national life? This would mean to pronounce a verdict of instantaneous disintegration on the people if they were so unwise as to listen to such a dangerous suggestion.

When the language problem is posed in all its ramifications and when it is clarified not from the viewpoint of one party or of one literary clique or another, but from the general national viewpoint, then there will be no place for such errors in this matter. Insofar as we recognize the merit of national existence in the Diaspora, we must also recognize the merit of Yiddish as one of the instruments of autonomy, together with Hebrew and the other factors of our culture.

May 1909.

Ninth Letter

*A HISTORIC MOMENT**
(*The Question of Emigration*)

I

Once again we are witnessing events[35] which testify that the path of history is cyclical and not linear in evolution. Jewish martyrology in southern Russia has now completed a cycle of development from the massacre of Uman to the slaughter of Kishinev, from 1768 to 1903.

Twenty-two years ago we who believed in the idea of unilinear progress for the first time noted with fright and perplexity that the straight road of history had been flagrantly perverted and forced into a direction which was bringing us closer to the starting point, to the days of the past and its terrors. The circle is now closed and the starting point and end point are one again.

We have reached a new boundary line drawn for us by the decree of fate. Most of the dividing lines in our history in the Diaspora are marked with deep stains of blood. The stations we pass through, which separate one epoch from another, are saturated with the blood of our martyred saints, heroes of passive resistance. The crusades, the Inquisition, the expulsions, the bloody massacres of Khmielnitski and the Haidamacks, oppression and persecutions by the Russian government, pogroms by the masses, these are the landmarks of our history. Each of them represents a turning point on our path of suffering.

Jewish hearts still ache from the pain of the frightful pogroms that passed over us and our eyes are still dim from profusion of tears; but at the same time a new stream of energy calling for action has become evident. There is a passionate current of national spirit such as stood us in good stead generation after generation in moments of severe crisis. The latest blow we received found us better prepared psychologically than we were during the pogroms of 1881. What can we

* This essay was written following the Kishinev pogrom in 1903.

still expect after twenty-two years in which "each and every day killed a hope and a dream?" . . . The past decades have taught us that our fate depends not on our environment but on ourselves, on our will and our national effort. The new pogroms have engraved the watchword "self-help" in flaming letters on the Jewish nation. It is as if a powerful electric charge had passed through the body of our humiliated people. . . . The principles of self-help and self-defense have never been as clear to all classes of our people, from the highest to the lowest strata, as at the present moment. What is the way of self-help? This is the consuming question which has not yet received a satisfactory answer from previous history and which now emphatically demands immediate solution.

II

The last twenty years bequeathed to us two forms of national self-help: (1) energetic work in the lands of the Diaspora; (2) mass exodus from the place of danger. The first is realized through an incessant and stubborn battle to secure civic and national rights in the old centers; the second is directed at improving the condition of the various national communities by transferring them from the old centers to countries which are better suited for civic, economic and national life. To this day there is no agreement regarding these two ways among the various parties in the Jewish community. On the question of internal help opinions are divided between those who strive only for the civic and economic emancipation of the Jews among the inhabitants of the state, and those who, in addition, strive also for Jewish national-cultural rights. Great difference of opinion also exists with respect to the purpose and direction of emigration. Some recognize only an economic goal and look with equanimity at the national effects of changes in location. Others wish to concentrate the masses of emigrants in definite areas where new national-cultural centers can be established, and one party makes the emigration question dependent on the hope for political revival (Zionism). But what is the real direction of emigration in the light of facts and figures?

The year 1881 inaugurated a new epoch in the history of Jewish migration second in importance only to the migrations following the expulsion of the Jews from Spain in 1492. In the last decades a mighty historic revolution has been taking place before our eyes: the transfer of the chief center of our people. Just as four hundred years ago the center of the Jewish people was transferred from western to eastern Europe and Jewish national hegemony passed from Spain to Poland, and then to Russia, so part of our great center is now being transferred by an uninterrupted exodus from Russia to other countries. Where is the main stream of migrants going? Not to our ancient homeland, Palestine, where, in spite of all our efforts, we succeeded in bringing only 20,000 persons during the last two decades (if the urban population is added to the agricultural); not to Argentina, where only several hundred families were settled on the land at the cost of millions of dollars, but to North America, especially to the United States. Close to a million Jews left Russia during the last twenty years and nine-tenths of this number went to North America. Prior to 1880 there were about 250,000 Jews in the United States,* now there are almost a million and a half. The Jewish community in New York alone numbers more than half a million.

The exodus to America continues without interruption and with astonishing regularity. It increases when civic and economic conditions of the Jews in Russia are aggravated, and it contracts when the crisis is less severe. According to statistics the average number of Jews emigrating from Russia to North America alone reached 25,000 annually during the period 1881-1897, and 35,000 annually during the four-year period from 1898-1902.† If the number of Jewish emigrants to other countries of the world is added to this figure, we arrive at an annual total of Jewish emigration from Russia during the last years of 50,000 persons. The natural increase of the Jews in Russia is estimated at 1.5 per cent;‡ that is, the natural increase of

* *Cf.* The article "America" in *The Jewish Encyclopedia* (New York, 1901), vol. i.

† *Ibid.*, vol. i, p. 506; "Jewish Emigration to the United States," in *Voskhod* (April 1903), pp. 104, 106, 111. *Cf.* Brockhaus-Efron, *Encyclopaedia*, vol. liv, p. 105.

‡ Brockhaus-Efron, vol. liv, p. 93 (Tables of population movements in the districts of the Pale).

five million Jews in Russia reaches 75,000 per year. It, therefore, follows that at present the equivalent of two-thirds of our annual natural increase leaves Russia.

Many signs indicate that the Kishinev catastrophe and the terror in the Jewish pale which came in its wake, together with our difficult civic position, will swell the emigration for this and the following year to an unparalleled degree. If the number of migrants reached almost 100,000 in 1891 (the year of the expulsion from Moscow and of other persecutions)* it will in no event be less than this figure during the next few years. In this manner a new average of annual emigration will be established which will more than double the previous average.† When the exodus reaches 100,000, not only the natural increase (75,000) but also 25,000 more from the basic Jewish population will leave Russia. At this point emigration will turn into a partial evacuation of the old Jewish center in Poland and Russia. Emigration on such a scale can, in time, lead to a diminution of the masses of our people in the Russian ghetto, but not to a complete exodus from it. In any case, the partial transfer of our great center from eastern Europe to North America is a living and permanent fact. This transfer is the most important event in contemporary Jewish history.

III

What does the Jew ask for when he escapes from the countries of oppression to the lands overseas? Bread and freedom? No, freedom and bread! Persecuted and humiliated, a member of the oldest cultural nationality made into a despised and lowly slave, the Jew asks first of all for freedom, and only then does he want bread, even if it be only the meager bread he had in the country which he left. He asks for human rights, without which it is impossible to live, as it is without air to breathe. He asks for security of person and property,

* In that year 76,000 emigrated to the United States ("Jewish Emigration . . . ," p. 106) while many others emigrated to Palestine, Argentina, South Africa and other countries during the same period.

† The facts have justified this estimate to a larger degree than we thought. The despair and the terror which gripped the Jewish population in Russia after the Kishinev pogrom, the Russo-Japanese War, and the wave of pogroms of 1905-1906 swelled the exodus to the astonishing annual figure of 150,000-200,000.

both of which were entirely lacking in his cruel homeland. . . . If persecution and oppression induced tens of thousands of emigrants to leave the country, terror and fright will force out hundreds of thousands. . . .

The main stream of Jewish emigration is directed to North America. Smaller streams branch out into Argentina, Palestine, South Africa and, to a small degree, also to the countries of western Europe. All these lesser streams, experience shows, absorb only small parts of the main stream. Whether this is desirable or not is another question. Even one who is not a political Zionist will welcome wholeheartedly the settlement of Jews in Palestine from a national point of view. By necessity, however, this settlement will be very gradual and, even under the best possible circumstances, will not be sufficient to fill the needs of the entire emigration. South America, with its Catholic, mostly Spanish, population, arouses suspicions concerning quiet and peaceful relations between the Jewish settlers and the "original" inhabitants. (Remember the Argentinean *gauchos.*) South Africa (the Cape, Transvaal) will always be of secondary importance as an immigration country, even after they remove the restrictions now placed in the way of Jewish immigrants. The Jews should be restrained from emigrating to the over-populated countries of western Europe because of their difficult living conditions and the dangers of anti-alien sentiment. Australia may perhaps become a branch of the American emigration movement in the course of time, but it has no value for the emigration problem at present.

If North America thus alone remains the center of emigration for us, the question arises: What must be done to organize the mass movement to this country so that the loss sustained by our national center in Russia will be made up by the growth of the new center overseas? In other words, how can we turn the quantitative center of Judaism in America into a qualitative center, or, at least, into one of several such centers? To this there is one answer: it is necessary to organize the exodus not merely as a socio-economic, but also as a national factor. The basic principle of our work must be, not to split up the Jewish Diaspora, not to scatter many small groups over a large area, but, on the contrary, to concentrate them in dense masses. It is necessary, however, to direct the masses of immigrants away from those places where concentration has reached its limits and where it may cause economic complications and social dangers to other not yet overcrowded areas. In New York, for example, and in the eastern states of America concentration has already reached the saturation point; for this reason groups of immigrants must be directed to the western states which are relatively less inhabited.

To realize these goals an organization must be established such as the "lovers of the people" dreamed of already in the 1880s. It should consist of a Central Committee for the Organization of Emigration, with branches in various places in Europe and America. In the Committee and its branches would be concentrated all emigration matters, such as providing information to emigrants, designation of the most suitable countries of entry, improvement of travel conditions through co-operation with shipping companies, the establishment of information bureaus for employment in countries of entry, and similar matters. Such an immense undertaking can be assumed only by an institution that disposes of large funds. Here the JCA (Jewish Colonization Association) automatically comes to mind. Up to now this organization has not been able to accomplish much with its capital of millions. The severe crisis through which we are passing should remind this Association of its prime duty: to organize the general Jewish emigration without giving one form of emigration preference over another. The emigration committee to be founded must assist in the organization not only of the main stream of the exodus, to North America, but also of the lesser streams flowing to Palestine, South Africa, Argentina, etc. This entire work must be basically, not simple philanthropy, but an organic effort toward a national emigration movement, that is, to the creation of large centers for our national-cultural life in the countries of entry. . . .

I am well aware of the characteristics of American culture which tend to blur the features of Jewish natioanl life rather than help to preserve them. This is true only, however, if emigration and entry are allowed to remain chaotic and unorganized. If the intellectual classes will assume active leadership, it will be possible to secure the freedom and opportunity needed for the realization of cultural autonomy. It is not possible, in accordance with the American constitution, to prevent communities from exercising free self-government, or organizing education in national schools, or setting up some general national organization of Jewry.* All these do not in the least contradict the duties imposed upon loyal citizens of the republic. What is needed for the strengthening of national Judaism in America are good will and united effort among the people and that the educated classes take the lead in this migration movement and find in America a wide field for their activities. In our present psychological state the intellectual classes, whose rights are curtailed, also feel the need to emigrate. An appreciable part of the intelligentsia will find moral satisfaction in leading the powerful movement which, in effect, will change the fate of Israel by changing its geographic distribution.

IV

We have already stated that even a mass emigration can only lead to a decrease of the Jewish population in the country of origin, the Russian Egypt, but not to a complete evacuation of its Jewish inhabitants. The majority of our people will stay in the countries they live in under extremely difficult material and spiritual conditions. Thus the basic problem of how to help ourselves and defend ourselves remains unchanged. . . . While we are concerned with organizing a mass emigration to new countries, we do not relinquish in any way our historical rights to those old centers in which we have carried on our cultural life for thousands of years. . . . Here we shall strive with all our strength to better and improve oui economic life and to obtain those civic rights which are refused us today. . . . If we are destined to continue to suffer for a long time, let us bear our suffering, but with strong aspirations for a better fate and not in humble resignation to existing reality. . . . In order to clarify all the issues connected with the two forms of self-help, self-help by emi-

* The example of the Jewish settlement of Woodbine, New Jersey, which developed into a "small Jewish town" with broad local autonomy, gives ground for the assumption that Jewish predominance in city government is also within the realm of possibility in a number of localities.

gration and political self-help, a general Jewish congress must be convened in the near future. . . .

The immense effort of self-help which we must undertake demands the utmost strengthening of all our national forces. The entire Jewish intelligentsia and all our trained youth must be mobilized and join ranks with all those assembled in this hour of emergency. However much the camp of the fighters for national emancipation has grown during the last decades, it still is small and weak compared to our intelligentsia remaining outside the camp. Thousands of educated and gifted Jews continue to labor in foreign vineyards, turn their backs on their lost brethren and defect to camps where their participation is not sought, perhaps also not desired. Since they were brought up in a spirit alien to Judaism, they are carried away by the social and literary currents of the alien environment. . . .

We like to hope that the new terrible catastrophe will force the uprooted among us to return from their path. In the face of danger, when a gigantic national effort is needed to save tens of thousands of our suffering brethren, we cannot afford to dissipate our social energies outside of our camp. Those who will look deeply into the complex chaos of our national catastrophe will not go over to the camp of the peaceful and the light-hearted, nor to the camp of those who dream of things that are remote from the burning needs of the hour. Our national catastrophe, which is as vast as the sea, must cure our estranged intelligentsia. It offers it a sacred and exalted ideal and will give meaning and purpose to its life.

May all the vital elements of our people, all those in whose souls "the spark of Judaism" is not yet extinguished, all those who strive for the preservation and revival of our nation, unite over the fresh graves of our new national martyrs! May every educated Jew look upon himself as a soldier in a united army, the only army in the world which has fought for two thousand years with spiritual weapons against powerful enemies, weapons which have sustained us and enabled us to reach this time.

May 1903.

Tenth Letter

THE MORAL OF STORMY DAYS
(Fragments)

I

*What Has Amalek Done to Us?**

A sea of blood storms and tosses,
A sea of tears for which the nation has no revenge,
Piercing and penetrating,
Bores the question into your innermost depth:
Why all these sufferings and victims?

—*Nadson*

Why these new frightful horrors, this return to the bloody dances of the Black Death and to the mass murder of Khmielnitski?[36] Why these thousands of victims, killed and maimed with ferocious cruelty in Odessa, Kiev, Yelisavetgrad, Kishinev, Kalarash, Romny, Orsha and numerous other cities in the north and south? Why this vandalistic destruction of hundreds of communities, streets drenched in blood and covered with shattered vessels, tens of thousands of families despoiled and left, like empty vessels, naked and deprived of everything?

Is it only in order that Russia might enter the epoch of its emancipation with the sign of Cain on its forehead, the sign of the savage or of the headstrong emancipated serf? Or is it perhaps a warning to the Jew that he who fought in the front ranks in the war for liberation is left, just as before, without defense and with curtailed rights; that he who labored more than anyone else for the revolution will enjoy its fruits less than all others, and that only one sad privilege will be his, to be the eternal victim of the counterrevolution and the scorn of the crude masses? What is this? A survival from a past not yet fully overcome, or an awesome foreboding of the future?

* This chapter was read before a memorial meeting in Vilna after the October pogroms in Russia (November 17, 1905).

The massacres of October 1905 were brought about not only as a result of the recent unrest. They came about as a result of the entire political system of Russia. They are the crowning achievement of a system of blood-and-iron that has weighed upon the Jews during the past quarter of a century. The rule of the knout in Russia set up two inquisitions for the Jewish population: oppression and curtailed rights as permanent institutions, and pogroms for extraordinary occasions. Here both ends of the stick were used, one end to smite and the other to kill; oppression on one side and extermination on the other. "Chief-butcher" Pobedonostsev and his henchmen issued special regulations for the Jews in order to introduce the old Spanish system in Russia. The motives of the regulations were perfectly clear: "The Jews are a cultured people and tend toward progress. This endangers our monarchical regime, our system of political apathy and the religious innocence of our ignorant masses. Therefore, let us oppress these aliens, let us not allow them to leave their pale of settlement, let us drive them from the villages into the overcrowded cities, take their livelihood from them, put out the light of their education, reduce them to the level of slaves, explain to the 'native' inhabitants that the Jews are outside the pale of the law, and if this influence is effective and leads to pogroms, let us not hasten to suppress the mobsters. Let the 'will of the people' run its course and teach those who are without rights that they are also without defense. And when they stagger under the burden of their life, let them go to America, to Palestine, to their hearts' desire!"

In 1881 the pogroms were officially designated in the words of Minister Ignatev as "popular justice." In 1905 they were again linked officially to "patriotic demonstrations." The earlier outbreaks were justified on the economic grounds that the Jews exploit the inhabitants of the state. Now they justify the pogroms on political grounds, that the Russian people are taking their revenge on the Jews for their part in the revolutionary movement. The motives have changed, changed also are the ways in which the pogroms are carried out, the latter for the worse. In the beginning the government looked on with indifference and did nothing. Now it aids openly or secretly in organizing the pogroms. During the first period they ransacked houses and plundered property; during the last years, from 1903 until this October, murder and massacre have been added, and those charged with "maintaining order," the police and the military, were given permission to destroy the Jewish self-defense. During the October days, police, soldiers, and Cossacks ganged up with robbers, murderers and assassins in perpetrating the pogroms. . . .

All this was the work of the "old" regime. And what does the new regime of Witte[37] do? It issues official statements on the pogroms which are based on the fabricated reports invented by the very government officials who had instigated or organized them. It does not bring the murderers to justice and it repudiates as "shameless" the report that the Russian envoy in Vienna had practically organized a collection for the benefit of the victims of the pogroms. In short, it has not condemned the atrocities even officially and thus there is ground for the belief that the new regime follows in this respect the ways of its predecessor. Clearly, the line dividing the old and the new Russia exists so far only in the imagination, at least with respect to matters concerning the Jews.

Such is the role the government has played in all that has befallen us. . . . And what did the people do? Did the savage mob assembled under the banner of the "Black Hundred"[38] only carry out the bidding of its leaders? Were the thousands and tens of thousands of workers, peasants and city-dwellers, who smashed Jewish heads, gouged the eyes of children, raped women, burned, robbed, looted and filled their homes with loot—were they all merely carrying out a counterrevolution? Not at all! They were doing what their fathers and brothers had done in years gone by, they will do it again in the future if conditions permit, and they will command their children and grandchildren to do the same until civilization has reached a higher level and has changed the wild beasts of the Black Hundred into human beings. It will take a long time to effect such a change, to re-educate the masses in the spirit of a state based on law and to eradicate the law of the fist which is so deeply rooted in Russian life. And even then, who will guarantee that in the improved environment we shall be accepted as equal citizens?

There is no room for hopeful confidence for the future on the basis of practical deeds. What have those who have risen above the savage and benighted regime done thus far? What are the reformers in Russian society doing, the liberals and the radicals? What a world of difference between their reactions against the October pogroms, on the one hand, and against the proclamation of a state of siege in Poland, on the other! . . . While the pogroms moved the progressive circles to nothing more than sighs of pity or bitter words, the persecution of the Poles led to an organized strike, to sharp protests and resolutions and, finally, even to energetic demands upon the government. Where are the committees to aid the victims of the pogroms which should have been organized by Russians at a time when such committees were being founded by Christians in England, France, Germany and other countries? Where are the protest meetings against a collective crime that shocked the entire civilized world? Where are the newspaper editorials to rain fire and brimstone upon the heads of the criminals? Where is the tremendous outcry against this St. Bartholomew Eve?

The liberated Russian press reacted with cold indifference to the cruel sufferings of the Jews, to the shame of Russia that has become the horror of the world. The leading proletarian newspaper, *Novaya Zhizn*,[39] passed over almost in silence the atrocities of the pogroms, as if they had been some minute episode in the revolutionary struggle. . . .

And how did the liberated Russian proletariat itself behave during the latest attack on the Jews? The Jewish worker had sacrificed himself in the revolutionary struggle together with the Russian worker, but when the counterrevolution vented its full fury on the Jews, where were the Russian "comrades"? After five days of bloodshed in Odessa, when the work of destruction and murder was completed, the Russian workers admitted publicly that they had done nothing to defend the unfortunates. Elsewhere even this belated admission was not forthcoming. Those few students and other Russians who took part in the Jewish self-defense, and paid with their lives while fulfilling their duty toward their fellow men, remain a bright exception to the shameful general rule.

After all this, is there any ground for optimism and confidence?

The terrible experiences of the recent past implanted in Russian Jewry a mortal hatred against an oppressive regime whose cruelty surpasses the Spanish Inquisition. Cursed be this contemptible regime which has abused our humane feelings and for decades has found pleasure in torturing a nation of six million people! The people, filled with anger and bitterness, have taken a sacred oath to fight incessantly against all remnants of the regime, which will not soon disappear from Russian life, and against every attempt to reintroduce the old order which has become an historic symbol of terror and abomination. The latest pogroms, unparalleled in their cruelty, through which the government tried to extinguish the fire of freedom that burns in us, will not achieve their purpose. On the contrary, they are likely to increase this spirit in us. We shall never forget the moral of these stormy days. "Remember what Amalek did unto thee by the way as ye came forth out of Egypt!" After twenty-five years of serfdom in Egypt, evil Amalek attacked us, and one heard the voice of Israel crying in the "wilderness of nations," the stifled moans of the dying, the groans of the maimed.

Who is the Amalek of our times? Not only the officials of the old despised order but also the ignorant masses who follow their lead. If the former stir up feelings of revenge and defiance in us, the latter arouse in us fear and apprehension for the future.

Will the hour of reconciliation and peace come soon? At the last congress of *zemstvos* in Moscow, one Russian speaker declared that a very long time will pass before the Polish people are able to feel love or good will toward Russia after the oppression Poland suffered under Russian rule for the past hundred years. If you consider the fact that it was only the Russian government and not the people that oppressed Poland, and that this people did not perpetrate pogroms or St. Bartholomew Eves upon the Poles, I suggest that you estimate how much time will have to pass before the Jewish people, the scapegoat of the Russian empire, is able to forget, to forgive, and to make peace with the descendants of those who oppressed and murdered it.

You specialists in political analysis will object to my remarks and cite "counterrevolution," "mass-psychosis," "line of least resistance," and other similar scholarly terms from the sociological dictionary. Let us admit for the moment that it is so. Let us restrain our pure emotion and submit to logical analysis, for the sake of our personal consolation and our unimpaired faith in the progress of the Russsian people. But how will you convince the Jewish masses who saw with their own eyes the horrors of all the Middle Ages in the span of one week? Can you obliterate the memory of all the thousands of innocent martyrs, or erase the sacred wrath of our generation and of our children's children? For many years to come the dead who were strangled and slain in the October days will be mourned by thousands of our families. For many years to come the crutches of the crippled, the sockets of gouged-out eyes, the mutilated hands and marred faces will remind us of the horrors of the days of fury. For a long time to come mothers will tell their children about "those days" when savages slew their fathers, brothers and sisters, ravaged their homes and condemned them to become childless and orphans, hungry, sick and poor, without end and without escape. Then the hearts of the people will be filled with grief, their eyes will flash forth anger and their fists will be clenched. Before such furious anger of the aggrieved we are powerless with all our cold logical analysis. When the heart of a people quakes, the sophistries and entreaties of the intellect are of no avail! Consider this feeling of the aggrieved nation, the state of mind of the suffering, the psychological ferments which move history more than abstract ideas! From all this you will deduce the following counsel of caution: "Do not put your trust in Amalek, neither Amalek's government nor its people, because the old Russia is bound to reappear in any Russia that is to come! . . ."

II

SLAVERY IN THE MIDST OF REVOLUTION

The outstanding characteristics of the forces active in present-day Russian Jewry are an exaggerated confidence in the political and national parties existing around us and a squandering of energies for general and often also alien causes, both of which characteristics are born of contempt for the most vital needs of the Jewish people. At a time when other suppressed nationalities in Russia fought under their own national flags during the revolution, most of the revolutionary Jews fought under a general Russian flag or under the flags of other nationalities around them. . . . The special revolutionary slogan of the Finns was the renewal of their autonomous constitution; that of the Poles, political autonomy, freedom of their national language and schools; the Armenians rose up against the limitations imposed upon their national freedom in church and educational affairs. . . . But in the strategy of the Jewish revolution, the special national protest was swallowed up in the general protest. The demand for equality of rights as one of the basic postulates of freedom was not emphasized among the general political or class demands. There was not even one special protest demonstration against the legal disabilities of Jews, or against the brash maltreatment of a cultural nationality for the last twenty-five years.[40] Up to the present time there have been no revolutionary actions in the name of the Jewish nationality. The desperation among Jews served as a cause of the revolutionary state of mind, but it did not stimulate revolutionary actions.

As a result of the incessant persecution by their oppressive government, a great force of resistance had accumulated within Russian Jewry. The revolutionary ferment penetrated into various circles of the persecuted people. It permeated even the souls of children, since the tyrannical regime also directed decrees against Jewish children and closed the doors of the schools to them. There is no other nationality in Russia that produced as large a number of revolutionary youth as the Jewish people. This was natural in the light of the terrible conditions under which we lived, but there were deplorable results, because it gave to the movement a tinge of recklessness and immaturity. Most of our energies were dissipated for needs other than our own. The old assimilationist tendencies of the active elements among our intelligentsia, on the one hand, and the political immaturity of many revolutionary fighters, on the other, had the effect of draining the Jewish protest of its individual content and of submerging it into the general Russian protest. The cries of our suffering brethren and the anguish of the prisoners of the ghetto were mixed with the general slogans. The fruit of our agonies, the best of our sacrifices were offered up on the general "altar of the fatherland." We have no revolutionary altar of our own, although other nationalities have taken their stand in the war against the old regime, each under its own banner. Our revolutionary groups either make common cause with like-minded organizations among other nationalities or set themselves apart in a special proletarian organization which can be called "Jewish" only in its ethnic composition and in the language of its propaganda material, but not in its national program.

The relationship of the Jewish members of the various Social-Democratic and revolutionary groups to Judaism has already been clarified sufficiently.

The strong contingent of young Jews taking an important place in the ranks of the Russian Social-Democratic Worker's Party, and even in its leadership, have formally severed all their ties to Judaism. Most of them are complete assimilationists.[41] Their people is the Russian and not the Jewish people, since for them a people is a political-territorial and not a cultural-historical concept. In their eyes the six million Jews wedged into the body of the Russian state are Russians who only temporarily are connected with the House of Israel. They are ready and willing to grant national autonomy to all the territorial nationalities in Russia but not to the Jewish nationality, since they believe that the Jewish river will empty into the Russian sea. The sight of the great stream of blood of their Jewish brethren spilled by Russians does not disturb the peace of mind of the Jewish members of the party . . . and they console themselves with the thought that all this is only a minor aspect of the "counterrevolution." These men do not realize that, in true lackey fashion, they are only carrying out the bidding of their masters, the bidding of the ruling nationality. They have not attained inner freedom even in revolution.

A more contemptible "bondage in the midst of revolution" was shown by the numerous Jews in the Polish Socialist Party (P.P.S.). These men, who struggle zealously for Polish autonomy and who at times come close to Polish chauvinism, strive for the complete assimilation of the Jews to their Polish environment (in some places they require the Jewish workers of their organization to learn the Polish language). . . . Following the example of their political opponents in the conservative and antisemitic National Democratic Party, the adherents of the P.P.S. demand of the Jews complete fusion with the Polish people. . . .

The Jewish members of the Socialist-Revolutionary Party (S.R.), whose minimalist platform is close to that of the left wing of the Constitutional-Democratic Party (Kadets), do not reject our national demands. But (with the exception of a few atypical individuals) they do not include them in their own political program. In their party program the agrarian question is much closer to their hearts than the Jewish question, which they consider as only one detail of the general Russian liberation movement. They live "like the just, by their faith," and they are confident that the time will come when antisemitism will disappear completely from the earth, and the Russian wolf will lie with the Jewish lamb in peace and security.

May we perhaps consider the Jewish Social-Democratic organization, the "Bund," which has acquired such an important role in the revolutionary movement of our times, as a defender of our national needs? It does, indeed, make claim "to represent the Jewish proletariat," but this claim is unfounded. As a party with an exclusively proletarian class program, the Bund consciously and knowingly works, not for the good of the Jewish people as a whole, but only for the good of one part, and the smallest part at that. For the Bund the struggle between the interests of the bourgeoisie and the proletariat completely displaces the struggle for our general national needs, which are more endangered from the outside. For the Bundists the essence of Jewishness is only an ethnic or folk quality, not national-cultural, with the exception only of the spoken language of the masses, Yiddish, whose rights they recognize. (They are absolutely opposed to Hebrew.) They talk of "the right to self-determination" and even of "national-cultural autonomy," among the principles of universal freedom, but they do not care for the concrete development of national Jewish culture, for the organization of autonomous communities, or for national education, as a shield against assimilation, which they consider a natural phenomenon.*

The Bundists are devoted sons of only one "nation," the proletarian class. They never join with national parties for any common cause. They do not believe in the totality of the Jewish community. They cut its living body in two and say: "This is ours, the proletariat's, and this belongs to the bourgeoisie, the Zionists, and the nationalists!" It is not enough for them that the scourge of oppression strikes at the proletarian, the capitalist and the small trader in equal measure and that the broken skulls of individuals from all three groups lie in the streets of their devastated cities. The alienation of these fanatical Marxists from Judaism left tragic marks during the recent disorder. The Bundists, who fancied themselves as the strong men of the general Russian revolution, tried hard to prove themselves "more Russian than the Russians" during the October demonstrations, but when these demonstrations were followed by Bartholomew Eves for the Jews, they said: "This is only an episode of the counterrevolution!" . . .

Our leftist parties must fight in the ranks of the revolutionary army, not under a Russian or Polish cloak, but as Jews who value the needs of their own people no less than the needs of the state in which they live.

* One of the ideological leaders of the party made the following statement: "We are not nationalists. . . . We are not assimilationists. We stand in the midst of a class war. . . . Here is the sphere of our duties, here the field of our aims. . . . If history has decreed that the Jews assimilate with the rest of the nations, we shall take no measures to hinder this process, nor shall we put ourselves out to help it along. We are neutral. . . . If history has assured the Jews a flowering of their own native culture, we shall do nothing to disturb this originality, nor shall we make any efforts in its behalf and for its success. We are neutral." Medem, Vladimir, "Social-Democracy and the National Question" (St. Petersburg, 1906, pp. 21-22; [this brochure is reprinted in its Yiddish version in *Vladimir Medem, tsum tsvantsiksten yortsayt*, New York, 1943, K. S. P.]). Toward the end of his life this leader reversed his views and followed more closely the national idea.

III

NATIONAL OR CLASS POLITICS?

Can national and class politics be combined? "Class politics" does not mean the economic struggle of the workers against the capitalists for the protection of their just interests. A struggle of this kind goes on incessantly under the iron laws of life and will not cease until all the rights of the workers are recognized to the fullest extent. In this constant struggle the usual means employed are: the organization of workers into trade-unions, strikes, and pressure on parliaments for the passage of laws favorable to the working class. However, the adherents of the idea of "class politics" mean something entirely different when they use this term. They mean the endeavor to bring all aspects of political and spiritual life within the framework of material class interests, the effort to divide the nation into two mutually antagonistic parts, the bourgeoisie and the proletariat, which are set apart from the economic viewpoint and have no unity from any other viewpoint. This represents the attempt to make the economic factors supreme in the historical process and to subordinate to it all social and spiritual developments with all their wide ramifications. This is not the place to point out the theoretical errors of historical materialism in its absolute form, which gained many adherents especially among the nation whose entire history is a violent protest against this doctrine. But this much is clear to us, that in practice class politics is opposed to every other kind of politics, especially national politics.

National politics, which aims to preserve and defend the nation as a whole, assumes the form of a struggle for existence for each cultural nationality which does not have the protective instruments of a definite territory or government of its own and which is a national minority in the midst of other peoples. It rises to the stage of high moral duty with a people whose stronger neighbors hate, persecute, and oppress it as a foreign national element. The Jewish people has been in such a state for many generations and will continue to be so for a long time to come. In Russia the oppression and the dangers inherent in such a condition reached a point where all the parties of the nation should have united to defend themselves in a war for national survival against the outside world and against all the evil forces surrounding it. What do we see, however? Instead of a policy of general national interests, which are in the greatest danger, they draw us into class politics which divides these common interests. The followers of one party proclaim the slogan, "Workers of the world, unite!" at a time when the salvation of the nation demands the unceasing call, "Jews of all classes and parties, unite!" The leaders of the Jewish proletariat declare that even the idea of common national interests, the principle that all Israel is one (*klal yisrael*), is bound to do harm to their aspirations in so far as it "weakens the class-consciousness of the proletariat." This narrow doctrine destroys the natural feeling of fraternity and friendship among the members of a nation which proceeds with astonishing strength on its path, the thorny path of history.

When class politics dominates a strong nation whose unity is assured by territory or government, it may perhaps be considered one-sided, but it presents no danger to the integrity of the nation. However, if the policy of class division spreads among the "smallest of all peoples," which has nothing but common cultural interests and at a time when it is exposed to the constant danger of being absorbed by the nations surrounding it, then such tactics constitute criminal guilt, since they must lead to national disruption. We see, for instance, that the Poles, although they are united by common territory and language and although they aspire to political autonomy in the near future, carry on a general national policy in all their parties. The Jews, on the other hand, who lack the protection of any territorial armor and who are subjected to the tyranny of powerful enemies, allow themselves the "luxury" of national division. Narrow class politics becomes anti-national in so far as it implants the idea in the Jewish proletariat that all its interests unite it with the proletariat of the other nationalities but separate it from the majority of its own people, from the masses of "bourgeoisie," so to speak, among whom the hungry outnumber the satisfied. . . .[42]

What political program is at present best suited for the majority of the active forces of Judaism and for the idea of national unity?

It is the program of political democracy, or of the Constitutional-Democratic Party, to which all the politically mature elements of Russian society adhere. . . . Our national interests demand that we join the party of democracy. The program of this party provides room for the maximum demands of the moderates and the minimum demands of the extremists, the Socialists, who can co-operate with the democrats until they have achieved their minimum. We shall obtain equal civic and political rights through an alliance with the healthy forces of the Russian people, who are concentrated in the Constitutional-Democratic Party and who are destined to play a leading role in the coming parliamentary system. Through a broad organization of our own forces we shall fight for the recognition of our national rights, such as communal self-government and cultural autonomy. We know perfectly well that, even after we have defeated the anti-semitism of the government, we will still have to fight against social antisemitism, and we do not minimize this struggle. However, we see a strong basis for this struggle only in the road to freedom provided by democracy.

The cornerstone for such an organization was laid in the spring of 1905, with the League for the Attainment of Equal Rights for the Jewish People in Russia. This society, which from the beginning stood on the platform of the Constitutional-Democrats, adopted as its goal the "attainment of full civic, political and national rights for the Jewish people." This was the first Jewish organization which raised the demand for "national rights" in conjunction with civic-political rights. "National rights," according to the published program of the League, meant "freedom of national-cultural self-determination in every form, especially broad communal autonomy, freedom of language and of education in the schools." These general objectives which were adopted at the preparatory meeting in Vilna, will still have to be clarified in detail and be formulated more exactly by the second meeting which will be convened in the near future. The second meeting has a double task: (1) to turn the League into a Jewish political organization to fight for the attainment of the rights of the Jewish people by unifying all the forces in the electoral contests and by creating a national group in the Russian Duma . . . ; (2) to prepare the ground for the creation of a general autonomous organization in the form of a "Union of Jewish Communities in Russia" which will elect a central committee for the administration of all internal affairs and for the realization of the principle of our national-cultural autonomy. . . .* Thus, the organization of our forces for the political struggle outside and for the national work within is the double motor with enough power to direct our lives into a new path, the path of civic and national emancipation.

* * *

Not all that our people can and should be told in this tragic hour of crisis can be said here. We are standing on the edge of a volcano which has already devoured tens of thousands of victims and which has not yet ceased smoking. . . . The October outbreaks have destroyed the mental balance of our people. The people have been thrown into a state of wild confusion. They flee for their lives from that country where the shadows of death overclouded the luster of freedom, where savagery was confused with revolution and where brute force won out over rational principles. Most of the refugees flee by the beaten path from the Russian Egypt across the Atlantic Ocean to the "Chosen Land," where they immediately attain freedom and, after a hard struggle, also their livelihood.

This movement has continued without interruption for the last twenty-five years. For twenty-five years the ships of the emigrants have plowed the waves of the ocean and have brought more than a million Jews from the land of slavery to the American republic. Even now, when Russia, while preparing to become a land of freedom, has not ceased to be a land of pogroms, our eternal wanderer is taking the beaten path across the ocean. Should you delay him, should you advise him to tarry a while, to postpone his hurried exodus from Egypt, to wait until Pharaoh is driven from his throne, until the "Black Hundred" will have been drowned in the waves of the Red Sea, until Egypt will have become a land of culture? No, do not offer such advice to the perplexed masses who are encircled

* A section containing a detailed program of the work of the League for the Attainment of Rights and the Union of the Communities is deleted at this point.

by the hordes of Amalek and who are looking for a place of refuge, depressed by the knowledge that their lot will never improve or at least not very soon. You are not in a position to promise them quick redemption or to heal their mortal wounds. You cannot give them a vision of a brilliant day once the dawn rises from a horizon of blood.

Our task is not to hinder but to organize this mighty migration movement. We will fight to free our people in our old homeland, which is drenched in the blood of our mutilated and our martyrs, but we will also think of the other part of Russian Jewry, which is creating a new national center overseas. Judaism is destined to develop in two great centers: in Russia and in America. The national hegemony must in due course be concentrated in these two centers, which are geographically two, but one in their historical value.

There is still another land on which the spring sun of our national life shines, the land of our fathers. Our hearts long for it, but our feet do not yet carry us there. Yearning has not yet turned into persistent will; desire has not yet been converted into determined action by the masses. Will this change ever come, and if it comes, will it bring the realization of the glorious dream of Zionism? Alas! The Diaspora will never end, unless we count on "the end of the days," the time of the Messiah. But to light up the darkness of the Diaspora, be it even with a small ray of light, which will fall on Zion, to create in the land where Judaism had its historic beginnings even a limited spiritual center, a model nursery of pure national culture, is a task which must have a place among all our other concrete tasks. This will be, not that Zionism which wants to conquer the entire national movement, but only that which recognizes itself as a part of this movement. The Zionism which will prove to be an important historical factor will not be the one which rejects life in the Diaspora and nurses the deceptive dream that the Diaspora will cease to exist, but rather that Zionism which adds one more task to the tasks of our national renaissance: to create in the land of our fathers an additional true source of spiritual strength which will provide nourishment to the Jews in the Diaspora who are battling for their existence with all their concentrated force.

November-December 1905.

Eleventh Letter

ON THE SUPREMACY OF NATIONAL POLITICS IN THE LIFE OF AN OPPRESSED NATIONALITY

(*A Commentary on the Tenth Letter*)

In my first collection of "Letters on Old and New Judaism" (1897-1902), I set down the following principal postulates emanating from the theory of spiritual or cultural nationalism: the demand for national and civic rights, autonomy in the communities and in cultural institutions, and national politics for the defense of Judaism in the Diaspora. I also developed in detail the relationship of this theory to assimilation on the one hand, and to Zionism on the other. In recent years, during which Socialism and class politics have made great strides, another question has come to demand our attention: whether national politics and class politics—two principles, each demanding supremacy in equal measure—can exist side by side under the special conditions of Jewish life. Investigation of this question and an examination of the work of our Socialist parties had led me to definite conclusions which I had intended to develop in detail in a series of new "Letters" based on the assumptions of the previous collection. As a result of the events of October 1905, I decided not to wait until the essays on this subject could be developed more systematically, but to heed the need of the hour—an hour of destruction and rebuilding—and to bring before the public a few fragments of these essays. This is the history of the preceding essay "The Moral of the Stormy Days."

I found it necessary to explain the origin of the essay on the "Moral" because the general title of the essay furnished my distinguished critic, S. A. Anski,[43] with a pretext for accusing me of having built my essay only on the "moral of troubled times," of having forced all the problems of the life of our people into a single framework, and of having found only one solution for them: national politics and national unity.* We must assume that my fellow-

* "The Moral of the Period of Storm," in *Voskhod* (1906), pp. 8-13.

contributor to the last number of the *Voskhod* forgot that the "Letters" which contained the "solution" he denounced had appeared long before the "stormy days" and as the resulting conclusion of a complete system; and from that it should be apparent that I could not have been influenced in these observations by the unfortunate events. On the other hand, it must also be presumed that the fragmentary form and occasionally also the method of presentation in the "Moral" leave room for misunderstanding my remarks and interpreting them incorrectly. . . .* This makes it necessary for me to present additional explanations to my "Moral of the Stormy Days," develop further my basic concepts and show a fair critic the difference between my real opinions and those ascribed to me.

My evaluation of our political parties was based on the following assumptions. National politics which strives to defend the integrity of the people and its free cultural development is the yardstick wherever the integrity of the people and its inner freedom are in danger. The Jewish people in the Diaspora finds itself in this respect in a state of constant danger because its unique condition exposes it to the assimilatory influence of foreign cultures. We learn from this that our national politics must always be the highest criterion for all parties and all classes which do not tend towards assimilation and the destruction of our national existence. Various political, social, and class parties can and must exist inside the nation, but they must all subordinate themselves to the highest of all principles, national survival. All Jewish history is one chain of incessant defensive wars for national survival and inner unity under conditions of external political and territorial fragmentation. This is both the tragedy and the supreme heroism in the annals of our life: the tragedy of a permanent "state of war" and the heroism of the beleaguered who defend their fortress. If you weaken this rallying of the forces of defense, Judaism will have no place left but in the museum of historical mummies. And you will arrive at this result if you substitute the class theory for the theory of "the whole of Israel" (*klal yisrael*).

Anski declares that he "does not see why oppression and perse-

* For example, a series of polemical articles in the Bund party newspaper, *Der Veker*, Vilna, January 1906.

cutions, even though they did take on a very severe form, should endanger our national unity just now." He says optimistically: "We do not see such danger either from external oppression or from internal division." He then explains that in every generation we were oppressed and persecuted, and Judaism nevertheless came out intact. As for internal division, insofar as it "manifests itself in a class struggle whose roots reach deep into the economic and social life of the people," it involves no danger of national disintegration since "the working class also defends the general national interests," even if it does not ally itself with the bourgeoisie. I would like to challenge my opponent to show me any instance in our past in which parts of the Diaspora, subjected to oppressive rule, were saved from destruction without determined assertion of national politics. As for the present, I agree with Anski's opinion, but only up to the point I set down in the essay on "Moral," which is that the class struggle within set limits does not contradict a general national policy. It does run counter to national policy, however, if it makes class politics dominate everything else, so that the entire social and spiritual life of the people is made subordinate to the idea of the economic antagonism between the bourgeoisie and the proletariat.

The leaders of the Jewish working class who preach eternal hatred against their "bourgeois" brothers, most of whom are just as poor and persecuted as they are, those leaders who keep telling the Jewish worker day in and day out that his community of interests with the proletariat of a foreign people is superior to the interests he shares with the "bourgeoisie" of his own people—those leaders destroy what is left of the consciousness of national unity and nullify all possibility for common action by our people, faced as we are by the combined hostility of the external enemies, the foreign bourgeoisie, and, sometimes, also the foreign proletariat. . . .

To those who preach this class separation I venture to oppose the "bourgeois" intelligentsia, so to speak, which, during the period of black reaction, endured our national suffering and labored in various ways to lighten it and to relieve its bitterness. What the representatives of the Socialist parties derisively call "bourgeois nationalism," "bourgeois Zionism," "movement of attainers" (taken from the program of the League for the Attainment of Rights), all these are movements which stand above one class, which aim to obtain rights, cultural autonomy, or even a separate territory for the people. The Jewish intelligentsia which created these movements always worked in a national spirit, favoring no one class over another, and it can look down with contempt on the senseless smears of "bourgeois psychology" brought against it by the Marxists, who have appropriated for themselves a "proletarian psychology." This intelligentsia strives to create a common political and national basis for a healthy life for all classes of our people and especially for those who are suffering from economic pressure.

It is the great mistake of Jewish Socialist politics that it measures our internal life by a foreign standard, that it exaggerates the class antagonism existing among us and that it draws upon this source for justification of its claim to power. Economically, the Jewish nationality in Russia resembles at present a magnetic field which has two poles at the ends and a large "neutral line" in the middle. The upper bourgeoisie and the organized proletariat occupy only small positions at the two extreme poles at this time, and the economic center does not rest in them but in the middle line, in that great mass of artisans and petty traders who, according to their standard of living, should be counted with the proletariat.* We are still in the early stages of the capitalist system, of whose bad effects our "class conscious individuals" read in the books of Marx and Engels. But they try to drag us by their Socialist rope towards the final stage, the stage close to the realization of the final goals of Socialism. Our Marxists, who have not penetrated deeply enough into the thought of Marx, will have just as little success with such a confused policy as with their slogan of the dictatorship of the proletariat and all the rest of their sudden revolutions.

To all the arguments that the class struggle is natural and necessary, I answer: Yes, it is natural and necessary in so far as it stems

* According to the figures of the "Collection of Materials Bearing on the Economic Condition of the Jews in Russia" (published by the JCA, 1904), the number of Jewish factory workers in the Pale is close to 45,000, the number of artisans more than 500,000, the number of petty traders even larger, while a fifth of the entire Jewish population belongs to no class or consists of homeless poor.

from the true relationship between the forces of capital and labor among our people; but it has not yet reached a stage of such decisive importance as to justify its claim to be the supreme principle and sole guide in our social and national life. The class struggle is one of the factors, but not the only factor and not even the most important factor in our life, and its influence on our national politics must be set in proper perspective and not be artificially exaggerated and inflated. Even if we grant that the class problem will become the chief factor for us in the distant future, even then national politics will not have to yield its supremacy to class politics if this entails a danger to the unity and integrity of the nation.

Anski, who admits at one point in his essay that economic antagonism "has a tendency to disrupt the national unity of the Jewish people," comforts us with the idea that internal national unity is not a necessary condition for national development, and he points to the example of a number of free territorial nationalities. Once more, I must stress the great difference between the Jews and other nationalities with territory and state. Nationalities which are united not only by spiritual but also by material factors (territory, state, military defense) face only the danger of conquest from without or political subjugation, and in moments of such danger they rally all their forces for the defense of the "fatherland," which protects their integrity and their freedom. But the Jewish people in the Diaspora, which lacks the protection of a territory, absorbs the blows with its very body. It is constantly exposed to the danger of being conquered from within: to decline and degenerate under the weight of social pressure or through cultural assimilation.

All through its history our people has fought against this perennial danger with one weapon only: the strengthening of the will for national survival in various forms adapted to the cultural level of each period. . . . Anyone who desires the continued existence of the Jewish nation must recognize the supremacy of its national politics, of that singular spiritual discipline of an uprooted people, of this substitute for the political and territorial unity that we lack. Without such comprehension, all ways open to us lead to exodus from Judaism. And if the number of those who leave us grows steadily from generation to generation we will share the fate of the Karaites or the Samaritans, and the history of the "Eternal People" will become the history of a dying and expiring people.

Now that I have explained the basic principle, the supremacy of national politics as the chief condition for national survival in times of oppression, I can turn to those objections of my opponent which touch upon the relationship of Jewish national politics to the contemporary Russian revolutionary movement.

In the first section of his essay, Anski contrasts the two periods of "pogroms," the present one and the one of the early 1880s, and he finds proof here for his views. "The pogroms of the eighties inspired the cry: Return! Return to religion, to national isolation, to the land of your fathers! The revolutionary movement budding among the youth faded as a result of the spirit of reaction. The pogroms of recent years (1903-1905), however, which began in the midst of a deep revolutionary ferment, did not weaken it. Only the slaughters of the last October days disturbed the spirit of the community, deepened the feeling of loneliness and confusion and, like twenty-five years earlier, aroused the need for isolation and withdrawal into the shell. It is only from this frightened part of the community that we now hear protests against the revolutionary movement." An echo of this reaction Anski senses in the latest essays by Ahad Ha-Am and by me.

I wonder how the author of *Pionern* . . . could have arrived at such a superficial historical confusion. . . . We do not find any indications of reaction in the movement of the 1880s. In that period a resistance developed among the intellectual classes against the previous assimilation, and many among our enlightened circles returned to their people with a firm determination to devote their energies to it. The national movement proceeded along two lines: the path of "Love of Zion" and the path of reform of the life of the old and new centers of the Diaspora. In the twenty years that have passed since the eighties, these two currents broadened and deepened. Both progressive nationalism and Zionism struck roots and branched out.

In the last few years the revolutionary and Socialist current also came to the fore. It was then that the question of the relationship of the three currents arose. The attitude of the nationalists and the Zionists to the new movement was not a negative one as long as the liberation movement embraced all Jews (Socialist groups of the type of the Poale-Zion, etc. were founded even in the camp of the Zionists). The nationalists, however, demand the supremacy of national politics in the struggle for freedom. It was the deviation from this principle that aroused the protest by Ahad Ha-Am and by me. We did not protest against the Jewish revolution, as a necessary reaction of an oppressed and humiliated people against its tormentors, but against our non-Jewish revolution, against the assimilation or the "slavery" in our revolutionary movement, against the contempt for our national purposes.* Anski's historical parallel should be rephrased as follows: In the eighties there was a protest against cultural assimilation, and in 1905 against political assimilation. And in the same way in which the former was not directed against culture in general, so the latter is not directed against revolution in general.

In my essay "The Moral" I specifically stated that I consider it to be more natural for an energetic revolutionary movement to exist among Jews than among any other nationality because the old system in Russia abused no other nationality as ruthlessly as it abused us. I specifically say abused, because it oppressed all peoples, but it despised us. If our people would yield to any other in its strong revolutionary fervor and its stubborn struggle against absolutist rule, I would no longer take pride in belonging to an ancient cultural people, the people of the Prophets who foretold the triumph of justice. The spirit of rebellion, nurtured by our severe sufferings during all the years of reaction, should have burst forth with the power of a stream that has been freed from its ice. Did we not all hope for this, did we not all pray that the hand of revenge would smite our tormentors, did we not all want to see the Jewish legion in the war of liberation, to hear in it the voices of Jewish heroes, the echo to the cries of our dead and martyred ones?

* Anski considers it sacrilege to associate the terms "slavery" and "revolution." It is clear to all, however, that the criticism implied in "slavery" or imitation is not directed against the participation of the forces of Judaism in the general revolutionary movement, but against their non-participation in the Jewish movement. The expression "Slavery in the Midst of Revolution" means the element of slavery even among those who fight for emancipation.

We waited and hoped—and what do we see? Where is our legion with our own banners? Were all national banners merged in the general battle against the armies of the old regime? By no means. We see Polish, Lithuanian, Armenian and Finnish banners fluttering. There is also a Jewish legion (the "Bund"), but it has no bright and flaming national banner of its own. This legion uses Russian slogans, even though its language of command is Yiddish. All our other zealots are fighting in the front ranks of the general revolutionary army. The slogans used in the liberation struggle of the most oppressed nationality ring strange in our ears. "Down with the Bourgeoisie! Long live the Dictatorship of the Proletariat!" As if not all classes of the Jewish people suffered and still continue to suffer under the yoke of violence, as if all the groans of suffering did not merge into one cry: "Freedom for the oppressed people!" The mistake in general strategy, which turned the political revolution prematurely into a social revolution, and the mistake of the Jewish fighters who concealed their Jewish banner—together brought about our present tragic condition. The former mistake did severe damage to the entire Russian liberation movement, the latter to its Jewish branch. . . .

The only ones who were free from this mistake were those who accepted the general political program of the Constitutional-Democratic Party (Kadet) and, in Jewish politics, the program of the League for the Attainment of Rights. . . . The more nationally conscious and mature section of our intelligentsia did not necessarily join the Kadet Party, but their ideas are very similar to the program of the Kadets, a program which cannot be imagined without the formal principle of equal national rights. This intelligentsia fights together with the Russian Kadets and, as a special legion under its own national banner, it must fight for the principles of a democratic constitution, without which equal rights can in no way be secured and guaranteed. However, this intelligentsia is not at all certain that our Russian allies, once liberation is achieved on paper, will not turn their backs on us as did the "Liberals" in western Europe. It could well be that after the honeymoon of freedom, antisemitic tendencies may develop among the Russian liberals. Be that as it may, we must rely only on our own forces if we want to secure our national rights, because we cannot rely on outside help in this respect and I do not expect it even from the Socialist parties, which, as a matter of principle, will advocate Jewish assimilation for a long time to come, even though they are free from the antisemitism that is transmitted from generation to generation.* . . .

To summarize: the supremacy of national politics is the correct expression of the idea of the indivisibility of all Israel (*klal yisrael*) in its modern form. National politics takes the place of territorial unity in the Diaspora, which faces the constant danger of conquest from within. . . . Under the condition in which the Jews find themselves in a gentile world, this idea has a unique significance which is different from the significance it has for the governments of strong nations. While for dominant nationalities "national politics" serves only as a means of oppressing subject peoples and curtailing their rights, for the persecuted nationalities true national politics will serve as a weapon to defend justice and right, the weak against the strong. . . .

April 1906†

* What has been said here can serve as proof how great is my "faith" in the Russian liberals, which Anski finds in me and which he contrasts with my suspicions towards the "populist Amalek." The expression "populist Amalek" I intended for the "Black Myriads," which will continue on in Russia for a long time, and for the consciously or unconsciously antisemitic masses in all political parties. I must explain at this point the limit to my agreement with Ahad Ha-Am's views. With all the respect I pay him for his forceful defense of our national politics in the newspapers and at the third meeting of the League for the Attainment of Rights, I do not agree with his conclusions that, for the defense of our liberty, we may ally ourselves with all Russian parties that recognize our rights, even those who do not belong to the forces of democracy. Strategy of this kind I find unnational from a Jewish point of view because the mass of our people is accustomed to consider all members of the rightist and even of the moderate Russian parties as its enemies. In western Europe the Jews never made common cause with the Conservatives. (The British Conservatives are unique and are therefore not in this category.) . . .

† Three years after this polemic with Anski, this member of the Socialist Revolutionary Party, who with all this is also an ardent Jewish democrat, joined our Folkspartay, whose program is explained in the following "Letter." Towards the end of his life he moved close to the Zionist movement.

Twelfth Letter

ON THE TASKS OF THE FOLKSPARTAY

The Jewish people is passing through one of the major crises in its history. The special character of this new crisis consists of the fact that in it are combined the revolutionary movement which promises equal rights to our persecuted nationality and elements of barbarous and reactionary antisemitism. The section of the Jewish people concentrated in Russia is placed in an unusual situation between inquisition and emancipation, between a St. Bartholomew's Eve and the light of dawning freedom. In the countries of western Europe, where the oppressed peoples won their freedom through political revolution, there was not even one section of our people that was in a comparable situation on the eve of its liberation. In the west, the period of emancipation was preceded by a regime characterized by absence of rights, but not by terror of pogroms and violence. In Russia mass pogroms accompany reaction as well as revolution. On the threshold of the new regime the whole "pale of settlement" is engulfed by flames and is devastated, destroyed and drenched with the blood of the pogrom victims.

The sufferings of oppression and the terrors of pogroms will, of course, not keep the active forces of Jewry from participating in the liberation movement. On the contrary, they will intensify the fervor of the revolutionary fighters, who connect the hope for salvation of our suffering nation with the success of the revolutionary movement. But what form should our participation in the liberation struggle take? What are the special goals of Jewry in this fight, and how can we unite all our national forces to achieve them? The various parties give different answers to these questions. The Folkspartay (Jewish People's Party) gives its own answers to these questions which, in its opinion, derive from a total synthesis of Jewish life in the past and its needs in the present.

The program of action of the Folkspartay is based on two principles: (a) the recognition of the common needs of all sections of

Jewry in the political, civic, and national-cultural fields; (b) the recognition that the Jews must carry on their fight for existence as members of one indivisible Jewish nationality, which, in the Diaspora, is divided into parts of different states, but not into parts of other nationalities.

The community of interests of the Jewish nationality is based upon positive historical, cultural and social factors, and not only upon the negative factor of the need for defense against the oppressive forces that manifest themselves in the form of antisemitism and hatred of Israel. However, to those who cannot or do not wish to probe into the matter of our national unity from a positive angle we must provide the negative argument that, wherever we find the whole people in danger from external pressure, we are entitled to demand the participation of all parties in its defense. A government and a society that are hostile to the Jews vent their wrath, not on this part or that part of our people, but on the entire people. Hatred against the Jews is indivisible no matter whether it is inherited or acquired through education, whether it springs from cold calculation or from savage revolt. It has assumed different masks in various periods: religious, national, economic, political, whatever suited the state of social climate prevailing at the moment.

The systematic antisemitic violence in contemporary Russia, which has taken on the form of a war of annihilation against the Jews, should have united the forces of all parties and currents into a general national defense. If the leader of the German Social Democratic Party declared that his party would fight shoulder to shoulder with the patriots of the bourgeoisie in case of danger,[44] if a foreign enemy should attack Germany, then what should Bebel's Jewish allies in Russia do when their own unfortunate nation is faced with danger that is greater than the one that would threaten Germany from attack by the French army? Did they join with all those who are fighting for the good of the nation? Did they desist at all from incitement to class dissension and take action in the revolutionary movement to save our people that stands like "a lamb amidst seventy wolves?" No such unity of active forces was achieved, not even in the present moment of grave crisis. We do not even have the temporary alliance often found in hours of danger among political enemies.

Even when the current danger will have passed and the new regime will have gained strength in Russia, shall we still not need special defense? . . . What is in store for us in Russia after we will have won equal rights on paper through the victory of the constitutional regime for which we now fight together with the emancipated Russian people? If paper-liberation has not yet given the Jews complete freedom even in western Europe, we can well imagine how much time will be required to secure it and establish it on a firm foundation in Russia, where the terrorist movement of the Black Hundred will continue for some time to fight against the recent gains in political liberty and against European civilization.

Furthermore, even if we should be freed from external danger in its crude forms of government oppression and mass pogroms, we shall still be confronted by the danger of internal national disruption, the force that is destroying the lives of our western brethren. Even if we secure our lives as citizens, we are not at all secure from national death, or, at least, from a national death struggle, unless we take measures to obtain assurances of cultural autonomy based on the same demands made by every national minority which does not wish to be assimilated by the alien environment of the majority.

We ourselves must answer the question as to whether we are fighting for survival as a motley group of individuals, forced into one compartment by common oppression, or as a united nationality with definite historical and cultural aims in a positive and decisive manner. We must decide whether we are merely concerned with the welfare of the individual Jewish citizen, who, after he has secured equal rights, may leave the Jewish community and align himself with the Russian, Polish or German nationality, or whether we want to reform and revitalize our whole people as a cultural historical body through the improvement of the social condition of the Jews. If we accept the former alternative we need not join together to wage a united political struggle. We can secure much greater advantages for the life of each individual if we disperse ourselves immediately among other national groups and among general international parties. By abandoning his affiliation with the oppressed nationality, each individual will cease to suffer from this oppression and all the other members of the nationality will be able to accept the principle of *sauve qui peut.* If we have not yet reached such a point of decline, if we have not yet become "national chaff" blown about by every wind, if we consider ourselves to be one nationality and not fragments of a nationality broken up into religious sects among other peoples, then we must everywhere defend our national identity in the same manner that all national minorities battle for their rights in a multi-national state—with those modifications, of course, which are inherent in the special characteristics of our historical position.

We must not repeat the mistake made by western Jews . . . in denying their nationality and in assimilating completely in all areas of life except religion. . . . We eastern Jews have seen all the terrors of the Middle Ages in the bright daylight of recent history and can, therefore, attain to deeper insights than our western brethren in the period preceding the rise of antisemitism. Moreover, we can also make use of their bitter experience. We have seen that there can be such things as semi-freedom and semi-emancipation and that under a system of formal equality of civic rights we may have a total rejection of equal status for Jewish national values. We have seen that not all hopes are realized quickly and not all sufferings will soon come to an end. We have jumped into the Russian revolutionary movement with the wrath of the despised and the vehemence of the insulted, but also with a strong determination to fight for our freedom to the end. Indeed, in the heat of the struggle against the terror-regime, which is the source of our sufferings and tears, the members of our extremist parties enrolled under general banners and did not set up our own national banner. They sounded general slogans in which the anguish of our own unhappy people was not audible. Psychologically, however, it was the Jewish protest that drove these revolutionaries into the fray. The angered masses felt that their chastising hand would give just due to the cursed regime and that with their blows they would break the fetters of slavery. These masses have the right to demand that the Jewish battle-cry be heard more forcefully in the legion of the revolutionary fighters which was recruited from the most humiliated and oppressed of all the peoples of Russia, and to insist that the Jewish demands be included in this battle-cry.

These demands must be proclaimed and will be proclaimed if not through all, then through the majority of our organized forces. The party that we are now founding under the name of Folkspartay will proclaim them and place these demands at the head of its program.[45]

The general political program and the special national program of the Folkspartay are adapted to the needs of the broad strata of the Jewish community. A democratic regime is a precondition for our civic emancipation. All discerning Jews in Russia understand the elementary truth that only a victory for the democratic constitution will give them freedom and equal rights, and that all parties to the right of this position will never agree to the full emancipation of the Jews. Thus not only our political aspirations, but our basic needs now force the majority of the Jews to join that current of democratic liberalism which assumed a special form in Russia in the program of the Constitutional-Democratic Party, which is the "party of national freedom."* For this reason the founders of the Folkspartay included the basic principles of the program of the Kadet party in the general part of their program, with the changes demanded by the national, economic, and spiritual characteristics of Jewish life. . . .† The founders of the party placed these basic problems at the head of their program because they recognize that the political struggle in Russia in the near future will center around the constitutional democratic basis and that the solution of the Jewish question depends on the outcome of this struggle. . . . Once the immediate aim is reached and the basis for a free democratic government and equal rights for all citizens established, then the time will be ripe for the solution of the other problems, including also those of extreme socialism.

* I refer to the "current" (in its different shades), and not to the party proper, since not all members of the Folkspartay need join the party. Every member of our circle may also join another party more to the left, as long as he accepts the Constitutional-Democratic program as a concrete minimum program for the immediate future.

† The general and national program of the Folkspartay was published early in 1907 in the newspapers and in separate pamphlets (in Russian and Yiddish), with this essay as an introduction.

The national part of the program is in line with the sections of the general political program which set down the principles of free self-determination for national minorities and the right to autonomy following from them. From these general principles are derived special and detailed provisions applicable to the conditions of Jewish life as well as the methods to be applied. . . . In our program of autonomy, the Folkspartay proposes to use the idea of communal self-administration that has been hallowed by the historical experience of many generations. Individual autonomy for every national minority not living as a compact territorial group is also recognized by contemporary political science. In all periods of the Diaspora, Jews in different countries had a substitute for territorial autonomy in the form of a more or less extensive communal organization. In the areas of Jewish settlement in Russia today and in the former Polish state there was a highly ramified organization of communities, unions of communities and councils of the lands. This old communal organization, however, was based on the civic inequality and complete isolation of the Jewish population. In addition, the main unit of self-administration was the religious community, the community of the synagogues. Finally the whole system of self-administration was vitiated by the plague of oligarchy (the rule of the hard-hearted rich).

The modern idea of self-administration differs from all the principles just mentioned: from the first—in the firm demand that the Jews take part in the civic and political life of the land as free men, since equality of rights cannot be visualized without this; from the second—in the secularization of the national idea, that is, its separation from the religious idea; and from the oligarchy—in that we should be protected by the democratic principles which would form the basis of the new communal autonomy. The unit of self-administration in our time can only be the free people's community (*Volksgemeinde*), with elected councils that administer the local cultural institutions, co-operatives, and philanthropic agencies. The communities would then be united in a Union of Jewish Communities in the Russian empire, which would create central institutions of self-administration in the sphere of Jewish national interests. Freedom of language and autonomy of the school are the most important of all "national rights," without which full civic equality before the law is impossible. . . . The Folkspartay does not demand territorial autonomy for a nationality which does not constitute a majority of the inhabitants in any area; but it will fight with all the strength it can muster for Jewish communal and national-cultural autonomy, which is derived from the principle of the freedom of cultural self-determination.

When we consider how difficult are the conditions for political development in Russia, we see how remote are the optimistic expectations that even this program, which may appear overly modest to extremist parties with their "programs for the future," will be realized quickly. It will be necessary to fight for every paragraph, first in the legislative assembly, and then in every locality. However, if we consider ourselves a nationality, a cultural body, we must present immediately all the demands of our program, the sum total of our civic and national rights, in concrete form, of course, that can be realized in practice. We must not ask timidly for the restoration of our human dignity "bit by bit" and with cautious "gradualism." Both our friends and our enemies must know what the Jewish people demands and for what it is fighting. Those opportunists who say: "Let us first win only civic emancipation and then we will present the demand for national rights" are saying in reality: "Let us secure equal rights for the individuals and conceal our nationality for the moment, and afterwards we will reveal the secret that we too are a 'nationality.' " These "clever" individuals are too short-sighted to understand that in so doing they brand upon their people the infamous mark of national inequality. How much a Jew must hate himself who recognizes the right of every nationality and language to self-determination but doubts it or restricts it for his own people, whose "self-determination" began three thousand years ago!

We do not delude ourselves with the hope that even the successful conclusion of our work will completely end the "Jewish emergency" in the Diaspora and will remove the incessant pressure to which other peoples and cultures subject us. We merely wish to indicate the only concrete way, justified by historical experience during two thousand years, that will lead to the weakening of this pressure and to the preservation and free development of the national Diaspora. Since we do not consider the Zionist "state of the future" to be within the realm of possibility, we are convinced that our work must be concentrated mainly on organizing our national existence in that world-Diaspora which, even after the future triumphs of Zionism, may decrease a little but will not vanish from this world.

The world Diaspora offers enough latitude to fight for the material and spiritual interests of Judaism. In those countries in which external oppression passes beyond the limits of endurance, our people will be aided by the outstanding factor in our history: emigration in its various stages, starting with the normal flight of groups of persecuted individuals, and ending with a partial or complete transfer of the center of the nation from the land of oppression to the land of freedom. Once emancipation is attained in the old homeland, the mass exodus of the Jews from Russia to America will have to be reduced substantially and the character of a panic flight eliminated. Even under more settled conditions, however, it will continue to serve as one of the most important factors in our life. . . . For this reason we include the organization of emigration among our national tasks (for they are not confined within the frontiers of one country only) so that this movement may not be reduced to fragments but flow to definite centers in fixed ways. We must concern ourselves especially with the two new future centers of Judaism, the land of Israel with its value as a spiritual center, and America with its value as a socio-economic center. This might well become our principal task if our broad program in Russia is disrupted by a temporary victory of the dark political reaction which plots to destroy and to obliterate the buds of the liberation movement. . . .

The nature of the program of the Folkspartay determines its relationship to all the other parties and organizations in Judaism. In the present historical moment we have a double criterion: the supremacy of general national politics and the realistic character of such politics serve as yardsticks for us of the political maturity of the parties. . . . Although we differ from the Zionists in the evaluation of all our cultural work in the Diaspora (they see it only as a stage preparatory to the migration to the Jewish "state of the future" while we trust that this powerful organic effort has inherent value for a people whose overwhelming majority will remain in the present centers of settlement and must live a full civic and national life there to the ultimate possible limits), we are nevertheless prepared to join with this party in its "concrete efforts" to improve the social condition of the Jews throughout the Diaspora. With the League for the Attainment of Rights we can work in harmony as long as it does not deviate from its democratic and national basis. With the leaders of our Jewish Socialist organizations we could go part of the way, up to a certain point, if they would renounce their objective to sharpen artificially the conflict between class and national politics and accept the supremacy of the latter. . . .

When parties with "programs for the future" arise to obscure the form of the nationality with its concrete needs of the moment, the defenders of the needs of *klal yisrael* must combine to secure the triumph of realistic national politics that correspond to the conditions of time and place. The Folkspartay is potentially, if not actually, the nucleus of the organized nation, because it takes the middle course between all camps—the way that unites them all. . . .

December 1906.

Thirteenth Letter

THE EMANCIPATION MOVEMENT AND THE EMIGRATION MOVEMENT

(*A Reply to Dr. Ch. D. Hurwitz*)[46]

With your "Open Letter" to me you did me a great favor by posing publicly the question of the relationship between the program of the Folkspartay, which is attuned to the emancipation movement in Russia, and the great emphasis I placed on the factor of emigration in our national life. I feel that so important a question deserves an answer, and your "Letter" made me decide to answer the question immediately.* . . .

You maintain that there is a basic contradiction between the fundamental ideas of our program and my explanatory essay. You find it difficult to understand how participation in the Russian emancipation movement in order to attain civic and national rights in our state and energetic efforts to organize a movement of emigration from this state can be joined in the same program. To you the matter appears as follows: if the Jews join the devoted ranks of Russian fighters for freedom and if they are filled with burning faith in their future liberation, how can they think of organizing a systematic emigration to other countries to which they were drawn earlier by oppression and bitter desperation? How can they combine bright hopes with gloomy despair? You find indications of such despair, or of "*galut* psychology," in my comments on the program of the party, especially in my statement that "we do not delude ourselves with the hope that even the successful conclusion of our work will completely end . . . the incessant pressure to which other peoples and cultures subject us," but that it will lead only to the weakening of this pressure.

It follows from your comments that the movement for liberty and

* After the preceding essay had been published as an introduction to the program of the Folkspartay, a piece entitled "Open Letter to S. Dubnow" appeared in the newspaper *Fraynd* over the signature of the well-known publicist Ch. D. Hurwitz. My reply to this "Open Letter," written in Yiddish, was published in the same newspaper (nos. 21-22, 1907).

the emigration movement are mutually contradictory. It is my view that they are two aspects of one movement directed toward the liberation of the Jewish nationality in every part of the Diaspora. I shall attempt to prove that one movement is impossible without the other under the present conditions of our people and, perhaps, also in the distant future.

You will not deny, of course, that of the two general causes of the exodus, the economic and the political, the economic cause will continue to affect the life of the Russian Jews for many years to come. The Germans and the Italians have many more privileges than we have and yet tens of thousands of them go to America every year, leaving their homeland for good or temporarily, because of poverty or unemployment. Many years will pass before the serious wounds of the last decades heal and before our economic situation in Russia becomes normalized. You surely will also agree that, even after the liberation movement triumphs in Russia, a sizable part of our Jewish masses will not lack political motives to leave their homeland to any lesser degree than the Irish or the Poles in their countries. If this is the case, if emigration from the Russian empire, even to a smaller extent, will continue, then we cannot fail to recognize the need to organize it as an important social factor. On this minimum, therefore, you also agree with me. Now let us clarify what appears to you to be the maximum of the emigration movement and to me—a necessity imposed by reality. . . .

Let us assume that the panic flight of the Jews from Russia, which became intensified after the pogroms of the last few years (1903-1906), will diminish in proportion to the improvement of our political and civic condition. No matter how much emigration will decrease, however, it will still be a more constant factor with us than with other peoples. Economically we shall not only continue to feel the effects of the old wounds, but shall also experience attacks by the new antisemitism which will develop as free Jewish competition in commerce and industry becomes stronger. We will, to be sure, obtain equal rights, but do you think that from that moment on we will live a life of peace and quiet and enjoy all the rights that were given us on paper? Do you know the troubles the Jews of Germany and Austria experienced before the civic and political rights guaranteed to them by their constitutions were actually put into force? And even today they still have not realized more than half of those privileges. Can you tell us in advance what distress and hardships we will continue to suffer from the gangs of "true Russians" and from the more cultured antisemites?

Do you seriously think that the victory of the liberation movement will put an end to oppression? True, terrible days like those of October, which are infrequent even in our history of pain and suffering, will perhaps not recur, but the Black Hundred still exists and will continue to exist for some time to come; and the followers of Krushevan[47] will not soon disappear from Holy Russia, and we shall still have to deal with this disease of the human species. Official antisemitism will perhaps be eliminated under a liberal regime, but social antisemitism will continue to manifest itself for a long time to come. . . . We shall obviously not give up, but stubbornly combat the social antisemitism as we fought official antisemitism before; yet there will be those who, unable to stand the pressure, will emigrate overseas. . . .

This is the most optimistic view of the situation once we obtain equal rights. But what will happen if the second Duma does not bring us the redemption to which we look forward with some dubiousness? What shall we do if this Duma, too, is unceremoniously dissolved, and if "they" begin to strengthen the constitution in "true Russian" fashion?* What will happen if the rowdies of the League of the Russian People triumph and take power into their bloodstained hands? Then the emigration of the earlier days of terror will be renewed. For the masses of our people there will be a new exodus from Egypt, if not to the Holy Land, at least to a land where people are not murdered. If those who pin all their hopes on the liberation movement now bury the emigration movement, they will be forced to exhume it later. And then they will really understand what vital and redeeming force is hidden in Jewish migration as it has been

* Soon afterwards this did happen, in June, 1907.

carried on for thousands of years from the time God said to Abraham: "Get thee out of thy country, and from thy kindred, and from thy father's house, unto the land that I will show thee!"

You think that the advocates of the emigration idea are sorry pessimists who weaken the hands of the people in the heat of the struggle for liberation. I say: "If you deprive the Jew of the hope of changing his place, the hope that he will be able to escape from danger, if things are bad, to a country where thousands of his brethren have found refuge, you will crush his soul into the dust. Then he will really despair because he will feel hemmed in on all sides and deserted by the whole world without refuge from oppression and persecution. What you say is quite true, the Jews stand with one foot in Russia and with the other in America; but if they were to stand with both feet on the Russian volcano, they would not have a firm foothold for fear of the possible terrors of the near future. . . .

It is here that you start finding faults, that is, contradictions and inconsistencies in our attitude. You accuse us of joining in the war of liberation without enthusiastic faith in its success, of offering the people a program for redemption with one hand and of directing it to America and Palestine with the other—of deepening the despair of the *galut* in the souls of the Jews. There is a considerable difference of opinion concerning this "despair." Who deepens it, he who shows the unfortunate two ways to freedom, or he who shows him only one? As far as our enthusiastic faith in the imminence of the messianic era in Russia is concerned, I believe that from the standpoint of realistic politics such romantic notions have no value for our goals. Our romantic youngsters in the Socialist parties think differently, but neither you nor I are political infants and we have not undertaken to build the "Kingdom Come" in the course of a few years. Ask the average Jew who thinks straight and clearly, whether he genuinely believes that we in Russia are on the threshold of happy days of liberty, equality and fraternity. Ask the mature intellectuals! Let us not deceive ourselves. We are living, not in bright hope, but 'twixt fear and hope, and it is certainly likely that we shall continue to live in such a condition for a long time to come.

We have in truth, as I said in my essay, "jumped into the Russian revolutionary movement with the wrath of the despised and the vehemence of the insulted." We could not have done otherwise: we, an ancient cultural people, cannot be the "slaves of slaves." If, however, we do not achieve our goal after a protracted struggle, if we receive the scroll of freedom in a cover of pogroms, if the Russian constitution remains the captive for some time to come of officers and gangs of the Black Hundred, then you will once more hear the call in the Jewish camp: "Get out of the Russian Egypt!" We have made and we shall continue to make sacrifices in the war of liberation, but if, after all our sacrifices, we remain like the old woman in the tale by Pushkin, with only a "broken old trough,"[48] we shall not maintain our position, and a large part of the masses of our people will go to distant lands. This hope of finding a refuge for part of our people in a distant country must be preserved by us for a day of trouble. It will give us greater strength and courage to struggle on here, in the old homeland.

Shall we try to deprive the Jews of this hope? Do you want to take away the wanderer's staff from a people which has relied on it for thousands of years? You disparage the "psychology of the wanderers." Try and tear it out of Ahasuerus' heart, and you will also tear out his soul! "A fugitive and a wanderer shalt thou be in the earth"— this curse, which was laid upon Ahasuerus the "Eternal Jew" in the Christian legend, turned into a blessing and an instrument of salvation for him. He would have vanished from this living earth a long time ago if he had not learned the lesson of migration. Ahasuerus would not have remained the "Eternal Jew" if he had not become the "Eternal Wanderer." Our ancestors understood this truth very well: "The Lord has done kindness to Israel in scattering it among the nations" (*Pesahim*, 87b). One of the medieval sages interprets the idea as follows: "A king in one country issues decrees against our money and our lives, while in another country another king has mercy and saves those who escape." From a religious point of view this is astonishing: the Lord could have saved the chosen people from ruin in a single country. But the saying contains a sound historical observation: without migration, not even a small remnant would have been left of the Jewish people after all the misfortunes, crusades, expulsions, persecutions, inquisitions and pogroms. And what would have been our fate in Russia during the last twenty years had we not been able to drill a hole in the boiling cauldron in which we were being roasted and let the steam escape! We would have been smothered in the land of slavery and pogroms, if we had not transferred a million and half Jews to North America, Palestine, Argentina, South Africa and other countries and if we had destroyed the hope that the opportunity exists to change our habitat and our fortune. And you want to place a lid over the hole in our cauldron! Beware and take heed: the cauldron is still boiling!

Our entire history is a chain of transfers of cultural centers from country to country, and in my historical works I have elaborated at some length upon this idea of changing centers. Palestine, Babylonia, Spain, Germany, Poland, Russia—these are the travels of the children of Israel, the great stations on the path of the wanderers. During the recent period a central station has been growing up in America and a smaller but beloved one in Palestine. I have already shown how the centers were transferred from the eastern to the western pole in our time (Letter Nine, IV), and recent events have proved that I was not mistaken.

There is something else that I must say to my critic. . . . You think that placing my hopes on the future of the two centers of Judaism, in America and Palestine, "means being taken in by facts that are not yet actual." In your opinion there is not the slightest proof that America will really become a strong economic and political center for us, and that the new settlement in Palestine will become a spiritual center. I gratefully acknowledge your "rebuke," your warning to adhere more closely to facts, because that is not a small thing at a time when political romanticists pursue distant aims and messianic ideals. . . . We members of the Folkspartay do not belong to the camp of the Zionists because we consider the final aim of political Zionism a chiliastic doctrine. But we, too, have a broad perspective which is also based on "facts that are in the making." When we see that within twenty-six years, twenty or thirty villages and tens of thousands of Jewish settlers have been added in our old homeland in Palestine, and that a new society of farmers, agricultural laborers and winegrowers is slowly coming into being there; when we hear that our ancient language is being renewed in the mouths of children, and that all subjects are being taught in this language in the schools, then we have a right to hope that in the course of time a spiritual center for the Jewish nation will rise in Eretz Yisrael.

Whether this center will be a large one or not is still a question, and I do not believe, as does Ahad Ha-Am, that the center in Palestine will have a magic power which will influence our whole national culture in the Diaspora. No, if we do not base our national autonomy firmly on civic freedom here in the Diaspora by ourselves, a handful of "Palestinian Jews" will not save us from the flood of assimilation. But we would not do right if we denied the moral influence of the Palestinian center. If even a small flame is kindled in Zion, too small to bring light to the entire world of Judaism, it is nevertheless clear to me that it will warm many Jewish hearts. This warm corner will always draw our hearts with magnetic force; it will awaken in us precious historical memories and, with all this, will also serve as a place of settlement. Everyone must support this practical colonization. It is not necessary to be a Zionist for this purpose, and a party like the Folkspartay, committed to national politics, must include this work in its program.

These words apply also to the youngest offshoot of Russian Jewry, which pulled down its home in the land of oppression and emigrated to a spacious though very distant dwelling place in North America. When we see that within twenty-five years a "Jewish America," numbering two million, was created, mainly by Russian emigrants, that New York City alone has close to 700,000 Jews, and that the main stream of our emigrants flows increasingly to the great republic across the sea, then we have the right to believe that in the course of time America will become the major center of Judaism alongside of Russia and, under certain conditions, may even surpass it. We must take this movement in hand and organize it as far as is possible. It is our duty—and this is also a national duty—to organize the emigration to America on firm foundations. We must see to it that our emigrants do not suffer unnecessarily from the vicissitudes of their journey, that they know where best to find work and sustenance in America without too great a dispersal. There as well as here we must concentrate all our forces so that our brethren will organize themselves in the free country on a broad basis of national autonomy which will protect them against cultural assimilation—the greatest danger in the United States. . . .

The Jewish settlement in America is from its birth an offshoot of our great center in Russia, and when the old mother is in bad and difficult circumstances she is drawn hopefully to her young daughter in the land of the free. We are strongly bound to that part of our national family that has moved across the sea. It is bone of our bone and flesh of our flesh. Our strength is the greater in that, in our war for liberation, we have two positions, one in Europe and one in America. If Esau falls upon one position, we will receive him properly; but in the event of the worst possible extremity, the second position will be left for Jacob and the "remaining camp will be able to escape." . . .

You find that we have no right to rebuke the other parties for placing their partisan aims above the general national aims. However, in uttering this rebuke in the introduction to our party program, I had in mind those class parties who disparage the hallowed watchword of Jewish unity, that "all Israel are brothers." Jews who use the term "general Jewish politics" (*klal Yīsroel politik*) with derision, who mock the noble concept of a national idea which has saved us for two thousand years, Jews who wish to shatter and split the scattered people and teach one-tenth of the oppressed people to hate the other nine-tenths as proletarians hate the "ruling bourgeoisie" (a "bourgeoisie" composed of millions of hungry or half-satisfied people, of which only a minority has enough to eat), such Jews truly deserve censure because they sacrifice the "nation" upon the altar of "class" or party.

You blame the Folkspartay for "avoiding long-range tasks and long-range ideals and for concentrating on the more immediate general affairs of Judaism." I accept your censure gratefully in the name of the party as a symbol of the praise we deserve. Indeed, we do not want to force the "end of the days" prematurely or to supplant the messiah. Do you know why? Because we can't do it. We have high ideals (what is comparable to the organization of the entire nation?), but we approach them with sure step and do not vacillate in mid-air. I believe that you, too, will say "Amen" to our prayer that we may be favored to attain "the immediate aims" of *klal yisrael*, proposed by the program of the Folkspartay, in at least fifty years, and then we will surely come to an agreement concerning the "long-range ideals!"

February 1907.

NEGATION AND AFFIRMATION OF THE DIASPORA IN AHAD HA-AM'S THOUGHT

Ahad Ha-Am occupies a unique position in the national movement of our time, a position very close to official Zionism and general Jewish nationalism. His great literary stature fills the entire gulf that separates those who have a negative attitude toward the Diaspora from those with a positive attitude. With the force of unfolding events and ideas, Ahad Ha-Am's doctrine of a "spiritual center" is becoming the mediating influence between those who are building Zion and those who are building the Diaspora in a national spirit. It can well serve as a bridge between the two extremes of the Jewish nationalist camp, unite all forces for national revival, and clear the ground for a nationalist synthesis.

In order to realize this end of uniting the various groupings in the national camp by means of the teaching of Ahad Ha-Am, we must clarify one basic idea which has not yet been adequately dealt with in the school of this writer: to what degree does the creator of this idea share the views of those who negate the Diaspora and how close has he moved to those who affirm it and demand organized national activity in all Jewish centers—activity for its own sake and not only for the sake of the unity of the "center" and its surroundings? The clarification of this question, as pointed out, is very important both theoretically and practically for the day when joint activity by nationalists and Zionists will be under discussion. From the day Ahad Ha-Am's theory was formulated, I have tried several times—in critical essays and in discussions with him—to clarify this question, but to this day I have not succeeded in arriving at a positive solution, even though we reached a point in our exchange very close to the desired solution.

My purpose in this brief essay is to discuss this point and help bring about an answer acceptable to both national views, for they have distinct spiritual affinity with each other. I should like to get beneath the surface of Ahad Ha-Am's ideas on this subject and see if we cannot come up with a general conclusion which he himself has as yet not formulated as a definite law, although it is already apparent in quite a number of the specific ideas set forth by our author in the course of the development of his views. After several decades of discussion between the proponents of spiritual Zionism and of spiritual nationalism, I feel the moral obligation to confirm the "lasting elements" (for "a dispute for the sake of Heaven must endure") to which we arrived at the end of our discussion and which contain a basis for a national synthesis for the future. Perhaps this small offering of mine will be favorably received in the issue of this magazine dedicated to our finest author—"a mixed offering" in which hopes for the future blend with memories of the past, a past of twenty-five years during which I observed at close range Ahad Ha-Am's growth and, together with him, the growth of the literature of the period.

For a long time Ahad Ha-Am was looked upon as an extremist in the negation of the Diaspora. The dark veil he spread over the *galut* in his first essays: "Slavery in the Midst of Freedom," "Fragments," and others, had the effect of engulfing all the hopes of the generation of emancipation and enlightenment in an "Egyptian darkness." Only one ray of light penetrated the darkness from afar: the idea of a "change of the center" in a form which, at the time, at the beginning of colonization in Palestine, was not yet felt nor had yet penetrated the heart. Indeed, anyone who looked into the teachings of Ahad Ha-Am, even in those days of the period of the Hoveve Tsiyon, could distinguish between negation of the Diaspora born out of the deep "distress of Judaism" and that superficial negation which came from the "distress of Jews," and which served as a sort of agitation for the dissemination of the idea of *Hibbat Tsiyon* in its immature form, the salvation of all the children of Israel through the colonization of Palestine. But the people of that generation did not sense this difference. Even Ahad Ha-Am himself, who presented the basic principles of his theory of the revival of the national spirit through the "renewal of a central point" in Eretz Yisrael with such clarity and precision, set no limits in the matter of the negation of the Diaspora.

Ahad Ha-Am set clearer limits to the negation when he began his polemics with the political Zionists. At the time of the early Zionist congresses, when enthusiasm for Herzl's faith was strongest, sobering words such as the following were heard: "The truth is bitter, but with all its bitterness it is better than illusion. We must admit to ourselves that the ingathering of the exiled is something beyond nature. It is quite reasonable to expect that after some time we shall establish a Jewish state and that the Jews will increase and multiply until the land is full of them. Even then, however, the majority of the Jewish people will remain scattered and dispersed in foreign countries. It is impossible to gather our exiled from the four corners of the earth. Only religion can promise this through miraculous salvation. If this is so and if the Jewish state does not mean the ingathering of the exiled but the settlement of a small part of the Jewish people in Palestine, then what about the physical distress of the majority of the Jewish people in the lands of the Diaspora? . . ." (*Al perashat derakhim*, vol. ii, pp. 24ff.)

After such an expression of opinion Ahad Ha-Am could no longer be satisfied with general arguments that the salvation of the national spirit in the Diaspora depended only on the creation and influence of the Zionist center. He felt the need to formulate practical principles for the work of revival in the Diaspora, which was a sort "affirmation of reality" (in an objective sense). Then, in his "Revival of the Spirit" (1903), he proposed a program of cultural activity: the strengthening of Hebrew literature and the striving to concentrate around it all the forces scattered among alien literatures, "the conquest of the schools" and of education in a national spirit, a series of communal activities in which many of the best Zionists and nationalists participated at the time.

Even with this, however, Ahad Ha-Am did not fulfill his obligation. When the question of national autonomy in the lands of the Diaspora began to burst upon our world, at first in literary form, then in the movements of parties in the Jewish community, the creator of the theory of the "spiritual center" had to clarify his relationship to this question and to define the degree of negation and affirmation of the Diaspora more precisely from the viewpoint of the "Spiritual Zionists." This answer came, although with some delay, in a short and spirited essay "The Negation of the Diaspora" (1909), one of his finest essays and one distinguished by brilliance of thought and style (*Al perashat derakhim*, vol. iv, pp. 106-116).

In this essay Ahad Ha-Am admits that, in an objective sense, the negation of the Diaspora, that is, the idea that our people cannot exist at all in the future as a separate nationality without a Jewish state, contradicts "the will to survive in the heart of the nation; for survival cannot be made dependent on any condition since the condition may not be fulfilled. The Jewish people as a whole feel that they have the will and the strength to survive whatever may happen, without any ifs or buts. Its natural instinct does not allow it to accept a theory that tells it that survival is conditional upon the ending of the Diaspora. Unconsciously it feels that this is a double condition, and that the acceptance of the first part of the condition leads also to the acceptance of the second part: If the attempt to leave the Diaspora does not succeed, you will surely die; and it wants life. . . ." Thus the affirmation of the Diaspora rooted in the hearts of the people forces it "to seek and find in every period the ways best suited for the preservation and development of its nationality in keeping with the conditions of life surrounding it." And what is the basis of national preservation? National autonomy in all the lands of the dispersion. But, Ahad Ha-Am asks at this point, "what degree of autonomy?" He assumes "as practically certain that the autonomists also concede that national autonomy (in the Diaspora) is not strong enough to give us a truly full and complete life. They contend, however, that the national will to survive demands that we struggle for national rights in the Diaspora in order to broaden the basis of our national life to the greatest possible extent. . . . And if we put the doctrine of autonomy in this modest form, I doubt whether any real Jew could be opposed to it from a subjective point of view, in the sense that he would not favor the extension of our national rights in the Diaspora and would not feel that it was necessary to work for it wherever possible. Opposition to it, wherever found, is based on the view that it is objectively impossible, that autonomy cannot be viewed from the standpoint of 'limits of possibility' but must extend beyond this limit, since in their opinion, our position among the nations is unique and is not at all such as to induce the major powers to recognize our national rights." It is here that Ahad Ha-Am sees the transition from the doctrine of autonomy to the theory of the spiritual center: "If this doctrine [of the autonomists] concedes that autonomy is not a complete solution but rather that we must try to attain it on the principle that 'half a loaf is better than none,' then it must also concede that we have the duty to look for still other, more 'radical' ways to strengthen our nationalism and to expand our national life on the other principle that 'a whole loaf is better than half a loaf.' " This is the way of the Zionist group that advocates a spiritual center, "which differs from the 'true' Zionists in that it does not believe in the ingathering of the exiled and does not deny existence in the Diaspora. On the contrary, since it considers the Diaspora as a permanent fixture which is beyond our power to eliminate, it insists that our national life in the Diaspora be strengthened, but it holds that this objective can only be realized by the creation of a definite center for our national life in the land of its natural existence." In the end, the autonomists too will be forced, according to Ahad Ha-Am, "to turn their eyes toward the East and to give to their doctrine a new formulation: Hold on to one thing, and do not withdraw your hand from the other. We must improve and expand our national life in the Diaspora to the utmost limits of possibility and, at the same time, search for the complete solution beyond the borders of the Diaspora."

I do not wish to renew the controversies between spiritual Zionism and national autonomism. I have already published my reply to Ahad Ha-Am's essay "The Negation of the Diaspora,"* and it may be said that in these two essays the two contending sides have gone as far as they can in their attempt to unite the divisions in the nationalist camp. We cannot speak of a "compromise" between the two sides, for on questions of basic principle there is no room for compromises. On the contrary, the question is how far each of the two systems forces its protagonists, through its principles, to accept from the related system the ideas that are common, potentially if not actually, to both. I have already expressed my opinions in the above-mentioned

* Affirmation of the Diaspora," in *Evreyskii mir* (1909) no. 5. [This is the Eighth Letter now in the present version of the *Letters*. See above, pp. 182-191 K. S. P.].

essay. Here I shall briefly summarize it. The autonomist nationalists recognize the value and influence of the cultural center in Eretz Yisrael and consider themselves obligated to work to strengthen and perfect it, on condition that this partial work be combined with the total activity directed toward strengthening our national culture and communal autonomy in all countries to the utmost limits of possibility. As I now study Ahad Ha-Am's *Torah* (for it is Torah and we must study it and also teach it according to the principle of "a specification requires a generalization"), I derive from it the conclusion which the author of this doctrine adumbrated but did not set up as a law, and I have the strong hope that, if he himself does not do it, his disciples will finish it and proclaim the law before their master.

Insofar as the spiritual Zionists "do not believe in the ingathering of the exiled and do not deny existence in the Diaspora but, on the contrary consider the Diaspora as a permanent feature . . . and that our national life in the Diaspora must be strengthened," they cannot and dare not see the "only way to this in the creation of a definite center for our national life in the land of its natural existence" (in the land of Israel), but as Ahad Ha-Am proclaimed to the autonomists, they must seize both: "improve and expand our national life in the Diaspora to the utmost limits of possibility and, at the same time, search for the complete solution beyond the borders of the Diaspora." This is equality of rights and equality of duties for the two sides in the dispute seeking completeness and integration of the national idea. In the last analysis, the work to perfect the spiritual center in Eretz Yisrael as one that will exercise its influence everywhere may also be counted among the activities carried out only "within the limits of possibility," only as far as we are able to dispose of the numerous political and cultural obstacles. Why does the Diaspora, fighting for its life against the "distress of Judaism," fighting as far as it is able with the means at its disposal and not only by emigration to Eretz Yisrael—why does it merit less consideration? To the same degree that the nationalist is obligated to participate in the revival of Eretz Yisrael, the Zionist who does not negate the Diaspora is obligated to participate in the revival of Israel in all countries in the world and to make use for this purpose of all the fighting weapons adopted by nations fighting for survival, even though he does not believe that the goal can be achieved in its entirety.

Many times the principle (which has been established as a definite psychological and historical law) has been advanced in Ahad Ha-Am's school that it is not the attainment of the goal that is the main thing but rather the striving for the goal. The striving for the creation of a spiritual center, will in itself lead to a greater concentration of forces in the Diaspora. This is indeed the supreme principle of all Jewish history, that our people has survived and will continue to survive in the Diaspora to the degree to which it has striven and will continue to strive for autonomy, for the self-regulation of its internal affairs, for a national culture everywhere in the dispersion, even though such striving may be far from the ideal goal. By such striving we carry on the thread of our national life. And if you should say: "Where will the striving, the will to a national life, come from?" we shall answer in Ahad Ha-Am's own words: "From the will to survive . . . which leads our people to believe in the possibility of its national survival in the Diaspora, and to search for the ways appropriate to the preservation and development of its nationality in accordance with the conditions of life surrounding it" (*Al perashat derakhim*, vol. iv, p. 109). And if this is so, are not both our aspirations really one: to bring about the revival of the majority of our people in the Diaspora and of a minority in Eretz Yisrael? Whoever takes hold of one of these aspirations dare not let go of the second, for both revivals are two sides of the same coin.

Ahad Ha-Am's inner understanding is profound and his teachings are clear. He never allows himself to become so intoxicated with an idea, no matter how taken he is with it, as to lose his sense of reality. That is why he has dared to deviate from the accepted path of his environment, the path of negation of the Diaspora. This "guide to the perplexed" has not yet completed his mission in life. Last year (1913) he brought his great book *Al perashat derakhim* to a close, but his teaching is not at an end. The Hebrew community has the right to expect new creative ideas from Ahad Ha-Am's pen, ideas concerning the great questions that move the Jewish world, the theory of the evolution of faith and knowledge, of ethics, and of the idea of nationalism. When Ahad Ha-Am ascends to the "summit," I trust that he will create there the nationalist synthesis, which will follow logically from his earlier teaching and will at the same time strike out on a path branching off from his *Perashat derakhim*.

I conclude with this greeting to Ahad Ha-Am on his literary anniversary: May it be God's will that his teaching reaches its highest perfection, and may its creator take his place in our midst as the mediator on whom the two branches of our nationalist camp lean. Then "*Ahad Ha-Am*" (One of the People) will become the "*Me'ahed Ha-Am*" (The Unifier of the People) and as such an important factor in the realization of our hope that "the throne may be complete" in the national development of Israel.

St. Petersburg, Shevat 5674 (1914).

PART II · ON HISTORY

JEWISH HISTORY

AN ESSAY IN THE PHILOSOPHY OF HISTORY

ISRAEL FRIEDLAENDER'S PREFACE TO THE GERMAN TRANSLATION

The author of the present essay, S. M. Dubnow, occupies a well-nigh dominating position in Russian-Jewish literature as an historian and an acute critic. His investigations into the history of the Polish-Russian Jews, especially his achievements in the history of hasidism, have been of fundamental importance in these departments. What raises Mr. Dubnow far above the status of the professional historian, and awakens the reader's lively interest in him, is not so much the matter of his books, as the manner of presentation. It is rare to meet with an historian in whom scientific objectivity and thoroughness are so harmoniously combined with an ardent temperament and plastic ability. Mr. Dubnow's scientific activity, first and last, is a striking refutation of the widespread opinion that identifies attractiveness of form in the work of a scholar with superficiality of content. Even his strictly scientific investigations, besides offering the scholar a wealth of new suggestions, form instructive and entertaining reading matter for the educated layman. In his critical essays, Mr. Dubnow shows himself to be possessed of keen psychologic insight. By virtue of this quality of delicate perception, he aims to assign to every historical fact its proper place in the line of development, and so establish the bond between it and the general history of mankind. This psychologic ability contributes vastly to the interest aroused by Mr. Dubnow's historical works outside of the limited circle of scholars. There is a passage in one of his books* in which, in his incisive manner, he expresses his views on the limits and tasks of historical writing. As the passage bears upon the methods employed in the present essay, and, at the same time, is a characteristic specimen of our author's style, I take the liberty of quoting:

> The popularization of history is by no means to be pursued to the detriment of its severely scientific treatment. What is to be guarded against is the notion that tedium is inseparable from the scientific method. I have always been of the opinion that the dullness commonly looked upon as the prerogative of scholarly inquiries, is not an inherent attribute. In most cases it is conditioned, not by the nature of the subject under investigation, but by the temper of the investigator. Often, indeed, the tediousness of a learned disquisition is intentional: it is considered one of the polite conventions of the academic guild, and by many is identified with scientific thoroughness and profound learning. . . . If, in general, deadening, hidebound caste methods, not seldom the cover for poverty of thought and lack of cleverness, are reprehensible, they are doubly reprehensible in history. The history of a people is not a mere mental discipline, like botany or mathematics, but a living science, a magistra vitæ, leading straight to national self-knowledge, and acting to a certain degree upon the national character. History is a science by the people, for the people, and, therefore, its place is the open forum, not the scholar's musty closet. We relate the events of the past to the people, not merely to a handful of archaeologists and numismaticians. We work for national self-knowledge, not for our own intellectual diversion.

These are the principles that have guided Mr. Dubnow in all his

* In the introduction to his "Istoricheskiya Sobscheniya," in Voskhod (1893), no. 7.

works, and he has been true to them in the present essay, which exhibits in a remarkably striking way the author's art of making "all things seem fresh and new, important and attractive." New and important his essay undoubtedly is. The author attempts, for the first time, a psychologic characterization of Jewish history. He endeavors to demonstrate the inner connection between events, and develop the ideas that underlie them, or, to use his own expression, lay bare the soul of Jewish history, which clothes itself with external events as with a bodily envelope. Jewish history has never before been considered from this philosophic point of view, certainly not in German literature. The present work, therefore, cannot fail to prove stimulating. As for the poet's other requirement, attractiveness, it is fully met by the work here translated. The qualities of Mr. Dubnow's style, as described above, are present to a marked degree. The enthusiasm flaming up in every line, coupled with his plastic, figurative style, and his scintillating conceits, which lend vivacity to his presentation, is bound to charm the reader. Yet, in spite of the racy style, even the layman will have no difficulty in discovering that it is not a clever journalist, an artificer of well-turned phrases, who is speaking to him, but a scholar by profession, whose foremost concern is with historical truth, and whose every statement rests upon accurate, scientific knowledge; not a bookworm with pale, academic blood trickling through his veins, but a man who, with unsoured mien, with fresh, buoyant delight, offers the world the results laboriously reached in his study, after all evidences of toil and moil have been carefully removed; who derives inspiration from the noble and the sublime in whatever guise it may appear, and who knows how to communicate his inspiration to others.

The translator lays this book of an accomplished and spirited historian before the German public. He does so in the hope that it will shed new light upon Jewish history even for professional scholars. He is confident that in many to whom our unexampled past of four thousand years' duration is now terra incognita, it will arouse enthusiastic interest, and even to those who, like the translator himself, differ from the author in religious views, it will furnish edifying and suggestive reading.

Introductory Note

What is Jewish History? In the first place, what does it offer as to quantity and as to quality? What are its range and content, and what distinguishes it in these two respects from the history of other nations? Furthermore, what is the essential meaning, what the spirit, of Jewish History? Or, to put the question in another way, to what general results are we led by the aggregate of its facts, considered, not as a whole, but genetically, as a succession of evolutionary stages in the consciousness and education of the Jewish people?

If we could find precise answers to these several questions, they would constitute a characterization of Jewish History as accurate as is attainable. To present such a characterization succinctly is the purpose of the following essay.

I

THE RANGE OF JEWISH HISTORY

> Le peuple juif n'est pas seulement considérable par son antiquité, mais il est encore singulier en sa durée, qui a toujours continué depuis son origine jusqu'à maintenant . . . S'étendant depuis les premiers temps jusqu'aux derniers, l'histoire des juifs enferme dans sa durée celle de toutes nos histoires.—PASCAL, Pensées, II, 7.

To make clear the range of Jewish history, it is necessary to set down a few general, elementary definitions by way of introduction.

It has long been recognized that a fundamental difference exists between historical and unhistorical peoples, a difference growing out of the fact of the natural inequality between the various elements composing the human race. Unhistorical is the attribute applied to peoples that have not yet broken away, or have not departed very far, from the state of primitive savagery, as, for instance, the barbarous races of Asia and Africa who were the prehistoric ancestors of the Europeans, or the obscure, untutored tribes of the present, like the Tartars and the Kirghiz. Unhistorical peoples, then, are ethnic groups of all sorts that are bereft of a distinctive, spiritual individuality, and have failed to display normal, independent capacity for culture. The term historical, on the other hand, is applied to the nations that have had a conscious, purposeful history of appreciable duration; that have progressed, stage by stage, in their growth and in the improvement of their mode and their views of life; that have demonstrated mental productivity of some sort, and have elaborated principles of civilization and social life more or less rational; nations, in short, representing not only zoologic, but also spiritual types.*

Chronologically considered, these latter nations, of a higher type, are usually divided into three groups: (1) the most ancient civilized peoples of the Orient, such as the Chinese, the Hindus, the Egyptians, the Chaldeans; (2) the ancient or classic peoples of the Occident, the Greeks and the Romans; and (3) the modern peoples, the civilized nations of Europe and America of the present day. The most ancient peoples of the Orient, standing "at the threshold of history," were the first heralds of a religious consciousness and of moral principles. In hoary antiquity, when most of the representatives of the human kind were nothing more than a peculiar variety of the class mammalia, the peoples called the most ancient brought forth recognized forms of

* "The primitive peoples that change with their environment, constantly adapting themselves to their habitat and to external nature, have no history. . . . Only those nations and states belong to history which display self-conscious action; which evince an inner spiritual life by diversified manifestations; and combine into an organic whole what they receive from without, and what they themselves originate." (Introduction to Weber's *Allgemeine Weltgeschichte*, i, pp. 16-18.)

social life and a variety of theories of living of fairly far-reaching effect. All these culture-bearers of the Orient soon disappeared from the surface of history. Some (the Chaldeans, Phoenicians, and Egyptians) were washed away by the flood of time, and their remnants were absorbed by younger and more vigorous peoples. Others (the Hindus and Persians) relapsed into a semi-barbarous state; and a third class (the Chinese) were arrested in their growth, and remained fixed in immobility. The best that the antique Orient had to bequeath in the way of spiritual possessions fell to the share of the classic nations of the West, the Greeks and the Romans. They greatly increased the heritage by their own spiritual achievements, and so produced a much more complex and diversified civilization which has served as the substratum for the further development of the better part of mankind. Even the classic nations had to step aside as soon as their historical mission was fulfilled. They left the field free for the younger nations, with greater capability of living, which at that time had barely worked their way up to the beginnings of a civilization. One after the other, during the first two centuries of the Christian era, the members of this European family of nations appeared in the arena of history. They form the kernel of the civilized part of mankind at the present day.

Now, if we examine this accepted classification with a view to finding the place belonging to the Jewish people in the chronological series, we meet with embarrassing difficulties, and finally arrive at the conclusion that its history cannot be accommodated within the compass of the classification. Into which of the three historical groups mentioned could the Jewish people be put? Are we to call it one of the most ancient, one of the ancient, or one of the modern nations? It is evident that it may lay claim to the first description, as well as to the second and the last. In company with the most ancient nations of the Orient, the Jewish people stood at the "threshold of history." It was the contemporary of the earliest civilized nations, the Egyptians and the Chaldeans. In those remote days it created and spread a religious world-idea underlying an exalted social and moral system surpassing everything produced in this sphere by its Oriental contemporaries. Again, with the classical Greeks and Romans, it forms the celebrated historical triad universally recognized as the source of all great systems of civilization. Finally, in fellowship with the nations of today, it leads a historical life, striding onward in the path of progress without stay or interruption. Deprived of political independence, it nevertheless continues to fill a place in the world of thought as a distinctly marked spiritual individuality, as one of the most active and intelligent forces. How, then, are we to denominate this omnipresent people, which, from the first moment of its historical existence up to our days, a period of thirty-five hundred years, has been developing continuously. In view of this Methuselah among the nations, whose life is co-extensive with the whole of history, how are we to dispose of the inevitable barriers between "the most ancient" and "the ancient," between "the ancient" and "the modern" nations—the fateful barriers which form the milestones on the path of the historical peoples, and which the Jewish people has more than once overstepped?

A definition of the Jewish people must needs correspond to the aggregate of the concepts expressed by the three group-names, most ancient, ancient, and modern. The only description applicable to it is "the historical nation of all times," a description bringing into relief the contrast between it and all other nations of modern and ancient times, whose historical existence either came to an end in days long past, or began at a date comparatively recent. And granted that there are "historical" and "unhistorical" peoples, then it is beyond dispute that the Jewish people deserves to be called "the most historical" (*historicissimus*). If the history of the world be conceived as a circle, then Jewish history occupies the position of the diameter, the line passing through its center, and the history of every other nation is represented by a chord marking off a smaller segment of the circle. The history of the Jewish people is like an axis crossing the history of mankind from one of its poles to the other. As an unbroken thread it runs through the ancient civilization of Egypt and Mesopotamia, down to the present-day culture of France and Germany. Its divisions are measured by thousands of years.

Jewish history, then, in its range, or, better, in its duration, presents a unique phenomenon. It consists of the longest series of events ever recorded in the annals of a single people. To sum up its peculiarity briefly, it embraces a period of thirty-five hundred years, and in all this vast extent it suffers no interruption. At every point it is alive, full of sterling content. Presently we shall see that in respect to content, too, it is distinguished by exceptional characteristics.

II

THE CONTENT OF JEWISH HISTORY

From the point of view of content, or qualitative structure, Jewish history, it is well known, falls into two parts. The dividing point between the two parts is the moment in which the Jewish state collapsed irretrievably under the blows of the Roman empire (70 C. E.). The first half deals with the vicissitudes of a nation which, though frequently at the mercy of stronger nations, still maintained possession of its territory and government and was ruled by its own laws. In the second half, we encounter the history of a people without a government, more than that, without a land, a people stripped of all the tangible accompaniments of nationality, and nevertheless successful in preserving its spiritual unity, its originality, complete and undiminished.

At first glance, Jewish history during the period of independence seems to be but slightly different from the history of other nations. Though not without individual coloring, there are yet the same wars and intestine disturbances, the same political revolutions and dynastic quarrels, the same conflicts between the classes of the people, the same warring between economical interests. This is only a surface view of Jewish history. If we pierce to its depths and scrutinize the processes that take place in its penetralia, we perceive that even in the early period there were latent within it great powers of intellect, universal principles, which, visibly or invisibly, determined the course of events. We have before us not a simple political or racial entity, but, to an eminent degree, "a spiritual people." The national development is based upon an all-pervasive religious tradition which lives in the soul of the people as the Sinaitic Revelation, the Law of Moses. With this holy tradition, embracing a luminous theory of life and an explicit code of morality and social converse, was associated the idea of the election of the Jewish people, of its peculiar spiritual mission. "And ye shall be unto me a kingdom of priests and a holy nation" is the figurative expression of this ideal calling. It conveys the thought that the Israelitish people as a whole, without distinction of rank and regardless of the social prominence of individuals, has been called to guide the other nations toward sublime moral and religious principles, and to officiate for them, the laity as it were, in the capacity of priests. This exalted ideal would never have been reached, if the development of the Jewish people had lain along hackneyed lines; if, like the Egyptians and the Chaldeans, it had had an inflexible caste of priests, who consider the guardianship of the spiritual treasures of the nation the exclusive privilege of their estate, and strive to keep the mass of the people in crass ignorance. For a time, something approaching this condition prevailed among the Jews. The priests descended from Aaron, with the Temple servants (the Levites), formed a priestly class and played the part of authoritative bearers of the religious tradition. But early, in the very infancy of the nation, there arose by the side of this official, aristocratic hierarchy, a far mightier priesthood, a democratic fraternity, seeking to enlighten the whole nation and inculcating convictions that make for a consciously held aim. The Prophets were the real and appointed executors of the holy command enjoining the "conversion" of all Jews into "a kingdom of priests and a holy nation." Their activity cannot be paralleled in the whole range of the world's history. They were not priests, but popular educators and popular teachers. They were animated by the desire to instill into every soul a deeply religious consciousness, to ennoble every heart by moral aspirations, to indoctrinate every individual with an unequivocal theory of life, to inspire every member of the nation with lofty ideals. Their work did not fail to leave its traces. Slowly but deeply idealism entered into the very pith and marrow of the national consciousness. This consciousness gained in strength and amplitude century by century, showing itself particularly in the latter part of the first period, after the crisis known as "the Babylonian Exile." Thanks to the exertions of the *Soferim* (Scribes), directed toward the broadest popularization of the Holy Writings and constituting the formal complement to the work of the Prophets, spiritual activity became an integral part of Jewish national life. In the closing centuries of its political existence, the Jewish people received its permanent form. There was imposed upon it the unmistakable hallmark of spirituality that has always identified it in the throng of the nations. Out of the bosom of Judaism went forth the religion that in a short time ran its triumphant course through the whole ancient world, transforming races of barbarians into civilized beings. It was the fulfilment of the Prophetical promise—that the nations would walk in the light of Israel.

At the very moment when the strength and fertility of the Jewish mind reached the culminating point, occurred a political revolution—the period of homeless wandering began. It seemed as though, before scattering the Jewish people to all ends of the earth, the providence of history desired to teach it a final lesson, to take with it on its way. It seemed to say: "Now you may go forth. Your character has been sufficiently tempered; you can bear the bitterest of hardships. You are equipped with an inexhaustible store of energy, and you can live for centuries, yea, for thousands of years, under conditions that would prove the bane of other nations in less than a single century. State, territory, army, the external attributes of national power, are for you superfluous luxury. Go out into the world to prove that a people can continue to live without these attributes, solely and alone through strength of spirit welding its widely scattered particles into one firm organism!"—And the Jewish people went forth and proved it.

This "proof," adduced by Jewry at the cost of eighteen centuries of privation and suffering, forms the characteristic feature of the second half of Jewish history, the period of homelessness and dispersion. Uprooted from its political soil, national life displayed itself on intellectual fields exclusively. "To think and to suffer" became the watchword of the Jewish people, not merely because forced upon it by external circumstances beyond its control, but chiefly because it was conditioned by the very disposition of the people, by its national inclinations. The extraordinary mental energy that had matured the Bible and the old writings in the first period, manifested itself in the second period in the encyclopedic productions of the Talmudists, in the religious philosophy of the middle ages, in Rabbinism, in the

Kabbala, in mysticism, and in science. The spiritual discipline of the school came to mean for the Jew what military discipline is for other nations. His remarkable longevity is due, I am tempted to say, to the acrid spiritual brine in which he was cured. In its second half, the originality of Jewish history consists, indeed, in the circumstance that it is the only history stripped of every active political element. There are no diplomatic artifices, no wars, no campaigns, no unwarranted encroachments backed by armed force upon the rights of other nations, nothing of all that constitutes the chief content—the monotonous and for the most part idea-less content—of many other chapters in the history of the world. Jewish history presents the chronicle of an ample spiritual life, a gallery of pictures representing national scenes. Before our eyes passes a long procession of facts from the fields of intellectual effort, of morality, religion, and social converse. Finally, the thrilling drama of Jewish martyrdom is unrolled to our astonished gaze. If the inner life and the social and intellectual development of a people form the kernel of history, and politics and occasional wars are but its husk,* then certainly the history of the Jewish Diaspora is all kernel. In contrast with the history of other nations it describes, not the accidental deeds of princes and generals, not external pomp and physical prowess, but the life and development of a whole people. It gives heartrending expression to the spiritual strivings of a nation whose brow is resplendent with the thorny crown of martyrdom. It breathes heroism of mind that conquers bodily pain. In a word, Jewish history is history sublimated.†

In spite of the noteworthy features that raise Jewish history above

* "History, without these (inner, spiritual elements), is a shell without a kernel; and such is almost all the history which is extant in the world." (Macaulay, on Mitford's "History of Greece," *Collected Works*, vol. i, p. 198, ed. A. and C. Armstrong and Son.)

† A Jewish historian makes the pregnant remark: "If ever the time comes when the prophecies of the Jewish seers are fulfilled, and nation no longer raises the sword against nation; when the olive leaf instead of the laurel adorns the brow of the great, and the achievements of noble minds are familiar to the dwellers in cottages and palaces alike, then the history of the world will have the same character as Jewish history. On its pages will be inscribed, not the warrior's prowess and his victories, nor diplomatic schemes and triumphs, but the progress of culture and its practical application in real life."

the level of the ordinary and assign it a peculiar place, it is nevertheless not isolated, not severed from the history of mankind. Rather is it most intimately interwoven with world-affairs at every point throughout its whole extent. As the diameter, Jewish history is again and again intersected by the chords of the historical circle. The fortunes of the pilgrim people scattered in all the countries of the civilized world are organically connected with the fortunes of the most representative nations and states, and with manifold tendencies of human thought. The bond uniting them is twofold: in the times when the powers of darkness and fanaticism held sway, the Jews were amenable to the "physical" influence exerted by their neighbors in the form of persecutions, infringements of the liberty of conscience, inquisitions, violence of every sort; and during the prevalence of enlightenment and humanity, the Jews were acted upon by the intellectual and cultural stimulus proceeding from the peoples with whom they entered into close relations. Momentary aberrations and reactionary incidents are not taken into account here. On its side, Jewry made its personality felt among the nations by its independent, intellectual activity, its theory of life, its literature, by the very fact, indeed, of its ideal staunchness and tenacity, its peculiar historical physiognomy. From this reciprocal relation issued a great cycle of historical events and spiritual currents, making the past of the Jewish people an organic constituent of the past of all that portion of mankind which has contributed to the treasury of human thought.

We see, then, that in reference to content Jewish history is unique in both its halves. In the first "national" period, it is the history of a people to which the epithet "peculiar" has been conceded, a people which has developed under the influence of exceptional circumstances, and finally attained to so high a degree of spiritual perfection and fertility that the creation of a new religious theory of life, which eventually gained universal supremacy, neither exhausted its resources nor ended its activity. Not only did it continue to live upon its vast store of spiritual energy, but day by day it increased the store. In the second "lackland" half, it is the instructive history of a scattered people, organically one, in spite of dispersion, by reason of its unshaken ideal traditions; a people accepting misery and hardship with stoic calm, combining the characteristics of the thinker with those of the sufferer, and eking out existence under conditions which no other nation has found adequate, or, indeed, can ever find adequate. The account of the people as teacher of religion—this is the content of the first half of Jewish history; the account of the people as thinker, stoic, and sufferer—this is the content of the second half of Jewish history.

A summing up of all that has been said in this and the previous chapter proves true the statement with which we began, that Jewish history, in respect to its quantitative dimensions as well as its qualitative structure, is to the last degree distinctive and presents a phenomenon of undeniable uniqueness.

III

THE SIGNIFICANCE OF JEWISH HISTORY

We turn now to the question of the significance to be attached to Jewish history. In view of its peculiar qualities, what has it to offer to the present generation and to future generations as a subject of study and research?

The significance of Jewish history is twofold. It is at once national and universal. At present the fulcrum of Jewish national being lies in the historical consciousness. In the days of antiquity, the Jews were welded into a single united nation by the triple agencies of state, race, and religion, the complete array of material and spiritual forces directed to one point. Later, in the period of homelessness and dispersion, it was chiefly religious consciousness that cemented Jewry into a whole, and replaced the severed political bond as well as the dulled racial instinct, which is bound to go on losing in keenness in proportion to the degree of removal from primitive conditions and native soil. In our days, when the liberal movements leavening the whole of mankind, if they have not completely shattered the religious consciousness, have at least, in an important section of Jewry, effected a change in its form; when abrupt differences of opinion with regard to questions of faith and cult are asserting their presence; when traditional Judaism developed in historical sequence is proving powerless to hold together the diverse factors of the national organism—in these days the keystone of national unity seems to be the historical consciousness. Composed alike of physical, intellectual, and moral elements, of habits and views, of emotions and impressions nursed into being and perfection by the hereditary instinct active for thousands of years, this historical consciousness is a remarkably puzzling and complex psychic phenomenon. By our common memory of a great, stirring past and heroic deeds on the battlefields of the spirit, by the exalted historical mission allotted to us, by our thorn-strewn pilgrim's path, our martyrdom assumed for the sake of our principles, by such moral ties, we Jews, whether consciously or unconsciously, are bound fast to one another. As Renan well says: "Common sorrow unites men more closely than common joy." A long chain of historical traditions is cast about us all like a strong ring. Our wonderful, unparalleled past attracts us with magnetic power. In the course of centuries, as generation followed generation, similarity of historical fortunes produced a mass of similar impressions which have crystallized, and have thrown off the deposit that may be called "the Jewish national soul." This is the soil in which, deep down, lies imbedded, as an unconscious element, the Jewish national *feeling*, and as a conscious element, the Jewish national *idea*.

It follows that the Jewish national idea and the national feeling connected with it have their origin primarily in the historical consciousness, in a certain complex of ideas and psychic predispositions. These ideas and predispositions, the deposit left by the aggregate of historical impressions, are of necessity the common property of the whole nation, and they can be developed and quickened to a considerable degree by a renewal of the impressions through the study of history. Upon the knowledge of history, then, depends the strength of the national consciousness.*

* A different aspect of the same thought is presented with logical clearness in another publication by our author. "The national *idea* and the national *feeling*," says Mr. Dubnow, "must be kept strictly apart. Unfortunately the difference between them is usually obliterated. National feeling is spontaneous. To a greater or less degree it is inborn in all the members of the nation as a feeling of kinship. It has its flood-tide and its ebb-tide in correspondence to external conditions, either forcing the nation to defend its nationality, or relieving it of the necessity for self-

But over and above its national significance, Jewish history, we repeat, possesses universal significance. Let us, in the first place, examine its value for science and philosophy. Inasmuch as it is preeminently a chronicle of ideas and spiritual movements, Jewish history affords the philosopher or psychologist material for observation of the most important and useful kind. The study of other, mostly dull chapters of universal history has led to the fixing of psychologic or sociologic theses, to the working out of comprehensive philosophic systems, to the determination of general laws. Surely it follows, without far-fetched proof, that in some respects the chapter dealing with Jewish history must supply material of the most original character for such theses and philosophies. If it is true, as the last chapter set out

---

defense. As this feeling is not merely a blind impulse, but a complicated psychic phenomenon, it can be subjected to a psychological analysis. From the given historical facts or the ideas that have become the common treasure of a nation, thinking men, living life consciously, can, in one way or another, derive the origin, development, and vital force of its national feeling. The results of such an analysis, arranged in some sort of system, form the content of the national idea. The task of the national idea is to clarify the national feeling, and give it logical sanction for the benefit of those who cannot rest satisfied with an unconscious feeling.

"In what, to be specific, does the essence of our Jewish national idea consist? Or, putting the question in another form, what is the cement that unites us into a single compact organism? Territory and government, the external ties usually binding a nation together, we have long ago lost. Their place is filled by abstract principles, by religion and race. Undeniably these are factors of first importance, and yet we ask the question, do they alone and exclusively maintain the national cohesion of Jewry? No, we reply, for if we admitted this proposition, we should by consequence have to accept the inference that the laxity of religious principle prevailing among free-thinking Jews, and the obliteration of race peculiarities in the 'civilized' strata of our people, bring in their train a corresponding weakening, or, indeed, a complete breaking up, of our national foundations—which in point of fact is not the case. On the contrary, it is noticeable that the latitudinarians, the *libres penseurs*, and the indifferent on the subject of religion, stand in the forefront of all our national movements. Seeing that to belong to it is in most cases heroism, and in many martyrdom, what is it that attracts these Jews so forcibly to their people? There must be something common to us all, so comprehensive that in the fact of multifarious views and degrees of culture it acts as a consolidating force. This 'something,' I am convinced, is the community of historical fortunes of all the scattered parts of the Jewish nation. We are welded together by our glorious past. We are encircled by a mighty chain of similar historical impressions suffered by our ancestors, century after century pressing in upon the Jewish soul and leaving behind a substantial deposit. In short, the Jewish national idea is based chiefly upon the historical consciousness." [Note of the German trl.]

to demonstrate, that Jewish history is distinguished by sharply marked and peculiar features, and refuses to accommodate itself to conventional forms, then its content must have an original contribution to make to philosophy. It does not admit of a doubt that the study of Jewish history would yield new propositions appertaining to the philosophy of history and the psychology of nations, hitherto overlooked by inquirers occupied with the other divisions of universal history. Inductive logic lays down a rule for ascertaining the law of a phenomenon produced by two or more contributory causes. By means of what might be called a laboratory experiment, the several causes must be disengaged from one another, and the effect of each observed by itself. Thus it becomes possible to arrive with mathematical precision at the share of each cause in the result achieved by several co-operating causes. This method of difference, as it is called, is available, however, only for a limited number of phenomena, only for phenomena in the department of the natural sciences. It is in the nature of the case that mental and spiritual phenomena, though they may be observed, cannot be artificially reproduced. Now, in one respect, Jewish history affords the advantages of an arranged experiment. The historical life of ordinary nations, such nations as are endowed with territory and are organized into a state, is a complete intermingling of the political with the spiritual element. Totally ignorant as we are of the development either would have assumed, had it been dissevered from the other, the laws governing each of the elements singly can be discovered only approximately. Jewish history, in which the two elements have for many centuries been completely disentangled from each other, presents a natural experiment, with the advantage of artificial exclusions, rendering possible the determination of the laws of spiritual phenomena with far greater scientific exactitude than the laws of phenomena that result from several similar causes.

Besides this high value for the purposes of science, this fruitful suggestiveness for philosophic thought, Jewish history, as compared with the history of other nations, enjoys another distinction in its capacity to exercise an ennobling influence upon the heart. Nothing so exalts and refines human nature as the contemplation of moral steadfastness, the history of the trials of a martyr who has fought and suffered for his convictions. At bottom, the second half of Jewish history is nothing but this. The effective educational worth of the biblical part of Jewish history is disputed by none. It is called "sacred" history, and he who acquires a knowledge of it is thought to advance the salvation of his soul. Only a very few, however, recognize the profound, moral content of the second half of Jewish history, the history of the Diaspora. Yet, by reason of its exceptional qualities and intensely tragic circumstances, it is beyond all others calculated to yield edification to a notable degree. The Jewish people is deserving of attention not only in the time when it displayed its power and enjoyed its independence, but as well in the period of its weakness and oppression, during which it was compelled to purchase spiritual development by constant sacrifice of self. A thinker crowned with thorns demands no less veneration than a thinker with the laurel wreath upon his brow. The flame issuing from the funeral pile on which martyrs die a heroic death for their ideas is, in its way, as awe-inspiring as the flame from Sinai's height. With equal force, though by different methods, both touch the heart, and arouse the moral sentiment. Biblical Israel the celebrated—medieval Judah the despised—it is one and the same people, judged variously in the various phases of its historical life. If Israel bestowed upon mankind a religious theory of life, Judah gave it a thrilling example of tenacious vitality and power of resistance for the sake of conviction. This uninterrupted life of the spirit, this untiring aspiration for the higher and the better in the domain of religious thought, philosophy, and science, this moral intrepidity in night and storm and in despite of all the blows of fortune—is it not an imposing, soul-stirring spectacle? The inexpressible tragedy of the Jewish historical life is unfailing in its effect upon a susceptible heart.* The wonderful exhibition of spirit triumphant, subduing the pangs of the flesh, must move every heart, and exercise uplifting influence upon the non-Jew no less than upon the Jew.

For non-Jews a knowledge of Jewish history may, under certain

* "If there are ranks in suffering, Israel takes precedence of all the nations—if the duration of sorrows and the patience with which they are borne ennoble, the Jews are among the aristocracy of every land—if a literature is called rich in the possession of a few classic tragedies, what shall we say to a National Tragedy lasting for fifteen hundred years, in which the poets and the actors were also the heroes?" (Zunz, *Die synagogale Poesie*. Translation by George Eliot in *Daniel Deronda*.)

conditions, come to have another, an humanitarian significance. It is inconceivable that the Jewish people should be held in execration by those acquainted with the course of its history, with its tragic and heroic past.* Indeed, so far as Jew-haters by profession are concerned, it is running a risk to recommend the study of Jewish history to them, without adding a word of caution. Its effect upon them might be disastrous. They might find themselves cured of their modern disease, and in the possession of ideas that would render worthless their whole stock in trade. Verily, he must have fallen to the zero-point of anti-semitic callousness who is not thrilled through and through by the lofty fortitude, the saint-like humility, the trustful resignation to the will of God, the stoic firmness, laid bare by the study of Jewish history. The tribute of respect cannot be readily withheld from him to whom the words of the poet (Pushkin) are applicable:

> "To die was not his hope; he fain
> Would live to think and suffer pain."

When, in days to come, the curtain rises upon the touching tragedy of Jewish history, revealing it to the astonished eye of a modern generation, then, perhaps, hearts will be attuned to tenderness, and on the ruins of national hostility will be enthroned mutual love,

* As examples and a proof of the strong humanitarian influence Jewish history exercises upon Christians, I would point to the relation established between the Jews and two celebrities of the ninteeenth century, Schleiden and George Eliot. In his old age, the great scientist and thinker accidentally, in the course of his study of sources for the history of botany, became acquainted with medieval Jewish history. It filled him with ardent enthusiasm for the Jews, for their intellectual strength, their patience under martyrdom. Dominated by this feeling, he wrote the two admirable sketches: *Die Bedeutung der Juden für Erhaltung und Wiederbelebung der Wissenschaften im Mittelalter* (1876) and *Die Romantik des Martyriums bei den Juden im Mittelalter* (1878). According to his own confession, the impulse to write them was "the wish to take at least the first step toward making partial amends for the unspeakable wrong inflicted by Christians upon Jews." As for George Eliot, it may not be generally known that it was her reading of histories of the Jews that inspired her with the profound veneration for the Jewish people to which she gave glowing utterance in "Daniel Deronda." (She cites Zunz, was personally acquainted with Emanuel Deutsch, and carried on a correspondence with Professor David Kaufmann. See *George Eliot's Life as related in her Letters and Journals.* Arranged and edited by her husband, J. W. Cross, vol. iii, ed. Harper and Brothers.) Her enthusiasm prompted her, in 1879, to indite her passionate apology for the Jews, under the title, "The Modern Hep! Hep! Hep!"

growing out of mutual understanding and mutual esteem. And who can tell—perhaps Jewish history will have a not inconsiderable share in the spiritual change that is to annihilate national intolerance, the modern substitute for the religious bigotry of the middle ages. In this case, the future task of Jewish history will prove as sublime as was the mission of the Jewish people in the past. The latter consisted in the spread of the dogma of unity of creation; the former will contribute indirectly to the realization of the not yet accepted dogma of the unity of the human race.

IV

THE HISTORICAL SYNTHESIS

To define the scope of Jewish history, its content and its significance, or its place among scientific pursuits, disposes only of the formal part of the task we have set ourselves. The central problem is to unfold the meaning of Jewish history, to discover the principle toward which its diversified phenomena converge, to state the universal laws and philosophic inferences deducible from the peculiar course of its events. If we liken history to an organic being, then the skeleton of facts is its body, and the soul is the spiritual bond that unites the facts into a whole, that conveys the meaning, the psychologic essence, of the facts. It becomes our duty, then, to unbare the soul of Jewish history, or, in scientific parlance, to construct, on the basis of the facts, the synthesis of the whole of Jewish national life. To this end, we must pass in review, by periods and epochs, one after another, the most important groups of historical events, the most noteworthy currents in life and thought that tell of the stages in the development of Jewry and Judaism. Exhaustive treatment of the philosophical synthesis of a history extending over three thousand years is possible only in a voluminous work. In an essay like the present it can merely be sketched in large outline, or painted in miniature. We cannot expect to do more than state a series of general principles substantiated by the most fundamental arguments. Complete demonstration of each of the principles must be sought in the annals that recount the events of Jewish history in detail.

The historical synthesis reduces itself, then, to uncovering the psychologic processes of national development. The object before us to be studied is the national spirit undergoing continuous evolution during thousands of years. Our task is to arrive at the laws underlying this growth. We shall reach our goal by imitating the procedure of the geologist, who divides the mass of the earth into its several strata or formations. In Jewish history there may be distinguished three chief stratifications answering to its first three periods, the Biblical period, the period of the Second Temple, and the Talmudic period. The later periods are nothing more than these same formations combined in various ways, with now and then the addition of new strata. Of the composite periods there are four, which arrange themselves either according to hegemonies, the countries in which at given times lay the center of gravity of the scattered Jewish people, or according to the intellectual currents there predominant.

This, then, is our scheme:

I. The chief formations:
   (a) The primary or Biblical period.
   (b) The secondary or spiritual-political period (the period of the Second Temple, 538 B. C. E. to 70 C. E.)
   (c) The tertiary or national-religious period (the Talmudic period, 70-500).

II. The composite formations:
   (a) The Gaonic period, or the hegemony of the Oriental Jews (500-980).
   (b) The Rabbinic-philosophical period, or the hegemony of the Spanish Jews (980-1492).
   (c) The Rabbinic-mystical period, or the hegemony of the German-Polish Jews (1492-1789).
   (d) The modern period of enlightenment (the nineteenth century).

V

THE PRIMARY OR BIBLICAL PERIOD

In the daybreak of history, the hoary days when seeming and reality merge into each other, and the outlines of persons and things fade into the surrounding mist, the picture of a nomad people, moving from the deserts of Arabia in the direction of Mesopotamia and western Asia, detaches itself clear and distinct from the dim background. The tiny tribe, a branch of the semitic race, bears a peculiar stamp of its own. A shepherd people, always living in close touch with nature, it yet resists the potent influence of the natural phenomena, which, as a rule, entrap primitive man, and make him the bond-slave of the visible and material. Tent life has attuned these semitic nomads to contemplativeness. In the endless variety of the phenomena of nature, they seek to discover a single guiding power. They entertain an obscure presentiment of the existence of an invisible, universal soul animating the visible, material universe. The intuition is personified in the patriarch Abraham, who, according to biblical tradition, held communion with God, when, on the open field, "he looked up toward heaven, and counted the stars," or when, "at the setting of the sun, he fell into benumbing sleep, and terror seized upon him by reason of the impenetrable darkness." Here we have a clear expression of the original, purely cosmical character of the Jewish religion.

There was no lack of human influence acting from without. Chaldea, which the peculiar semitic shepherds crossed in their pilgrimage, presented them with notions from its rich mythology and cosmogony. The natives of Syria and Canaan, among whom in the course of time the Abrahamites settled, imparted to them many of their religious views and customs. Nevertheless, the kernel of their pure original theory remained intact. The patriarchal mode of life, admirable in its simplicity, continued to hold its own within the circle of the firmly-knitted tribe. It was in Canaan, however, that the shepherd people hailing from Arabia showed the first signs of approaching disintegration. Various tribal groups, like Moab and Ammon, consolidated themselves. They took permanent foothold in the land and submitted, with more or less readiness, to the influences exerted by the indigenous peoples. The guardianship of the sublime traditions of the tribe remained with one group alone, the "sons of Jacob" or the "sons of Israel," so named from the third patriarch, Jacob. To this group of the Israelites composed of smaller, closely united divisions, a special mission was allotted; its development was destined to lie along peculiar lines. The fortunes awaiting it were distinctive, and for thousands of years have filled thinking and believing mankind with wondering admiration.

Great characters are formed under the influence of powerful impressions, of violent convulsions, and especially under the influence of suffering. The Israelites early passed through their school of suffering in Egypt. The removal of the sons of Jacob from the banks of the Jordan to those of the Nile was of decisive importance for the progress of their history. When the patriarchal Israelitish shepherds encountered the old, highly complex culture of the Egyptians, crystallized into fixed forms even at that early date, it was like the clash between two opposing electric currents. The pure conception of God, of *Elohim*, as of the spirit informing and supporting the universe, collided with the blurred system of heathen deities and crass idolatry. The simple cult of the shepherds, consisting of a few severely plain ceremonies transmitted from generation to generation, was confronted with the insidious, coarsely sensual animal worship of the Egyptians. The patriarchal customs of the Israelites were brought into marked contrast with the vices of a corrupt civilization. Sound in body and soul, the son of nature suddenly found himself in unsavory surroundings fashioned by culture, in which he was as much despised as the inoffensive nomad is by "civilized" man of settled habit. The scorn had a practical result in the enslavement of the Israelites by the Pharaohs. Association with the Egyptians acted as a force at once of attraction and of repulsion. The manners and customs of the natives could not fail to leave an impression upon the simple aliens, and invite imitation on their part. On the other hand, the whole life of the Egyptians, their crude notions of religion, and their immoral ways, were calculated to inspire the more enlightened among the Israelites with disgust. The hostility of the Egyptians toward the "intruders," and the horrible persecutions in which it expressed itself, could not but bring out more aggressively the old spiritual opposition between the two races. The antagonism between them was the first influence to foster the germ of Israel's national consciousness, the consciousness of his peculiar character, his individuality. This early intimation of a national consciousness was weak. It manifested itself only in the chosen few. But it existed, and the time was appointed when, under more favorable conditions, it would develop and display the extent of its power.

This consciousness it was that inspired the activity of Moses, Israel's teacher and liberator. He was penetrated alike by national and religious feeling, and his desire was to impart both national and religious feeling to his brethren. The fact of national redemption he connected with the fact of religious revelation. "I am the Lord thy God who have brought thee forth out of the land of Egypt" was proclaimed from Sinai. The God-idea was nationalized. Thenceforth "Eternal" became the name peculiar to the God of Israel. He was, indeed, the same *Elohim,* the Creator of the world and its Guide, who had been dimly discerned by the spiritual vision of the Patriarchs. At the same time, He was the special God of the Israelitish nation, the only nation that avouched Him with a full and undivided heart, the nation chosen by God Himself to carry out, alone, His sublime plans.* In its wanderings, Israel became acquainted with the chaotic religious systems of other nations. Seeing to what they paid the tribute of divine adoration, Israel could not but be dominated by the consciousness that it alone from of old had been the exponent of the religious idea in its purity. The resolution must have ripened within Israel to continue for all time to advocate and cherish this idea. From that moment Israel was possessed of a clear theory of life in religion and morality, and of a definite aim pursued with conscious intent.

Its originators designed that this Israelitish conception of life should serve not merely theoretically, as the basis of religious doctrine, but also practically, as the starting point of legislation. It was to be realized in the daily walks of the people, which at this very time attained to political independence. Sublime religious conceptions were not to be made the content of a visionary creed, the subject of

* This is the true recondite meaning of the verses Exodus 6.2-3: "And God spake unto Moses, and said unto him, I am the Eternal: and I appeared unto Abraham, unto Isaac, and unto Jacob, as *El-Shaddai* (God Almighty), but by my name Eternal I was not known unto them."

dreamy contemplation, but, in the form of perspicuous guiding principles, were to control all spheres of individual and social life. Men must beware of looking upon religion as an ideal to be yearned for, it should be an ideal to be applied directly, day by day, to practical contingencies. In "Mosaism," so-called, the religious and the ethical are intimately interwoven with the social and the political. The chief dogmas of creed are stated as principles shaping practical life. For instance, the exalted idea of one God applied to social life produces the principle of the equality of all men before the one Supreme Power, a principle on which the whole of biblical legislation is built. The commands concerning love of neighbor, the condemnation of slavery, the obligation to aid the poor, humane treatment of the stranger, sympathy and compassion with every living being—all these lofty injunctions ensue as inevitable consequences from the principle of equality. Biblical legislation is perhaps the only example of a political and social code based, not upon abstract reasoning alone, but also upon the requirements of the feelings, upon the finest impulses of the human soul. By the side of formal right and legality, it emphasizes, and in a series of precepts makes tangible, the principle of justice and humanity. The Mosaic Law is a "propaganda by deed." Everywhere it demands active, more than passive, morality. Herein, in this elevated characteristic, this vital attribute, consists the chief source of the power of Mosaism. The same characteristic, to be sure, prevented it from at once gaining ground in the national life. It established itself only gradually, after many fluctuations and errors. In the course of the centuries, and keeping pace with the growth of the national consciousness, it was cultivated and perfected in detail.

The conquest of Canaan wrought a radical transformation in the life of the Israelitish people. The acquiring of national territory supplied firm ground for the development and manifold application of the principles of Mosaism. At first, however, advance was out of the question. The mass of the people had not reached the degree of spiritual maturity requisite for the espousal of principles constituting an exalted theory of life. It could be understood and represented only by a thoughtful minority, which consisted chiefly of Aaronites and

Levites, together forming a priestly estate, though not a hierarchy animated by the isolating spirit of caste that flourished among all the other peoples of the Orient. The populace discovered only the ceremonial side of the religion; its kernel was hidden from their sight. Defective spiritual culture made the people susceptible to alien influences, to notions more closely akin to its understanding. Residence in Canaan among related semitic tribes that had long before separated from the Israelites, and adopted altogether different views and customs, produced a far greater metamorphosis in the character of the Israelites than the sojourn in Egypt. After the first flush of victory, when the unity of the Israelitish people had been weakened by the particularistic efforts of several of the tribes, the spiritual bonds confining the nation began to relax. Political decay always brings religious defection in its train. Whenever Israel came under the dominion of the neighboring tribes, it also fell a victim to their cult. This phenomenon is throughout characteristic of the so-called era of the Judges. It is a natural phenomenon readily explained on psychologic grounds. The Mosaic national conception of the "Eternal" entered more and more deeply into the national consciousness, and, accommodating itself to the limited mental capacity of the majority, became narrower and narrower in compass—the lot of all great ideas! The "Eternal" was no longer thought of as the only one God of the whole universe, but as the tutelar deity of the Israelitish tribe. The idea of national tutelar deities was at that time deeply rooted in the consciousness of all the peoples of western Asia. Each nation, as it had a king of its own, had a tribal god of its own. The Phoenicians had their Baal, the Moabites their Kemosh, the Ammonites their Milkom. Belief in the god peculiar to a nation by no means excluded belief in the existence of other national gods. A people worshiped its own god, because it regarded him as its master and protecting lord. In fact, according to the views then prevalent, a conflict between two nations was the conflict between two national deities. In the measure in which respect for the god of the defeated party waned, waxed the number of worshipers of the god of the victorious nation, and not merely among the conquerors, but also among the adherents of other religions.* These crude, coarsely materialistic conceptions of God gained entrance with the masses of the Israelitish people. If Moab had his Kemosh, and Ammon his Milkom, then Israel had its "Eternal," who, after the model of all other national gods, protected and abandoned His "clients" at pleasure, in the one case winning, in the other losing, the devotion of His partisans. In times of distress, in which the Israelites groaned under the yoke of the alien, the enslaved "forgot" their "conquered" "Eternal." As they paid the tribute due the strange king and yielded themselves to his power, so they submitted to the strange god and paid him his due tribute of devotion. It followed that liberation from the yoke of the stranger coincided with return to the God of Israel, the "Eternal." At such times the national spirit leaped into flaming life. This sums up the achievements of the hero-Judges. But the traces of repeated backsliding were deep and long visible, for, together with the religious ideas of the strange peoples, the Israelites accepted their customs, as a rule corrupt and noxious customs, in sharp contrast with the lofty principles of the Mosaic Law, designed to control social life and the life of the individual.

The Prophet Samuel, coming after the unsettled period of the Judges, had only partial success in purifying the views of the people and elevating it out of degradation to a higher spiritual level. His work was continued with more marked results in the brilliant reigns of Saul, David, and Solomon. An end was put to the baleful disunion among the tribes, and the bond of national tradition was strengthened. The consolidated Israelitish kingdom triumphed over its former oppressors. The gods of the strange peoples cringed in the dust before the all-powerful "Eternal." But, with the division of the kingdom and the political rupture between Judah and Israel, the period of

* "Ye have forsaken me," says God unto Israel, "and served other gods; wherefore I will deliver you no more. Go and cry unto the gods which ye have chosen: let them deliver you in the time of your tribulations" (Judges 10.13-14). The same idea is brought out still more forcibly in the arguments adduced by Jephthah in his message to the king of Ammon (more correctly, Moab), who had laid claim to Israelitish lands: "Thou," says Jephthah, "mayest possess that which Kemosh thy god giveth thee to possess, but what the Lord our God giveth us to possess, that will we possess" (Judges 11.24). Usually these words are taken ironically; to me they seem to convey literal truth rather than irony.

efflorescence soon came to an end. Again confusion reigned supreme, and customs and convictions deteriorated under foreign influence. Prophets like Elijah and Elisha, feverish though their activity was, stood powerless before the rank immorality in the two states. The northern kingdom of Israel, composed of the Ten Tribes, passed swiftly downward on the road to destruction, sharing the fate of the numberless oriental states whose end was inevitable by reason of inner decay. The inspired words of the early Israelitish Prophets, Amos, Hosea, and Micah, their trumpet-toned reproofs, their thrilling admonitions, died unheeded upon the air—society was too depraved to understand their import. It was reserved for later generations to give ear to their immortal utterances, eloquent witnesses to the lofty heights to which the Jewish spirit was permitted to mount in times of general decline. The northern kingdom sank into irretrievable ruin. Then came the turn of Judah. It, too, had disregarded the law of "sanctification" from Sinai and had nearly arrived at the point of stifling its better impulses in the morass of materialistic living.

At this critical moment, on the line between to be and not to be, a miracle came to pass. The spirit of the people, become flesh in its noblest sons, rose aloft. From out of the midst of the political disturbances, the frightful infamy, and the moral corruption, resounded the impressive call of the great Prophets of Judah. Like a flaming torch carried through dense darkness, they cast a glaring light upon the vices of society, at the same time illuminating the path that leads upward to the goal of the ethical ideal. At first the negative, denouncing element predominated in the exhortations of the Prophets: unsparingly they scourged the demoralization and the inquity, the social injustice and the political errors prevalent in their time; they threatened divine punishment, that is, the natural consequences of evil-doing, and appealed to the reason rather than the feelings of the people. But gradually they elaborated positive ideals, more soul-stirring than the ideals identified with the old religious tradition. The Prophets were the first to touch the root of the evil. It is clear that they realized that alien influences and the low grade of intelligence possessed by the masses were not the sole causes of the frequent backsliding of the people. The Jewish doctrine itself bore within it the germ of error. The two chief pillars of the old faith—the nationalizing of the God-idea, and the stress laid upon the cult, the ceremonial side of religion, as compared with moral requirements—were first and foremost to be held responsible for the flagrant departures from the spirit of Judaism. This was the direction in which reform was needed. Thereafter the sermons of the Prophets betray everywhere the intense desire, on the one hand, to restore to the God-idea its original universal character, and, on the other hand, while strongly emphasizing the importance of morality in the religious and the social sphere, to derogate from the value of the ceremonial system. The "Eternal" is no longer the national God of Israel, belonging to it exclusively; He becomes the God of the whole of mankind, the same *Elohim*, Creator and Preserver of the world, Whom the Patriarchs had worshiped and to Whom, being His creatures, all men owe worship. His precepts and His laws of morality are binding upon all nations; they will bring salvation and blessing to all without distinction.* The ideal of piety consists in the profession of God and a life of rectitude. The time will come when all nations will be penetrated by true knowledge of God and actuated by the noblest motives; then will follow the universal brotherhood of man. Until this consummation is reached, and so long as Israel is the only nation formally professing the one true God and accepting His blessed law, Israel's sole task is to embody in itself the highest ideals, to be an "ensign

* Two biblical passages, the one from Deuteronomy, the other from Deutero-Isaiah, afford a signal illustration of the contrast between the religious nationalism of the Mosaic law and the universalism of the Prophets. Moses says to Israel: "Thou art a holy people unto the Lord thy God: the Lord thy God hath chosen thee to be a special people unto himself, above all people that are upon the face of the earth. The Lord did not set his love upon you, nor choose you, because ye were more in number than any people: for ye were the fewest of all people. But because the Lord loved you . . ." (Deut. 7.6-8). And these are the words of the prophecy: "Listen, O isles, unto me, and hearken, ye people, from far! The Lord hath called me . . . and said unto me, Thou art my servant, O Israel, in whom I will be glorified! But I had thought, I have labored in vain, I have spent my strength for nought, and in vain; yet surely my judgment is with the Lord, and my work with my God. For now said the Lord unto me . . . It is too light a thing that thou shouldest be my servant to raise up the tribes of Jacob and to restore the preserved of Israel: no, I will also give thee for a light to the Gentiles, that my salvation may reach unto the end of the earth" (Isa. 39.1-6).

to the nations," to bear before them the banner of God's law, destined in time to effect the transformation of the whole of mankind. Israel is a missionary to the nations. As such it must stand before them as a model of holiness and purity. Here is the origin of the great idea of the spiritual "Messianism" of the Jewish people, or, better, its "missionism," an eternal idea, far more comprehensive than the old idea of national election, which it supplanted.

These sublime teachings were inculcated at the moment in which Judah was hastening to meet its fate. It had become impossible to check the natural results of the earlier transgressions. The inevitable happened; Babylon the mighty laid her ponderous hand upon tiny Judah. But Judah could not be crushed. From the heavy chastisement, the Jewish nation emerged purified, reborn for a new life.

VI

THE SECONDARY OR SPIRITUAL-POLITICAL PERIOD

The rank and file of a people are instructed by revolutions and catastrophes better than by sermons. More quickly than Isaiah and Jeremiah, Nebuchadnezzar brought the Jews to a recognition of their tasks. The short span of the Babylonian Exile (586-538 B. C. E.) was a period of introspection and searching self-examination for the people. Spiritual forces hitherto latent came into play; a degree of self-consciousness asserted itself. The people grasped its mission. At last it comprehended that to imitate inferior races, instead of teaching them and making itself a model for them to follow, was treason to its vocation in life. When the hour of release from the Babylonian yoke struck, the people suddenly saw under its feet "a new earth," and to "a new heaven" above it raised eyes dim with tears of repentance and emotion. It renewed its covenant with God. Like the exodus from Egypt, so the second national deliverance was connected with a revelation. But the messages delivered by the last Prophets—especially by "the great unknown," the author of the latter part of the Book of Isaiah—were too exalted, too universal in conception, for a people but lately emerged from a severe crisis to set about their realization at once. They could only illumine its path as a guiding-star, inspire it as the ultimate goal, the far-off messianic ideal. Meanwhile the necessity appeared for uniform religious laws, dogmas, and customs, to bind the Jews together externally as a nation. The moralizing religion of the Prophets was calculated to bring about the regeneration of the individual regardless of national ties; but at that moment the chief point involved was the nation. It had to be established and its organization perfected. The universalism of the Prophets was inadequate for the consolidating of a nation. To this end outward religious discipline was requisite, an official cult and public ceremonies. Led by such considerations, the Jewish captives, on their return to Jerusalem, first of all devoted themselves to the erection of a Temple, to the creating of a visible religious center, which was to be the rallying point for the whole nation.

The days of the Prophets were over. Their religious universalism could apply only to a distant future. In the present, the nation, before it might pose as a teacher, had to learn and grow spiritually strong. Aims of such compass require centuries for their realization. Therefore, the spiritual-national unification of the people was pushed into the foreground. The place of the Prophet was filled by the Priest and the Scribe. Zerubbabel, Ezra, and Nehemiah were permeated by the purpose to make religion and the cult subservient to the cause of national union and isolation. The erection of the Temple, the solemn service with the singing of Psalms and the public reading from the "Book of the Law" (the Pentateuch, which underwent its final redaction at that time), the removal of whatever might arouse the remembrance of strange and heathen institutions—these were the levers of their unifying activity. At first sight this activity might appear almost too one-sided. But if we summon to mind a picture of the conditions prevailing in those days, we are forced to the conclusion that, in the interest of national restoration, a consistent course was imperative. In point of fact, however, some of Ezra's innovations testify to the broad-minded, reformatory character of this activity; as, for instance, the public reading of the Pentateuch, introduced with a view to making the people see the necessity of obtaining detailed knowledge of the principles of its religion and obeying the precepts of the Law, not blindly, but with conscious assent. The object steadily aimed at was the elevation of the whole body of the people to the plane of spirituality, its transformation, in accordance with the biblical injunction, into a "kingdom of priests."

This injunction of civilizing import became the starting point of the activity of all of Ezra's successors, of the so-called school of the *Soferim*, the Scribes, those versed in the art of writing. The political calm that prevailed during the two centuries of the Persian supremacy (538-332 B. C. E.) was calculated to an eminent degree to promote spiritual development and the organization of the inner life of the people. During this period, a large part of the writings after the Pentateuch that have been received into the Bible were collected, compiled, and reduced to writing. The immortal thoughts of the Prophets clothed themselves in the visible garb of letters. On parchment rolls and in books they were made accessible to distant ages. The impressive traditions transmitted from earliest times, the chronicles of the past of the people, the Psalms brought forth by the religious enthusiasm of a long series of poets, all were gathered and put into literary shape with the extreme of care. The spiritual treasures of the nation were capitalized, and to this process of capitalization solely and alone generations of men have owed the possibility of resorting to them as a source of faith and knowledge. Without the work of compilation achieved by the *Soferim*, of which the uninstructed are apt to speak slightingly, mankind today had no Bible, that central sun in world-literature.

These two centuries may fitly be called the school-days of the Jewish nation; the Scribes were the teachers of Jewry. In the way of original work but little was produced. The people fed upon the store of spiritual food, of which sufficient had been laid up for several generations. It was then that the Jews first earned their title to the name, "the People of the Book." They made subservient to themselves the two mightiest instruments of thought, the art of writing and of reading. Their progress was brilliant, and when their schooling had come to an end and they stepped out into the broader life, they were at once able to apply their knowledge successfully to practical contingencies. They were prepared for all the vicissitudes of life. Their spiritual equipment was complete.

Nothing could have been more opportune than this readiness to assume the responsibilities of existence, for a time of peril and menace was again approaching. From out of the west, a new agent of civilization, Hellenism, advanced upon the east. Alexander the Great had put an end to the huge Persian monarchy, and brought the whole of western Asia under his dominion (332 B. C. E.). His generals divided the conquered lands among themselves. With all their might, the Ptolemies in Egypt and the Seleucidae in Syria hellenized the countries subject to their rule. In the old domain of the Pharaohs, as in Babylonia, Phoenicia, and in Syria, the Greek language was currently spoken, Greek ceremonies were observed, the Greek mode of life was adopted. Athens ceded her rights of primogeniture to New Athens, Alexandria, capital of Egypt and cosmopolitan center of the civilized world. For a whole century Judea played the sad part of the apple of discord between the Egyptian and the Syrian dynasty (320-203 B. C. E.). By turns she owned the sway of the Ptolemies and the Seleucidae, until finally, in 203, she was declared a Syro-Macedonian province. Here, as in the others parts of their realm, the rulers devoted themselves energetically to the dissemination of Greek culture. Meeting with resistance, they had resort to main force. At first, indeed, a large part of the people permitted itself to be blinded by the "beauty of Japheth" and promoted assimilation with the Greeks. But when the spread of Hellenism began to threaten the spiritual individuality of Judaism, the rest of the nation, endowed with greater capacity of resistance, arose and sturdily repulsed the enemy.

Hellenism was the first gravely dangerous opponent Judaism had to encounter. It was not the ordinary meeting of two peoples, or of two kinds of civilization. It was a clash between two theories of life that stood abruptly opposed to each other, were, indeed, mutually exclusive. It was a duel between "the Eternal" on the one side, and Zeus on the other—between the Creator of the universe, the invisible spiritual Being who had, in a miraculous way, revealed religious and ethical ideals to mankind, and the deity who resided upon Olympus, who personified the highest force of nature, consumed vast quantities of nectar and ambrosia, and led a pretty wild life upon Olympus and elsewhere. In the sphere of religion and morality, Hellene and Judean could not come close to each other. The former deified nature herself, the material universe; the latter deified the Creator of nature, the spirit informing the material universe. The Hellene paid homage first and foremost to external beauty and physical strength; the Judean to inner beauty and spiritual heroism. The Hellenic theory identified the moral with the beautiful and the agreeable and made life consist of an uninterrupted series of physical and mental pleasures. The Judean theory is permeated by the strictly ethical notions of duty, of purity, of "holiness"; it denounces licentiousness and sets up as its ideal the controlling of the passions and the infinite improvement of the soul, not of the intellect alone, but of the feelings as well. These differences between the two theories of life showed themselves in the brusque opposition in character and customs that made the Greeks and the Jews absolute antipodes in many spheres of life. It cannot be denied that in matters of the intellect, especially in the field of philosophy and science, not to mention art, it might have been greatly to the advantage of the Jews to become disciples of the Greeks. Nor is there any doubt that the brighter aspects of Hellenism would make an admirable complement to Judaism. An harmonious blending of the Prophets with Socrates and Plato would have produced a many-sided, ideal *Weltanschauung*. The course of historical events from the first made such blending, which would doubtless have required great sacrifices on both sides, an impossible consummation. In point of fact, the events were such as to widen the abyss between the two systems. The meeting of Judaism and Hellenism unfortunately occurred at the very moment when the classical Hellenes had been supplanted by the hellenized Macedonians and Syrians, who had accepted what were probably the worst elements of the antique system, while appropriating but few of the intellectual excellencies of Greek culture. There was another thwarting circumstance. In this epoch, the Greeks were the political oppressors of the Jews, outraging Jewish national feeling through their tyranny to the same degree as by their immoral life they shocked Jewish ethical feeling and Jewish chastity.

Outraged national and religious feeling found expression in the insurrection of the Maccabees (168 B. C. E.). The hoary priest Mattathias and his sons fought for the dearest and noblest treasures of Judaism. Enthusiasm begets heroism. The Syrian-Greek yoke was thrown off, and, after groaning under alien rule—the Persian, the Egyptian, and the Syro-Macedonian—for four hundred years, Judea became an independent state. In its foreign relations, the new state was secured by the self-sacrificing courage of the first Maccabean brothers, and from within it was supported by the deep-sunk pillars of the spiritual life. The rise of the three famous parties, the Sadducees, the Pharisees, and the Essenes, by no means testifies, as many would have us believe, to national disintegration, but rather to the intense spiritual activity of the people. The three tendencies afforded opportunity for the self-consciousness of the nation to express itself in all its variety and force. The unbending religious dogmatism of the Sadducees, the comprehensive practical sense of the Pharisees in religious and national concerns, the contemplative mysticism of the Essenes—they are the most important offshoots from the Jewish system as held at that time. In consequence of the external conditions that brought about the destruction of the Maccabean state* after a century's existence (165-63 B. C. E.), the Pharisee tendency, which had proved itself the best in practice, won the upper hand. When Judea was held fast in the clutches of the Roman eagle, all hope of

* The external causes of the downfall of the Maccabean state, dynastic quarrels, are well known. Much less light has been thrown upon the inner, deeper-lying causes of the catastrophe. These are possibly to be sought in the priestly-political dualism of the Judean form of government. The ideal of a nation educated by means of the Bible was a theocratic state, and the first princes of the Maccabean house, acting at once as regents and as high priests, in a measure reached this ideal. But the attempts of other nations had demonstrated conclusively enough that a dualistic form of government cannot maintain itself permanently. Sooner or later one of the two elements, the priestly or the secular, is bound to prevail over the other and crush it. In the Judean realm, with its profoundly religious trend, the priestly element obtained the ascendency, and political ruin ensued. The priestly-political retreated before the priestly-national form of government. Though the religious element was powerless to preserve the *state* from destruction, we shall see that it has brilliantly vindicated its ability to keep the *nation* intact.

escape being cut off, the far-seeing leaders of the people gained the firm conviction that the only trustworthy support of the Jewish nation lay in its religion. They realized that the preservation of national unity could be effected only by a consistent organization of the religious law, which was to envelop and shape the whole external life of the people. This explains the feverish activity of the early creators of the Mishna—of Hillel, Shammai, and others—and it interprets also the watchword of still older fame, "Make a fence about the Law." If up to that moment religious usage in its development had kept abreast of the requirements of social and individual life, the requirements out of which it had grown forth, it now became a national function, and its further evolution advanced with tremendous strides. For the protection of the old "Mosaic Laws," a twofold and a threefold fence of new legal ordinances was erected about them, and the cult became more and more complicated. But the externals of religion did not monopolize all the forces. The moral element in the nation was promoted with equal vigor. Hillel, the head of the Pharisee party, was not a legislator alone, he was also a model of humane principles and rare moral attainments.

While Judaism, in its native country was striving to isolate itself, and was seizing upon all sorts of expedients to insure this end, it readily entered into relations, outside of Judea, with other systems of thought and accepted elements of the classical culture. Instead of the violent opposition which the Palestinian Judaism of the pre-Maccabean period, that is, the period of strife, had offered to Hellenism, the tendency to make mutual concessions, and pave the way for an understanding between the two theories of life, asserted itself in Alexandria. In the capital city of the hellenized world, the Jews constituted one of the most important elements of culture. According to Mommsen, the Jewish colony in Alexandria was not inferior, in point of numbers, to the Jewish population of Jerusalem, the metropolis. Influenced by Greek civilization, the Jews in turn exercised decisive influence upon their heathen surroundings and introduced a new principle of development into the activity of the cultivated classes. The Greek translation of the biblical writings formed the connecting link between Judaism and Hellenism. The Septuagint, the translation of the Pentateuch, in use since the third century before the Christian era, had acquainted the classical world with Jewish views and principles. The productions of the Prophets and, in later centuries, of the other biblical authors, translated and spread broadcast, acted irresistibly upon the spirit of the cultivated heathen and granted him a glimpse into a world of hitherto unknown notions. On this soil sprang up the voluminous Judeo-Hellenic literature, of which but a few, though characteristic, specimens have descended to us. The intermingling of Greek philosophy with Jewish religious conceptions resulted in a new religio-philosophic doctrine, with a mystic tinge, of which Philo is the chief exponent. In Jerusalem, Judaism appeared as a system of practical ceremonies and moral principles; in Alexandria, it presented itself as a complex of abstract symbols and poetical allegories. The Alexandrian form of Judaism might satisfy the intellect, but it could not appeal to the feelings. It may have made Judaism accessible to the cultivated minority, to the upper ten thousand with philosophic training; for the masses of the heathen people Judaism continued unintelligible. Yet it was pre-eminently the masses that were strongly possessed by religious craving. Disappointed in their old beliefs, they panted after a new belief, after spiritual enlightenment. In the decaying classical world, which had so long filled out life with materialistic and intellectual interests, the moral and religious feelings, the desire for a living faith, for an active inspiration, had awakened and was growing with irresistible force.

Then, from deep out of the bosom of Judaism, there sprang a moral, religious doctrine destined to allay the burning thirst for religion and bring about a reorganization of the heathen world. The originators of Christianity stood wholly upon the ground of Judaism. In their teachings were reflected as well the lofty moral principles of the Pharisee leader as the contemplative aims of the Essenes. But the same external circumstances that had put Judaism under the necessity of choosing a sharply-defined, practical, national policy, made it impossible for Judaism to fraternize with the preachers of the new doctrine. Judaism, in fact, was compelled to put aside entirely the thought of universal missionary activity. Instead, it had to devote its powers to the more pressing task of guarding the spiritual unity of a nation whose political bonds were visibly dropping away.

For just then the Jewish nation, gory with its own blood, was struggling in the talons of the Roman eagle. Its sons fought heroically, without thought of self. When, finally, physical strength gave out, their spiritual energy rose to an intenser degree. The state was annihilated, the nation remained alive. At the very moment when the Temple was enwrapped in flames, and the Roman legions flooded Jerusalem, the spiritual leaders of Jewry sat musing, busily casting about for a means whereby, without a state, without a capital, without a Temple, Jewish unity might be maintained. And they solved the difficult problem.

VII

THE TERTIARY, TALMUDIC OR NATIONAL-RELIGIOUS, PERIOD

The solution of the problem consisted chiefly in more strictly following out the process of isolation. In a time in which the worship of God preached by Judaism was rapidly spreading to all parts of the classical world, and the fundamental principles of the Jewish religion were steadily gaining appreciation and active adherence, this intense desire for seclusion may at first glance seem curious. But the phenomenon is perfectly simple. A foremost factor was national feeling, enhanced to a tremendous degree at the time of the destruction of Jerusalem. Lacking a political basis, it was transferred to religious soil. Every tradition, every custom, however insignificant, was cherished as a jewel. Though without a state and without territory, the Jews desired to form a nation, if only a spiritual nation, complete in itself. They considered themselves then as before the sole guardians of the law of God. They did not believe in a speedy fulfilment of the prophetical promise concerning "the end of time" when all nations would be converted to God. A scrupulous keeper of the Law, Judaism would not hear of the compromises that heathendom, lately entered into the bosom of the faith, claimed as its due consideration. It refused to sacrifice a single feature of its simple dogmatism, of its essential ceremonies, such as circumcision and Sabbath rest. Moreover, in the period following close upon the fall of the Temple, a part of the people still nursed the hope of political restoration, a hope repudiating in its totality the proclamation of quite another messianic doctrine. The delusion ended tragically in Bar Kokhba's hapless rebellion (135 C. E.), whose disastrous issue cut off the last remnant of hope for the restoration of an "earthly kingdom." Thereafter the ideal of a spiritual state was replaced by the ideal of a spiritual nation, rallying about a peculiar religious banner. Jewry grew more and more absorbed in itself. Its seclusion from the rest of the world became progressively more complete. Instinct dictated this course as an escape from the danger of extinction, or, at least, of stagnation. It was conscious of possessing enough vitality and energy to live for itself and work out its own salvation. It had its spiritual interests, its peculiar ideals, and a firm belief in the future. It constituted an ancient order, whose patent of nobility had been conferred upon it in the days of the hoary past by the Lord God Himself. Such as it was, it could not consent to ally itself with *parvenus*, ennobled but today, and yesterday still bowing down before "gods of silver and gods of gold." This white-haired old man, with a stormy past full of experiences and thought, would not mingle with the scatter-brained crowd, would not descend to the level of neophytes dominated by fleeting, youthful enthusiasm. Loyally this weather-bronzed, inflexible guardian of the Law stuck to his post—the post entrusted to him by God Himself—and, faithful to his duty, held fast to the principle *j'y suis, j'y reste.*

As a political nation threatened by its neighbors seeks support in its army and provides sufficient implements of war, so a spiritual nation must have spiritual weapons of defense at its command. Such weapons were forged in great numbers and deposited in the vast arsenal called the Talmud. The Talmud represents a complicated spiritual discipline, enjoining unconditional obedience to a higher invisible power. Where discipline is concerned, questions as to the necessity for one or another regulation are out of place. Every regulation is necessary, if only because it contributes to the desired end, namely, discipline. Let no one ask, then, to what purpose the innumerable religious and ritual regulations, sometimes reaching the extreme of pettiness, to what purpose the comprehensive code in which every step in the life of the faithful is foreseen. The talmudic religious provisions, all taken together, aim to put the regimen of the nation on a strictly uniform basis, so that everywhere the Jew may be able to distinguish a brother in faith by his peculiar mode of life. It is a uniform with insignia, by which soldiers of the same regiment recognize one another. Despite the vast extent of the Jewish Diaspora, the Jews formed a well-articulated spiritual army, an invisible "state of God" (*civitas dei*). Hence these "knights of the spirit," the citizens of this invisible state, had to wear a distinct uniform and be governed by a suitable code of army regulations.

As a protection for Jewish national unity, which was exposed to the greatest danger after the downfall of the state, there arose and developed, without any external influence whatsoever, an extraordinary dictatorship, unofficial and spiritual. The legislative activity of all the dictators—such as, Rabbi Johanan ben Zakkai, Rabbi Akiba, the Hillelites, and the Shammaites—was formulated in the Mishna, the "oral law," which was the substructure of the Talmud. Their activity had a characteristic feature, which deserves somewhat particularized description. The laws were not laid down arbitrarily and without ceremony. In order to possess binding force, they required the authoritative confirmation to be found in the Mosaic books. From these, whether by logical or by forced interpretation of the holy text, its words, or, perchance, its letters, they had to be derived. Each law, barring only the original "traditions," the *Halakha le-Moshe mi-Sinai*, was promulgated over the supreme signature, as it were, that is, with the authentication of a word from the Holy Scriptures. Or it was inferred from another law so authenticated. The elaboration of every law was thus connected with a very complicated process of thought, requiring both inductive and deductive reasoning and uniting juridical interpretation with the refinements of casuistry. This legislation was the beginning of talmudic science, which from that time on, for many centuries, growing with the ages, claimed in chief part the intellectual activity of Jewry. The schools and the academies worked out a system of laws at once religious and practical in character, which constituted, in turn, the object of further theoretic study in the same schools and academies. In the course of time, however, the means became the end. Theoretic investigation of the law, extending and developing to the furthest limits, in itself, without reference to its practical value, afforded satisfaction to the spiritual need. The results of theorizing often attained the binding force of law in practical life, not because circumstances ordered it, but simply because one or another academy, by dint of logic or casuistry, had established it as law. The number of such deductions from original and secondary laws increased in geometric progression, and practical life all but failed to keep up with the theory. The "close of the Mishna," that is, its reduction to writing, had no daunting effect upon the zeal for research. If anything, a new and strong impetus was imparted to it. As up to that time the text of the Holy Scriptures had been made the basis of interpretation, giving rise to the most diverse inferences, so the rabbis now began to use the law book recently canonized as a new basis of interpretation, and to carry its principles to their utmost consequences. In this way originated first the "Palestinian Gemara." Later, when the Patriarchate in Palestine was stripped of its glory by persecutions, and, in consequence, the center of activity had to be transferred from the Talmud academies of Palestine to those of Babylonia, supreme place and exclusive dominion were obtained by the "Babylonian Gemara," put into permanent form about the year 500 C. E., a gigantic work, the result of two hundred years of mental labor.

This busy intellectual activity was as comprehensive as it was thoroughgoing. Talmudic legislation, the Halakha, by no means confines itself to religious practices, extensive as this field is. It embraces the whole range of civil and social life. Apart from the dietary laws, the regulations for the festivals and the divine service, and a mass of enactments for the shaping of daily life, the Talmud elaborated a comprehensive and fairly well-ordered system of civil and criminal law, which not infrequently bears favorable comparison with the famous *rationi scriptæ* of the Romans. While proceeding with extreme rigor and scrupulousness in ritual matters, the Talmud is governed in its social legislation by the noblest humanitarian principles. Doubtless this difference of attitude can be explained by the fact that religious norms are of very much greater importance for a nation than judicial regulations, which concern themselves only with the interests of the individual and exercise but little influence upon the development of the national spirit.

The most sympathetic aspects of the Jewish spirit in that epoch are revealed in the moral and poetic elements of the Talmud, in the Agada. They are the receptacles into which the people poured all its sentiments, its whole soul. They are a clear reflex of its inner world, its feelings, hopes, ideals. The collective work of the nation and the trend of history have left much plainer traces in the Agada than in the dry, methodical Halakha. In the Agada the learned jurist and formalist appears transformed into a sage or poet, conversing with the people in a warm, cordial tone, about the phenomena of nature, history, and life. The reader is often thrown into amazement by the depth of thought and the loftiness of feeling manifested in the Agada. Involuntarily one pays tribute of reverence to its practical wisdom, to its touching legends pervaded by the magic breath of poesy, to the patriarchal purity of its views. But these pearls are not strung upon one string, they are not arranged in a complete system. They are imbedded here and there, in gay variety, in a vast mass of heterogeneous opinions and sentiments, naive at times and at times eccentric. The reader becomes aware of the thoughts before they are consolidated. They are still in a fluid, mobile state, still in process of making. The same vivacious, versatile spirit is revealed in the Midrashim literature, directly continuing the Agada up to the end of the middle ages. These two species of Jewish literature, the Agada and the Midrashim, have a far greater absolute value than the Halakha. The latter is an official work, the former a national product. Like every other special legislation, the Halakha is bound to definite conditions and times, while the Agada concerns itself with the eternal verities. The creations of the philosophers, poets, and moralists are more permanent than the work of legislators.

Beautiful as the Agada is, and with all its profundity, it lacks breadth. It rests wholly on the national, not on a universal basis. It would be vain to seek in it for the comprehensive universalism of the Prophets. Every lofty ideal is claimed as exclusively Jewish. So far from bridging over the chasm between Israel and the other nations, knowledge and morality serve to widen it. It could not be otherwise, there was no influx of air from without. The national horizon grew more and more contracted. The activities of the people gathered intensity, but in the same measure they lost in breadth. It was the only result to be expected from the course of history in those ages. Let us try to conceive what the first five centuries of the Christian era, the centuries during which the Talmud was built up, meant in the life of mankind. Barbarism, darkness, and elemental outbreaks of man's migratory instincts, illustrated by the "great migration of races," are characteristic features of those centuries. It was a wretched transition period between the fall of the world of antique culture and the first germinating of a new Christian civilization. The Orient, the center and hearth of Judaism, was shrouded in impenetrable darkness. In Palestine and in Babylonia, their two chief seats, the Jews were surrounded by nations that still occupied the lowest rung of the ladder of civilization, that had not yet risen above naive mysticism in religion, or continued to be immersed in superstitions of the grossest sort.

In this abysmal night of the middle ages, the lamp of thought was fed and guarded solely and alone by the Jews. It is not astonishing, then, that oblivious of the other nations they should have dispensed light only for themselves. Furthermore, the circumstance must be considered that, in the period under discussion, the impulse to separate from Judaism gained ground in the Christian world. After the Council of Nicaea, after Constantine the Great had established Christianity as the state-church, the official breach between the Old Testament and the New Testament partisans became unavoidable.

Thus the Jews, robbed of their political home, created a spiritual home for themselves. Through the instrumentality of the numberless religious rules which the Talmud had laid down, and which shaped the life of the individual as well as that of the community, they were welded into a firmly united whole. The Jewish spirit—national feeling and individual mental effort alike—was absorbed in this pursuit of unification. Head, heart, hands, all human functions of the Jew, were brought under complete control and cast into fixed forms by these five centuries of labor. With painful exactitude, the Talmud prescribed ordinances for all the vicissitudes of life, yet, at the same time, offered sufficient food for brain and heart. It was at once a religion and a science. The Jew was equipped with all the necessaries. He could satisfy his wants from his own store. There was no need for him to knock at strange doors, even though he had thereby profited. The consequences of this attitude, positive as well as negative consequences, asserted themselves in the further course of Jewish history.

VIII

THE GAONIC PERIOD, OR THE HEGEMONY OF THE ORIENTAL JEWS (500-980)

With the close of the Talmud, at the beginning of the sixth century, the feverish intellectual activity abated. The Jewish center of gravity continued in Babylonia. In this country, in which the Jewish race had heard its cradle song at the dawn of existence, and later on *Judæa capta* had sat and wept remembering Zion, Judaism, after the destruction of the second Temple and hundreds of years of trials, was favored with a secure asylum. In the rest of the Diaspora, persecution gave the Jews no respite; but in Babylonia, under Persian rule, they lived for some centuries comparatively free from molestation. Indeed, they enjoyed a measure of autonomy in internal affairs, under a chief who was entitled Exilarch (*Resh-Galutha*). The Law and the word of God went forth from Babylonia for the Jews of all lands. The Babylonian Talmud became the authoritative code for the Jewish people, a holy book second only to the Bible. The intellectual calm, that supervened at the beginning of the sixth century and lasted until the end of the eighth century, betrayed itself in the slackening of independent creation, though not in the flagging of intellectual activity in general. In the schools and academies of Pumbeditha, Nahardea, and Sura, scientific work was carried on with the same zest as before, only this work had for its primary object the sifting and exposition of the material heaped up by the preceding generations. This was the province of the Sabureans and the Geonim, whose relation to the Talmud was the same as that of the Scribes (the *Soferim*) of the Second Temple to the Bible. In the later period, as in the earlier, the aim was the capitalization of the accumulated spiritual treasures, an undertaking that gives little occasion for movement and life, but all the more for endurance and industry.

This intellectual balance was destroyed by two events: the appearance of Islam and the rise of Karaism. Islam, the second legitimate offspring of Judaism, was appointed to give to religious thought in the slumbering Orient the slight impulse it needed to start it on its rapid career of sovereign power. Barely emancipated from swaddling clothes, young Hotspur at once began to rage. He sought an outlet for his unconquerable thirst for action, his lust for world-dominion. The victorious religious wars of the followers of Allah ensued. This foreign movement was not without significance for the fate of the Jews. They were surrounded no longer by heathens but by Moslems, who believed in the God of the Bible, and through the mouth of their prophet conferred upon the Jews the honorable appellation of "the People of the Book." In the eighth century the wars ceased, and the impetuous energy of the rejuvenated Orient was diverted into quieter channels. The Bagdad Caliphate arose, the peaceful era of the growth of industry, the sciences, and the arts was inaugurated. Endowed with quick discernment for every enlightening movement, the Jews yielded to the vivifying magic of young Arabic culture.

Partly under the influence of the Arabic tendency to split into religio-philosophic sects, partly from inner causes, Karaism came into being in the second half of the eighth century. Its active career began with a vehement protest against the Talmud as the regulator of life and thought. It proclaimed the creators of this vast encyclopedia to be usurpers of spiritual power, and urged a return to the biblical laws in their unadulterated simplicity. The weakness of its positive principles hindered the spread of Karaism, keeping it forever within the narrow limits of a sect and consigning it to stagnation. What gave it vogue during the first century of its existence was its negative strength, its violent opposition to the Talmud, which aroused strenuous intellectual activity. For a long time it turned Judaism away from its one-sided talmudic tendency and opened up new avenues of work for it. True to their motto: "Search diligently in the Holy Scriptures," the adherents of Karaism applied themselves to the rational study of the Bible, which had come to be, among the Talmudists, the object of casuistic interpretation and legendary adornment. By the cultivation of grammar and lexicography as applied to the biblical thesaurus of words, they resuscitated the Hebrew language, which, ousted by the Aramaic dialect, had already sunk into oblivion. By the same means they laid the foundation of a school of rejuvenated poetry. In general, thought on religious and philosophic subjects was promoted to a higher degree by the lively discussions between them and the Talmudists.

By imperceptible steps talmudic Judaism, influenced at once by the enlightened Arabs and the protesting Karaites, departed from the "four ells of the Halakha," and widened its horizon. Among the spiritual leaders of the people arose men who occupied themselves not only with the study of the Talmud but also with a rational exegesis of the Bible, with philology, poetry, philosophy. The great Gaon Saadia (892-942) united within himself all strands of thought. Over and above a large number of philological and other writings of scientific purport, he created a momentous religio-philosophic system, with the aim to clarify Judaism and refine religious conceptions. He was an encyclopedic thinker, a representative of the highest Jewish culture and of Arabic culture as well—he wrote his works in Arabic by preference. In this way Jewish thought gained ground more and more in the Orient. It was in the West, however, that it attained soon after to the climax of its development.

Gradually the center of gravity of Jewry shifted from Asia Minor to western Europe. Beginning with the sixth century, the sparsely sown Jewish population of occidental Europe increased rapidly in numbers. In Italy, Byzantium, France and Visigothic Spain, important Jewish communities were formed. The medieval intolerance of the church, though neither so widespread nor so violent as it later became, suffered its first outbreak in that early century. The persecutions of the Jews by the Visigothic kings of Spain and the bishops Avitus of Clermont and Agobard of Lyons in France (sixth to the ninth century) were the prelude to the more systematic and the more bloody cruelties of subsequent days. The insignificant numbers of the European Jews and the insecurity of their condition stood in the way of forming an intellectual center of their own. They were compelled to acknowledge the spiritual supremacy of their oriental brethren in faith. With the beginning of the tenth century the situation underwent a change. Arabic civilization, which had penetrated to Spain in previous centuries, brought about a radical transformation in the character of the country. The realm of the fanatic Visigoths, half barbarous and wholly averse to the light of progress, changed into the prosperous and civilized Caliphate of the Ommiades. Thither the best forces of oriental Jewry transferred themselves. With the growth of the Jewish population in Arabic Spain and the strengthening of its communal organization, the spiritual center of the Jewish people gradually established itself in Spain. The academies of Sura and Pumbeditha yielded first place to the high schools of Cordova and Toledo.

The Jewry of the East resigned the national hegemony to the Jewry of the West. The Geonim withdrew in favor of the Rabbis. After centuries of seclusion, the Jewish spirit once more asserted itself and enjoyed a period of efflorescence. The process of national growth became more complex, more varied.

IX

THE RABBINIC-PHILOSOPHICAL PERIOD, OR THE HEGEMONY OF THE SPANISH JEWS (980-1492)

The five centuries, marked at their beginning by the rise of Arabic-Jewish civilization in Spain and at their end by the banishment of the Jews from Spain (980-1492), offer the Jewish historian an abundance of culture manifestations and intellectual movements so luxuriant that it is well-nigh impossible to gather them up in one formula. The monotony formerly prevailing in Jewish national life, both in its external and in its internal relations, was succeeded by almost gaily checkered variety. Swept along by the movement toward enlightenment that dominated their surroundings, the Jews of Arabic Spain threw themselves into energetic work in all the spheres of life and thought. While they had political ground more or less firm under their feet, and for the most part enjoyed peace and liberty, the Jews in the Christian lands of Europe stood upon volcanic soil, every moment threatening to swallow them up. Exposed constantly to persecutions, they lived more or less isolated and devoted themselves to one-sided though intense intellectual activity. Somber shadows and streaks of bright light alternate with each other in this period. In its second half, the clouds massed themselves heavily upon the darkening horizon. Even the "privileged" Spanish Jews suffered an untoward change in their affairs at the beginning of the thirteenth century: gradually they were withdrawn from under the sovereignty of the Arabs and made subject to the power of the Catholic monarchs. They became thenceforward the equal partners of their brethren in faith in the rest of Europe. All without distinction had a share in the spiritual martyrdom which is the greenest bayleaf in the crown of Jewish history. To think and to suffer became the watchword of the whole nation.

At first, as we have said, a considerable portion of the Jewish people enjoyed the happy possibility of thinking. This was during the classical epoch of the Arabic-Jewish renaissance, which preceded the Italian renaissance by four centuries. There is a fundamental difference between the two renaissance periods: the earlier one was signalized by a rebirth of the sciences and of philosophy, the later one pre-eminently of the arts and of literature. The eleventh and twelfth centuries marked the meridian of the intellectual development of medieval Judaism. As once, in Alexandria, the union of Judaic with Hellenic culture brought in its train a superabundance of new ideas of a universal character, so again the amalgamation, on Spanish soil, of Jewish culture with Arabic gave rise to rich intellectual results, more lasting and fruitful than the Alexandrian, inasmuch as, in spite of their universal character, they did not contravene the national spirit. The Jewish people dropped its misanthropy and its leaning toward isolation. The Jews entered all sorts of careers: by the side of influential and cultivated statesmen, such as Hasdai ibn Shaprut and Samuel Hanagid, at the courts of the Caliphs, stood a brilliant group of grammarians, poets, and philosophers, like Jonah ibn Ganach, Solomon ibn Gabirol, and Moses ibn Ezra. The philosophic-critical scepticism of Abraham ibn Ezra co-existed in peace and harmony with the philosophic-poetic enthusiasm of Judah Halevi. The study of medicine, mathematics, physics, and astronomy went hand in hand with the study of the Talmud, which, though it may not have occupied the first place with the Spanish Jews of this time, by no means disappeared, as witness the compendium by Alfassi. Unusual breadth and fulness of the spiritual life is the distinction of the epoch. This variety of mental traits combined in a marvelous union to form the great personality of Maimonides, the crown of a glorious period. With one *Strong Hand*, this intellectual giant brought order out of the talmudic chaos, which at his word was transformed into a symmetrical, legal system; with the other, he "guided the perplexed" through the realm of faith and knowledge. For rationalistic clarity and breadth of view no counterpart to the religio-philosophic doctrine which he formulated can be found in the whole extent of medieval literature. The main feature of the philosophy of Maimonides and of the systems based upon it is rationalism—not a dry, scholastic, abstract rationalism, but a living rationalism, embracing the whole field of the most exalted psychic phenomena. It is not philosophy pure and simple, but religious philosophy, an harmonization, more or less felicitous, of the postulates of reason with the dogmas of faith. It is reason mitigated by faith, and faith regulated by reason. In the darkness of the middle ages, when the Roman Church impregnated religion with the crudest superstitions, going so far as to forbid its adherents to read the Bible, and when the greatest philosopher representatives of the Church, like Albertus Magnus, would have rejected offhand, as a childish fancy or, indeed, as an heretical chimera, any attempt to rescue the lower classes of the people from their wretched state of spiritual servitude—in a time like this, the truly majestic spectacle is presented of a philosophy declaring war on superstition, and setting out to purify the religious notions of the people.

Not a breath of this ample spiritual development of the Jews of Arabic Spain reached the Jews living in the Christian countries of Europe. Their circumstances were too grievous, and in somberness their inner life matched their outer estate. Their horizon was as contracted as the streets of the Jewries in which they were penned. The crusades (beginning in 1096) clearly showed the Jews of France and Germany what sentiments their neighbors cherished toward them. They were the first returns which Christianity paid the Jewish people for its old-time teaching of religion. The descendants of the "chosen people," the originators of the Bible, were condemned to torture of a sort to exhaust their spiritual heritage. Judaism suffered the tragic fate of King Lear. Was it conceivable that the horrors—the rivers of blood, the groans of massacred communities, the serried ranks of martyrs, the ever-haunting fear of the morrow—should fail to leave traces in the character of Judaism? The Jewish people realized its imminent danger. It convulsively held fast to its precious relics, clung to the pillars of its religion, which it regarded as the only asylum. The Jewish spirit again withdrew from the outer world. It gave itself up wholly to the study of the Talmud. In northern France and in Germany, talmudic learning degenerated into the extreme of scholastic pedantry, the lot of every branch of science that is lopped off from the main trunk of knowledge and vegetates in a heavy, dank atmosphere, lacking light and air. Rashi (1064-1105), whose genial activity began before the first crusade, opened up Jewish religious literature to the popular mind, by his systematic commentaries on the Bible and the Talmud. On the other hand, the Tossafists, the school of commentators succeeding him, by their petty quibbling and hairsplitting casuistry, made the talmudic books more intricate and less intelligible. Such being the intellectual bias of the age, a sober, rationalistic philosophy could not assert itself. In lieu of an Ibn Ezra or a Maimonides, we have Jehuda he-Hasid and Eliezer of Worms, with their mystical books of devotion, *Sefer Hasidim, Rokeah*, etc., filled with pietistic reflections on the other world, in which the earth figures as a "vale of tears." Poetry likewise took on the dismal hue of its environment. Instead of the varied lyrical notes of Gabirol and Halevi, who sang the weal and woe, not only of the nation, but also of the individual, and lost themselves in psychologic analysis, there now fall upon our ear the melancholy, heart-rending strains of synagogue poetry, the harrowing outcries that forced themselves from the oppressed bosoms of the hunted people, the prayerful lamentations that so often shook the crumbling walls of the medieval synagogues at the very moment when, full of worshipers, they were fired by the inhuman crusaders. A mighty chord reverberates in this poetry: *Morituri te salutant.*

One small spot there was, in the whole of Europe, in which Jews could still hope to endure existence and enjoy a measure of security. This was southern France, or the Provence. The population of Provence had assimilated the culture of the neighboring country, Arabic Spain, and become the mediator between it and the rest of Europe. This work of mediation was undertaken primarily by the Jews. In the twelfth century several universities existed in Provence, which were frequented in great numbers by students from all countries. At these universities the teachers of philosophy, medicine, and other branches of science were for the most part Jews. The rationalistic philosophy of the Spanish Jews was there proclaimed *ex cathedra.* The Tibbonides translated all the more important works of the Jewish thinkers of Spain from Arabic into Hebrew. The Kimchis devoted themselves to grammatical studies and the investigation of the Bible. In Montpellier, Narbonne, and Lunel, intellectual work was in full swing. Rational ideas gradually leavened the masses of the Provençal population. Conscience, freed from intellectual trammels, began to revolt against the oppression exercised by the Roman clergy. Through the Albigensian heresy, Innocent III, founder of the papal power, had his attention directed to the Jews, whom he considered the dangerous protagonists of rationalism. The "heresy" was stifled, Provence in all her magnificence fell a prey to the Roman mania for destruction, and, on the ruins of a noble civilization, the Dominican Inquisition raged with all its horrors (1213).

Thenceforward the Catholic Church devoted herself to a hostile watch upon the Jews. Either she persecuted them directly through her Inquisition, or indirectly through her omnipotent influence on kings and peoples. In the hearts of the citizens of medieval Europe, the flame of religious hatred was enkindled, and religious hatred served as a cloak for the basest passions. Jewish history from that time on became a history of uninterrupted suffering. The Lateran Council declared the Jews to be outcasts, and designed a peculiar, dishonorable badge for them, a round patch of yellow cloth, to be worn on their upper garment (1215). In France the Jews became by turns the victims of royal rapacity and the scapegoats of popular fanaticism. Massacres, confiscations, banishments followed by dearly purchased permission to return, by renewed restrictions, persecutions, and oppressions—these were the measures that characterized the treatment of the Jews in France until their final expulsion (1394). In Germany the Jews were not so much hated as despised. They were *servi cameræ*, serfs of the state, and as such had to pay oppressive taxes. Besides, they were limited to the meanest trades and to usury and peddling. They were shut up in their cramped Jewries, huddled in wretched cabins, which clustered about the dilapidated synagogue in a shamefaced way. What strange homes! What gigantic misery, what boundless suffering dumbly borne, was concealed in those crumbling, curse-laden dwellings! And yet, how resplendent they were with spiritual light, what exalted virtues, what lofty heroism they harbored! In those gloomy, tumbledown Jew houses, intellectual endeavor was at white heat. The torch of faith blazed clear in them, and on the pure domestic hearth played a gentle flame. In the abject, dishonored son of the ghetto was hidden an intellectual giant. In his nerveless body, bent double by suffering, and enveloped in the shabby old cloak still further disfigured by the yellow wheel, dwelt the soul of a thinker. The son of the ghetto might have worn his badge with pride, for in truth it was a medal of distinction awarded by the papal Church to the Jews, for dauntlessness and courage. The awkward, puny Jew in his way was stronger and braver than a German knight armed cap-a-pie, for he was penetrated by the faith that "moves mountains." And when the worst came to the worst, he demonstrated his courage. When his peaceful home was stormed by the bestialized hordes of Armleder, or the drunken bands of the Flagellants, or the furious avengers of the Black Death, he did not yield, did not purchase life by disgraceful treason. With invincible courage he put his head under the executioner's axe, and breathed forth his heroic spirit with the enthusiastic cry: "Hear, O Israel, the Lord our God is One."

At length the turn of the Spanish Jews arrived. For the unbroken peace they had enjoyed, they had to atone by centuries of unexampled suffering. By degrees, the Arabs were forced out of the Pyrenean peninsula, and the power they had to abdicate was assumed by the Catholic kings of Castile and Aragon. In 1236 occurred the fall of Cordova, the most important center of Arabic Jewish culture. Thereafter Arab power held sway only in the province of Granada. The fortunes of the Spanish Jews underwent a calamitous change. The kings and the upper ten thousand were, indeed, favorably disposed toward them. At the courts of Castile and Aragon, the Jews were active as ministers, physicians, astronomers. But the people, incited by the propaganda of the clerics, nursed frightful hatred against the Jews, not only as "infidels," but also as intellectual aristocrats. The rage of the populace was the combustible material in the terrific explosions that occurred periodically, in the bloody saturnalia of the Pastouraux (1320), in the Black Death riots (1348), in the massacre of Seville (1391).

Dire blows of fortune were unable to weigh down the Spanish Jew, accustomed to independence, as they did the German Jew. He carried his head proudly on high, for he was conscious that in all respects he stood above the rabble pursuing him, above its very leaders, the clerics. In spite of untoward fate his mental development proceeded; but inevitably it was modified by the trend of the times. By the side of the philosophic tendency of the previous age, a mystical tendency appeared in literature. The Kabbala, with its mist-shrouded symbolism, so grateful to the feelings and the imagination, chimed in better than rationalistic philosophy with the depressed humor under which the greater part of the Jews were then laboring. Another force antagonistic to rationalistic philosophy was the Rabbinism transplanted from France and Germany. The controversy between Rabbinism and philosophy, which dragged itself through three-quarters of a century (1232-1305), ended in the formal triumph of Rabbinism. However, philosophic activity merely languished, it did not cease entirely; in fact, the three currents for some time ran along parallel with one another. Next to the pillars of Rabbinism, Asheri, Rashba, Isaac ben Sheshet, loomed up the philosophers, Gersonides (Ralbag), Crescas, and Albo, and a long line of Kabbalists, beginning with Nahmanides and Moses de Leon, the compiler of the *Zohar*, and ending with the anonymous authors of the mysterious *Kana and Pelia*.

The times grew less and less propitious. Catholicism steadily gained ground in Spain. The scowling Dominican put forward his claim upon the Jewish soul with vehement emphasis, and made every effort to drag it into the bosom of the alone-saving Church. The conversion of the Jews would have been a great triumph, indeed, for Catholicism militant. The conversion methods of the Dominican monk were of a most insinuating kind—he usually began with a public religious disputation. Unfortunately, the Jews were experts in the art of debate, and too often by their bold replies covered the self-sufficient dignitaries of Rome with confusion. The Jews should have known, from bitter experience, that such boldness would not be passed over silently. From sumptuous debating hall to Dominican prison and scaffold was but a short step. In 1391, one of these worthy soul-catchers, Bishop Ferdinando Martinez, set the fanatical mob of Seville on the Jews, and not without success. Terrorized by the threat of death, many accepted Catholicism under duress. But they became Christians only in appearance; in reality they remained true to the faith of their fathers, and, in secret, running the risk of loss of life, they fulfilled all the Jewish ordinances. This is the prologue to the thrilling marrano tragedy.

Finally, the moment approached when gloomy Catholicism attained to unchallenged supremacy in the Pyrenean peninsula. On the ruins of the enlightened culture of the Arabs, Ferdinand the Catholic and Isabella of Castile reared the reactionary government of medieval Rome. The Inquisition was introduced (1480). Torquemada presided as high priest over the rites attending the human sacrifices. *Ad gloriam ecclesiæ*, the whole of Spain was illuminated. Everywhere the funeral pyres of the Inquisition flared to the skies, the air was rent by the despairing shrieks of martyrs enveloped in flames or racked by tortures, the prisons overflowed with marranos,—all instruments of torture were vigorously plied.

At last the hour of redemption struck: in 1492 all Jews were driven from Spain, and a few years later from Portugal. Jewish-Arabic culture after five centuries of ascendancy suffered a sudden collapse. The unhappy people again grasped its staff and wandered forth into the world without knowing whither.

X

THE RABBINIC-MYSTICAL PERIOD, OR THE HEGEMONY OF THE GERMAN-POLISH JEWS (1492-1789)

The expulsion from Spain was a stunning blow. The hoary martyr people which had defied so many storms in its long life was for a moment dazed. The soil of Europe was quaking under its feet. At the time when the medieval period had formally come to a close for occidental Christendom, and the modern period had opened, the middle ages continued in unmitigated brutality for the Jews. If anything, the life of the Jews had become more unendurable than before. What, indeed, had the much-vaunted modern age to offer them? In the ranks of the humanistic movement Reuchlin alone stood forth prominently as the advocate of the Jews, and he was powerless before the prejudices of the populace. The Reformation in Germany and elsewhere had illuminated the minds of the people, but had not softened their hearts. Luther himself, the creator of the Reformation, was not innocent of hating the followers of an alien faith. The Jews especially did not enjoy too great a measure of his sympathies. The wars growing out of the Reformation, which in the sixteenth and seventeenth centuries devastated Europe in the name of religion, were not calculated to favor the spread of tolerance and milder manners. The conflict raging in the bosom of the Church and setting her own children by the ears, was yet insufficient to divert her maternal care from her "unbelieving" stepchildren. In Spain and Portugal, stakes continued to burn two centuries longer for the benefit of the marranos, the false Christians. In Germany and Austria, the Jews were kept in the same condition of servitude as before. Their economic circumstances were appalling. They were forced to emigrate *en masse* to Poland, which offered the adherents of their faith a comparatively quiet life, and by and by was invested with the Jewish hegemony. Some of the smaller states and independent towns of Italy also afforded the Jews an asylum, though one not always to be depended upon. A group of hard-driven Spanish exiles, for instance, under the leadership of Abarbanel had found peace in Italy. The rest had turned to Turkey and her province Palestine.

For a time, indeed, the Jewish spiritual center was located in Turkey. What Europe, old, Christian, and hardhearted, refused the Jews, was granted them by Turkey, young, Moslem, and liberal. On hearing of the banishment of the Jews from Spain, Sultan Bajazet exclaimed: "How can you call Ferdinand of Aragon a wise king, the same Ferdinand who has made his land poor and enriched ours?" His amazement characterizes the relation of Turkey to the Jews of the day. The one-time marrano, Joseph Nassi, rose to be a considerable dignitary at the court of Sultan Selim (1566-1580). Occasionally he succeeded, by diplomatic means, in wreaking vengeance upon European courts in retaliation for the brutal tortures inflicted upon his people. With the generosity of a Maecenas, he assembled Jewish scholars and poets, and surrounded himself with a sunlit atmosphere of intellectuality and talent. All other Jewish communities looked up to that of Constantinople. Now and again its rabbis played the part of patriarchs of the synagogue. To this commanding position the rabbis of Palestine especially were inclined to lay claim. They even attempted to restore the Patriarchate, and the famous controversy between Jacob Berab and Levi ben Habib regarding the *semikha* is another evidence of the same assertive tendency. Among the Spanish exiles settled in the Holy Land a peculiar spiritual current set in. The storm-tossed wanderers, but now returned to their native Jordan from the shores of the blood-stained Tagus and Guadalquivir, were mightily moved at the sight of their ancestral home. Ahasuerus, who on his thorn-strewn pilgrim's path had drained the cup of woe to the dregs, suddenly caught sight of the home of his childhood razed level with the ground. The precious, never-to-be-forgotten ruins exhaled the home feeling, which took possession of him with irresistible charm. Into his soul there flowed sweet memories of a golden youth, past beyond recall. The impact of these emotions enkindled passionate "longing for Zion" in the heart of the forlorn, homeless martyr. He was seized by torturing thirst for political resurrection. Such melancholy feelings and vehement outbursts found expression in the practical Kabbala, originating with Isaac Luria and his famous Safed school. A mystical belief in the coming of Messiah thenceforward became one of the essential elements of the Jewish spirit. It vanquished the heart of the learned Joseph Karo, who had brought Rabbinism to its climax by the compilation of his celebrated ritual code, the *Shulhan Arukh.* With equal force it dominated the being of Solomon Molcho, the enthusiastic youth who, at one time a marrano, on his public return to Judaism proclaimed the speedy regeneration of Israel. He sealed his faith in his prophecy with death at the stake (1532). The marranos beyond the Pyrenees and the unfortunate Jews of Italy, who, in the second half of the sixteenth century had to bear the brunt of papal fanaticism, on the increase since the Reformation, were kept in a state of constant excitement by this messianic doctrine, with its obscure stirrings of hope. A mournful national feeling pervades the Jewish literature of the time. Recollections of torments endured enflamed all hearts. A series of chronicles were thus produced that record the centuries of Jewish martyrdom—*Johasin, Shebet Jehuda, Emek ha-bakha,* etc. The art of printing, even then developed to a considerable degree of perfection, became for the dispersed Jews the strongest bond of spiritual union. The papal *index librorum prohibitorum* was impotent in the face of the all-pervading propaganda for thought and feeling carried on by the printing press.

After Palestine and Turkey, Holland for a time became the spiritual center of the scattered Jews (in the seventeenth century). Holland was warmly attached to the cause of liberty. When it succeeded in freeing itself from the clutches of fanatical Spain and her rapacious king, Philip II, it inaugurated the golden era of liberty of conscience, of peaceful development in culture and industry, and granted an asylum to the persecuted and abandoned of all countries. By the thousands the harassed ghetto sons, especially the marranos from Spain and Portugal, migrated to Holland. Amsterdam became a second Cordova. The intellectual life was quickened. Freedom from restraint tended to break down the national exclusivism of the Jew, and intercourse with his liberal surroundings varied his mental pursuits. Rabbinism, the Kabbala, philosophy, national poetry—they all had their prominent representatives in Holland. These manifold tendencies were united in the literary activity of Manasseh ben Israel, a scholar of extensive, though not intensive, encyclopedic attainments. Free thought and religious rationalism were embodied in Uriel Acosta. To a still higher degree they were illustrated in the theory of life expounded by the immortal author of the *Theologico-Political Tractate* (1640-1677). This advanced state of culture in Holland did not fail to react upon the neighboring countries. Under the impulse of enthusiasm for the Bible, Puritan England under Cromwell opened its portals to the Jews. In Italy, in the dank atmosphere of rabbinical dialectics and morbid mysticism, great figures loom up—Leon de Modena, the antagonist of Rabbinism and of the Kabbala, and Joseph del Medigo, mathematician, philosopher, and mystic, the disciple of Galileo.

These purple patches were nothing more than the accidents of a transition period. The people as a whole was on the decline. The Jewish mind darted hither and thither, like a startled bird seeking its nest. Holland or Turkey was an inadequate substitute for Spain, if only for the reason that but a tiny fraction of the Jews had found shelter in either. The Jewish national center must perforce coincide with the numerical center of the dispersed people, in which, moreover, conditions must grant Jews the possibility of living undisturbed in closely compacted masses, and of perfecting a well-knit organization of social and individual life. Outside of Spain these conditions were fulfilled only by Poland, which gradually, beginning with the sixteenth century, assumed the hegemony over the Jewry of the world. This marks the displacement of the Sephardic (Spanish, in a broader sense, Romanic) element, and the supremacy of the Ashkenazic (German-Polish) element.

Poland had been a resort for Jewish immigrants from Germany since the outbreak of the Crusades, until, in the sixteenth century, it rose to the position of a Jewish center of the first magnitude. As the merchant middle class, the Jews were protected and advanced by the kings and the *shlakhta*. The consequent security of their position induced so rapid a growth of the Jewish element that in a little while the Jews of Poland outnumbered those of the old Jewish settlements in occidental Europe. The numerous privileges granted the Jews, by Boleslaus of Kalish (1246), Casimir the Great (1347-1370), Witowt (1388), Casimir IV (1447), and some of their successors, fortified their position in the extended territory covered by Poland, Lithuania, and the Ukraine. Their peculiar circumstances in Poland left an impress upon their inner life. An intense mental activity was called forth. This activity can be traced back to German beginnings, though at the same time it is made up of many original elements. For a space Rabbinism monopolized the intellectual endeavors of the Polish Jews. The rabbi of Cracow, Moses Isserles, and the rabbi of Ostrog, Solomon Luria (d. 1572), disputed first place with the foremost rabbinical authorities of other countries. Their decisions and circular letters regarding religious and legal questions were accorded binding force. Associates and successors of theirs founded Talmud academies throughout the country, and large numbers of students attended them. Commentators upon the Talmud and expounders of classical works in Jewish theological literature appeared in shoals. Jewish printing establishments in Cracow and Lublin were assiduous in turning out a mass of writings, which spread the fame of the Polish rabbis to the remotest communities. The large autonomy enjoyed by the Polish and Lithuanian Jews conferred executive power upon rabbinical legislation. The *kahal*, or Jewish communal government, to a certain degree invested with judicial and administrative competence, could not do without the guiding hand of the rabbis as interpreters of the law. The guild of rabbis, on their side, chose a "college of judges," with fairly extensive jurisdiction, from among their own members. The organization of the Rabbinical Conferences, or the Councils of the Four Lands, formed the keystone of this intricate social-spiritual hierarchy. The comprehensive inner autonomy and the system of Talmud academies (*yeshiboth*) that covered the whole of Poland remind one of the brilliant days of the Exilarchate and the Babylonia of the Geonim. One element was lacking, there was no versatile, commanding thinker like Saadia Gaon. Secular knowledge and philosophy were under the ban in Poland. Rabbinism absorbed the whole output of intellectual energy. As little as the Poles resembled the Arabs of the "golden age," did the Polish Jews resemble their brethren in faith in the Orient at Saadia's time or in the Spain of Gabirol and Maimonides. Isolation and clannishness were inevitable in view of the character of the Christian environment and the almost insuperable barriers raised between the classes of Polish society. But it was this exclusiveness that gave peculiar stability and completeness to the life of the Jew as an individual and as a member of Jewish society, and it was the same exclusiveness that afforded opportunity for the development of a sharply defined culture, for its fixation to the point of resisting violent shocks and beyond the danger point of extinction through foreign invasion.

The fateful year 1648 formed a turning point in the history of the Polish Jews, as in the history of the countries belonging to the Polish crown. The Cossack butcheries and wars of extermination of 1648-1658 were the same for the Polish Jews that the Crusades, the Black Death, and all the other occasions for carnage had been for the Jews of western Europe. It seemed as though history desired to avoid the reproach of partiality and hastened to mete out even-handed justice by apportioning the same measure of woe to the Jews of Poland as to the Jews of western Europe. But the Polish Jews were prepared to accept the questionable gift from the hands of history. They had mounted that eminence of spiritual stability on which suffering loses the power to weaken its victim, but, on the contrary, endows him with strength. More than ever they shrank into their shell. They shut themselves up more completely in their inner world, and became morally dulled against the persecutions, the bitter humiliations, the deep scorn, which their surroundings visited upon them. The Polish Jew gradually accustomed himself to his pitiable condition. He hardly knew that life might be other than it was. That the Polish lord to whom he was a means of entertainment might treat him with a trace of respect, or that his neighbors, the middle-class merchant, the German guild member, and the Little Russian peasant, might cherish kindly feelings toward him, he could not conceive as a possibility. Seeing himself surrounded by enemies, he took precautions to fortify his camp, not so much to protect himself against hostile assaults from without—they were inevitable—as to paralyze the disastrous consequences of such assaults in his inner world. To compass this end he brought into play all the means suggested by his exceptional position before the law and by his own peculiar social constitution. The *kahal*, the autonomous rabbinical administration of communal affairs, more and more assumed the character of an inner dictatorship. Jewish society was persistently kept under the discipline of rigid principles. In many affairs the synagogue attained the position of a court of final appeal. The people were united, or rather packed, into a solid mass by purely mechanical processes—by pressure from without, and by drawing tight a noose from within. Besides this social factor tending to consolidate the Jewish people into a separate union, an intellectual lever was applied to produce the same result. Rabbinism employed the mystical as its adjutant. The one exercised control over all minds, the other over all hearts. The growth of mysticism was fostered both by the unfortunate conditions under which the Polish Jews endured existence and by the messianic movements which made their appearance among the Jews of other countries.

In the second half of the seventeenth century, mysticism reached its zenith in Turkey, the country in which had stood the cradle of the "practical Kabbala." The teachings of Luria, Vital, and the school established by them spread like wildfire. Messianic extravagances intoxicated the baited and persecuted people. In Smyrna appeared the false messiah, Sabbatai Zevi. As by magic he attracted to himself a tremendous company of adherents in the East and in the West. For a quarter of a century (1650-1676), he kept the Jewish communities everywhere in a state of quivering suspense.

The harassed people tossed to and fro like a fever patient and raved about political rebirth. Its delirious visions still further heated its agitated blood. It came to its senses but slowly. Not even the apostasy and death of Sabbatai Zevi sufficed to sober all his followers. Under the guise of a symbolic faith in a messiah, many of them, publicly or secretly, continued the propaganda for his doctrines.

This propaganda prepared the fertile soil from which, in the eighteenth century, shot up messianic systems, tending to split Judaism into sects. Nowhere did the mystical teachings evoke so ready a response as in Poland, the very center of Judaism. At first an ally of the rabbinical school, mysticism, grown passionate and uncontrollable, now and again acted as the violent opponent of Rabbinism. Secret devotion to the Sabbatian doctrines, which had made their home in Poland, sometimes led to such extremes in dogma and ethics that the rabbis could not contain themselves. Hayim Malach, Jehuda he-Hasid, and other Galician mystics, in the second decade of the eighteenth century, brought down upon themselves a rabbinical decree of excommunication. The mystical tendency was the precursor of the heretical half-Christian sect of Frankists, who ventured so far as to lift a hand against the fundamentals of Judaism: they rejected the Talmud in favor of the *Zohar* (1756-1773). At the same time a much more profound movement, instinct with greater vitality, made its appearance among the Polish-Jewish masses, a movement rooted in their social and spiritual organization. The wretched, debased condition of the average Jew, conjoined with the traditions of the Kabbala and the excrescences of Rabbinism, created a foothold for hasidic teaching. Hasidism replaced talmudic ratiocination by exalted religious sentiment. By the force of enthusiasm for faith, it drew its adherents together into a firmly welded unit in contrast with Rabbinism, which sought the same goal by the aid of the formal law. Scenting danger, the rabbinical hierarchy declared war upon the Kabbala. Emden opposed Eibeschütz, the Polish Sabbatians and Frankists were fought to the death, the Vilna Gaon organized a campaign against the hasidim. Too late! Rabbinism was too old, too arid, to tone down the impulsive outbreaks of passion among the people. In their religious exaltation the masses were looking for an elixir. They were languishing, not for light to illumine the reason, but for warmth to set the heart aglow. They desired to lose themselves in ecstatic self-renunciation. Hasidism and its necessary dependence upon the *tsaddik* offered the masses the means of this forgetfulness of self through faith. They were the medium through which the people saw the world in a rosy light, and the consequences following upon their prevalence were seen in a marked intensification of Jewish exclusiveness.

The same aloofness characterizes the Jews of the rest of the eighteenth century Diaspora. Wherever, as in Germany, Austria, and Italy, Jews were settled in considerable numbers, they were separated from their surroundings by forbidding ghetto walls. On the whole, no difference is noticeable between conditions affecting Jews in one country and those in another. Everywhere they were merely tolerated, everywhere oppressed and humiliated. The bloody persecutions of the middle ages were replaced by the burden of the exceptional laws, which in practice degraded the Jews socially to an inferior race, to citizens of a subordinate degree. The consequences were uniformly the same in all countries: spiritual isolation and a morbid religious mood. During the first half of the "century of reason," Jewry presented the appearance of an exhausted wanderer, heavily dragging himself on his way, his consciousness clouded, his trend of thought obviously anti-rationalistic. At the very moment in which Europe was beginning to realize its medieval errors and repent of them, and the era of universal ideals of humanity was dawning, Judaism raised barricades between itself and the world at large. Elijah Gaon and Israel Baal Shem Tob were the contemporaries of Voltaire and Rousseau. Apparently there was no possibility of establishing communication between these two diametrically opposed worlds. But history is a magician. Not far from the Poland enveloped in medieval darkness, the morning light of a new life was breaking upon slumbering Jewry in German lands. New voices made themselves heard, reverberating like an echo to the appeal issued by the "great century" in behalf of a spiritual and social regeneration of mankind.

XI

THE MODERN PERIOD OF ENLIGHTENMENT
(The Nineteenth Century)

Two phenomena signalized the beginning of the latest period in Jewish history: the lofty activity of Mendelssohn and the occurrence of the French Revolution. The man stands for the spiritual emancipation of the Jews, the movement for their political emancipation. At bottom, these two phenomena were by no means the ultimate causes of the social and spiritual regeneration of the Jewish people. They were only the products of the more general causes that had effected a similar regeneration in all the peoples of western Europe. The new currents, the abandonment of effete intellectual and social forms, the substitution of more just and energetic principles, the protest against superstition and despotism—all these traits had a common origin, the resuscitation of reason and free thought, which dominated all minds without asking whether they belonged to Jew or to Christian. It might seem that the rejuvenation of the Jews had been consummated more rapidly than the rejuvenation of the other peoples. The latter had had two centuries, the period elapsing since the middle ages, that is, the period between the Reformation and the great Revolution, in which to prepare for a more rational and a more humane conduct of life. As for the Jews, their middle ages began much later, and ended later, almost on the eve of 1789, so that the revolution in their minds and their mode of life had to accomplish itself hastily, under the urgence of swiftly crowding events, by the omission of intermediate stages. But it must be taken into consideration that long before, in the Judeo-Hellenic and in the Arabic-Spanish period, the Jews had passed through their "century of reason." In spite of the intervening ages of suffering and gloom, the faculty of assimilating new principles had survived. For the descendants of Philo and Maimonides the rationalistic movement of the eighteenth century was in part a repetition of a well-known historical process. They had had the benefit of a similar course of studies before, and, therefore, had no need to cram on the eve of the final examination.

In point of fact, the transformation in the life of the Jews did take place with extraordinary swiftness. It was hastened in France by the principles of the Revolution and the proclamation of the civil equality of Jews with the other citizens. In Germany, however, it advanced upon purely spiritual lines. Mendelssohn and Lessing, the heralds of spiritual reform, who exposed old prejudices, carried on their labors at a time in which the Jews still stood beyond the pale of the law, a condition which it did not occur to Frederick II, "the philosopher upon the throne," to improve. A whole generation was destined to pass before the civil emancipation of the German Jews was accomplished. Meantime their spiritual emancipation proceeded apace, without help from the ruling powers. A time so early as the end of the eighteenth century found the German Jews in a position to keep step with their Christian fellow-citizens in cultural progress. Enlightened Jews formed close connections with enlightened Christians, and joined them in the universal concerns of mankind as confederates espousing the same fundamental principles. If they renounced some of their religious and national traditions, it was by no means out of complaisance for their neighbors. They were guided solely and alone by those universal principles that forced non-Jews as well as Jews to reject many traditions as incompatible with reason and conscience. Non-Jews and Jews alike yielded themselves up to the fresh inspiration of the time, and permitted themselves to be carried along by the universal transforming movement. Mendelssohn himself, circumspect and wise, did not move off from religious-national ground. But the generation after him abandoned his position for that of universal humanity, or, better, German nationality. His successors intoxicated themselves with deep draughts of the marvelous poetry created by the magic of Goethe and Schiller. They permitted themselves to be rushed along by the liberty doctrines of 1789; they plunged head over heels into the vortex of romanticism and took an active part in the conspicuous movements of Europe, political, social, and literary, as witness Börne, Heine, and their fellow-combatants.

The excitement soon evaporated. When the noise of the liberty love-feasts had subsided, when the cruel reaction (after 1814) had settled heavily upon the Europe of the nineteenth century, and God's earth had again become the arena of those agents of darkness whom dreamers had thought buried forever beneath the ruins of the old order, then the German Jews, or such of them as thought, came to their senses. The more intelligent Jewish circles realized that, in devotion to the German national movement, they had completely neglected their own people. Yet their people, too, had needs, practical or spiritual, had its peculiar national sphere of activity, circumscribed, indeed, by the larger sphere of mankind's activities as by a concentric circle, but by no means merged into it. To atone for their sin, thinking Jews retraced their steps. They took in hand the transforming of Jewish inner life, the simplification of the extremely complicated Jewish ritual, the remodeling of pedagogic methods, and, above all, the cultivation of the extended fields of Jewish science, whose head and front is Jewish historical research in all its vastness and detail. Heine's friend, Zunz, laid the cornerstone of Jewish science in the second decade of the nineteenth century. His work was taken up by a goodly company of zealous and able builders occupied for half a century with the task of rearing the proud edifice of a scientific historical literature, in which national self-consciousness was sheltered and fostered. At the very height of this reforming and literary activity, German Jewry was overwhelmed by the civil emancipation of 1848. Again a stirring movement drew them into sympathy with a great general cause, but this time without drawing them away from Jewish national interests. Cultural and civil assimilation was accomplished as an inner compelling necessity, as a natural outcome of living. But spiritual assimilation, in the sense of a merging of Judaism in foreign elements, was earnestly repudiated by the noblest representatives of Judaism. It was their ideal that universal activity and national activity should be pursued to the prejudice of neither, certainly not to the exclusion of one or the other, but in perfect harmony with each other. In point of fact, it may be asserted that, in spite of a frequent tendency to go to the one or the other extreme, the two currents, the universal and the national, co-exist within German Jewry, and there is no fear of their uniting, they run parallel with each other. The Jewish genius is versatile. Without hurt to itself it can be active in all sorts of careers: in politics and in civil life, in parliament and on the lecture platform, in all branches of science and departments of literature, in every one of the chambers of mankind's intellectual laboratory. At the same time it has its domestic hearth, its national sanctuary; it has its sphere of original work and its self-consciousness, its national interests and spiritual ideals rooted in the past of the Jew. By the side of a Lassalle, a Lasker, and a Marx towers a Riesser, a Geiger, a Graetz. The leveling process unavoidably connected with widespread culture, so far from causing spiritual desolation in German Judaism, has, on the contrary, furnished redundant proof that even under present conditions, so unfavorable to what is individual and original, the Jewish people has preserved its vitality to the full.

An analogous movement stirred the other countries of western Europe—France, Italy, and England. The political emancipation of the Jews was accomplished earlier in them than in Germany. The reconstruction of the inner life, too, proceeded more quietly and regularly, without leaps and bounds, and religious reform established itself by degrees. Yet even here, where the Jewish contingent was insignificant, the spiritual physiognomy of the Jews maintained its typical character. In these countries, as in Germany, the Jew assimilated European culture with all its advantages and its drawbacks. He was active on diplomatic fields, he devoted himself to economic investigations, he produced intellectual creations of all kinds—first and last he felt himself to be a citizen of his country. Nonetheless he was a loyal son of the Jewish people considered as a spiritual people with an appointed task. Crémieux, Beaconsfield, Luzzatti are counterbalanced by Salvador, Franck, Munk, Reggio, and Montefiore. All the good qualities and the shortcomings distinctive of the civilization of modern times adhere to the Jew. But at its worst modern civilization has not succeeded in extinguishing the national spirit in Jewry. The national spirit continues to live in the people, and it is this spirit that quickens the people. The genius of Jewish history, as in centuries gone by, holds watch over the sons of the "eternal people" scattered to all ends of the earth. West-European Jewry may say of itself, without presumption: *Cogito ergo sum.*

Russian Jewry, the Jewry that had been Polish, and that is counted by the millions, might, if necessary, prove its existence by even more tangible marks than occidental Jewry. To begin with, the center of gravity of the Jewish nation lies in Russia, whose Jews not only outnumber those of the rest of Europe, but continue to live in a compact mass. Besides, they have preserved the original Jewish culture and their traditional physiognomy to a higher degree than the Jews of other countries. The development of the Russian Jews took a course very different from that of the Jews of the West. This difference was conditioned by the tremendous contrast between Russian culture and west-European culture, and by the change which the external circumstances of Jews outside of Russia underwent during the modern period. The admission of the Polish provinces into the Russian empire at the end of the eighteenth century found the numerous Jewish population in an almost medieval condition, the same condition in which the non-Jewish population of Russian Poland was at that time. The Polish regime, as we saw above, had isolated the Jews alike in civil and spiritual relations. The new order did not break down the barriers. The masses of Jews cooped up in the Pale of Settlement were strong only by reason of their inner unity, their firmly established patriarchal organization. The bulwark of Rabbinism and the citadel of hasidism protected them against alien influences. They guarded their isolation jealously. True to the law of inertia, they would not allow the privilege of isolation to be wrested from them. They did not care to step beyond the ramparts. Why, indeed, should the Jews have quitted their fortress, if outside of their walls they could expect nothing but scorn and blows? The unfortunates encaged in the sinister Pale of Settlement could have been lured out of their exclusive position only by complete civil emancipation combined with a higher degree of culture than had been attained by Russian society, an impossible set of circumstances in the first half of the nineteenth century. The legislative measures of the time, in so far as they relate to the Jews, breathe the spirit of police surveillance rather than of enlightenment and humanity. To civilizing and intellectual influences from without the way was equally barred. Yet all this watchfulness was of no avail. Nothing could prevent the liberty principles espoused by the Jews of western Europe from being smuggled into the Pale, to leaven the sad, serried masses. A sluggish process of fermentation set in and culminated in the literary activity of Isaac Ber Levinson and of the Vilna reformers of the second and fourth decades of the nineteenth century. They were the harbingers of approaching spring.

When spring finally came (after 1855), and the sun sent down his genial rays upon the wretched Jewry of Russia, life and activity began to appear at once, especially in the upper strata. As in Germany, so in Russia spiritual emancipation preceded political emancipation. Still shorn almost entirely of the elementary rights of citizens, the Russian Jews nevertheless followed their ideal promptings and participated enthusiastically in the movement for enlightenment which at that time held the noblest of the Russians enthralled. In a considerable portion of the Russian Jewish community a process of culture regeneration began, an eager throwing off of outworn forms of life and thought, a swift adoption of humane principles. Jewish young men crowded into the secular schools, in which they came in close contact with their Christian contemporaries. Influenced by their new companions, they gave themselves up to Russian national movements, often at the cost of renunciation of self. Some of them, indeed, in one-sided aspiration strove to become, not Russians, but men. The influence exercised by literature was more moderate than that of the schools. Rabbinic and hasidistic literature, on the point of dying out as it was, abandoned the field to the literature of enlightenment in the Hebrew language, a literature of somewhat primitive character. It consisted chiefly of naive novels and of didactic writings of publicists, and lacked the solid scientific and historical element that forms the crown of western Jewish literature. It is indisputable, however, that it exerted an educational influence. Besides, it possesses the merit of having resuscitated one of the most valuable of Jewish national possessions, the Hebrew language in its purity, which in Russia alone has become a pliant instrument of literary expression. A still greater field was reserved for the Jewish-Russian literature that arose in the "sixties." It was called into being in order to present a vivid and true picture of the social and spiritual interests of the Jews. Proceeding from discussions of current political topics, this literature gradually widened its limits so as to include Jewish history, Jewish science, and the portrayal of Jewish life, and more and more approached the character of a normal European literature. All this was in the making, and the most important work had not yet begun. The lower strata of the people had not been touched by the fresh air. In time, if all had gone well, they, too, would have had their day. And if the minority of the Jewish people in the West in a short span of time brought forth so many notable workers in so many departments of life and thought, how much superior would be the cultural achievements of the Eastern majority! How vigorously the mighty mental forces latent in Russian Jewry would develop when their advance was no longer obstructed by all sorts of obstacles, and they could be applied to every sphere of political, social, and intellectual life!

Nothing of all this came to pass; exactly the opposite happened. Not only were the barriers in the way of a prosperous, free development of Jewry not removed, but fresh hindrances without number were multiplied. Some specter of the middle ages, some power of darkness, put brakes upon the wheel of history. It first appeared in the West, under the name antisemitism, among the dregs of European society. But in its earliest abode it was and is still met with an abrupt rebuff on the part of the most intelligent circles, those whom even the present age of decadence has not succeeded in robbing of belief in lofty moral ideals. Antisemitism in the West is in *anima vili*. Its cult is confined to a certain party which enjoys a rather scandalous reputation. But there are countries in which this power of darkness, in the coarser form of Judophobia, has cast its baleful spell upon the most influential members of society and upon the press. There it has ripened noxious fruit. Mocking at the exalted ideals and the ethical traditions of religious and thinking mankind, Judophobia shamelessly professes the dogma of misanthropy. Its propaganda is bringing about the moral ruin of an immature society, not yet confirmed in ethical or truly religious principles. Upon its victims, the Jews, it has the same effect as the misfortunes of the middle ages, which were meted out to our hoary people with overflowing measure, and against which it learnt to assume an armor of steel. The recent severe trials are having the same result as the persecutions of former days: they do not weaken, on the contrary, they invigorate the Jewish spirit, they spur on to thought, they stimulate the pulse of the people.

> "The hammer shivers glass,
> But iron by its blows is forged." (Pushkin)

The historical process Jewry has undergone repeatedly, it must undergo once again. But now, too, in this blasting time of confusion and dispersion, of daily torture and the horrors of international conflict, "the keeper of Israel slumbereth not and sleepeth not." The Jewish spirit is on the alert. It is ever purging and tempering itself in the furnace of suffering. The people which justly bears the name of the veteran of history withdraws and falls into a reverie. It is not a narrow-minded fanatic's flight from the world, but the concentrated thought of a mourner. Jewry is absorbed in contemplation of its great, unparalleled past. More than ever it is now in need of the teachings of its past, of the moral support and the prudent counsels of its history—its four thousand years of life crowded with checkered experiences.

XII

THE TEACHINGS OF JEWISH HISTORY

Let us return now to the starting point of our discussion, and endeavor to establish the thoughts and lessons to be deduced from the course of Jewish history.

Above all, Jewish history possesses the student with the conviction that Jewry at all times, even in the period of political independence, was pre-eminently a spiritual nation, and a spiritual nation it continues to be in our own days, too. Furthermore, it inspires him with the belief that Jewry, being a spiritual entity, cannot suffer annihilation: the body, the mold, may be destroyed, the spirit is immortal. Bereft of country and dispersed as it is, the Jewish nation lives, and will go on living, because a creative principle permeates it, a principle that is the root of its being and an indigenous product of its history. This principle consists first in a sum of definite religious, moral, or philosophic ideals, whose exponent at all times was the Jewish people, either in its totality, or in the person of its most prominent representatives. Next, this principle consists in a sum of historical memories, recollections of what in the course of many centuries the Jewish people experienced, thought, and felt in the depths of its being. Finally, it consists in the consciousness that true Judaism, which has accomplished great things for humanity in the past, has not yet played out its part, and, therefore, may not perish. In short, the Jewish people lives because it contains a living soul which refuses to separate from its integument, and cannot be forced out of it by heavy trials and misfortunes such as would unfailingly inflict mortal injury upon less sturdy organisms.

This self-consciousness is the source from which the suffering Jewish soul draws comfort. History speaks to it constantly through the mouth of the great apostle who went forth from the midst of Israel eighteen hundred years ago: "Call to remembrance the former days, in which, after ye were enlightened, ye endured a great conflict of sufferings; partly, being made a gazing-stock both by reproaches and afflictions; and partly, becoming partakers with them that were so used. . . . Cast not away therefore your boldness, which hath great recompense of reward" (Epistle to the Hebrews, 10.32-34, 35).

Jewish history, moreover, arouses in the Jew the desire to work unceasingly at the task of perfecting himself. To direct his attention to his glorious past, to the resplendent intellectual feats of his ancestors, to their masterly skill in thinking and suffering, does not lull him to sleep, does not awaken a dullard's complacency or hollow self-conceit. On the contrary, it makes exacting demands upon him. Jewish history admonishes the Jews: "*Noblesse oblige*. The privilege of belonging to a people to whom the honorable title of the 'veteran of history' has been conceded, puts serious responsibilities on your shoulders. You must demonstrate that you are worthy of your heroic past. The descendants of teachers of religion and martyrs of the faith dare not be insignificant, not to say wicked. If the long centuries of wandering and misery have inoculated you with faults, extirpate them in the name of the exalted moral ideals whose bearers you were commissioned to be. If, in the course of time, elements out of harmony with your essential being have fastened upon your mind, cast them out, purify yourselves. In all places and at all times, in joy and in sorrow, you must aim to live for the higher, the spiritual interests. But never may you deem yourselves perfect. If you become faithless to these sacred principles, you sever the bonds that unite you with the most vital elements of your past, with the first cause of your national existence."

The final lesson to be learned is that in the sunny days of mankind's history, in which reason, justice, and philanthropic instinct had the upper hand, the Jews steadfastly made common cause with the other nations. Hand in hand with them, they trod the path leading to perfection. But in the dark days, during the reign of rude force, prejudice, and passion, of which they were the first victims, the Jews retired from the world, withdrew into their shell, to await better days. Union with mankind at large, on the basis of the spiritual and the intellectual, the goal set up by the Jewish Prophets in their sublime vision of the future (Isa., 2, and Micah, 4), is the ultimate ideal of

Judaism's noblest votaries. Will their radiant hope ever attain to realization?

If ever it should be realized,—and it is incumbent upon us to believe that it will—not a slight part of the merits involved will be due to Jewish history. We have adverted to the lofty moral and humanitarian significance of Jewish history in its role as conciliator. With regard to one-half of Jewish history, this conciliatory power is even now a well-established fact. The first part of Jewish history, the biblical part, is a source from which, for many centuries, millions of human beings belonging to the most diverse denominations have derived instruction, solace, and inspiration. It is read with devotion by Christians in both hemispheres, in their houses and their temples. Its heroes have long ago become types, incarnations of great ideas. The events it relates serve as living ethical formulas. But a time will come—perhaps it is not very far off—when the second half of Jewish history, the record of the two thousand years of the Jewish people's life after the biblical period, will be accorded the same treatment. This latter part of Jewish history is not yet known, and many, in the thrall of prejudice, do not wish to know it. But ere long it will be known and appreciated. For the thinking portion of mankind it will be a source of uplifting moral and philosophical teaching. The thousand years' martyrdom of the Jewish people, its unbroken pilgrimage, its tragic fate, its teachers of religion, its martyrs, philosophers, champions, this whole epic will in days to come sink deep into the memory of men. It will speak to the heart and the conscience of men, not merely to their curious mind. It will secure respect for the silvery hair of the Jewish people, a people of thinkers and sufferers. It will dispense consolation to the afflicted, and by its examples of spiritual steadfastness and self-denial encourage martyrs in their devotion. It is our firm conviction that the time is approaching in which the second half of Jewish history will be to the noblest part of *thinking* humanity what its first half has long been to *believing* humanity, a source of sublime moral truths. In this sense, Jewish history in its entirety is the pledge of the spiritual union between the Jews and the rest of the nations.

THE SURVIVAL OF THE JEWISH PEOPLE

The Secret of Survival and the Law of Survival

1. *Reflections on the Secret of Survival*

When we try to assess the "prospects of Judaism" from a general and abstract point of view, contemplating the form rather than the content of its history, we are confronted by a great and hidden mystery. We try to penetrate the depths of this mystery, the secret of the survival of the Jewish people, and fathom the forces operating within the soul of the people, forces whose results lie open before us but whose inner workings are shrouded in darkness, like all basic forces operating in the soul of both individual and community. We shall direct our attention to general principles before we study the development of the specific details. We shall search for a cause, not for causes—for the "first cause."

Let us examine this matter briefly.

It is difficult even for a discerning investigator to estimate the value of the powerful forces stored in the soul of a nation which has traversed the earth's surface for thousands of years. Every generation in Israel carries within itself the remnants of worlds created and destroyed during the course of the previous history of the Jewish people. The generation, in turn, builds and destroys worlds in its form and image, but in the long run continues to weave the thread that binds all the links of the nation into the chain of generations. The spirit of each generation turns about continually in its circuit and the spirit returns again to its circuit, the point of the nation's existence. The soul of each generation (a generation is for a nation what an individual is for society) emanates from the soul of the (collective) "body" of all the preceding generations, and what endures, namely, the strength of the accumulated past, exceeds the wreckage, the strength of the changing present. If it sometimes seems to us that the destroyed elements exceed those that endure, that is only because of an aberration of our vision, which comes about because a moving point close by hides from view the fixed area, the firm rock in the background which all the winds will not move from its place.

Thus each generation in Israel is more the product of history than it is its creator. Every individual member of a generation, who is not like a dry branch or a leaf fallen from the tree, carries the "burden of the heritage" of the chain of generations; and he carries it willingly or unwillingly, knowingly or unknowingly. He is nursed and fed by the national forces accumulated in the past even when he rebels against the very means through which the forces were accumulated and even when he strives to destroy them, or to alter their form, or "reform" them.

As we look at the Jewish nation from the beginning of history up to the present we see a thread of eternity woven through it all. We, the people of Israel living today, continue the long thread that stretches from the days of Hammurabi and Abraham to the modern period. We have before us a firmly-molded body in which the depths of history are congealed, a body which is indestructible because it has a "second soul," and around it, wherever it goes, the wheel of history revolves: nations rise and fall, grow and wither. We see further that during the course of thousands of years the nations of the world have borrowed from our spiritual storehouse and added to their own without depleting the source. In hundreds of languages throughout the four corners of the earth men read with awe and reverence the Book which our people created in ancient times, and thousands of hearts are still filled with emotion while thus reading. They use the songs of the Psalms in prayer and tears well from their eyes at the sound of the words that came forth from the heart of an ancient Israelite whose "soul was cast down within him" among the hills of Judah and Ephraim. And when free thinkers among Christian scholars wish to glorify the origins of their faith, they rely on the teachings of our Prophets and credit their "Saviour" with being the heir of the Prophets, although the difference between the two teachings is more than obvious.

The causes of all these phenomena in the history of the development of the world religions are well known, but we cannot accept the notion that the basis of it all is to be found in a chain of accidents and not in inner forces.

We find in the history of Israel a spiritual attracting force and a repelling force. The Jewish people goes its own unique way, attracting and repelling, beating out for itself a unique path among the routes of the nations of the world, a path that continues on from the beginning of history, to go on perhaps to its end. And when we ask: "Are the days of this people indeed like the days of the heavens above the earth?," a voice comes out from the depths of history and replies: "They are, indeed!"

This is the product of the reflections interpreting the secret of Jewish survival. Bound up in this interpretation are the feelings and experiences of countless generations, accumulated and crystallized into the decisive answer: a people that was, is, and will be. The answer flows from the depths of the soul, from the source of "mysteries." But what is a speculative "mystery" if not a "manifest phenomenon" whose source is hidden?

A voice speaks to us out of the clouds and discloses the mystery. But our critical reason says: "Do not talk out of the clouds! Mysteries are for the faithful; rational knowledge is for those who understand and ponder." We must recognize our creator, the forces of the past that created us and our national soul, that have kept us alive and sustained us up to this time. Before we can penetrate the mystery of our survival, we are obliged to get to know and to recognize the law of survival of the people of Israel, the way of its history which, even though it be miraculous and unique, is subject to fixed laws and branches out into thousands of causes and effects—links forged into a chain.

Let us see what non-esoteric theory teaches us.

2. *The Law of Survival Considered*

We have viewed the people of Israel as a creation of history; now let us view it as the creator of its history. Let us examine the content and methods of its creativity.

Here we have "primeval matter" (in a historical, not a philosophical sense), a people among the peoples of the ancient East. In the beginning it is a *tribal* creation, one of the tribes of the East. It is then removed, like an egg, from several shells: from among the tribes of the Semites, the Aramaeans, the Hebrews, until we reach the central kernel "Israel." A nomadic people develops into a nation settled on its own territory and then into a political nation. As a political nation, Israel is constantly influenced by its environment, or even subjugated by the powerful empires growing and decaying in this environment. In its spiritual development, Israel, from the beginning, forges ahead on its beaten path: it creates for itself a God in its own form and image, a national God, a "ruler of the nation," amidst a family of rulers of the nations of the world. In its moral position, too, it is influenced by its environment and enjoys the taste of the "sins of youth." In time, however, before the people as a whole has attained a specific world view, there arise in its midst men "who sought after God" in ways other than those followed by the lawgivers and prophets of other nations. After a long internal struggle, there takes shape in Israel a spiritual tendency unique in kind, the tendency to create a people in the form and image of God, the Exalted Ideal. This is the fruit of the spirit of the Prophets. The God of the Prophets is the universal God and not merely a ruler of the nation. He created and continues to direct the universe and all nations by moral laws based on truth and justice. For several centuries the Prophets of truth and justice are active among the Hebrew people, while the prophets of other peoples extol power and beauty. Slowly the seedlings mature in the soil of the nation and a unique historical creation arises before us: a people that is small and weak in its political structure, but great in its spiritual form. It stands amidst a raging sea and struggles for survival. Branches of the nation are cut off by the sword of Assyria and by the exile of the Kingdom of Israel, and only the "trunk" remains. Judah is exiled to Babylonia, returns and experiences a rebirth on its own soil, and also strikes roots in the lands of the Diaspora. Instead of contracting, Judaism expands. In the period of Greek and Roman rule, Judea is surrounded by a wreath of Jewish centers in Egypt, Babylonia, and Syria. Hebrew culture wrestles with Greek culture, the culture representing "truth and justice" (ethicism) with the one representing "power and beauty" (estheticism). In the land of Israel, Jewish national culture wins out over Hellenism and is preserved in purity, walled in and contracted. In the centers of the Diaspora it is only half victorious: it penetrates into Greek culture and creates a strong ferment, but it also receives considerable influences from Hellenic civilization. Thus syncretism develops a mixture of Judaism and Hellenism which prepares the ground for the acceptance of Christianity, a mixture of the principles of Judaism with principles opposed to it.

Then comes the destruction of the Second Temple. The political center in Judea is destroyed and replaced by a regime which has no parallel in world history: a regime of "nomocracy," the rule of laws, "hedges" and "fences." Israel lays aside the weapons of the zealots, the defenders of political freedom, and takes up other weapons which in fact it wielded in a limited way even before the fall, and which it uses now almost exclusively "to fence itself in." The people armed with the sword are defeated by the armies of Titus and Hadrian, but the people armed with religious and national laws and fences win the struggle for survival. The land still remains on the ruins of the state. The Patriarchs and heads of the communities and academies provide leadership for the remnant of Israel in its land. They protect its inner autonomy in the same way the zealots protected its external freedom during the last days of the Temple. The sun of the center in Eretz Yisrael is not yet set when the sun of the autonomous center in Babylonia rises. Heads of the Diaspora, heads of academies and geonim, nearly eight hundred years of national life and autonomous administration in the "sacred communities" and unions of communities—these are the forces that strengthen the nation outside of Palestine. The nation acquires more powerful weapons: the Talmud is the arsenal for the camp of Israel.

The Jewish people thus armed enters the countries of the West after the destruction of its centers in the East. Here it erects new centers on the foundations of the old ones. The national thread continues to be woven. National hegemony passes from center to center: from Spain to France and Germany, from there to Poland and Russia. In and around each center the Jewish nationality fights for its individual character. In the same way that the synagogue had become a "miniature Temple" the autonomous community becomes part of a living, self-supporting body—a token (surrogate) for the state, a miniature state. Each community is a division of the great army that is united in our dispersion. Unions of communities and associations of unions—this is what "ingathering of the exiled" means in the Diaspora. Armament by laws and "fences" grows stronger to the degree that hatred against Israel in the countries of the West grows stronger. Israel thus clad in its armor passes between the lines of the hostile armies surrounding us. The armor does not protect the body from blows, but it protects the spirit, even though it is occasionally forced to shrink and contract. The armor represses the individuals in the nation, but it protects the community "in the state of siege" in which it finds itself. The nation is surrounded by a wall of its own within the wall erected by others. Cultural isolation from the environment is the way of life in the western Diaspora in times of war; social isolation and defense of communal autonomy in times of peace. Thus the Jewish people fights for its existence for a thousand years until it comes to the threshold of modern times, the period of revolution and emancipation in Europe.

This was "the law of survival" in the past: adaptation to all ways of life without destroying the national form, arming the nation with spiritual weapons after the loss of the political weapon, the struggle for survival through isolation from the environment, through internal self-rule, and through preservation of specific cultural possessions. "Autonomism"—existence that is self-determined and the striving for inner national freedom—this is the name of the law, this is the revealed secret of the survival of the people of Israel.

3. *Our Future: The Manifest and the Hidden*

A revolution came to the western world that was both political and cultural, the period of liberation—emancipation—or the striving for liberation. In most states the external wall isolating Jews from Gentiles was demolished and Jews for their part tore down the internal wall which their fathers had built.

They laid down their weapons, the national "fences" in their religion. They leave the camp, enter the alien environment, and absorb alien principles into their spirit. The emancipated Jew exchanges his national freedom for civic freedom. To a certain extent he is forced to this in line with the statement heard in the National Assembly in Paris during the great Revolution: "Give all the rights to the Jews as men, but give them nothing as sons of a specific nation!" This formulation by Clermont-Tonnerre, a partisan of emancipation, became the cornerstone of the emancipation structure in all countries. The emancipators demanded clearly: "Since citizenship has been introduced we must dissolve all national institutions: autonomous administration of the communities (except in religious affairs), schools that are not like the general state-schools, the use of Hebrew or Yiddish in the life of the community, etc." Thus emancipation liberates the Jew from both his bondage and his Judaism at one and the same time. It seems as if the dreaded end of Israel has come; limb after limb is swept into the stream and swallowed up in the abyss of the Gentile world.

Then the tempest comes from the north and the wheel turns back. The hatred against the eternal people that appeared to have subsided rises again. The war is renewed, in a cultural form in western Europe and in a savage form in the East. The Jewish masses who did not lay down their old weapons meet their enemies with the well-tested strategy of their fathers. But those who already have acquiesced in the environment and remain naked and without national armor—what about them?

The answer is heard in all corners of the Diaspora, one answer consisting of two parts: (1) return to national Judaism in a form appropriate to modern humanitarian culture; (2) return to Eretz Yisrael in order to build a pure national culture. Once more a period of construction succeeds a period of destruction. But there is no peace among the builders nor is there faith in the hearts of many of their number. Those who call for an ingathering of the exiled in the land of Israel despair of spiritual salvation in the lands of the Diaspora and sentence all the dispersed of Israel to national death; and the spiritual nationalists do not believe in a miraculous ingathering of the exiled through the new "messianic" idea. Voices rise to proclaim either the "end of the nation," or the "revival of Israel," and they deafen the ears and confuse the minds.

There is one remedy for the faint-hearted and for those who cling to vain illusions—detailed and thorough study of the law of survival of the Jewish people. This law will come and smite the faces of those who despair of the spiritual revival and say to them: "You view only the limited range of modern history and are frightened of what you see. You imagine that there never was a period like this before in Jewish history—a period of assimilation and wholesale conversions. You are wrong. In just the same way the sword of the Diaspora wrought havoc in Alexandria and Syria 'in front of the Temple' (despite the influence of the center in Judea), in the lands under Moslem rule in the eastern Caliphate, in Arab and Christian Spain—yet with all this the law of survival never ceased to pursue its work. Apart from this, are you not also my witnesses yourselves, you members of a generation that saw the withering of assimilation and the growth of the national idea in all its many shades? Your parents saw groups of Jews who denied their Jewish nationality in order to receive civic freedom—while you have seen myriads of Jews fighting for both civic and national freedom in the Diaspora centers and raising the banner on which was inscribed: 'National Rights!' They have not yet won the struggle, but do you not see the 'way of the spirit,' the trend toward building up the nation, not toward tearing it down and destroying it?* What is this if not a phenomenon often repeated in our history: in the hour of danger, the enduring elements win out over the disruptive elements; the national force accumulated in the past triumphs over the destructive force and restores the national group to its position. Out of the depths of the Jewish soul the gigantic force of the past bursts into the open and combines with the forces of the nation that are currently active and leads them to the cleared path, the path of life.

If this is so, one might ask, is not everything predetermined and don't we merely have to place our trust in the favors of history? Must we have complete faith in the survival of the Jewish nation despite all the frightening spectacles that pass before us?

Yes and no. If faith in the survival of Judaism is not just a vague belief, but a conclusion derived from the knowledge of all causes and effects in our history; if the understanding of the secret of survival flows from the understanding of the law of survival, from a knowledge of the conditions on which it depends, then this faith is tied to action, to practical commandments, although not those derived from the *Shulhan Arukh*. The principles of the national commandments are known: perennial struggle for communal autonomy—autonomy of the cells that make up the body of the nation—in a form that is appropriate to the conditions of the time; a struggle for national education at home and in schools established for this purpose—education in the ancient national language and the vernacular languages developed in the Diaspora which unite the entire people or large sections of it; a struggle for the cultivation of all basic national possessions and their adaptation to universal culture without damaging their own individuality. The believers who declare themselves free from such practical commandments harbor a dead faith in their hearts, and they will not awake to the national revival. We demand a living, active, and effective faith that stirs the will to life and does

* After I had completed this essay, I received an issue of *Hashiloah* (Tevet 5672), containing an article by A. Kaminka "Is Judaism Rising or Declining?" This article is worth taking to heart because it represents a new voice among the complaints of those who negate the Diaspora who have condemned western Jewry to national destruction.

not lull it to sleep. Perseverance in the "will to survive"—this is the goal of our labors.

But the faint-hearted object even to this "refined faith" that depends on knowledge and understanding, and assert: "We doubt that the will to a national life in the Diaspora will endure. National feeling is decreasing under the impact of the alien environments; the Jewish community will be swept into the midst of the life of the ruling nations, and the national will—the basis of our survival—will be weakened accordingly. The Jewish nationality is approaching its end in the Diaspora; only *in* the land of Israel, in a national environment, can we remain alive, or, at least *by means of* the land of Israel and its influence on the Diaspora."

To objections of this kind I answer: If you do not believe that the will to a national life in the Diaspora will endure (that is in something that is borne out by the events and experience of thousands of years), how can you believe that the will to revive the land of Israel can be strengthened to the degree required for a tremendous ingathering of the exiled—unparalleled since the time of the destruction of the Second Temple—or even for a center small in quantity but great in quality, for the creation of a center in Eretz Yisrael that would spread its influence over the Diaspora? If the source of the will in the Diaspora is destroyed, where will the revival come from? And if you say: "We are satisfied with a partial ingathering of the exiled, while the rest perish in the desert of the nations," are you not decreeing the destruction of the majority of the Jewish people? If our ancestors had entertained such notions, Israel would already have ceased to exist. Your error stems from the fact that you base your conclusions on a theoretical and not on a historical analogy.

History teaches us to believe that the national will must endure everywhere and to carry on by the power of this faith. National faith and activity are two sides of one coin, and if the image is rubbed off one side, the reverse side will also be effaced. Only after we realize that the national will can endure in all the lands of our dispersion and that it can give strength to the national centers, can we believe that from it as the source, there will come forth a striving to build a cultural center for a part of the Jewish people in Eretz Yisrael; then we can also work toward the end that this center will be established and will influence appreciably the lands of the Diaspora as a shining example of pure national culture, free of alien admixtures. But far be it from us to put all our hopes upon this influence alone and to divert our attention from the overwhelming majority of our people. As long as Zionism continues to pursue the path of the "negation of the Diaspora" (which embraces also the cultural possessions of the Diaspora which have become active national forces, like the spoken vernacular, etc.), it is bound to destroy with one hand what it builds with the other. "Hatred of the *galut*," rooted in the hearts of many in order to honor "love for Zion," is dangerous. Love that springs from hatred generally is suspect, but especially so if the hatred is directed against a powerful historical phenomenon that is part of our very being and that, under the historical conditions in which we find ourselves, cannot be severed from the body of the nation without wounding its soul.

From all this we conclude that there is great danger in the "serenity of the righteous," and the quietism of those who believe that Israel exists through a miracle, whether they be adherents of the "mission" idea or mummies of *Wissenschaft des Judentums* who have not tasted of its elixir of life. They are those who are afflicted with the plague of assimilation and preach "sweet sermons" on the immortality of the soul just as it is leaving the body and those who proclaim: "Let the Jewish nationality die and long live Judaism!" But danger may also come from those who reject completely the existence of the Jewish nationality in the Diaspora, who direct their efforts only toward the goal of exodus and "redemption," and who out of despair are prepared to condemn all the Jews in the Diaspora, that is, the entire people, to death by assimilation. We share neither the serenity of the "believers" nor the troubled spirit of the deniers. We demand a faith as closely linked to action as fire is to coal. Our history (living, not mummified, history) teaches us what to do and what to believe, and it says: "You are sons (*banim*) of your people in the measure that you are its builders (*bonim*), to the degree that you combine faith with action and fight with dedication for the survival of our nation and for its inner autonomy in all the lands in which it is dispersed."

THE SOCIOLOGICAL VIEW OF JEWISH HISTORY

(Introduction to the *Weltgeschichte*)

(*1925*)

1. *The General Conception of Jewish History*

"World History of the Jewish People" is perhaps an unusual title, but it corresponds fully to the content and scope of this unusual segment of the history of mankind. It is customary to speak of "World History" in conjunction with the general history of highly developed nations, as distinguished from the history of single countries and peoples. The destiny of the Jewish people, however, has unfolded in such a way that it possesses a world history of its own in the literal sense of the word. It embraces in a physical sense almost the entire civilized world (except India and China) and it coincides chronologically with the whole course of the historical existence of mankind. Judaism represents a true historical microcosm, and thus there is excellent justification for speaking of a world history of the Jewish people.

The dominant method for the world history of Jewry, as for the world history of mankind, must be that of synthesis. The major task of the historian is to clarify the general goals and paths of historical life in varying times and places, and to uncover the organic connection among the individual fragments of time and space, distributed over three thousand years of national development. The historian who follows the synthetic method, and deals with materials already collected and more or less analyzed, must not shirk the labors of independent analysis, of critical examination of the sources and of a re-examination of the facts. On their long historical way, these sources were bound to diminish considerably in reliability and completeness, and without strict re-examination they are bound to cause distorted generalizations. Still, the chief task consists in bringing to the fore the main outlines of the historical process that lie behind the great mass of facts, to draw up a carefully worked-out plan of procedure and then to erect the towering structure of history in keeping with the plan. The first condition for such a work of synthesis, however, is a clear general conception of Jewish history, a clear idea of its bearer or subject, the Jewish people, a conception that is not marred by dogmatic and scholastic concepts; and this in turn will determine in advance the pertinent methods of scientific research.

Until quite recently there were great obstacles in the way of such a scientific conception of the history of the "most historical" of peoples. With regard to the most ancient part of Jewish history, the part which occupies the exceptional position of "sacred history," the theological conception still dominates the minds not only of the orthodox, who accept the religious pragmatism of the historical books of the Bible without reservations, but also of the advocates of free biblical criticism, who substitute their own, no less theological pragmatism, for that of the Bible. In the treatment of the medieval and modern history of the Jews, we likewise find the dominance of a one-sided spiritualistic conception that is based on the axiom that a people deprived of state and territory can play an active role in history only in the field of intellectual life, while elsewhere, in its social life, it is condemned to being a passive object of the history of the peoples among whom it lives. Jewish historiography initiated by Zunz and Graetz thus paid attention mainly to two basic factors in presenting the history of the Diaspora: it dealt mostly with intellectual activities and with heroic martyrdom (*Geistes-und Leidensgeschichte*).

The main content of the entire life of the people was thus usually reduced to a history of literature, on the one hand, and to a martyrology on the other. The horizon of history was confined within these limits. The division into epochs, too, was adapted to this one-sided view of "post-biblical" history. The periods set up were the Talmudic, Gaonic, Rabbinic, Mystical and Enlightenment periods—a periodization valid for the history of a literature, but not for the history of a nation.

Only recently have we arrived at a more comprehensive and more strictly scientific conception of Jewish history that may be termed "sociological." Basic to this conception is the idea derived from the totality of our history, that the Jewish people has at all times and in all countries, always and everywhere, been the subject, the creator of its own history, not only in the intellectual sphere but also in the general sphere of social life. During the period of its political independence as well as in its stateless period, the Jews appear among the other nations, not merely as a religious community, but with the distinctive characteristics of a nation. This nation, endowed with perennial vitality, fought always and everywhere for its autonomous existence in the sphere of social life as well as in all other fields of cultural activity. Even at the time of the existence of the Judean state, the Diaspora had already attained high development and had its autonomous communities everywhere. Later on, it also had central organs of self-administration, its own legislative institutions (corresponding to the Sanhedrin, the Academies and Patriarchs in Roman-Byzantine Palestine; Exilarchs, Geonim, and legislative academies in Babylonia; the *aljamas* and congresses of communal delegates in Spain; *kahals* and *vaads*, or congresses of *kahals*, in Poland and Lithuania, etc.). The latest national movement among the Jews, linked as it is with this historical process and combining the older heritage of autonomism with the modern principle of national minority rights, testifies to the immortality of this eternal driving force of Jewish history. Even during the epoch of assimilation and of revolutionary change in the life of the people, it has been able to assert itself.

The causes of the one-sided conception of Jewish history, which was still widespread in the recent past, are obvious. Scientific Jewish historiography originated in western Europe in the middle of the nineteenth century, when the dogma of assimilation held complete sway there. This dogma asserted that Jewry is not a nation, but a religious community. Jewish historiography was also carried away by the general current and therefore concerned itself more with the religion of Judaism than with its living creator, the Jewish people. Even an opponent of this universally accepted dogma, like Graetz, was not able to go counter to this current. The profound revolution of national consciousness which characterizes our age inevitably wrought a transformation in our conception of the historical process. The secularization of the Jewish national idea was bound to effect the secularization of historical writing, liberating it from the shackles of theology and, subsequently, of spiritualism or scholasticism. A new conception of Jewish history came into being, a conception much more appropriate for the content as well as the scope of this history. Slowly the awareness grew that the Jewish people had not been entirely absorbed all these centuries by its "thought and suffering," but that it had concerned itself with constructing its life as a separate social unit, under the most varied conditions of existence, and that, therefore, it was the foremost task of historiography to try to understand this process of building the life of the Jewish people.

The subject of scientific historiography is the people, the national individuality, its origin, its growth, and its struggle for existence. In the course of a succession of centuries, the initially amorphous national cell became differentiated from the surrounding milieu of the peoples of the ancient Orient, took on a firmly outlined national form, established its own state and then lost it again, integrated in its own way the elements of universal culture which it had absorbed and, while so doing, lifted its spiritual creativity to the heights of the Prophetic movement. The movement toward the final formation of the national type coincided with that of the first political catastrophe (The Babylonian Exile), and the succeeding Persian, Greek, Hasmonaean and Roman epochs were marked by the rivalry between theocracy and the secular state. The second political catastrophe, brought on by the irresistible onslaught of Rome, gave rise to new forms of struggle by the dispersed people for its national unity. The indomitable urge to autonomous life and to the preservation of the greatest measure of social and cultural individuality while amidst alien peoples found expression, not in political, but in other social forms. The entire spiritual vitality of the nation came to be directed to this goal. The religion of Judaism was fashioned in accordance with the image of social conditions of the nation's existence, and not the reverse.

From the realistic and sociological conception of Jewish history there follows of necessity a new evaluation of many of the important individual historical events, which have previously been interpreted from the theological or scholastic point of view. We shall cite a few especially appropriate examples to illustrate the difference between the new and the older conception of interpreting the outstanding problems of Jewish history.

The older historiography was in hopeless confusion regarding the problem of the Pharisees and Sadducees, whose mutual relations were so decisive for the national life during the Hasmonaean and Roman periods. Even the historians who were not influenced by theology attributed the origin of these parties to religious-ritualistic and dogmatic controversies. These historians, basing their interpretation on the Hellenistic and philosophically colored history of Flavius Josephus, and also on the later talmudic traditions in which the political element had already become disintegrated, converted the most significant national controversy—the controversy over the very character of the national type itself, that is, whether the Jewish people should be a worldly or a spiritual nation, a nation like the average member of the international family or a unique type of people—into a struggle between "sects" or "schools." The controversy between the two parties, however, also had a social background. The Sadduceean aristocracy, which clung to political power, fought against the Phariseean democracy, which was chiefly interested in its spiritual influence upon the masses of the people. This sociological view of the origin and activity of these parties, which is elaborated in the second volume of this history, follows necessarily from everything we know about the political and spiritual conflict between the Pharisees and the Sadducees and from their entire record of activity from the Hasmonaean epoch down to the collapse of the state of Judea. The religious and ritualistic differences were merely incidental to the profound national and social antagonisms of both parties. Their conflicting attitude toward the Oral Law was only a consequence of their difference of opinion on the vital question of the propriety of Judea's creating a fence around itself and isolating itself from the surrounding culture and way of life of the Graeco-Roman world.

Another instance of distortion of true historical perspective in the older viewpoint is the generally accepted evaluation of the significance of the Sanhedrin at Jamnia. At the moment of the greatest upheaval in Jewish history, after the destruction of the Jewish state by the Romans, a center of self-administration was formed in a town close to devastated Jerusalem. Historians accepting the naive though beautiful legend, according to which Rabbi Johanan ben Zakkai escaped with the permission of the Romans from beleaguered Jerusalem and founded an academy for the study of the Torah in Jamnia, estimate in various ways the significance of this new establishment for the subsequent destiny of the Jews. While some glorify the heroic raising of the banner of scholarship upon the ruins of statehood, others see in it the beginning of national decay and of the ossification of Judaism in the letter of the Law. In reality both are wrong, since the idea that the center established in Jamnia was primarily a scholarly academy is wholly erroneous. What really happened there was one of the most significant acts of national and social reorganization. Not an academy was established in Jamnia, but a center of nomocracy, a center of administration by means of the authority of the Law. The academy for talmudic law was identical with the legislative body or the Sanhedrin which, after the destruction of the state, was called upon to weld together and unite the scattered fragments of the Jewish people by the ties of homogeneous laws regulating the entire internal life on an autonomous basis. From here resounded the call to reorganize the defeated national army and to substitute a new social order for the shattered forms of political life. This is, above all, a chapter in the history of national reconstruction and only secondarily of the history of religion, learning and literature.*

Other complex historical problems can likewise be brought closer

* See vol. iii of the *Weltgeschichte* and the "Concluding Remark" to this Introduction.

to solution by means of the sociological approach. Thus the antinomy between nationalism and universalism and the conflict between political and spiritual forces in the activity of the Prophets become intelligible. This conflict between two principles, which was caused by Israel's position among the states of the ancient Orient, is resolved in the great synthesis of the Prophetic movement. The nation is the core and the state is merely the shell, and if the shell is broken the core remains nonetheless intact. If the core is sound the nation will succeed in maintaining its autonomy against the heteronomy of its surrounding environment, and it will stand as a "banner for nations" and as a model of spiritual steadfastness.* The exact opposite of this doctrine was later preached by the prophet and apostles of Christianity. They held that only the individual religious personality has worth and not the collective historical individuality in the form of the nation. These new prophets wanted to plunge the Jewish nation into the abyss of nonexistence at the very moment it was locked in a life and death struggle with insatiable, all-devouring Rome, and, in consequence, the prophets of national suicide were particularly unpalatable to the healthy national instincts of self-preservation.† This also clarifies the deep meaning of Talmudism, and its iron national discipline of religious sanctions, for all subsequent Jewish history. The Talmud is above all the literary monument of the national hegemony of the Jewish autonomous centers in Roman Palestine and Persian Babylonia, the perpetual expression of centuries-long efforts made by national leaders who made it their most important goal to clothe the softening national core with the firm cover of the Law.‡

I am fully persuaded that the general conception presented here is the only possible presupposition for a scientifically objective methodology of Jewish historiography. This conception provides a way out for our historiography from the labyrinth of theological and metaphysical theories and places it upon a firm bio-sociological foundation. The subject of investigation is not an abstraction but

* Vol. i, sections 49, 55, 60-62, 69, of the *Weltgeschichte*.

† Vol. ii, last chapter of the *Weltgeschichte*.

‡ See vol. iii of the *Weltgeschichte*.

a living organism which has developed out of an original biological germ, the "tribe," into a complex cultural historical whole, the nation. The method of investigation is strictly evolutionary. The period of the formation of the national individuality is to be examined first; then, after this individuality has assumed a more fixed form, the period of its struggle for separate existence, for the preservation and unfolding of its characteristic national traits and of the cultural treasures it accumulated in the course of centuries. In presenting this dual process of individuation and struggle for the emerging individuality, we start from the basic assumption that a strong and clearly molded national collective personality as the product of historical evolution is, not only a natural phenomenon, but also represents a high cultural value. This, however, by no means implies that the historian must consider as valuable all those direct or winding paths that led to the preservation of the collective personality. If, for example, he is forced to recognize normal separation as an indispensable condition of national existence, he must not fail, on the other hand, to point out those periods during which cultural isolation—even though it was often necessary for the purpose of self-preservation—led to deplorable excesses, culminating in the complete alienation of the Jewish people from the valuable achievements of universal culture. It is incumbent upon him to present a vivid description of the struggle between centripetal and centrifugal forces that no national organism can escape, as well as the tragic conflicts in the life of the people induced thereby. The historian, however, who starts with the firm acceptance of national individuality as a cultural value, will evaluate the end results of the centripetal and constructive efforts differently from the centrifugal and destructive tensions.

Another obvious postulate of the sociological method is that due consideration be given in historiography, not only to the social and national, but also to the socio-economic factors which were so badly neglected by the old school. This is not to be interpreted as a concession to the materialist interpretation of history, which seeks to reduce all historical facts to the evolution of the economic conditions of life. We do not reject the antiquated, spiritualistic conception of history only to become captives of the opposite doctrine, the no-less-one-sided materialistic view of history which equally obscures all historical perspective. The economic order, like the cultural order, is but one element of the natural and social conditions of the nation's life. Commanding sovereignty over the life of the nation is exercised by the totality of all social and spiritual factors it creates. Consideration of the reciprocal relations between the individual factors shows that there is interdependence as well as conflict among them. We find nowhere, however, that all these varied functions of life are subordinate to any one single factor.

The full value of this new conception of Jewish history is especially apparent to those who, like the author of this work, had themselves previously strayed along the crooked path of the old Jewish historiography. I myself at one time acclaimed the generally accepted principles without reservation. I myself passed through all the above-mentioned phases of historical thinking, in my search for a comprehensive synthesis of Jewish history, a synthesis which I pursued unceasingly from the first day of my scientific research. In my first and as yet immature work,* which was permeated by an outspokenly religious-reformist tendency, I attempted to apply the theological method in reverse. In a series of later works, in which the tendency to secularize Jewish historiography was already patent,† I still was not able to free myself completely from the spell of the ideologically

* "Some moments in the History of the Evolution of Jewish Thought," in *Russkii evrei* (1881), nos. 16-36.

† "On the Study of the History of Russian Jews," in *Voskhod* (1891), nos. 4-9; "The Historian of Judaism: Graetz, His Life and Work," in *Voskhod* (1892), nos. 2-9; "What is Jewish History?" in *Voskhod* (1893), nos. 10-12. The latter essay was intended originally as an introduction to a Russian edition of Graetz's *Geschichte der Juden*, which was planned but did not materialize at the time. This explains the dominance of Graetz's ideology in this one-sided study in the philosophy of history. The Russian original was never reprinted in book form; but, by coincidence, it was widely disseminated (which it did not deserve) in German and English editions. The German translation by Israel Friedlaender (*Die jüdische Geschichte. Ein geschichts-philosophischer Versuch*) saw two editions (Berlin 1898; Frankfort 1921); an English translation by Henrietta Szold from the German edition appeared simultaneously in America and England in 1903 (*Jewish History. An Essay in the Philosophy of History*. Philadelphia, Jewish Publication Society of America [Reprinted in this volume, pp. 253-324]).

colored views of the school of Zunz and Graetz. My only innovation at that time consisted of an attempt to force the national-social program into the old frame of the history of ideas. The deficiencies of the old method became increasingly clear to me only after I had spent many years in detailed examination of the sources of general Jewish history, and after I had to write a history of the Jewish nation and not only of its literature. At the same time, the frame of investigation and generalization was visibly broadened and the historical horizon opened up until what was once hidden behind the veil of scholastic mystification finally came to the fore.* Then I undertook to check the results I had arrived at inductively by the opposite, the deductive method, and I found that my conclusions, which had thus turned into assumptions, were fully confirmed when applied to the historical materials.

2. *Periodization and the Organization of Materials*

The new general conception which we have described also involves a new arrangement of the materials of Jewish history and a new classification of the periods of the historical process. The division of the history of the Jewish people into periods and epochs must follow national and social rather than religious or literary criteria. These criteria are suggested primarily by the historical environment of the Jewish nation in the various periods, and then by the hegemony of one or another segment of the nation emerging in the ever-changing national center. Thus the history of the period of statehood, which many writers still divide into the "epoch of the First Temple" and the "epoch of the Second Temple," should rather be subdivided in accordance with political considerations and along lines that correspond to the changing position of Palestine amidst the world mon-

* *Cf.* "Letters on Old and New Judaism," especially Letter One (St. Petersburg, 1907); "The Processes of Humanization and Nationalization in Recent Jewish History," in *Evreyskii mir* (1909), no. 1; Lecture before the Jewish Historical-Ethnographical Society of St. Petersburg, February 21, 1910 (report in *Evreyskii starina* [1910], no. 1); "Intoduction" to vol. i of my *General Jewish History*, 2d ed. (St. Petersburg, 1910). I elaborated my historical system in great detail in a general course on Jewish history which I gave in St. Petersburg for many years, first at the Institute for Oriental Studies (1908-1916) and later at the Jewish Academy (1919-1922).

archies of the ancient Orient: Egypt, Assyria, Babylonia, Persia, the Hellenistic kingdoms of the Ptolemies and Seleucids, and the Roman empire. The history of the stateless period, on the other hand, after the Jews had lost their unified center, must be subdivided in accordance with clear-cut geographical considerations and along lines corresponding to shifts in the center of national hegemony within the Jewish people. Each epoch is determined by the fact that the dispersed nation possessed within this period one main center, or sometimes two co-existing centers, which assumed the leadership of all other parts of the Diaspora because they were able to achieve far-reaching national autonomy and a high state of cultural development.

The world history of the Jewish people may, therefore, be divided into the following two main periods: (a) the oriental period, when the chief national centers were located in the Near East and in North Africa, in Palestine, Syria, Mesopotamia, Egypt; and (b) the western period, when these centers shifted to Europe where colonies of the Jewish Diaspora gradually began to flourish. Within the oriental period three further epochs must be distinguished, which were determined by political and cultural conditions: (1) the epoch of purely oriental milieu, which includes the periods of the conquest of Canaan, the kingdoms of Judah and Israel, and the supremacy of the three successive world-monarchies, Assyria, Babylonia, and Persia (1200-332 B.C.E.); (2) the epoch of mixed oriental and western environment and of Graeco-Roman rule, which includes the intermediate episodes of an independent Judea under the Hasmonaeans up to the fall of the Jewish state (332 B.C.E.-70 C.E.); (3) the epoch of dual hegemony, of Roman-Byzantine Palestine and Persian-Arab Babylonia, between the two newly emerged world-historical forces, Christianity and Islam. In the latter epoch, after Judea's defeat in the struggle with Rome, the following changes in the hegemony of Jewish centers occurred: the hegemony of Palestine during the time of pagan Rome (second and third centuries C.E.) was replaced at first by the dual Palestinian-Babylonian hegemony, while Byzantium and the new Persia dominated the Orient (fourth-sixth centuries). In the older historiography this sequence of epochs in the second millennium of Jewish history was usually treated under the general heading of "The Talmudic Period," and under additional scholastic subheadings of epochs of the Mishna, the Gemara, the Tannaim, the Amoraim, the Saburaim, and the Geonim. In reality it was determined by the great epoch-making turns in world history.

This second millennium of the oriental period of Jewish history, which coincides with the first Christian millennium, was, however, also a period of colonization for the European Diaspora, a period which paved the way for the shift of national hegemony from East to West. The eleventh century of the Christian era thus forms the dividing line between two great periods of Jewish history, the oriental and the occidental. National hegemony now starts its migration through the centers of great Jewish mass settlements in Europe. In the Middle Ages the hegemony of Judaism fell to the lot of the Jews of Arab and, later, Christian Spain (eleventh-fourteenth centuries). Concurrently the Jews of southern and, later, of northern France (thirteenth-fifteenth centuries), and soon also the Jews of Germany (thirteenth-fifteenth centuries) took the lead. In "modern times" (sixteenth-eighteenth centuries) Germany and the autonomous Jewish center in Poland shared the hegemony. Finally, at the end of the eighteenth century, under the impact of the Enlightenment, the Jewish cultural hegemony assumed a dual form. German Jewry took the leadership of the progressive movement in the West, while Polish-Russian Jewry remained the citadel of the old, traditional culture, until it, too, was swept into the vortex of the latest currents in the second half of the nineteenth century.

The "recent history" of the Jews (1789-1914) was marked by profound social and cultural crises. These were caused by the fact that, on the one hand, short periods of emancipation and reaction followed each other closely and continuously in the general civic life, and that, on the other hand, these were paralleled by conflicts between assimilationist and nationalist tendencies within the Jewish communities of western and eastern Europe. In the latest phase of this recent history (1881-1914), in the epoch of growing antisemitism on the one hand and of the Jewish national movement on the other, Jewish national life took a new and significant turn of fate with the beginning of the exodus from eastern Europe. One group of emigrants established a new great Diaspora center in America within the short span of three decades, while the other, numerically far smaller, laid the cornerstone for the revived national center in the old homeland, in Palestine. The devastation of the World War and the Russian Revolution (1914-1920) dealt a severe blow to the largest of the previous Jewish centers, the Russian center, and, now, at the new dividing line of history, the sphinx of the Jewish people's future raises its double face, simultaneously looking toward the West and toward the East. In the wake of the two great periods of Jewish world history, the oriental and the occidental, the prospects for the future indicate, if not a total turn toward the Orient, in the form of a resuscitated Palestine, at least a rivalry for national hegemony between East and West, between Palestine and the European-American Diaspora. The historian must halt at this dividing line caused by the world conflagration of 1914; our *History* does not go beyond this point.

The organization of the materials, covering thousands of years of the history of the world-historical people, presents special difficulties. In the case of the most ancient period, these difficulties can be overcome since we have to cope only with the synchronous existence of the kingdoms of Israel and Judah after the division of the realm, and with a limited Diaspora in the period of Persian rule. The difficulties increase with the further extension of the Diaspora, first in the Orient, then also in the West. Already in the Graeco-Roman period the historian's attention is divided between Judea and the "great Diaspora," as it is later, in the Roman-Byzantine and Persian-Arab periods, between the two centers of Palestine and Babylonia, on the one hand, and the ever-expanding European Diaspora, on the other. As we approach the history of the western period, the difficulties become immeasurably greater. Here we are faced with an enormous number of countries, in each of which the destiny of the Jewish population is intertwined with the most diverse political and cultural conditions. The historian has the choice between the two possible ways of presentation, both of which, however, appear equally inexpedient. He may arrange the history of the Jewish people according to the countries in which it was scattered, and thus present it as a purely external collection of monographs, or he may treat the history of the Jews in all countries concurrently and, converting the history into chronicle, he may present a chronological record of events that coincide in time but differ fundamentally in character and local conditions. The first master of Jewish historiography, Graetz, preferred, in the main, the latter method of synchronism. The sudden transitions (*kefizot ha-derekh*) from one country to the other within the same chapter often alienate the reader of his grandly conceived work. Although this artificial stringing together of most heterogeneous events has something of the plasticity of synoptic tables, it nevertheless lacks what is indispensable for a scientific synthesis, a concatenation of events with local conditions. This is completely obscured in such a chronicle-like presentation. With Graetz the confusion is further augmented by his method of throwing together political, socio-economic, and literary data in the narrowest sense of the word into a single chapter.*

The only way to avoid all these limitations is to divide the materials according to the threefold principle of time, place and subject matter. The history of each epoch must be presented according to the country in which it occurs, and within each country according to the order of causal connections that link the external conditions with those of internal life. Within the limits of each period, the history of the different segments of the nation are presented in such a way that the main center of national hegemony comes first and is then followed by the other countries according to their importance

* *Cf.*, as proof, an abstract of a chapter of vol. vi of Graetz's *Geschichte*, which bears the characteristic scholastic heading, "Fourth Rabbinical Era:" "The Jews in Spain. Toledo . . . The poet Charisi. The Martyrdom and Death of Abraham ibn-Daud and the Jewess Formosa Rachel. The Traveller Benjamin of Tudela. *Provence:* Narbonne, Abraham b. Isaac, and the Kimchi Family. The Communities of Beziers, Montpellier, and Lunel . . . Philipp Augustus and the First Expulsion of the Jews from Northern France. The Tossaphist Isaac the Elder, the Martyrs of Bray. Judah he-Hasid and the *Sefer hasidim*. The Jews of England," etc. The next chapter juxtaposes Germany, Italy, Byzantium, Syria, and Palestine, the Caliphate of Bagdad, Persia, India and Arabia, and deals with the following topics: the German *servi camerales*, rabbinism, martyrology, the minnesinger, Roman Popes, eastern exilarchs, the pseudo-messiah David Alroy, Tartars, Egyptian Karaites, etc.

for the total national history. Sometimes, however, it appears unavoidable to begin the presentation of a particular section with a central event, for example, with a political or social movement that affected several countries simultaneously and impressed its character upon an entire period. Examples of such events are the first crusades and their significance for France and Germany, the new settlements of the Sefardim after their expulsion from Spain, the spread of the Sabbatian messianic movement from Turkey, the first French Revolution and the beginning of Jewish emancipation and, finally, the German antisemitism of the last decades of the nineteenth century. The treatment of each epoch in the present work is prefaced by a "general survey," which presents the leading characteristics of the center of each period as well as of its peripheral areas. In the presentation proper, the external political events are distinguished as far as possible from the internal social phenomena, on the one hand, and from the data of literary history, on the other. In each chapter dealing with a particular center of the Diaspora, the material is usually arranged in the following way: political conditions, self-administration in the Jewish communities, intellectual life and literature. For purposes of a "History of the Jewish People" we are interested in literary history only in so far as it influenced the social dynamics or was itself a product of social movements. We are concerned far less with individual works of literature than with literary movements that are expressive of the general orientation of the national spirit. History of literature in the narrowest sense of the word is outside the scope of this work.

Since I am publishing my work in the country in which the first foundations for scientific Jewish historiography were laid a century ago, I cannot refrain from observing that I consider this, as it were, a symbol of continuity. Even though I differ from my predecessors in my general conception of Jewish history as well as in many details, I am always conscious of the fact that, without the labor of a century of scholars of the school of Zunz, Geiger, Graetz and Frankel, we could never have reached the present stage of Jewish historiography. As regards the history of the most ancient period, the achievements of German Christian scholars, like Wellhausen, Kittel and Schürer, must be accorded special recognition. They far outdistanced their Jewish colleagues in their critical analysis of the sources, even though their criticism was not entirely free of theological bias. If we are able today to see the entire course of Jewish history from a wholly different viewpoint than that of our predecessors of the school of Graetz, we must thank them for their work, which was for us a stimulus to further research. The historic events of our stormy epoch have enriched our historiographical experience. The last two generations of intellectuals have themselves traversed part of the historic road on which they were able to perceive both the dark abysses of the Middle Ages and the effects of the confusion of ideas brought about by the recent past. The historian of today leans on the work of his predecessors and can, therefore, look farther into the recesses of history than they were able to. But he in turn will be superseded by his successors if our historiography continues to experience a normal course of development.

Concluding Remark

The general conception of Jewish history presented above was at one time the subject of scientific controversy, and may in the future become so again. To avoid misunderstanding and useless polemics it seems to me imperative to add several additional explanatory comments at this point.

1. I use the much too ambiguous term "sociological conception" only and exclusively in the sense indicated above: the sense of a conception of the subject of Jewish history as a living national organism. This conception must not be confused with the sociological method. The well-known sociologist Max Weber recently applied the sociological method to the ancient Jewish people (*Das antike Judentum*, 1923); but this did not prevent him from conceiving of Jewish history in a theological and metaphysical spirit (his basic idea of the Jews as a "pariah nation," his views on the "sect" of the Pharisees, etc.). I could perhaps have avoided the confusion of terms by choosing the term "national conception" to characterize my view; but in this case, I still would have to add that I mean national only in the sense

of recognizing the nation as the subject of history but not in the sense of a subjective nationalistic evaluation of all historical phenomena, which would be wholly tendentious in every respect. It is perfectly possible to recognize the eternal nation as the bearer, or active subject, of Jewish history and yet at the same time condemn all extreme nationalistic excesses in the development of this people without reservation or, at best, to justify them as acts of self-defense.

2. In emphasizing the one-sidedness of the general conception of the majority of our historians, I did not intend to deny that their works contain many sociological elements. It is not the factual content, but the general view of history that is in question here. Of all Jewish historians, Graetz was closest to the national conception in the sense just indicated. He saw clearly the political element in the activities of the Pharisees and Sadducees and he vigorously opposed the narrow dogmatists. This did not prevent him, however, from characterizing these two parties, together with the Essenes, as "three sects" or "three heresies" ("Das Trihaeresion," *Geschichte*, vol. iii, note 12). Graetz perceived the motives of nomocracy in the work of Johanan ben Zakkai and the "Academy" at Jamnia, and yet he could not get himself to carry through this idea in the fourth volume of his work, but represented this entire period in an academic light, as a chain of "generations of Tannaim and Amoraim." The inconsistency of Graetz's general conception appears especially glaring in two contradictory theses formulated in the introduction to the fifth volume of his work. (1) "The history of the post-talmudic period still bears, therefore, a national character. It is in no way merely the history of a religion or of a church, because its subject is not merely the course of development of a doctrine, but also a particular national group . . ." (2) "History has never yet provided the example of a people that laid down its weapons of war and dedicated itself wholly to the peaceful pursuit of knowledge and art . . ." etc. Our most eminent historian undoubtedly proceeded in the direction of a scientific conception of Jewish history, but he could not free himself from the impervious dogmas of his generation even though he was practically anathematized for his minute deviations by both the right

and the left (Samson Raphael Hirsch, Abraham Geiger, the assimilationists, after the publication of vol. ix of Graetz's work).

3. It is also appropriate at this point to warn against another misleading confusion of two terms which must be kept absolutely apart: the *conception* of history, on the one hand, and the *content* of history, on the other hand. We exclude neither the religious nor the ideological elements as such from the content of history and they are given the most careful attention in the present "History." What we do insist on is the priority of the scientific-evolutionary over the dogmatic conception of history, a priority that is based upon the simple truth that the whole complex of ideas called Judaism must be considered a product of the organic growth of the nation and of its adaptation to wholly unique and distinctly characteristic historical conditions of life.

WHAT SHOULD ONE DO IN HAMAN'S TIMES?

(A *Letter to the Editors* of Oyfn Sheydveg)
(*1939*)

Dear Friends:

The year 1937 marked the passing of two thousand years since the Roman General Pompey brought the first Jewish captives from Jerusalem to Rome (63 B.C.E.). This was the beginning of Jewish settlement in Europe. Several years later the captives were freed and we have the testimony of Cicero that Jews were already occupying a prominent role in the social life of Rome. We could, therefore, be celebrating now the two-thousandth anniversary of our coming to Europe, if not for the fact that the beginning of our third millenium is marred by the reincarnation of those Germanic barbarians who were still in a semi-civilized state in the days of Pompey and Caesar. The past two years of the Hitler regime (1938-1939) have led many people to the impression that this is the beginning of the destruction of European Jewry and that the dominant center of our people will be transferred overseas, either to America or to Asia.

We are now passing through one of the gravest crises in our history. The years 5698-5699 (1938-1939) will be recorded in the list of gruesome historical dates: 4856 (the Crusades, 1096), 5108-5109 (the Black Death, 1348-1349), 5252 (expulsion from Spain, 1492), 5408-

5409 (Khmielnitski, 1648-1649), 5641-5642 and 5663-5664 (Russian pogroms, 1881-1882, 1903-1904), 5679-5680 (Ukrainian Petlurist pogroms, 1919-1920). The anti-Jewish measures in central Europe today combine all the sufferings of the previous periods with the most modern system of cruelty, vandalism and torture that only the inquisitorial fantasy of a Hitler, Goering or Streicher could create. We are in truth living in Haman's times. Hitler's "system of extermination" is simply a translation of Haman's plan "to destroy, to slay, and to cause to perish, all Jews." There is but one difference. In the earlier instance it never got beyond the planning stage, for the Jewish people organized resistance to the plan and Haman was led to the gallows. Hitler, on the other hand, has almost realized his plan. One million Jews in Germany, Austria and Czechoslovakia are destroyed, plundered and mutilated; about half are driven out and the other half are still in Hitler's land as prisoners or hostages, being subjected to slow and painful destruction. Over all continents and oceans are heard the cries of thousands of "exiles from Germany" knocking at the doors of all the nations and being barred because of immigration restrictions or plain hostility.

What should one do in such times? When the knife is at the throat we must hasten to stay the hand of the murderer and save the victim. We must create a world organization to combat this band of murderers and we must also set up organizations to find emigration lands for the exiles and refugees. For a number of years now, work has been carried out along these lines by both Jews and non-Jews. More recently throughout the world a militant struggle has been initiated against the Nazi-Fascist alliance—a combination which represents just as grave a danger for humanity at large as it does for its Jewish part. All active forces of Jewry must join in this tremendous battle, in order to pull Europe out of the mud and save European Jewry from extinction. First must come the salvaging action, later will come the measures to reconstruct our shattered world and our own little world foundations of justice and liberty, human and national progress.

In these days of confusion and war-scare, among bundles of newspapers that are full of the outcries of Hitler victims, I received the first issue of your journal *Oyfn Sheydveg* (At the Crossroad). In normal times I would have derived great pleasure from it, but today it elicits critical thoughts in me. I would have applauded the very fact that people stop "At the Crossroad" to ponder over the question whether the previous paths taken by our Jewish intelligentsia were the right ones and whether we might not better change some things in our ideology of the nineteenth and twentieth centuries. Is this the time *now*, however, to stop for ideological revision, now when we are engaged in a battle for physical survival, for human dignity, when each day wrenches from our ranks thousands of victims, when a million of our brethren are so overwhelmed by terrible sufferings that many are led either to suicide or to insanity? It seems to me that we are not at the spiritual crossroad, but rather upon a battlefield, where beaten and tortured human beings are falling around us.

The question may be asked: What can unarmed Jewish masses accomplish upon the battlefield? A great deal! An international people of millions of adherents, full of hatred of fascism and Nazism, can serve as a powerful ferment to stir up the world against these murderous movements and arouse the conscience of mankind. We have achieved quite a bit already through our boycott of German goods, especially in America, where we find allies in the non-Jewish laboring masses. The latest statistics show a decline in German exports due to the Jewish boycott; Hitler and his agents were forced to admit that world Jewry has inflicted damage upon Nazi Germany. To take away the bread and butter from the murderer's mouth means tearing from his hand the sword with which he aims to kill us. We thus give aid to the *economic* blockade which the anti-aggressor Great Powers are creating around Hitler and Mussolini. Through our propaganda we also help create the *moral* blockade of these two plundering nations. If a world war breaks out, enthusiastic Jewish volunteers will fight in armies of the anti-aggressor bloc.

This is one aspect of our battle. The other is still more important—to find homes for our refugee brethren who are searching for a roof over their heads in all parts of the world. Here too we have a bitter struggle to wage: in Palestine with the Arab terrorists and the pro-Arab elements in the British government; in the other countries of immigration, with the guardians of the closed gates. In those countries of immigration in which some elements of Nazism have taken root and which seek to get rid of their Jewish population, we must continue to wage the old battle for civic rights.

All in all we have pressing work to do, more than we can handle with the forces at our disposal. And amidst all this, you come to us with expressions of despair and frustration, with confessions and searching for God. This is not the first time that we hear such sentiments of contrition. Even in the past sixty years—from the Russian to the German pogroms—we have gone through several revisions of our ideals: *Hibbat tsiyon*, political and spiritual Zionism, Diaspora autonomism, territorialism and Socialist combinations of all these "isms." You are quite right, my friends, when you say (*Oyfn Sheydveg*, no. 1, p. 5): "After every great catastrophe in the life of the people there would arise from the ruins a new vitality and a spiritual stock-taking." Yes, *after* the catastrophe, but not *in the very midst* of the catastrophe. We are not yet done with it, for it is of longer duration and more severe than all previous catastrophes during the past century. When the "German Expulsion" will have come to an end and we will have settled all our hundreds of thousands of refugees in other countries, we will then have to review the degree to which the assimilationist trend has been eradicated from our midst, after the storm of racism and Hitlerism, and we will have to consider what spiritual measures we can take to salvage the bare souls of the new generation. Right now, however, we must save their bodies. First Jews—then Judaism. Right now we must do battle with the plague of antisemitism in its Nazi form and with the plans for new expulsions and persecutions in eastern Europe.

In our epoch of counter-emancipation we dare not pose the ironic question: "Well, what has emancipation brought us?" True, it brought assimilation, but also freedom and human dignity. It revived the free person in the Jew. The task of our great national movement in the past fifty years consisted of the struggle for emancipation *without* assimilation, for both civic and national rights. We succeeded in winning such liberty after World War I, but only in a juridic sense, in the treaties of the League of Nations with the east-European states. Hardly had this *total* emancipation been realized, when the Hitlerite plague came upon the scene to poison the minds of the people in those countries in which there were large Jewish centers. Does this mean that we were deceived by emancipation? We must fight against the spirit of counter-emancipation, against the vicious plans of "emancipating" millions of Jews from the countries which Jews helped to build up for many centuries together with the Christian population. We must fight against the plague of the Hitler expulsions and not drop our hands and sigh that "emancipation has deceived us!" You will say that the "German Expulsion" may be duplicated in eastern Europe, but here they have already tasted of Hitlerism and they had to line up with the anti-aggression bloc of the democratic countries against these world bandits. When the anti-aggression movement succeeds in liberating Europe, its Jewish part will also be liberated.

Now, at a time of the most terrible counter-revolution, we celebrate the 150th anniversary of the great French Revolution, which established a new epoch in world history. And the progressive circles of our people will celebrate with enthusiasm the first symbol of "our festival of freedom." Two years from now we will commemorate our first emancipation (1791)—and we will remind the world that during the most recent period we added to this elementary civic emancipation national or auto-emancipation. We stand or fall with the progress or regress of entire mankind as a whole, and not with a few of its degenerate parts.

The call "Back to the Ghetto" is not a new one. We have heard it several times during the past decades. Insofar as this means "Back to Jewish culture," or to "Judaism in the modern sense," it is part of the program of the national movement. But progressive Jews will never return to the *medieval* ghetto and its Judaism. The call "Back to God, to our Traditional Orthodoxy" will have as much success as similar calls issued by Christian Churches to their peoples. The religious masses will remain true to their faith, but the progressives will not be dragged back into the synagogue or the church.

A hundred years ago Samson Raphael Hirsch, the founder of neo-orthodoxy, proclaimed in his *Nineteen Letters* the following severe demand: "It is not the Torah that has to adapt itself to life, but life must adapt itself to the Torah." Yet recent generations have demonstrated that the pure core of Judaism can be preserved only by making adjustments to modern life. We now have a religious Judaism and a national Judaism, or a combination of the two. Let each party go its way. But no one has the right to claim a monopoly of all of Judaism for himself. Our divisions of opinion were created by the great historical processes which every living people experiences. The free competition of ideas must continue and the instinct of national survival will direct the oldest historical nation to the right path for its continued existence.

We will talk about all these internal matters as soon as the insane world has calmed down, after the new "anti-aggression alliance" has triumphed over the robber nations in that struggle in which the Jewish nation, plundered and mutilated more than all others, must participate actively to the full limit of its powers.

Notes to the Biographical Essay

[1] The chief sources for the life of Dubnow are Dubnow's autobiography and the biography by his daughter, Sophie Dubnow-Ehrlich, which first appeared in Russian (New York, 1950) and then was issued in Yiddish translation by Moshe Ferdman, together with a number of additional materials, under the title of *Dos Lebn un shafn fun Shimen Dubnov* (Mexico City, 1952). Dubnow's own autobiography was published in three volumes, in Riga (1934-35), under the title *Kniga zhizni*. Selections from the autobiography dealing with the period up to 1880 and between 1890 and 1894 appeared in Yiddish translation in the *Zukunft*, vol. xxxvii (1932), pp. 536-43, 609-16, 645-52, 719-25; vol. xxxviii (1933), pp. 271-73, 356-59, 413-19, 472-77; vol. xxix (1934), pp. 32-35, 105-108, 204-207, 281-84, 343-45, 420-22 and 476-78. Selections from the period 1880-1922 appeared in German translation by Elias Hurwicz, in Dubnow, S., *Mein Leben* (Berlin, 1937). Valuable material for Dubnow's biography is also to be found in the *Sefer Shimon Dubnov*, edited by Simon Rawidowicz (London, 1954), which includes a collection of Hebrew letters by Dubnow and a number of essays by students and friends. A bibliography of all of Dubnow's published works up to 1930 was compiled by Joseph Meisel and is included in the *Festschrift* for Dubnow's 70th birthday, edited by Ismar Elbogen, Joseph Meisel and Mark Wischnitzer (Berlin, 1930). Joseph Meisel also compiled a bibliography of all published works by Dubnow in the Hebrew language, which appears in the *Sefer Shimon Dubnov*, cited above, pp. 236-39. The same bibliography also includes works about Dubnow in Hebrew literature.

[2] See the Introduction to his *Weltgeschichte*, in which he criticizes the *Geistes- und Leidensgeschichte* of his predecessors. A very similar approach, perhaps even sharper, was developed by Salo W. Baron in his essay, "Ghetto and Emancipation," published in the *Menorah Journal* in 1927. It was here that Prof. Baron first coined the term "lacrymose historiography."

[3] See Dubnow, S., "Zhitlovsky's autonomizm," in *Zhitlovski zamlbukh* (Warsaw, 1929), pp. 190-95.

[4] Quoted from Horodetzky, S. A., "The Genealogy of Simon Dubnow," in *Yivo Annual of Jewish Social Science*, vol. vi (1952), p. 15.

[5] Dubnow-Ehrlich, p. 91.

[6] Horodetzky, *op. cit.*, pp. 17-18.

[7] Dubnow-Ehrlich, p. 28.

[8] *Ibid.*, p. 31.

[9] *Mein Leben*, pp. 64-67.

[10] *Ibid.*, pp. 68-69.

[11] When Dubnow was having difficulties in settling in St. Petersburg and was full of bitterness at the reactionary regime, he made the following entry in his diary: "Were I alone and physically strong I would go to America for good. I'd rather chop wood in a free country than be a writer in the land of absolutism, slavery and despotism" (Dubnow-Ehrlich, p. 68). I would interpret this as an

expression of momentary resentment rather than as serious consideration of the possibility of emigration.

[12] *Cf.* Charney-Niger, S., "Simon Dubnow as a Literary Critic," in *Yivo Annual of Jewish Social Science*, vol. i (1946), pp. 305-18.

[13] Dubnow-Ehrlich, pp. 66-67.

[14] *Ibid.*, pp. 77-78.

[15] *Zukunft* (1934), p. 204.

[16] Dubnow-Ehrlich, p. 85.

[17] *Mein Leben*, p. 130.

[18] *Ibid.*, p. 110.

[19] *Sefer Shimon Dubnov*, p. 269.

[20] *Zukunft* (1934), p. 204.

[21] It is republished in the present volume, see pp. 253-324.

[22] Quoted from Mark Wischnitzer, "Shimen Dubnow, der organizator fun der yidisher geshikhtsvisenschaft in rusland," in *Zukunft* (1931), p. 58.

[23] Dubnow-Ehrlich, *op. cit.*, p. 192.

[24] *Ibid.*

[25] *Ibid.*, pp. 128-29.

[26] Dubnow-Ehrlich, *op. cit.*, p. 149.

[27] *Ibid.*, pp. 172-73.

[28] *Sefer Shimon Dubnov*, p. 262.

[29] Dubnow-Ehrlich, pp. 160-61.

[30] Davis, Moshe, "Jewry, East and West. The Correspondence of Israel Friedlaender and Simon Dubnow," in *Yivo Annual of Jewish Social Science*, ed. by Koppel S. Pinson, vol. ix (1954), pp. 19-20. This essay and the collection of letters provides an illuminating exposition of the relationship between the two scholars and in this way also an important link in the influence of Dubnow in the United States.

[31] Dubnow-Ehrlich, *op. cit.*, p. 187.

[32] *Mein Leben*, p. 207.

[33] *Ibid.*, p. 208.

[34] *Ibid.*, pp. 211-12.

[35] *Ibid.*, p. 225.

[36] Dubnow-Ehrlich, pp. 212-13.

[37] *Mein Leben*, p. 249.

[38] *Ibid.*, pp. 254-55.

[39] *Sefer Shimon Dubnow*, p. 277.

[40] From the very valuable archives of Maxim Vinaver, now in the Yiddish Scientific Institute. See *Yedies fun Yivo*, no. 35 (December 1949).

[41] *Sefer Shimon Dubnov*, p. 279.

[42] *Ibid.*, p. 389, n. 2.

[43] In a letter to S. Feigin in the United States, dated October 27, 1934, Dubnow writes that the German edition as completed in 1929 "is now the chief edition from the point of view of completeness and latest *editorial changes*." *Sefer Shimon Dubnov*, p. 381.

[44] *Cf.* also the Preface to the German edition, vol. i, p. 15.

[45] Quoted by Abraham Levinson in *Sefer Shimon Dubnov*, p. 188.

[46] *Ibid.*, p. 188.

[47] Dubnow-Ehrlich, p. 263.
[48] *Ibid.*, p. 265.
[49] *Sefer Shimon Dubnov*, p. 290.
[50] *Ibid.*, p. 374.
[51] Dubnow-Ehrlich, p. 275.
[52] *Ibid.*, p. 306.
[53] *Ibid.*, p. 305.
[54] See below, pp. 354-59.
[55] Translated, by kind permission of Dr. Joseph Meisel, from *Kiryat Sefer*, vol. xx (1943), pp. 178-79.
[56] The two most reliable accounts of these last days of Dubnow are by Hillel Melamed, "Vi azoy di nazis hobn dermordet professor S. Dubnov," in *Zukunft*, vol. li (1946), pp. 320-21, and Max Kaufmann, *Die Vernichtung der Juden Letlands* (Munich, 1947).
[57] The main body of this section was published in my article "The National Theories of Simon Dubnow," in *Jewish Social Studies*, vol. x (1948), and I wish to express my thanks to the Board of Editors of the journal for permission to use it here.
For a critique of Dubnow's national theories see Kaufman, Ezekiel, *Gola venekhor* (Tel-Aviv, 1929-31), vol. iii, pp. 300-18; see also Janowsky, Oscar I, *The Jews and Minority Rights, 1898-1919* (New York, 1933) and Friedlaender, Israel, "Dubnow's Theory of Jewish Nationalism," first published in 1905 and then reprinted in his *Past and Present* (Cincinnati, 1919).
[58] "The Survival of the Jewish People," see below, p. 332.
[59] *Letters* . . . p. 79. All subsequent references are to pages in this volume.
[60] Ibid., p. 102.
[61] *Ibid.*, p. 103.
[62] *Ibid.*, p. 127-30.
[63] *Ibid.*, p. 175.
[64] See Janowsky, *op. cit.*
[65] *Letters* . . . , p. 141.
[66] *Ibid.*, p. 80.
[67] *Ibid.*, p. 89.
[68] *Zukunft* (1934), p. 343.
[69] *Weltgeschichte*, vol. ii, p. 157. See also pp. 123-24, 143-47.
[70] *Letters* . . . , p. 130.
[71] *Ibid.*, p. 181.
[72] "The Survival of the Jewish People," below, p. 326.
[73] *Letters* . . . , p. 91.
[74] *Vom Sinn des Judentums* (Frankfurt a.M. 1925), pp. 44-47; the Hebrew original appeared in *Haolam*, Dec. 24, 1924.
[75] At the same time it is interesting to note that Dubnow took issue with Ahad Ha-Am on the question of the Jewish attitude toward the political parties in Russia after the 1905 revolution. Ahad Ha-Am said he was ready to accept the aid of any political party, even the most reactionary, for the sake of the Jewish cause. Dubnow rejected such allies and identified the aspirations of the Jews only with the progressive parties (See *Letters* . . . , p. 223n.).
[76] Dubnow, "Vegn der izolatsye fun Bund," in *Zukunft* (1938), p. 329.

[77] *Letters . . .*, p. 84.
[78] *Ibid.*, pp. 84-85.
[79] Dubnow, *Pinkas hamedina* (Berlin, 1925), p. xi. See also his *History of the Jews in Russia and Poland*, vol. iii, pp. 53-54.
[80] *Letters . . .*, p. 240.
[81] *Ibid.*, p. 137.
[82] *Ibid.*, p. 136.
[83] *Geschichte des Chassidismus*, vol. 1 (Berlin, 1931), pp. 14-16.
[84] Dubnow, S., *Fun zhargon tsu yiddish* (Vilna, 1929), p. 3.
[85] *Letters . . .*, pp. 190-91.
[86] *Fun zhargon tsu yiddish*, pp. 13-14.
[87] Dubnow-Ehrlich, *op. cit.*, p. 163.
[88] *Zhitlovski zamlbukh* (Warsaw, 1929), p. 194.
[89] *Fun zhargon tsu yiddish*, p. 3.
[90] *Letters . . .*, p. 157.
[91] *Ibid.*, p. 164.
[92] *Ibid.*, p. 166.
[93] *Ibid.*
[94] See Dubnow's memoirs in *Zukunft* (1934) and his *Fun zhargon tsu yiddish*, especially the section on Mendele. See also Tschernowitz, Ch., *Hakhmei Odessa* (New York, 1945).
[95] Dubnow's side of this debate is found in his seventh and eighth letters and his article "Shelilat hagalut vehiyuba betorat Ahad Ha-Am"; see also his obituary on Ahad Ha-Am in *Haolam* (1926), no. 1. For Ahad Ha-Am's side see his "Shalosh madregot" and "Shelilat hagalut" in *Al perashat derakhim*, 4 vols. (Berlin, 1921), vol. ii, p. 57-65 and vol. iv, p. 106-16, and his *Igarot*, 6 vols. (Tel Aviv, 1922-25).
[96] See also Kaufman, *op. cit.*
[97] Ahad Ha-Am, *Al perashat derakhim*, vol. ii, p. 65.
[98] *Letters . . .*, p. 180.
[99] *Ibid.*, pp. 185-86.
[100] *Ibid.*, p. 189.
[101] *Fun zhargon tsu yiddish*, p. 104.
[102] *Oyfn Sheydveg*. See below, p. 356.
[103] He was, however, in general an admirer of Tolstoi and wrote a beautiful essay on Tolstoi ("Yesod ha-yahadut shebetorat Tolstoy," in *Hashiloah*, vol. xxv (1911), pp. 627-28.
[104] Croce, B., *History as the Story of Liberty* (New York, 1945).
[105] *Oyfn Sheydveg*, see below, pp. 357-58; see also Dubnow's review of Salo Baron's *Social and Religious History of the Jews* in *Zukunft* (1937), p. 767.
[106] Ahad Ha-Am, *Al perashath derakhim*, vol. ii, p. 62.
[107] *Zukunft* (1935), p. 397.
[108] "A Community Theory of American Life," in *Menorah Journal*, vol. vi (1920), pp. 311-21.
[109] *Ninth Letter*, p. 199.
[110] *Zukunft* (1933), p. 357.
[111] *Mein Leben*, pp. 85-86.
[112] On the relations between Dubnow and his Hebrew translator, Abraham Levinson, see the latter's illuminating essay, "Beyn hamehaber limetargemo," in

Sefer Shimon Dubnov, pp. 184-201, and in the letters by Dubnow to Levinson in the same volume (pp. 364-68), in which Dubnow expresses his complete satisfaction with the work of his Hebrew translator. Dubnow, incidentally, always took great pains with his translators and supervised their work carefully. Interesting comments by him on the art of translation are found in a letter to David Movshovitch, of London, which is found in the archives of the Yivo. See *News of the Yivo*, no. 28 (1947).

[113] See below, p. 344.

Notes to Dubnow's Writings

1. The German translation was prepared by Dr. Elias Hurwicz for the Jüdischer Verlag but was never published. The full story of these translations may be found in Dubnow's letters to Abraham Levinson, in *Sefer Shimon Dubnov*, ed. by Simon Rawidowicz (London, 1954), pp. 364-68.

2. At the time Dubnow was writing, the terms "race" and "racial" had not yet acquired the unsavory and indeed tragic associations and connotation that they possess today. They were used frequently and rather loosely by scholars and writers and often interchangeably for "nation" and "national." The terms also occur frequently in Dubnow's "Letters," but they never have the meaning of the inextricable connection between mental and physical characteristics that is the distinguishing mark of true racial doctrine. Dubnow's primacy of the spiritual and cultural factors as the product of historical development is just the opposite of racialism. When using the term "race," he is merely referring to the biological and physical factors in man. In Dubnow, as in Ahad Ha-Am, there is no mystical doctrine of "blood" and "blood relationship" such as is found among German-Jewish writers like Moses Hess, Martin Buber, Walther Rathenau and others.

3. See further discussion of this in the Introduction to his *Weltgeschichte*, below, pp. 340-41.

4. *Aljama* is the term used to designate the autonomous community of the Jews in Spain.

5. Omitted here is a lengthy comment on the definition of nationalism as found in Springer's *Der Kampf der oesterreichischen Nationen* (1902).

6. The Russian original carries a footnote at this point which reads as follows: "Supporters of assimilation usually claim Moses Mendelssohn as one of their own, while opponents of assimilation, on the basis of this assumption, denounce the great thinker. This is a great historical error which, unfortunately, took root in our journalism since the days of Smolenskin. It is true that Mendelssohn did not consider the Jews to be a secularized cultural nation—he who so vigorously fought for the separation of church and state nevertheless rejected the separation of nationality from the synagogue—and it was not he who created the notion that Jews are a religious group capable of merging with other national groups. Mendelssohn, in his great work *Jerusalem*, in his philosophy of history as well as in his own personal life, showed that he viewed the Jews as a religious nation that will never be merged with other nationalities. He differed from the old orthodoxy only in the fact that he believed that, with the progress of culture and education, closer friendship in the field of civic life would develop between Jews and the other nations.

7. The Russian text has "indisputable dogmatism" in place of "holiness."

8. The Russian original includes at this point a footnote on the Jewish member of the Duma, Herzenstein, who after embracing Christianity still registered as an "orthodox Christian of the Jewish nationality."

9. Peter Lavrovich Lavrov (1823-1900) was one of the outstanding Russian social philosophers of the nineteenth century and a powerful influence on the development of the revolutionary movement in Russia. His famous "Historical Let-

ters" (1869) are available in German translation (Berlin, 1901) and also in French translation (Paris, 1903). Lavrov was also an important influence in molding the thought of Russian Jewish intellectuals of the time. Aaron Lieberman, Chaim Zhitlovsky as well as Dubnow acknowledged their debt to the works of Lavrov. *Cf.* E. Tscherikower, "Peter Lavrov and the Jewish Socialist Emigrés," in *Yivo Annual of Jewish Social Science*, vol. vii (1952), pp. 132-45.

10. The Russian original contains the following footnote at this point: "The well-known Jewish journalist Matthias Acher recently formulated this distinction in the two terms "Machtnationalismus" and "Kulturnationalismus" (*Voskhod*, 1906, no. 2, p. 36). As an opponent of Zionism, Acher accepts the formula of spiritual nationalism ("Judaism as spiritual potentiality" *ibidem*) and now actively advocates national cultural autonomy for the Jews in Austria.

11. The Russian original includes at this point a lengthy quotation from Wilhelm Windelband's *Präludien*.

12. The Russian text includes the following:

"This natural feeling of love of fatherland is within everyone of us, regardless of whether we were happy or unhappy there. We cherish the place of our birth, where we grew up and were nourished by its nature, and to which a long chain of reminiscences of our youth, our family and historical events, be they happy or sad, are linked. Places where we suffered and went through hardships are just as dear to us as those in which we lived happily. Who does not know of the deep devotion of the Jews of Spain and Portugal to their fatherland for many centuries after they had been exiled from it in the fifteenth century. In our own day, we see the Russian Jewish emigrants to the United States still cherishing the land of their birth, Russia, from which they were exiled. Birth is not the only factor that binds us to a country. It is also the cherished national relics, the graves of our ancestors, our sacred places, our historical monuments, the places connected with poetic folklore which so often in our youth filled us with joy or sadness—all these and many more are the factors that nourish deep devotion to our fatherland."

13. Konstantin Petrovich Pobednostsev (1827-1907) was Procurator of the Holy Synod and tutor in the Russian royal family. He was one of the chief exponents of the philosophy of political absolutism and of enforced Russification.

14. Vladimir Sergeyevich Solovyev (1853-1900) was Russia's greatest religious and social philosopher. He was a humanitarian nationalist who subordinated attachment to nationality to the dedication to universal humanity. His essays on "The National Question in Russia" represent one of the most forceful and penetrating assaults on extreme nationalism as found in Russian Slavophilism. Solovyev was also a militant defender of Jews and Judaism and raised his voice frequently to denounce antisemitism and the persecution of Jews in Russia. See Hans Kohn, *Pan-Slavism. Its History and Ideology* (Notre Dame, 1953), pp. 175-79; *idem. The Mind of Modern Russia* (New Brunswick, 1955), pp. 212-31; Paul Berline, "Russian Religious Philosophers and the Jews," in *Jewish Social Studies*, vol. ix (1947), pp. 271-86.

15. The Russian text includes at this point a more extended discussion of the changes in Socialist ideology with respect to nationalism. A long quotation from the German Social Democratic leader August Bebel is cited with approval by Dubnow, who also cites the Italian Enrico Ferri and the Austrian Pernerstorfer as examples of Socialists who have adopted a sounder policy on this problem. Kautsky

and Plekhanov are, according to Dubnow, only beginning to understand the real nature of the problem.

16. The Russian text contains an interesting footnote, which runs as follows: "When this Letter was written (1901), the great work by the Austrian jurist, Springer, *Der Kampf der oesterreichischen Nationen um den Staat*, Part I, 1902, had not yet been published, and his brochure, *Staat und Nation* (Vienna, 1899), published under the pseudonym of Synopticus, was not known to me. Upon acquainting myself with these two works, I note with pleasure that this expert on the very complicated national problems of Austria has reached conclusions quite similar to my own regarding Jewish autonomy. In his analysis, Springer maintains that the guiding principle to be used in establishing autonomous forms for minority groups be that of person rather than that of territory. . . . Thus an Austrian and a Jewish autonomist arrive at the same conclusions regarding the problem of the national community and the type of unit for self-determination, one by the experience of the present and the other by the experience of the past. . . . In recent years certain elements of "autonomism" were included in the program of the Bund and members of the party have been frequently referred to as "autonomists." This designation is hardly appropriate, since the Bund has to this date not formulated a definite attitude on the question of Jewish self-rule and not even on the Jewish national idea itself. In the program of the Bund this is rather tolerated (in a very vague form) than recognized."

17. Samuel Lublinski (1868-1910) was a German-Jewish literary critic, essayist and poet. His earlier works dealt with Jewish subject matter, but he later turned to general German and cosmopolitan subjects. His best known work was *Literatur und Gesellschaft im 19. Jahrhundert*, 4 vols. (Berlin, 1899-1900).

18. Ludwig Jacobowski (1868-1900) was a prominent literary figure in Germany in his day. He was the editor of the literary review *Die Gesellschaft*, author of *Loki* (1896) and a volume of poetry that attracted considerable attention after his death. Besides his novel *Werther der Jude*, discussed by Dubnow, he also published a study on *Der Juden Anteil am Verbrechen* (Berlin, 1892). Cf. *Ludwig Jacobowski im Lichte des Lebens*, ed. by Marie Stoma (Breslau, 1901).

19. Georg Moris Cohen Brandes (1842-1927) was perhaps the leading literary critic in Europe during the pre-World War era. Born in Denmark and attached to his native country, he made the entire area of European literature his domain. His *Main Currents of Literature in the 19th Century* was translated into all European languages and is a classic of literary criticism. Brandes' interest in Jewish life was distant and lukewarm and he was frequently taken to task by Yiddish and Hebrew writers for not reacting to Jewish persecution and suffering. In his later years he evinced a little more interest, but still as a distant observer. See his article "Meine Stellung zum nationalen Judentum," in *Der Jude*, vol. ii (1918), pp. 592-94.

20. Marcus Ehrenpreis (1869-1945), chief rabbi of Sweden, was active in the world Zionist movement from its inception and was the author and translator of numerous works of and about Hebrew literature.

21. The Russian text contains the parenthetical remark, "I would not call it a national movement, since it hardly reached the wide masses of the people."

22. The Russian text includes here a more lengthy exposition and interpreta-

tion of the origins of Zionism and especially of Zionism as a secularized form of religious mysticism.

23. Moshe Leyb Lilienblum (1843-1910) was one of the fighting champions of the Haskala in Russian Jewry. His autobiography, *Hatat neurim* ("The Sins of Youth") was a scathing and unvarnished exposé of the obscurantism, fanaticism and intolerance against which the "enlightened" Jewish youth of his day battled. He later became one of the chief ideologues of the *Hibbat Tsiyon* movement and was associated with Pinsker in Odessa in furthering Jewish colonization in Palestine.

24. Leo Pinsker (1821-1891) was the author of the famous *Auto-Emancipation* (1882), one of the basic documents in the development of modern Zionism. Pinsker, a practicing physician in Odessa, became one of the leading figures in the Zionist movement in Russia.

25. Baron Edmund James Rothschild (1845-1934) was the head of the Paris branch of the Rothschild family and the munificent benefactor of the first period of Jewish colonization in Palestine.

26. The Kattowitz Conference was called by Dr. Leo Pinsker in 1884 to mobilize all the followers of the *Hibbat Tsiyon* movement. Out of it came the formation of the Odessa Committee for the furtherance of Jewish colonization in Palestine.

27. Ahad Ha-Am (Asher Ginzberg, 1856-1927) was the leading theorist of "spiritual Zionism," with its criticism of political Zionism and its championing of the idea of Palestine as a cultural center that would infuse the rest of world Jewry with new life and with Jewish creative energy. As these "Letters" by Dubnow show, Ahad Ha-Am and Dubnow were not only close personal friends but were also closely allied in their assault on assimilationism and in their primary concern with the spiritual and cultural aspects of Judaism. The intimacy of the two scholars, which began with Dubnow's coming to Odessa in 1890, lasted down to Ahad Ha-Am's death and can be followed in the fascinating exchange of correspondence as found in the *Iggarot* of Ahad Ha-Am and in *Sefer Shimon Dubnov*, ed. by Simon Rawidowicz (London, 1954), pp. 245-85. English translations of the important essays by Ahad Ha-Am are found in *Selected Essays* (Philadelphia, 1912), *Ten Essays on Judaism and Zionism* (London, 1922) and *Ahad Ha-Am. Essays, Letters, Memoirs* (Oxford, 1946), all three volumes translated by Leon Simon.

28. Max Nordau (1849-1923) was a distinguished social philosopher, publicist and Zionist leader. Of his numerous literary and philosophical works those that received widest circulation were *Die conventionellen Lügen der Kulturmenschheit* (1883); *Paradoxe* (1885) and *Entartung* (1892-93). He was one of the first associates of Herzl in the Zionist movement and remained till his death a leading exponent of active political Zionism. Following World War I he advocated mass Jewish emigration to Palestine as opposed to the gradualism of the official Zionist policy. See M. Ben-Horin, *Max Nordau* (New York, 1956).

29. The Russian text has the following: "The success of political Zionism among the educated Jewish youth in the West and in Russia can be attributed to the increased awakening of Jewish national consciousness, on the one hand, and estrangement from Judaism and ignorance regarding its unique historical destiny, on the other hand. Rejected by the antisemitism of Christian society and previously estranged from Jewish culture, these Jewish young people embrace political Zionism as a means of salvation. They cherish their nation because they hope it

will soon become just like the other political nations of the world. This is 'external assimilation' which has replaced the former 'internal assimilation.' To realize this goal, a specific philosophy of Jewish history is being created, adjusted to the latest models of historical materialism or to the 'transvaluation of values,' and which has but one fault, nonconformity to the stubborn course of Jewish history which does not submit to different theories prepared in advance and refuses to be subjected to radical surgery."

30. In the Russian text there follows a long section, of which the following excerpts are the more interesting.

"We shall turn now from the estranged youth to the Zionists of the older generation and to those who are closer to Jewish life. Here the success of Zionism is caused by varying motives of lower or higher order. In one category it is evoked by a limited (I would call it commercial) practicality. Strange as it may sound, many see in the Zionist utopia the 'business' aspect, the element of bold and daring enterprise. The Jewish people in its historical aspect stands very low in this market. How often do we hear in these circles frank avowals that they themselves despise the Jews as a 'feeble' nation, nourished as it is only by the strength of spirit, and that they will respect it only when it becomes strong materially, when it acquires the status of the wealthy. Thus if Jewry becomes a political nation, its continued existence will be justified; if not, there is no point to its existence. A people which is incapable of creating a good 'career' of its own is good for nothing. . . . From these 'conventional' Jews we expect nothing. Should political Zionism fail, they will turn their backs on the Jewish national idea.

"Another category embraces Zionism because it titillates their social instincts. They are attracted by the opportunity to 'make politics,' to play the role of creators of the future state. The program of the spiritual nationalists requires more serious groundwork, special knowledge and slow labor. In the Zionist movement none of these requirements are necessary. It is sufficient to make believe that the Jewish state is just around the corner. The intelligent or semi-intelligent masses follow the prevailing current of the moment merely by instinct. Where these people will find themselves after the crash of Zionism it is difficult to predict. Should another 'fashionable movement' arise at that time, they will most likely join it. If not, they will remain 'unemployed.' . . .

"There is still another large category of Zionists, whom I would classify as 'simple-minded citizens,' good people who see no difference between political Zionism and cultural nationalism. They include everything in their program: the colonization of Palestine, a plan for a Jewish state, the revival of the national spirit —in general, all activities which are for the good of the nation. For them, Zionism is the banner of Jewish national self-help. For this group the failure of political Zionism would not be harmful, for they still have certain spiritual ideals in store. But there are also among the Zionists a large number of self-sacrificing national workers who should be respected deeply, even though we may not share their partisan convictions. These genuinely honest individuals know the Jewish people, carry the burden of its sufferings together with them; they were caught in the Zionist camp as a result of despair. They are deeply stirred by the revival of national consciousness among the youth, whom they had already considered as lost to our people. They are thrilled by the fact that 'fathers and sons' enemies only yesterday, are united in the same cause, and they hesitate to let go of this banner lest the general cause be harmed. . . .

"Still closer to our historical doctrine are those 'spiritual Zionists' whom I have discussed above. . . .

"As stated already, spiritual nationalists have full sympathy with the gradual colonization of Palestine, provided this colonization of small groups is not viewed as the salvation of the general Jewish problem and provided it does not divert millions of Jews, who will not find themselves in Palestine, from their spiritual and material needs.

"Thus we have much in common for purposes of practical work, although there are differences in principle. As to principles, time will eventually tell who was right and who acted more in keeping with the historical evolution of the Jewish people and who with the accidental trends of external development." . . .

31. The peace treaties after World War I imposed upon the succession states of the Austro-Hungarian and Russian empires provisions for according national minority rights to Jews and other minority groups. The Committee of Jewish Delegations in Paris was an important factor in establishing these principles in international law and there is no doubt that the theories of Dubnow had a great deal to do with shaping the thought of the Jewish leaders. See Oscar I. Janowsky, *The Jews and Minority Rights, 1898-1919* (New York, 1933), and *Were the Minorities Treaties a Failure?* by Jacob Robinson *et al.*, published by the Institute of Jewish Affairs of the World Jewish Congress (New York, 1943).

32. Three entire Letters in the original Russian version are here omitted.

Letter VIII in the Russian original is entitled "Changing Trends in Russian-Jewish Journalism." It is a survey of the important Jewish periodicals in the Russian language appearing during the last half of the nineteenth century (*Razsvet, Zion, Dyen, Voskhod,* etc.) and their respective ideological positions with respect to Jewish emancipation and to independent Jewish national life.

Letter IX in the original Russian edition is called "A Divided and a United National Party." In this essay Dubnow classifies the various groupings in Jewish life among assimilationists, Jewish nationalists and waverers, draws some interesting analogies with party groupings in earlier Jewish history, and concludes with a call for a united party of all those who have a positive attitude toward Jewish nationalism.

Letter X in the original Russian edition is entitled "The Confused Intelligentsia." It is a polemical essay, directed against the ideological proponents of assimilation among Russian Jewish intellectuals of the time. The Russian-Jewish journalist, M. G. Margulies, who had published several critical articles on Dubnow's theory of autonomism, is the chief object of Dubnow's attention in this essay.

33. The reference here is to the rabbinic principle of "placing a fence around the Torah," which meant setting up precautionary measures, in addition to those prescribed by Scripture, in order to prevent man from even getting near possible violations of divine law.

34. Daniel Pasmanik (1869-1930) was a problematic and controversial figure in the history of the Zionist movement and among the Russian Jewish intelligentsia. He alternated between radicalism, Mizrachi and Poale Zionism and ended his life as an associate of the reactionary monarchist elements of the Russian

emigration in Paris. At the time of Dubnow's "Letters," he was a practicing physician in Odessa and an active Zionist journalist.

35. The Kishinev pogrom of 1903 was the most notorious and most brutal instance of government-fostered antisemitism in tsarist Russia, intended by the autocratic regime as a counter-measure to the revolutionary movement. Inflamed by the constant calls to violence of the antisemitic sheet *Bessarabets*, published by Krushevan, and undoubtedly organized by police and government agents, the mob perpetrated on April 6 and 7 one of the bloodiest pogroms in pre-war Russia upon the defenseless Jews of the capital of Bessarabia. During those two days, 45 Jews were killed, 86 severely wounded or crippled, 500 slightly wounded, 1500 homes and stores looted and destroyed and an unknown number of women raped. Humanitarians all over the world, including Tolstoi and Korolenko inside Russia, cried out in protest against the outbreak. The Yiddish poet Shimen Frug and the Hebrew poet Bialik gave poetic expression to the poignancy of the Jewish tragedy (especially Bialik's immortal *Be-ir ha-harega*). Movements of self-defense, emigration and Jewish nationalism were all intensified as a result of this new wave of persecution.

36. The Revolution of 1905 in Russia was accompanied in April of that year by a series of pogroms on the Jews. Even more savage, however, were the pogroms that ushered in the counterrevolution. During the week between October 18th and 25th, 1905, there were more than fifty bloody pogroms in various Jewish centers and several hundred "bloodless" pogroms, involving plunder and property damage. Dubnow's reference to the "Black Death" pertains to the anti-Jewish outbreaks in central Europe in the fourteenth century, and his allusion to Khmielnitski refers to the massacres of Jews in Poland and the Ukraine during the uprising of Bogdan Khmielnitski in 1648.

37. Count Serge Witte (1849-1915), who was taken to represent the more "liberal" and constitutional supporters of the tsarist regime, was called to head the ministry under the new constitutional order initiated after the revolution of 1905. He was dismissed early in 1906.

38. The "Black Hundred" was the more popular name for the organization officially known as the League of the Russian People founded in 1904. It was the most active agent of violence against the Jews in Russia. It was headed by Dr. Dubrovin, Vladimir Purishkevich, Markov the Second and numerous government and police officials. Tsar Nicholas II gave his personal support to the activities of the Black Hundred. On December 23, 1905, he said to a delegation of the organization: "Unite the Russian people. I count on you." In addition to organizing pogroms, the Black Hundred helped spread the *Protocols of the Elders of Zion* and later engineered the notorious Mendel Beilis ritual murder trial in 1913. See Marc Vishniak, "Antisemitism in Tsarist Russia," in *Essays on Antisemitism*, edited by Koppel S. Pinson (2d ed. New York, 1946), pp. 138ff.

39. The *Novaya Zhizn* was a Bolshevik newspaper edited by Maxim Gorky. Lenin was also a member of the editorial board.

40. The Russian text adds the following to the sentence at this point: "with the exception of the protest by Dashevski after the Kishinev pogrom and also, in part, after the Lekert affair."

41. Among the more prominent Russian-Jewish Social Democrats of that period

were Pavel Akselrod, Juri Martov-Zederbaum, Leo Deytch, Theodor Dan, Aaron Zundelevich and Leon Trotsky-Bronstein.

42. The Russian text has the following footnote at this point: "An unsuccessful attempt to combine class politics with national politics was made by the new groups which developed a kind of strange combination of socialism and Zionism (Zionists-Socialists, Poale-Zion Social-Democrats, etc.). By means of talmudic *pilpul,* these groups are attempting to combine in their theories the basic elements of two completely different systems, forgetting at the moment that the essence of the dispute is which policy should be the dominant one, the national or the class policy, since both cannot rule at the same time. Here too, in practice, victory is on the side of socialism. Both the Zionist-Socialists and the Poale Zion consider the class struggle to be the paramount issue. These groups are constantly bickering with each other and with the other socialist parties, each one trying to prove that it is closer to 'true Marxism' or to the ideal of the 'proletariat.' These eclectic theories carry within themselves the seeds of destruction and they remind us of the confusion which prevailed in certain circles of our youth during our transition period."

43. S. Anski (1863-1920) is best known as the author of *The Dybuk.* In his youth he came under the influence of the radical movement of the *narodniki* and later, together with Chaim Zhitlovsky, was active in the Socialist Revolutionary Party. He served as secretary to Peter Lavrov from 1894 to Lavrov's death in 1900. After the revolution of 1905, he turned his attention more actively to Jewish affairs and to Yiddish literature, taking special interest in the collection of Jewish folklore in Russia. He was an anti-Bolshevik and left Russia in 1918. He died in Vilna in 1920.

44. August Bebel (1840-1913) was the parliamentary leader of the German Social Democratic Party before World War I. In numerous speeches and articles he affirmed the resolution of the Socialists in Germany to defend their fatherland if it is a victim of foreign aggression. At the party congress in 1907, he declared: "If indeed we should have to defend our Fatherland some day, we would defend it because it is our Fatherland, whose soil we live upon, whose language we speak, whose customs we possess, because we wish to make this, our Fatherland, a land unexcelled in this world for perfection and beauty." (Quoted from A. Joseph Berlau, *The German Social Democratic Party, 1914-1921,* New York, 1949, pp. 46-47.)

45. In March 1905, in Vilna, there was organized the League for the Attainment of Equal Rights for the Jewish People in Russia, which comprised all the leading democratic non-Socialist Jewish groups. Dubnow was associated in this work with M. Vinaver, L. Bramson, H. Slyozberg, Shmaryahu Levin, and others. In 1907 the coalition was dissolved and four separate groups were formed. The Folkspartay was the group that adhered to Dubnow's national-autonomist program. It remained active only for a short period. It was revived again in Poland after World War I.

46. Chaim Dov Hurwitz was at the time a prominent Hebrew and Yiddish publicist. He was one of the leading contributors to the Yiddish newspaper *Der Fraynd* and it was here that he published his "Letter to Dubnow."

47. P. A. Krushevan was the reactionary antisemitic journalist and leader of the Black Hundred who was the chief instigator of the Kishinev pogrom. He started

his activities with the publication of a local antisemitic paper, *Bessarabets* (The Bessarabian) and also came to St. Petersburg where he received financial support from Plehve to publish the newspaper *Znamya* (The Banner). A Jewish youth, Pinhas Dashevski, made an attempt on Krushevan's life on June 4, 1903, but inflicted only a minor wound. The *Protocols of the Elders of Zion* were first published in Russia in the *Znamya*, from August 28 to September 7, 1903, under the title "A Jewish Program to Conquer the World."

48. Dubnow refers here to the popular "Tale of the Fisherman and the Fish," by Alexander Pushkin, which tells the story of a greedy woman who, starting her life in an old mud hut, was not satisfied with the more modest gifts bestowed upon her by a miraculous fish, but kept egging her poor husband on to extract from the fish gifts of palaces, changes in social and economic status and regal powers until she broke the magic spell by her extravagant demands. The gift-dispensing fish "splashed the water, off she went to the depths of the sea," and the old man returned to his wife. "He beheld his old mud hut; at the threshold his woman is sitting, and before her—the broken old trough." (Eng. trans. in *The Russian Wonderland*, by Boris Brasol, New York, 1936, pp. 15-24.)

INDEX

INDEX

MERIDIAN BOOKS

published by The World Publishing Company
2231 West 110 Street, Cleveland 2, Ohio

JEWISH PUBLICATION SOCIETY SERIES

JP1 FOR THE SAKE OF HEAVEN *by Martin Buber*
JP2 STUDENTS, SCHOLARS AND SAINTS *by Louis Ginzberg*
JP3 A HISTORY OF MEDIAEVAL JEWISH PHILOSOPHY *by Isaac Husik*
JP4 JEWISH LIFE IN THE MIDDLE AGES *by Israel Abrahams*
JP5 STUDIES IN JUDAISM *by Solomon Schechter*
JP6 HISTORY OF THE JEWISH PEOPLE *by Max Margolis and Alexander Marx*
JP7 GOD IN SEARCH OF MAN *by Abraham Joshua Heschel*
JP8 INTRODUCTION TO THE TALMUD AND MIDRASH *by Hermann L. Strack*
JP9 KIDDUSH HA-SHEM *and* SABBATAI ZEVI *by Sholem Asch*
JP10 JUDAISM AND MODERN MAN *by Will Herberg*
JP11 PRINCE OF THE GHETTO *by Maurice Samuel*
JP12 A HISTORY OF THE MARRANOS *by Cecil Roth*
JP13 THREE JEWISH PHILOSOPHERS *edited by Hans Lewy, Alexander Altmann, and Isaak Heinemann*
JP14 THE JEW IN THE MEDIEVAL WORLD *by Jacob R. Marcus*
JP15 THE JEW IN THE LITERATURE OF ENGLAND *by Montagu Frank Modder*
JP16 A HISTORY OF THE CONTEMPORARY JEWS *by Solomon Grayzel*
JP17 THE ZIONIST IDEA *edited by Arthur Hertzberg*
JP18 MODERN NATIONALISM AND RELIGION *by Salo W. Baron*
JP19 GERMANY'S STEPCHILDREN *by Solomon Liptzin*
JP20 NATIONALISM AND HISTORY: ESSAYS ON OLD AND NEW JUDAISM *by Simon Dubnow*
JP21 THE CONFLICT OF THE CHURCH AND THE SYNAGOGUE *by James Parkes*

MERIDIAN BOOKS

published by The World Publishing Company
2231 West 110 Street, Cleveland 2, Ohio

MERIDIAN GIANTS

MG1 MYSTICISM *by Evelyn Underhill*
MG2 MEDIEVAL PANORAMA *by G. G. Coulton*
MG3 PROLEGOMENA TO THE STUDY OF GREEK RELIGION *by Jane Harrison*
MG4 MY LIFE IN ART *by Constantin Stanislavski*
MG5 THE ROMANTIC AGONY *by Mario Praz*
MG6 PHILOSOPHIES OF INDIA *by Heinrich Zimmer*
MG7 PLATO: THE MAN AND HIS WORK *by A. E. Taylor*
MG8 FRANCE AGAINST HERSELF *by Herbert Luethy*
MG9 THE LITERATURE OF THE SPANISH PEOPLE *by Gerald Brenan*
MG10 FILM FORM *and* THE FILM SENSE *by Sergei Eisenstein*
MG11 LITERATURE IN AMERICA *edited by Philip Rahv*
MG12 THE DISSOCIATION OF A PERSONALITY *by Morton Prince*
MG13 A TREASURY OF YIDDISH STORIES *edited by Irving Howe and Eliezer Greenberg*
MG14 CHINESE CIVILIZATION *by Marcel Granet*
MG15 THE ORIGINS OF TOTALITARIANISM *by Hannah Arendt*
MG16 THE PHILOSOPHY OF SPINOZA *by Harry Austryn Wolfson*
MG17 THE MAN OF THE RENNAISSANCE *by Ralph Roeder*
MG18 NEW YORK PLACES & PLEASURES *by Kate Simon*
MG19 THE PLACE OF VALUE IN A WORLD OF FACTS *by Wolfgang Köhler*
MG20 FROM THE N.R.F. *edited by Justin O'Brien*
MG21 JAIL KEYS MADE HERE AND OTHER SIGNS *photographs by Lee Boltin*
MG22 FRANK LLOYD WRIGHT: WRITINGS AND BUILDINGS *selected by Edgar Kaufmann and Ben Raeburn*
MG23 THE CHILDHOOD OF MAN *by Leo Frobenius*
MG24 THE MYSTIC ROSE *by Ernest Crawley*
MG25 WEBSTER'S NEW WORLD DICTIONARY OF THE AMERICAN LANGUAGE (CONCISE EDITION)
MG27 FOLKSONGS AND FOOTNOTES: AN INTERNATIONAL SONGBOOK *by Theodore Bikel*
MG28 THE SOUL AFIRE *edited by H. A. Reinhold*
MG29 AN INTRODUCTION TO THE LITERATURE OF THE OLD TESTAMENT *by S. R. Driver*
MG30 EARLY GREEK PHILOSOPHY *by John Burnet*

MG31 ROMAN SOCIETY IN THE LAST CENTURY OF THE WESTERN EMPIRE *by Samuel Dill*

MG32 THE HISTORY OF ROME *by Theodor Mommsen*

MG33 THE NEW ARCHITECTURE OF EUROPE: AN ILLUSTRATED GUIDEBOOK AND APPRAISAL *by G. E. Kidder Smith*

MG34 A DICTIONARY OF CLASSICAL ANTIQUITIES *by Oskar Seyffert*

MG35 PROLEGOMENA TO THE HISTORY OF ANCIENT ISRAEL *by Julius Wellhausen*

MG36 A HISTORY OF AESTHETIC *by Bernard Bosanquet*

MG37 AN ENCYCLOPEDIA OF RELIGION AND RELIGIONS *by E. Royston Pike*